written and edited by

Casey A. Barrio Minton
Donna M. Gibson
Carrie A. Wachter Morris

Evaluating
Student Learning
Outcomes in
Counselor Education

AMERICAN COUNSELING
ASSOCIATION
6101 Stevenson Avenue, Suite 600
Alexandria, VA 22304
www.counseling.org

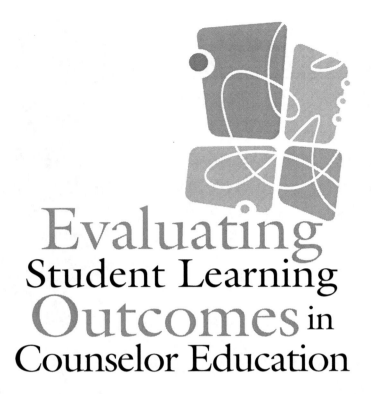

Evaluating Student Learning Outcomes in Counselor Education

American Counseling Association
6101 Stevenson Avenue, Suite 600
Alexandria, VA 22304

Associate Publisher • Carolyn C. Baker

Digital and Print Development Editor • Nancy Driver

Senior Production Manager • Bonny E. Gaston

Copy Editor • Tyler Krupa

Cover and text design by Bonny E. Gaston

Library of Congress Cataloging-in-Publication Data
Names: Barrio Minton, Casey A., author. | Gibson, Donna M., author. | Wachter Morris, Carrie A., author.
Title: Evaluating student learning outcomes in counselor education / Casey A. Barrio Minton, Donna M. Gibson, Carrie A. Wachter Morris.
Description: Alexandria, VA : American Counseling Association, [2016] | Includes bibliographical references and index.
Identifiers: LCCN 2015049928 | ISBN 9781556203374 (pbk. : alk. paper)
Subjects: LCSH: Student counselors—Training of—Evaluation.
Classification: LCC LB1731.75.B37 2016 | DDC 371.4—dc23 LC record available at http://lccn.loc.gov/2015049928

To our fellow counselor educators, past, present, and future.
You give of yourselves to train talented professional counselors
who will change the world one client at a time.
This is beyond measure!

● ● ●

Table of Contents

Part III • Moving Forward

Part IV • Applications

Acknowledgments

We wish to acknowledge the following individuals and groups for making this book possible:

- The Council for Accreditation of Counseling and Related Educational Programs (CACREP), for working toward unity and high standards in the counseling profession. Unless otherwise cited, the ideas and recommendations expressed in this book are those of the authors and do not represent the opinions or policy of CACREP. Yet, our experiences as students in CACREP-accredited programs and now as scholars of the profession help us understand how to develop curricula that can meet the ever-changing needs of our students and their future clients.
- The Association for Assessment and Research in Counseling, for partnering in this work and embracing a vision that advances the counseling profession by promoting best practices in assessment, research, and evaluation in counseling.
- Paula Swindle, doctoral student, University of North Carolina at Greensboro, for her service as managing editor throughout the review process.
- Sharon Bruner, doctoral student, University of Tennessee, Knoxville, for her technical support throughout the revision process.
- Julia Taylor, doctoral student, Virginia Commonwealth University, for editing as a "future consumer" in the early writing days for this project.
- Finally, our families, for their love and support throughout not only our writing process but also our journeys as counselors and counselor educators.

About the
Editors

Casey A. Barrio Minton, PhD, NCC, is an associate professor of counselor education at the University of Tennessee in Knoxville, Tennessee. She served as president (2013–2014) and secretary (2010–2012) for the Association for Assessment and Research in Counseling (AARC). Casey has published more than two dozen journal articles in professional counseling venues, three books, and nearly as many chapters and works. She presents regularly at local, state, and national conferences and serves the profession through her editorship of the *Journal for Counselor Leadership and Advocacy* and through her presence on editorial boards, including *Counselor Education and Supervision* and *The Professional Counselor.* In all, her presentations, publications, and leadership reflect her research interests in building a strong profession through research and program evaluation, evidence-based teaching, and crisis intervention.

Donna M. Gibson, PhD, LPC, NCC, is an associate professor and program coordinator of counselor education at Virginia Commonwealth University in Richmond, Virginia. She served as president (2007–2008) and member-at-large for membership (2001–2004) for AARC and is serving currently as the AARC governing council representative of the American Counseling Association. In addition to more than 100 peer-refereed professional state, regional, national, and international presentations, Donna has more than 40 professional publications, including peer-refereed journal articles, book chapters, and books. Her presentations and publications reflect her research interests in program evaluation, professional identity development, leadership and leadership identity development, and advocacy in counseling.

Carrie A. Wachter Morris, PhD, NCC, ACS, is an associate professor of counseling and educational development at the University of North Carolina at Greensboro, where she coordinates the school counseling track. She served as president (2015–2016) and secretary (2012–2014) for AARC. Carrie has published nearly two dozen articles in national peer-refereed journals, one book, and an additional 10 chapters and works. She presents regularly at state, regional, and national conferences on topics related to the scholarship of teaching and learning in counselor education, crisis, and school counselor education. She serves the profession on the editorial boards of *Counselor Education and Supervision* and *Professional School Counseling.* Carrie's engagements reflect her commitments to innovation in counselor education pedagogy, program evaluation, professional advocacy, and crisis prevention and intervention.

About the
Contributors

Nick R. Abel, EdD, is an assistant professor of school counseling at Butler University in Indianapolis, Indiana. He has a special interest in school counselor preparation and teaches many related courses, including professional orientation, legal/ethical issues, and comprehensive school counseling.

L. DiAnne Borders, PhD, LPC, NCC, ACS, is Burlington Industries Excellence Professor at the University of North Carolina at Greensboro, where she teaches the doctoral course in clinical supervision and oversees the supervision interns. She has published numerous studies on supervisor training and the supervision process. She is coauthor of *The New Handbook of Clinical Supervision* and the editor of *The Clinical Supervisor*.

Ryan G. Carlson, PhD, LMHC, NCC, is an assistant professor of counselor education at the University of South Carolina in Columbia, South Carolina. His research focuses on interventions for high-risk couples and families. Ryan teaches master's students in the marriage, couples, and family counseling track, including the introduction to family counseling and couples counseling courses.

Catherine Y. Chang, PhD, LPC, NCC, CPCS, is a professor at Georgia State University in Atlanta, Georgia, and she is a program coordinator for the Counselor Education and Practice doctoral program. Her primary areas of interest include social justice and advocacy, multicultural counseling competence, supervision, and counseling implications related to Asian American and Korean American clients.

M. Kristina DePue, PhD, NCC, is an assistant professor of counselor education at the University of Florida in Gainesville, Florida. Her clinical specialty is addictions counseling.

Melissa J. Fickling, PhD, LPC, NCC, is an assistant professor of clinical mental health counseling at the University of Memphis in Memphis, Tennessee. Her specialties include career counseling, college counseling, and adult career transitions; she is particularly interested in intersections of work and mental health.

Laura M. Gonzalez, PhD, is an assistant professor in counseling and educational development at the University of North Carolina at Greensboro. She has research interests in supports and barriers to college access for Latino immigrant families, and she teaches in the college counseling/career counseling and researcher development areas.

Kristopher M. Goodrich, PhD, LMHC, NCGC-I, is an associate professor and program coordinator of the Counselor Education Program at the University of New Mexico in Albuquerque, New Mexico. He has specialty interests in lesbian, gay, bisexual, transgender, questioning, and intersex issues in counseling and addictions, and he teaches courses in substance abuse, mental health, and sexuality in counseling. He currently serves as the president of the Association for Lesbian, Gay, Bisexual, and Transgender Issues in Counseling (2015–2016) and has a part-time clinical practice at the Evolution Group—an addictions counseling agency in Albuquerque, New Mexico.

Tyler M. Kimbel, PhD, is Vice President, Research and Advocacy & Outreach, at the Council for Accreditation of Counseling and Related Educational Programs in Alexandria, Virginia. He also serves as an adjunct professor at Palo Alto University in Palo Alto, California, where he teaches research and program evaluation, career counseling, and capstone writing. His specialty interests include school counseling, program evaluation, research, accreditation policy, counselor identity, and professional issues.

Margaret R. Lamar, PhD, LPC, is an assistant professor at Palo Alto University in Palo Alto, California. She has specialty interests in researcher identity development, and she teaches professional orientation, ethics, and research.

A. Stephen Lenz, PhD, LPC, is an assistant professor and chair of the Counseling Outcome Research and Program Evaluation Academy at Texas A&M University–Corpus Christi. He has been nationally recognized for his work with program evaluation and development for adolescents and young adults as well as for his contributions to the body of empirical evidence regarding trauma-focused treatments. He is president-elect of the Association for Assessment and Research in Counseling.

C. Peeper McDonald, EdS, LPC, NCC, is a doctoral candidate in the Counselor Education and Practice program at Georgia State University in Atlanta, Georgia. She has specialty interests in professional identity, social justice, and advocacy issues as well as multicultural issues in counseling. She has experience teaching both online and in-person courses with a heavy emphasis on basic and advanced counseling skills.

Rebecca A. Newgent, PhD, LCPC, NCC, is a professor at Western Illinois University–Quad Cities in Moline, Illinois. She has specialty interests in measurement and evaluation, clinical interventions and supervision, and peer victimization, and she teaches assessment, ethics, practicum, diagnosis, and professional orientation. She is also the editor-in-chief of *Counseling Outcome Research and Evaluation*.

Jonathan H. Ohrt, PhD, is an assistant professor at the University of South Carolina in Columbia, South Carolina. He has specialty interests in group counseling and adolescent well-being, and he teaches a variety of school counseling and helping skills classes.

Brandie M. Oliver, EdD, is an assistant professor of school counseling at Butler University in Indianapolis, Indiana. Her specific areas of interest include bullying prevention and intervention, grief and loss, data-driven school counseling, restorative practices, and advocating for an increased focus on culturally responsive education. She sees her role as a resource and support for school counselors as well as an advocate and source of positive change for all students, parents, and educators.

Maria Adele Paredes, PhD, LPCS, CEDS, is a visiting assistant professor at the University of North Carolina at Greensboro. She has specialty interests in eating disorders, body image, grief counseling, clinical supervision, and English language learners. She teaches a wide range of core and elective courses, and she enjoys continuing to provide counseling to the community.

Elizabeth A. Prosek, PhD, NCC, is an assistant professor of counseling at the University of North Texas in Denton, Texas. Her research areas include diagnosis and assessment, co-occurring disorders, and issues in counselor education; her specialty area is interventions for veterans. She teaches clinical mental health counseling curriculum, including diagnosis and treatment planning, professional orientation and ethics, and mental health systems.

Heather C. Sands, MS, MEd, LMHC, NCC, is a doctoral student of anthropology at the University of New Mexico in Albuquerque, New Mexico. She has specialty interests in the commodification of race, gender, and sexuality surrounding situations of migration, border politics, and trauma embedded in the modes of neoliberal and late liberal politics of help in the United States. In her scholarship and practice, she hopes to deepen her understanding of mental health as it relates to peoples, places, and politics.

Marie F. Shoffner, PhD, is an associate professor at Virginia Commonwealth University in Richmond, Virginia. She teaches master's-level and doctoral career development courses and is passionate about facilitating doctoral students' development as researchers and scholars. She has specialty interests in career transitions, work and mental health, and girls and women in STEM (science, technology, engineering, and mathematics), and she enjoys volunteering her counseling expertise at Richmond's Fan Free Clinic.

Cortney Stark is a doctoral student in counselor education at the University of New Mexico in Albuquerque, New Mexico. Her work with individuals struggling with substance abuse includes the utilization of harm reduction strategies and motivational interviewing in individual counseling, medication-assisted treatment of opiate dependence, and coordination and facilitation of Acudetox group treatment sessions. As an educator, she seeks to meet the individual learning needs of each student by being adaptable and by utilizing the self as an instrument in the evolution of students' perceptions, beliefs, and personal meaning.

Jacqueline M. Swank, PhD, LMHC, LCSW, RPT-S, is an assistant professor at the University of Florida in Gainesville, Florida. She has specialty interests in assessment, outcome research, counselor development/competency, children and adolescents, and creative and nature-based interventions. She teaches counseling courses in the areas of assessment, research, child and adolescent counseling, and play therapy.

Paula J. Swindle, MA, NCC, LPCS, is a doctoral student at the University of North Carolina at Greensboro. She plans to become a counselor educator and has specialty interests in religious/spiritual abuse and wellness issues. She has returned to pursue her PhD after 15 years in the counseling field.

Jodi L. Tangen, PhD, NCC, is an assistant professor of counselor education at North Dakota State University in Fargo, North Dakota. Her dissertation research focused on ways in which counselors facilitate moments of emotional depth with clients. She has a background in educational psychology and has special interests in counseling supervision.

Michael J. Walsh, PhD, LPC, CRC, CPRP, is an assistant professor of neuropsychiatry and behavioral science for the Rehabilitation Counseling program at the University of South Carolina in Columbia, South Carolina. He has specialty interests in psychiatric rehabilitation.

Molly Watkins, MSEd, NCC, is a professional school and family counselor at Ames Middle School in Ames, Iowa. She has specialty interests in child and adolescent counseling and at-risk factors for youths. She is the former editorial assistant for *Counseling Outcome Research and Evaluation.*

Joshua C. Watson, PhD, LPC, NCC, ACS, is an associate professor at Texas A&M University–Corpus Christi. He has specialty interests in counseling student–athletes and the college adjustment experiences of underserved student populations. He is a former president of the Association for Assessment and Counseling and Research, and he serves as the editor for the *Journal of College Counseling.*

Kelly L. Wester, PhD, NCC, LPC, is an associate professor at the University of North Carolina at Greensboro. She has specialty interests in research training as well as nonsuicidal self-injury. She teaches in research methodology, the research process, counseling theories, and sexual abuse, and she also provides supervision.

Part I
Context

• • •

If you are reading this book, you have likely found yourself navigating expectations within the third decade of accountability in higher education. Perhaps you are here because you are enthusiastic about the possibility of learning creative ways to find what your students know and can do. If so, that is wonderful, and we welcome you! We believe that student learning outcome (SLO) assessment can be surprisingly meaningful and rewarding if done well. More likely, you cracked this book open because you understand your need to show evidence of student learning for some reason or another. Maybe there is an expectation that you generate effectiveness data for promotion, tenure, or merit purposes. Or maybe you are helping to establish an SLO assessment plan to meet expectations of administrators, accrediting bodies, or key stakeholders. If so, you are in good company.

At its heart, SLO assessment involves going beyond traditional, input-based measures of productivity (e.g., how many courses and students we taught, what syllabi we provided, whether students were satisfied with their experiences) to outcome-based measures of effectiveness. These measures of effectiveness help us understand what students know and can do as a result of their educational endeavors (Council for Higher Education Accreditation, 2011; Urofsky, 2009).

Part I includes three chapters designed to lay a foundation for understanding the SLO assessment process. In Chapter 1, we provide a brief overview of the SLO movement. In Chapter 2, we outline the bigger picture of academic program evaluation. Chapter 3 includes practical strategies for identifying SLOs and mapping them to curricula in intentional ways. After you have reviewed these foundations, you will be ready to turn your attention to Part II, where we provide concrete and practical guidance for developing direct and indirect measures of student learning. Part III is focused on technical assistance for gathering, storing, reporting, making meaning of, and implementing changes on the basis of SLO data. Finally, Part IV includes several assignments and rubrics that your colleagues have developed to help you think of options for assessing student learning throughout core areas of the counselor education curriculum. Because we are counselor educators who are writing to an audience largely composed of counselor educators, we looked to the Council for Accreditation of Counseling and Related Educational Programs (CACREP) 2016 Standards to frame the presentation of our work and organization of the application; at the same time, we trust you will find the material relevant even if you are in a program that is not accredited or that is accredited by a specialty body other than CACREP.

Chapter 1

The SLO Movement

The emphasis on evaluating SLOs in higher education began with a focus on institutional account-ability and overall undergraduate program improvement (New Leadership Alliance for Student Learning and Accountability, 2012). Over time, key players have shifted from state government to federal government to accrediting bodies. The now-famous Commission on the Future of Higher Education (also known as the Spellings Commission) admonished higher education institutions for not being more forthcoming about SLOs, which marked a pivotal point in the accountability movement in higher education. The Commission on the Future of Higher Education (2006) wrote the following:

> We are disturbed by evidence that the quality of student learning at U.S. colleges and universities is inadequate and, in some cases, declining . . . Colleges and universities must become more transparent about cost, price, and student success outcomes, and must willingly share this information with students and families. (pp. 3–4)

Today, accreditation is the "primary vehicle for quality assurance in American higher education and the major driver of learning outcomes assessment" (Kuh & Ewell, 2010, p. 23), and faculty members across programs are becoming more involved in the process of assessing SLOs and using data to promote learning (Ewell, Paulson, & Kinzie, 2011; Kuh, Jankowski, Ikenberry, & Kinzie, 2014). Indeed, after examining assessment practices across countless institutions, Kuh et al. (2014) concluded the following:

> U.S. higher education has turned a corner in the assessment of student learning. Carrying out this important work is no longer primarily an act of compliance but more appropriately and promisingly is driven by a balance of compli-ance and institutional desire to improve. (p. 5)

In this chapter, we provide a brief review of accountability and SLO assessment movements in higher education to provide context for the tasks that we discuss in the remainder of the book. First, we review key developments and stakeholders in this movement. Later, we provide a synopsis of the current state of SLO assessment procedures, challenges, and opportunities. We end the chapter with resources that you may find helpful for understanding the greater context of assessment and accountability in higher education.

A Brief History

In a reflection on major changes over the first 25 years of the SLO assessment movement, Ewell (2009) noted several major changes and strides nationwide. First, over time, faculty members have increased buy-in and improved perspectives regarding the legitimacy of the movement. Second, there is ongoing and increased government and policy concern regarding the importance of transparency and attention to learning outcomes in higher education. Third, although accountability expectations began with mandates from state governments, expectations related to SLO assessment procedures have transitioned to regional and specialty accrediting bodies operated for and by educators. Finally, the last two decades have brought rapid advances in technology and resources to facilitate the SLO assessment process.

While reflecting on trends in the first 25 years of the SLO movement, Ewell (2009) called attention to four main players:

1. *State governments.* Although funding models are changing, state governments traditionally held the purse strings for public higher education institutions. The accountability movement in higher education began with short-lived, state government mandates for standardized testing and reporting.
2. *Federal government.* Traditionally, the federal government had limited involvement in higher education, although it plays an important role in financial aid. The formation of the Commission on the Future of Higher Education marked an important turning point in the role of federal government in higher education accountability.
3. *Accrediting bodies.* Over time, regulation of accountability and expectations for SLO assessment has transitioned to regional accrediting bodies. Program or specialty accrediting bodies are now quite active in setting expectations for SLO assessment.
4. *Customers, public opinion, and press.* Ultimately, institutions of higher education are accountable for providing the products and processes that constituents need to thrive in a changing world.

With a focus on demonstrating that higher education programs are effective, accreditation standards of agencies and professional accrediting organizations provide the primary motivation to engage in evaluation. These happen on two primary levels: regional accreditation and program accreditation. The Council for Higher Education Accreditation, which is the accrediting body for accrediting bodies, stated in 2010 that accreditors must "require institutions or programs routinely to provide reliable information to the public on their performance, including student achievement as determined by the institution or program" (Policies and Procedures Standard 12.B.1, p. 5).

In the United States, seven regional, nonprofit, self-regulatory accrediting commissions are responsible for determining accreditation status of most institutions of higher education. These regional accrediting bodies are more alike than different when it comes to expectations for SLO assessment. Provezis (2010) found that all seven regional accreditors (a) were following the Council of Regional Accrediting Commissions' (2003) *Principles for Good Practices* related to SLO assessment, (b) expected institutions to design and assess SLOs, and (c) expected public disclosure of findings. All but one accrediting commission expected faculty involvement in the SLO assessment process. All accrediting commissions reported concerns regarding the state of SLO assessment, all but one accrediting commission provided support for institutions in the SLO assessment process, and none of the accrediting commissions prescribed how institutions were to go about the task.

Higher education personnel acknowledge that recognizing only the accomplishments of programs and students is not adequate for growth, change, and transparency (Kuh & Ikenberry, 2009). In an effort to be more transparent, more than 300 colleges and universities are now collecting and reporting SLOs along with other information as part of the Voluntary System of Accountability. Many accrediting organizations require programs to be transparent with SLOs by publishing this information to constituent groups and the public. Utilizing systematic assessment approaches that include the measurement of students' knowledge, competencies, and dispositions allows higher education program faculty and personnel to determine where improvement is needed at classroom, program, and institution levels. When educators make changes based on this information, they are published or otherwise made transparent so that stakeholders can understand quality improvement processes at play.

As SLO evaluation has evolved in higher education, more undergraduate and graduate programs are engaging in this level of assessment (Kuh & Ikenberry, 2009). Programmatic accrediting bodies ranging from business to nursing to medicine all require their constituents to engage in SLO assessment practices. CACREP joined the accountability movement in 2009 when it introduced the requirement that programs attend to SLOs as part of their systematic program assessment plans and that programs document student knowledge and skills specific to various specialty areas within the profession. At the same time, Kuh and Ikenberry (2009) reported that "American higher education is far from where it needs to be in assessing student learning and in using the results to improve outcomes" (p. 4). It appears that counselor education programs are in the learning curve with much of higher education in regard to measuring SLOs to make useful meaning and application of what is learned in these evaluations.

Current State of SLO Assessment

As we have settled into the accountability movement, we are shifting attention to more meaningful assessment of SLOs in a way that goes beyond reporting and defending one's practices to outside parties. Rather, the process may be used for "preserving and developing the institutions' internal capacity for evidence-based continuous improvement" (Ewell, 2009, p. 14). In a 2008 foundational work, the Association of American Colleges and Universities (AACU) made a strong argument that SLO assessment practices must be situated in context and must focus on capturing the most authentic, meaningful student work. "We must hold ourselves accountable for assessing our students' best work, not generic skills and not introductory levels of learning" (AACU, 2008, p. 3). This involves a holistic process, including being proactive in response to legitimate external concern, documenting action on assessment findings, locating assessment activities at major gateways or transition points, and embedding assessment throughout the curriculum (Ewell, 2009).

In attempts to capture the current state of SLO assessment, Kuh et al. (2014) gathered data from 1,202 institutions of higher education in the United States. They found that SLO assessment was the norm across institutions and that participants placed high importance on requirements for regional accreditation and moderate-to-high importance on program accreditation. Institutions were using a broad range of approaches to SLO assessment (Kuh et al., 2014). Rated from most to least frequently used, methods included national student surveys, rubrics, classroom-based performance assessments, alumni surveys, incoming student placement examinations, locally developed surveys, capstones, locally developed knowledge and skills measures, general knowledge and skills measures, employer surveys, portfolios, and externally situated performance assessments. When comparing the types of activities used in the SLO process with activities used 5 years prior, Kuh et al. noted more than a threefold increase in use of rubrics (to 69% of institutions) and a fourfold increase in use of external performance assessments, such as internships (to 40% of institutions) and portfolios (to 41% of institutions). Because this study captures current practice in big-picture SLO assessment, we include a summary of key findings here:

- Stated learning outcomes for students are now the norm in American higher education.
- The prime driver of assessment remains the same: expectations of regional and program or specialized accredited agencies.
- There is significantly more assessment activity now than a few years ago.
- The range of tools and measure to assess student learning has expanded significantly.
- Meeting accreditation expectations heads the list of how institutions use assessment evidence, but internal use by campuses is growing and is considered *far more important* than external use.
- Institutions more frequently report assessment results internally than to external audiences.
- Provosts perceive substantial support on their campuses for assessment.
- In general, institutional selectivity is negatively related to assessment activity.
- Faculty are key to moving assessment work forward. (Kuh et al., 2014, pp. 3–4)

Examination of program-level SLO assessment practices parallels Kuh et al.'s (2014) findings in several ways (Ewell et al., 2011). In a 2010 survey of department or program chairs across 2,719 institutions, participants reported program improvement and accreditation as the greatest drivers of SLO assessment. Most program leaders noted that their units had established SLOs, and programs were using a wide variety of assessment methods. Two thirds of programs used capstone assessments; two thirds used rubrics; more than one half used performance assessments or final projects; and about one third used portfolios, comprehensive examinations, and external examinations. Faculty members in accredited programs appeared to be more involved in SLO assessment work, and those in accredited programs reported greater use of data obtained from the SLO assessment process. Although some chairs reported staff support, responses from participants indicated that SLO assessment work appeared to be an add-on responsibility for many faculty members.

Taken together, findings from accrediting bodies and scholars of SLO assessment at institutional and program levels all point in one direction: SLO assessment is a reality of work across higher education. Participating in accountability and quality assurance practices is part of what it means to be a faculty member in higher education today. This participation will require a more sophisticated understanding of best practices for meaningful, authentic assessment of student learning in a manner that exceeds historical examination of syllabi, student satisfaction, or general indicators such as pass rates on standardized or instructor-developed examinations.

Although educator buy-in and collaboration are central to SLO assessment success, not all educators are enthused about this increased focus on learning outcomes (Barrio Minton & Gibson, 2012; Hutchings, 2010; Kuh et al., 2014; Miller, 2012). In a humorous account of the process of incorporating attention to SLOs into practice, Miller (2012) compared the accountability movement over the last 25 years with Kübler-Ross's (1969) stages of grief. She noted that faculty members initially engaged in denial followed by angry rejection and reactivity, bargaining for minimal compliance with standards in exchange for being left alone, depression, and finally acceptance that perhaps we can learn something valuable from the exercise. Faculty members may feel threatened and disconnected from the SLO evaluation process, perhaps because initial rationale for SLO assessment was less than welcoming and was imposed by individuals outside of programs and institutions (Hutchings, 2010). Others have argued that the SLO assessment process inevitably violates faculty members' academic freedom (see Cain, 2014). Faculty involvement and engagement are key for changing culture and for moving SLO assessment forward in meaningful ways (Hutchings, 2010; Kuh et al., 2014). Consider Hutchings's (2010, pp. 13–16) six suggestions for involving faculty in SLO assessment:

- Build assessment around the regular, ongoing work of teaching and learning.
- Make a place for assessment in faculty development.
- Build assessment into the preparation of graduate students.
- Reframe the work of assessment as scholarship.
- Create campus spaces and occasions for constructive assessment conversation and action.
- Involve students in assessment.

Moving Forward

We believe SLO assessment is here to stay. When done well, faculty members can use the process to optimize quality of counselor education programs and, in turn, quality of services offered to counseling consumers across settings. By demystifying the SLO assessment process, providing practical resources, and helping faculty members align program evaluation with their values, we hope to spark curiosity regarding what is working in our programs, how we might improve our programs, and, ultimately, how we might best prepare students for the world of practice. If we are proactive in establishing our SLOs, we can use them to expand beyond just meeting accreditation requirements to building stronger programs, serving clients more effectively, and increasing the rigor of the scholarship of teaching and learning (SoTL) in counselor education.

In Chapter 2, we discuss SLO assessment expectations unique to counselor education and provide you with a model for program development and evaluation. Throughout the remainder of the text, we discuss practical strategies for managing each stage of the model.

Resources

Cain, T. R. (2014). *Assessment and academic freedom: In concert, not conflict.* Retrieved from http://www.learningoutcomesassessment.org/documents/OP2211-17-14.pdf

Council for Higher Education Accreditation: http://www.chea.org/

Council for Higher Education Accreditation. (2003). *Statement of mutual responsibilities for student learning outcomes: Accreditation, institutions, and programs.* Retrieved from http://www.chea.org/pdf/StmntStudentLearningOutcomes9-03.pdf

Council of Regional Accrediting Commissions. (2003). *Regional accreditation and student learning: Principles for good practices.* Retrieved from https://www.msche.org/documents/regnlsl.pdf

Council of Regional Accrediting Commissions. (2004). *Regional accreditation and student learning: A guide for institutions and evaluators.* Retrieved from http://www.sacscoc.org/pdf/handbooks/GuideForInstitutions.pdf

Ewell, P. T. (2009). *Assessment, accountability, and improvement: Revisiting the tension.* Retrieved from http://www.learningoutcomeassessment.org/documents/PeterEwell_005.pdf

Ewell, P., Paulson, K., & Kinzie, J. (2011). *Down and in: Assessment practices at the program level.* Retrieved from http://www.learningoutcomesassessment.org/documents/NILOAsurvey-report2011.pdf

Hutchings, P. (2010). *Opening the doors to faculty involvement in assessment.* Retrieved from http://www.learningoutcomesassessment.org/documents/PatHutchings_0004.pdf

Kuh, G. D., Ikenberry, S. O., Jankowski, N. A., Cain, T. R., Ewell, P. T., Hutchings, P., & Kinzie, J. (2015). *Using evidence of student learning to improve higher education.* San Francisco, CA: Jossey-Bass.

Kuh, G. D., Jankowski, N. A., Ikenberry, S. O., & Kinzie, J. (2014). *Knowing what students know and can do: The current state of learning outcomes assessment at U.S. colleges and universities.* Retrieved from http://www.learningoutcomeassessment.org/documents/2013%20Survey%20Report%20Final.pdf

National Institute for Learning Outcomes Assessment: http://www.learningoutcomesassessment.org/

Urofsky, R. I. (2009, Fall). CACREP board issues guiding statements on student learning outcomes. *The CACREP connection.* Retrieved from http://www.cacrep.org/wp-content/uploads/2012/07/Connection-Fall-20091.pdf

Chapter 2

The Bigger Picture
of Program Evaluation

Be honest—is the purpose of having a program assessment plan simply to satisfy the administration and your external accreditation organization? Or is there genuine interest in the ongoing process of identifying the strengths and weaknesses in the program as reflected through student performance? A plan created to appease the accrediting agency or administration is very different from an assessment plan that was created with the intent to implement and learn from it. (Hatfield, 2009, p. 1)

• • •

In the most general sense, a program is "a set of resources and activities directed toward one or more common goals, typically under the direction of a single manager or management team" (Newcomer, Hatry, & Wholey, 2010, p. 5). Programs may be simple or complex. Within higher education, one could conceptualize any of the following as a program: courses, tracks or specialty areas, degree programs, entire academic units, colleges, or universities.

> Program evaluation is the application of systematic methods to address questions about program operations and results. It may include ongoing monitoring of a program as well as one-shot studies of program processes or program impact. The approaches used are based on social science research methodologies and professional standards. (Newcomer et al., 2010, pp. 5–6)

In counselor education, program evaluation involves using systematic and reasoned approaches to understanding operations of courses, specialty areas, and the department or program as a whole.

The CACREP 2016 Standards are clear regarding evaluation expectations with regard to the overall program, students, as well as faculty and supervisors. These standards include the specific nature of data to be considered alongside requirements for annual, public reporting of performance and evidence of use of data. The Standards do not, however, specify processes for engaging in this systematic evaluation process. In this chapter, we provide a general program evaluation model to serve as a foundation for the remainder of this book, illustrate ways in which these processes link with the types of data you will utilize in program evaluation, and identify resources for learning more about the big-picture program evaluation process. In the remainder of the book, we focus on best practices for engaging in specific components of the program and the SLO evaluation process.

CACREP 2016 Standards—Section 4: Evaluation in the Program

Evaluation in the program includes opportunities for counselor education program faculty to comprehensively evaluate overall program effectiveness. Assessment of students' knowledge, skills, and professional dispositions is integral. Evaluation data will help program faculty reflect on aspects of the program that work well and those that need improvement and will inform programmatic and curricular decisions.

The following Standards apply to all entry-level and doctoral-level programs for which accreditation is being sought unless otherwise specified.

Evaluation of the Program

A. Counselor education programs have a documented, empirically based plan for systematically evaluating the program objectives, including student learning. For each of the types of data listed in 4.B, the plan outlines (1) the data that will be collected, (2) a procedure for how and when data will be collected, (3) a method for how data will be reviewed or analyzed, and (4) an explanation for how data will be used for curriculum and program improvement.

B. The counselor education program faculty demonstrate the use of the following to evaluate the program objectives: (1) aggregate student assessment data that address student knowledge, skills, and professional dispositions; (2) demographic and other characteristics of applicants, students, and graduates; and (3) data from systematic follow-up studies of graduates, site supervisors, and employers of program graduates.

C. Counselor education program faculty provide evidence of the use of program evaluation data to inform program modifications.

D. Counselor education program faculty disseminate an annual report that includes, by program level, (1) a summary of the program evaluation results, (2) subsequent program modifications, and (3) any other substantial program changes. The report is published on the program website in an easily accessible location, and students currently in the program, program faculty, institutional administrators, and personnel in cooperating agencies (e.g., employers, site supervisors) are notified that the report is available.

E. Counselor education program faculty must annually post on the program's website in an easily accessible location the following specific information for each entry-level specialty area and doctoral program: (1) the number of graduates for the past academic year, (2) pass rates on credentialing examinations, (3) completion rates, and (4) job placement rates.

Assessment of Students

F. The counselor education program faculty systematically assesses each student's progress throughout the program by examining student learning in relation to a combination of knowledge and skills. The assessment process includes the following: (1) identification of key performance indicators of student learning in each of the eight core areas and in each student's respective specialty area(s) (for doctoral programs, each of the five doctoral core areas), (2) measurement of student learning conducted via multiple measures and over multiple points in time, and (3) review or analysis of data.

G. The counselor education program faculty systematically assesses each student's professional dispositions throughout the program. The assessment process includes the following: (1) identification of key professional dispositions, (2) measurement of student professional dispositions over multiple points in time, and (3) review or analysis of data.

H. The counselor education program faculty has a systematic process in place for the use of individual student assessment data in relation to retention, remediation, and dismissal.

Evaluation of Faculty and Supervisors

I. Written procedures for administering the process for student evaluations of faculty are available to the counselor education program faculty.

J. Students have regular, systematic opportunities to formally evaluate counselor education program faculty.

K. Students have regular, systematic opportunities to formally evaluate practicum and internship supervisors.

Note. From *2016 Standards*, by the Council for Accreditation of Counseling and Related Educational Programs, 2016, *Section* 4: Evaluation in the Program. Copyright 2016 by the Council for Accreditation of Counseling and Related Educational Programs. Reprinted with permission.

A General Framework for Program Evaluation

As noted earlier, program evaluation involves systematic investigation using research principles. The credibility of a program evaluation is related directly to the intentionality with which it is designed. As with good research, this includes attention to measurement validity, measurement reliability, internal validity, external validity, statistical conclusion validity, and strength of reporting (Newcomer et al., 2010). This also means that strong program evaluation involves starting with a clear understanding of questions to be investigated and ways in which they are meaningful to constituents. In academic program evaluation, this includes stakeholders such as students, faculty, accrediting bodies, university administration, agency and school personnel served by program graduates, and the public at large. Stakeholders may have some unifying interests, but the specific nature of needs and questions will be uniquely theirs.

The Program Logic Model is a longstanding tool for helping program personnel conceptualize programs in a meaningful and ordered way (McLaughlin & Jordan, 2010; Taylor-Powell, Jones, & Henert, 2002). A Logic Model provides a structure for telling the story of a program with special attention to the human, financial, and material resources that go into a program (inputs); program activities (outputs); program participants; and short-, medium-, and long-term program outcomes. In addition to naming tangible and intangible components of the program, the Logic Model helps program planners and evaluators conceptualize relationships and processes throughout the program.

Understanding Logic Models and Logic Model processes is essential to articulating a coherent program evaluation plan. If you are not yet familiar with Logic Models, we encourage you to take a time out and participate in the free University of Wisconsin extension course *Enhancing Program Performance With Logic Models* (see http://www.uwex.edu/ces/lmcourse). Participating in this program will help you best understand the language used throughout most evaluation resources, and it will provide a strong foundation for program evaluation planning processes.

It is a short step from articulating how a program works via a Logic Model to identifying elements of the program to be evaluated. In the online Logic Model course, Taylor-Powell et al. (2002) specified key evaluation questions for each component of the Logic Model. For example, one can evaluate inputs (e.g., What are characteristics of program applicants? Staff? Students? Learning resources?), outputs (e.g., What is the effectiveness of teaching and supervision within the program?), and outcomes (e.g., What do students know as a result of their participation in the program? What are students able to do as a result of their time in the program?).

Evaluation questions may be focused on needs, process, or outcomes. Needs assessment includes attention to understanding the community and university context and using that understanding to shape the overall objectives and nature of the program. For example, a counselor education program located near major military operations may use needs assessment data to incorporate a special program focus related to needs of veterans or military families; faculty members may also use student feedback to structure a program in a way that allows maximum flexibility for students in military families. Process evaluation may include attention to how things happen within the program. In our field, that may include attention to student satisfaction with teaching, supervision quality, alumni perceptions of program support after graduation, or site supervisor perceptions of program support. Outcome evaluation attends to actual products of learning. The bulk of this book is focused on the process of gathering and evaluating evidence of SLOs in courses and field experiences. This outcome evaluation may also include attention to effectiveness in work with clients and program graduate accomplishments. In all, the CACREP 2016 Standards include both process and outcome evaluation.

In a related work, Praslova (2010) adapted Kirkpatrick's (1959) four-level model of training criteria to program evaluation in academia, noting four criteria of interest: reaction, learning, behavior/transfer, and results. *Reaction* is process-oriented, is focused on students' perceptions regarding the program, and is most clearly articulated in student evaluations. *Learning* is outcome-oriented, is focused on direct measures of student learning, and includes attention to the types of assessments that we describe in the chapters focused on course-based assessments (Chapter 4) and comprehensive examinations (Chapter 6). *Behavior/transfer* relates to evidence of competency demonstrated in the most authentic, culminating work conducted outside the traditional class context; this includes field experience performance (Chapter 5), overarching portfolios (Chapter 7), and theses or dissertations (Chapter 8). Finally, the *results* criterion is impact-oriented and is focused on career and academic outcomes as well as more global contributions to the field and society at large; these are often assessed via alumni and employer surveys (Chapter 10) as well as examination of awards and recognitions earned by graduates. All of these elements are important in a strong program evaluation plan.

Program evaluation is continuous and systematic. On the basis of the components required of the evaluation, everything from student characteristics, site supervisor program perceptions, employers' perceptions of their employees who recently graduated, SLOs, and area standards are included. In this way, assessment and evaluation of the program begin following admission of each student and continue at different points throughout the program until the program graduates are employed.

To ensure a meaningful big-picture evaluation plan, program faculty should look beyond specific CACREP (2016) requirements for program evaluation to determine what additional information is needed to make evaluative decisions about students, curricula, and the program. In addition to content considerations, this will include answers to questions such as the following:

- When is this information needed?
- How will faculty utilize the information?
- What does this mean for individual students and the program as a whole?

For example, a program faculty may decide to assess dispositions of individual students often because of the developmental nature of counselor education programs. Students may need extra support as they progress through a program and prepare to provide counseling services during practicum and internship. Additional measures to assess this level of preparation may be required prior to students delivering those services to the public.

Organizing the multiple pieces of information required in program evaluation can be quite complex. Mizikaci (2006) offered a technical systems approach to understanding program evaluation in higher education. A technical system "includes a transformation process as the 'interaction' among the input, resources, and output" (Mizikaci, 2006, p. 48). These three elements are influenced by external environment entities, such as accreditation standards and stakeholders (i.e., students, professional counselors, clients). However, counselor educators can determine when information should be collected through examination of this systemic process. The section that follows identifies suggested assessment points expanded from R. G. Lewis and Smith's (1994) description of the interaction among the three elements of inputs, resources, and outputs.

Data Collection in Counselor Education Programs

Inputs

Program inputs include the following considerations:

- *Student characteristics* (academic, demographic, need and expectations, interests): Collected through admission information to include undergraduate grade point average (GPA), graduate GPA, standardized test scores, gender, ethnicity, disabilities, admission interview documentation, and initial disposition measure with student.
- *Faculty characteristics* (demographic, advising load, research accomplishments): Collected every year through updated vitas, advising logs, and so forth.
- *Financial resources* (sufficient, effectively used, not available): Documented every year through faculty meeting minutes and program/department budgets.
- *Facilities* (classrooms, library holdings/subscriptions, instructional equipment, clinic facilities/access): Documented every year though faculty meeting minutes and classroom rosters.
- *Programs, curriculum, courses, and schedules*: Documented every semester/year through faculty minutes, program summary reports, course schedules, and faculty program/department/college/school minutes.

Transformation Process

Transformation process includes the following considerations:

- *Design* (courses, programs, schedules, inputs, class size): Documented through faculty/department/college/school minutes as well as course schedules and rosters.
- *Delivery* (methods to deliver course material to the students): Documented through course syllabi and student/program handbooks (revised consistently).

- *Measurement of the outputs* (includes the measures used to document program standards and SLOs): Documented through faculty meeting regarding the CACREP assessment plan.
- *Evaluation of the program, the courses, and the professors* (student surveys, alumni, employers, site supervisors): Faculty teaching evaluations and faculty/site supervisor evaluations are collected when students complete courses and/or practicum/internship. Alumni and employer surveys are typically collected one or more years after students graduate from the program. Graduation surveys are collected of current graduates. Site supervisors of practicum and internship students are surveyed regarding preparedness of students for clinical experiences after their completion of the field experience.

Outputs

Program outputs include the following considerations:

- *Academic achievement, SLOs, and dispositions* (success rates, skill development competency): Measures designed to assess specific specialty area CACREP Standards are collected as students complete specific assignments or are observed to demonstrate specific skills (rubrics, observations). Comprehensive exams, academic portfolios, and dispositions may be collected every semester or once a year for each student while matriculating. Note that programs may require a passing score on a comprehensive exam or standardized counseling assessment prior to students entering practicum and/or internship.
- *Program completion data* (graduation, dropout, failure): Documented in grades, faculty program meeting minutes, and the registrar's office.
- *Student professional accomplishments* (pass rates on professional certification/licensure exams, publications/presentations, employment as counselor/counselor educator): Information is typically sent to the program or college/school for professional examinations. Current students and alumni are surveyed once a year for scholarship achievements. Recent graduates are surveyed each year for current employment.
- *Employment achievements* (on-the-job accomplishments, employer satisfaction): Alumni are surveyed once a year regarding their career accomplishments. Employer surveys of alumni at least one year postgraduation may focus on satisfaction with graduates' skills and/or level of preparedness of graduates to conduct the work appropriately.

Putting Program Evaluation Into Action

Now that you understand the key components of bigger picture program evaluation, it may help to develop a more ordered, concrete model for creating meaningful program evaluation plans. It is necessary to break down the who, what, when, where, and how of program assessment and evaluation. Although this task may seem daunting, it demystifies the process for the subsystems of faculty, students, higher education administrators, and external stakeholders. Furthermore, it demonstrates the systemic nature of the process, as all the subsystems are interacting continuously in this effort. Because of this level of interaction and interdependence, strong, effective communication is imperative. Buy-in to the process in which all subsystem members have some level of responsibility in the program evaluation makes for success. Hence, feedback to and from those leading the process should be elicited. This is not a "telling to" process—doing so will alienate these individuals. Program administrators may want to consider some measure of consistent feedback about the process and make adjustments as necessary.

   Another point to consider is that program evaluation is not a product. CACREP (2016) requires self-study reports and yearly vital statistics reports, but these are reflections of the larger process. Although the words "outcomes" and "outputs" may indicate a product, they are one part of the total picture of the program. The old adage "the whole is greater than the sum of its parts" could apply to this example. Delineating measures to use, scheduling when those measures are used, and designating who will collect those measures are parts of the whole picture of program evaluation. The results should tell a story about the program from beginning to end, with the faculty, students, supervisors, and administrators authoring the story. Considering this, there is a need for flexibility during the evaluation process. Timing may need to change on the basis of feedback or measures that do not adequately assess specific skills or behaviors. Similarly, programs may need to update (and document) changes to when and how measures are used throughout the process. Good program evaluation promotes good practice and innovation, but it also helps program constituents advocate for the specific needs related to their program.

Hatfield (2009) provided 14 key questions that will help evaluation planners keep focused when creating plans:

1. Why are we doing assessment?
2. What kind of plan are we writing?
3. Who is responsible for assessment in our program?
4. Is administration supportive of assessment?
5. Is there a common language for talking about assessment?
6. Have we identified program-level SLOs?
7. Does the plan rely on direct measures of student learning?
8. Are the assessment methods appropriate to the outcomes?
9. Is there a systematic approach to implementing the plan?
10. What is the method for collecting and organizing data?
11. How are faculty trained to use assessment tools?
12. Do the assessment tools distinguish among levels of achievement?
13. What happens to the data after having been collected?
14. Have we used the data to improve learning and teaching?

These questions include attention to understanding specific program processes and outcomes of focus as well as consideration of reliability and validity. We strongly recommend this free, short, and logical work for grounding understanding in academic program evaluation.

As the program faculty sits together to create the bigger picture program evaluation plan, they may find a roadmap helpful in this process. In addition to providing strong worksheets and foundations in the online Logic Model course (Taylor-Powell et al., 2002), Taylor-Powell, Steele, and Douglah (1996) provided an excellent, free guide to program evaluation planning. The guide includes clear and simple questions to help users identify purposes of the evaluation and stakeholders involved in the process. Further, the authors provided worksheets to help users articulate purposes, key stakeholders, necessary information, methods for collecting information, analysis and reporting procedures, target dates, responsible parties, and resources needed. We expect that you will find these worksheets especially helpful for thinking through the overarching process in a meaningful way.

The bigger program evaluation picture includes activities geared toward understanding how characteristics, qualities, strengths, and opportunities for those who participate in the program (e.g., students, faculty, staff, supervisors) and program processes as a whole (e.g., admission, course sequencing, field experiences) contribute to student outcomes. This book is primarily dedicated to the specific process of evaluating SLOs within counselor education courses and programs.

As is illustrated in Figure 2.1, the program and SLO evaluation process will begin with the process of identifying objectives of interest. After mapping curricula and processes to understand where and how these elements take place (Chapter 3), program faculty members are ready to select assessments or indicators of learning (Chapters 4–9). After these indicators have been identified, faculty members will turn attention to measuring—through rubrics, rating forms, or other objective measures—both direct and indirect assessments of learning (Chapters 10 and 11). After this plan is in place, program faculty will invest time and energy in collecting and managing data (Chapter 12), analyzing data (Chapter 13), and reporting data to constituents (Chapter 14). After data are obtained, the faculty arrives at the single-most important program and SLO evaluation step: making meaning of the data to inform work with students and overall enhancements to the program. Chapters 15–17 include focused attention to use of data in developing programs, supporting students, and informing research. After you have this foundation, you will be ready to delve into Part IV, where you will find several SLO assessments and measures that you may find helpful for thinking about SLO evaluation in your counselor education program or course.

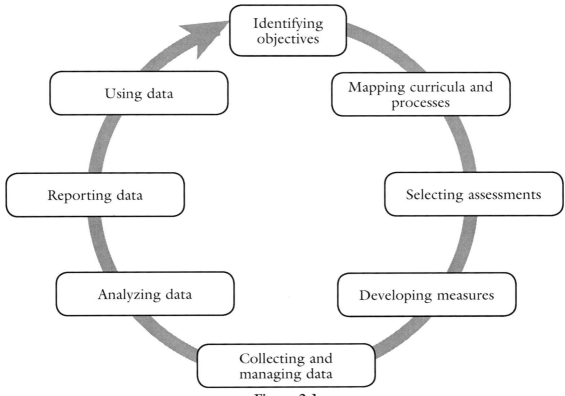

Figure 2.1
The Student Learning Outcome Evaluation Process

Resources

Driscoll, A., & Wood, S. (2007). *Developing outcomes-based assessment for learner-centered education: A faculty introduction.* Sterling, VA: Stylus.

Gardiner, L. R., Corbitt, G., & Adams, S. J. (2010). Program assessment: Getting to a practical how-to model. *Journal of Education for Business, 85,* 139–144. doi:10.1080/08832320903258576

Hatfield, S. (2009). *Assessing your program-level assessment plan.* Manhattan, KS: IDEA Center.

Richman, W. A., & Ariovich, L. (2013). *All-in-one: Combining grading, course, program, and general education outcomes assessment* (Occasional Paper No.19). Retrieved from http://www.learning-outcomesassessment.org/documents/Occasional%20Paper%2019%20FINAL.pdf

Taylor-Powell, E., & Henert, E. (2008). *Developing a Logic Model: Teaching and training guide.* Retrieved from http://www.uwex.edu/ces/pdande/evaluation/pdf/lmguidecomplete.pdf

Taylor-Powell, E., Jones, A. L., & Henert, E. (2002). *Enhancing program performance with Logic Models.* Retrieved from http://www.uwex.edu/ces/lmcourse/

Taylor-Powell, E., Steele, S., & Douglah, M. (1996). *Planning a program evaluation* (G3658-1). Retrieved from http://learningstore.uwex.edu/assets/pdfs/G3658-1.PDF

U.S. Department of Health and Human Services, Centers for Disease Control and Prevention. (2011). *Introduction to program evaluation for public health programs: A self-study guide.* Retrieved from http://www.cdc.gov/eval/guide/CDCEvalManual.pdf

Wholey, J. S., Hatry, H. P., & Newcomer, N. E. (2010). *Handbook of practical program evaluation* (3rd ed.). San Francisco, CA: Jossey-Bass.

Chapter 3

Identifying Objectives
and Mapping Curricula
and Processes

Now that we have attended to context for the accountability movement in higher education and have explored the program evaluation process more broadly, it is time to turn attention to what this means for the day-to-day practice of making meaning of student learning in counselor education. In this chapter, we explore what we mean by SLOs and discuss the process of creating SLOs to guide program and course assessment processes. After we have developed a clear understanding of how we want students to develop during their programs, we turn attention to curriculum mapping as a means for ensuring that curricula include the types of experiences students need to develop SLOs. We end this chapter with attention to procedures and tools for crafting broad-based, curriculum-linked, SLO-focused assessment plans. By the time you are done reading this chapter, you should understand the SLO assessment process in enough depth to begin diving into specific options for gathering evidence of student learning, measuring this evidence with rubrics and rating forms, making meaning of data, and using the data to inform program development. These more task-oriented steps compose the remainder of the book.

Creating Meaningful SLOs

Consider the following definitions of SLOs:

- "a stated expectation of what someone will have learned during an academic experience" (Driscoll & Wood, 2007, p. 5);
- "what should our students be able to DO 'out there' that we are responsible for 'in here'" (Stiehl & Lewchuk, 2008a, p. 23); and
- "clearly articulated, collective conception" of the ideal candidate so that programs may use "intentionality and coherence . . . to cultivate those qualities" (AACU, 2008, p. 1).

Each definition captures an element of learning, and the last two definitions highlight the beauty of meaningful assessment practices. Meaningful SLOs are focused on the world of practice in a way that comes alive and helps tell a story about students' growth toward developing the knowledge, skills, and dispositions needed to be effective as professional counselors.

As discussed in Chapter 1, recent movements within higher education require that programs, colleges, and universities include attention to SLOs in their evaluation procedures. Beginning with the release of the 2009 Standards, CACREP required that counselor education programs assess learning related to broad core curricular areas, and they provided specific SLOs for accredited programs to assess within each specialty area (e.g., clinical mental health counseling, school counseling). In the 2016 Standards, CACREP retained the expectation for SLO assessment, added an expectation that programs assess broad categories of SLOs at multiple times and using multiple measures, and discontinued providing specific SLOs for entry-level programs. The more recent revision provides programs flexibility in articulating their overall program goals and SLOs.

Initial Identification of SLOs

The process of creating meaningful SLOs starts with faculty members coming together to determine what a student who is successful in the program should look like. More specifically, this may include attention to *cognitive* domains (i.e., what students should know or how they should think), *affective* domains (i.e., how students feel, what students care about), and *behavioral* domains (i.e., what students can do) at the end of the course or program (Office of Academic Planning and Assessment, 2001). In counseling, cognitive domains include SLOs oriented toward foundational knowledge, case conceptualization, and critical thinking abilities. Affective domains may include cultivation of personal characteristics associated with effective practitioners, internalized sense of professional identity, and commitment to professional values such as wellness and human dignity. Examples of the behavioral domain include enacting core conditions of counseling, facilitating the assessment or testing process, and delivering large group lessons as part of a comprehensive developmental guidance plan.

There is no one right or best way to begin identifying SLOs. Indeed, most program administrators will find themselves drawing from many sources and using several procedures in the development process. Inspiration for SLOs may include, but is not limited to, the following:

- CACREP 2016 Standards;
- state licensure and certification requirements;
- professional best practice documents;
- competency standards;
- professional literature;
- university or college values, mission, vision, or priorities;
- unique characteristics of local populations or specialized program considerations (e.g., rural mental health, urban mental health, veterans or military families);
- faculty professional values, judgments, or identities; and
- existing program information and data sources.

This list of sources includes accreditation standards, and it goes beyond minimal standards by highlighting the opportunity to develop SLOs aligned with more aspirational standards or unique focus areas.

The program faculty must come together to determine SLOs that are most central to the program and that will become the heart of the SLO evaluation plan. This is no easy feat, especially as faculty members may have a sense that everything is important, and identification of too many SLOs is likely to be overwhelming and counterproductive, perhaps even paralyzing (Hatfield, 2009). If you are at this stage in the SLO development process, the resource list at the end of this chapter includes several sources that have practical exercises and creative techniques for engaging program faculty in collaborative exploration and decision making around SLOs.

For example, in *Program-Based Review and Assessment: Tools and Techniques for Program Improvement*, the Office of Academic Planning and Assessment (2001) provided prompts for facilitating open discussions with program faculty members, a suggestion to clarify values by attempting to reduce SLOs by 25%, goal inventory methods, and a discussion technique that may be particularly helpful for identifying those things that are most important to the programs. They also reminded readers to glean insights into overall priorities by reviewing syllabi, instructional materials, program literature, academic catalogs, and goals of peer and aspirational programs. Similarly, Stiehl and Lewchuk (2008a) provided a series of course- and program-level brainstorming activities that involved utilizing post-it notes to brainstorm "what's good," collecting ideas from variety of sources, and assembling thoughts into more meaningful and broad-level clusters that faculty can then convert into official SLOs.

Whatever SLO identification methods you choose, give adequate time, care, and attention to this SLO process. Resist the urge to shortcut the process. The SLOs you identify should have meaning for the faculty and students as a whole, and the most recent CACREP Standards provide a great deal of program flexibility in determining what these look like. The more faculty members are engaged in the identification process and find meaning in the identified SLOs, the more likely the SLOs are to be authentic in the ways they capture student outcomes and the more likely the faculty members are to be creative and constructive in the remainder of the SLO assessment process.

In the 2016 Standards, CACREP requires that "the counselor education program faculty systematically assesses each student's progress throughout the program by examining student learning in relation to a combination of knowledge and skills" (Standard 4.F, p. 16). Standard 4.F also notes that assessment should include indicators in each core area and students' respective areas. To keep the number of SLOs manageable yet transparent, program faculty may wish to consider aligning overarching SLOs with the major domains identified by CACREP (2016).

Core Curricular Areas for Entry-Level Programs

The following list includes CACREP core curricular areas for entry-level programs:

- professional counseling orientation and ethical practice,
- social and cultural diversity,
- human growth and development,
- career development,
- counseling and helping relationships,
- group counseling and group work,
- assessment and testing, and
- research and program evaluation.

Entry-Level Specialty Areas

Examples of specialty areas include addiction counseling, career counseling, clinical mental health counseling, clinical rehabilitation counseling, college counseling and student affairs, couple and family counseling, and school counseling. CACREP entry-level special areas include three main areas:

- foundations,
- contextual dimensions, and
- practice.

Core Curricular Areas for Doctoral Programs

CACREP includes five core curricular areas for doctoral programs:

- counseling,
- supervision,
- teaching,
- research and scholarship, and
- leadership and advocacy.

Articulating SLOs

After program faculty members have come to agreement regarding what they hope students will gain from the program, it is time to articulate those hopes in a more formal manner. In this section, we discuss levels of SLOs; characteristics of strong SLOs; and tips for writing clear, measurable SLOs.

Whether at the course or the program level, you should work to limit the number of SLOs to only a handful of the most important or central outcomes (Carriveau, 2010; Hatfield, 2009). This may be challenging given the complexity of master's professional programs and the requirement that accredited programs assess eight major areas for all students and three major sets of areas for students in each specialty programs. Counselor educators may find it helpful to organize their thinking into levels of SLOs. Although Carriveau (2010) focused on course-level SLOs and linking SLOs to examinations, we can easily adapt his recommendations to program-level SLOs to the following:

1. *Goals* are overall or "super SLOs" that capture broad areas of interest to educators. Goals are often more complex and conceptual in nature. We may find attention to goals within program mission and vision statements, in catalogs, and in more general literature. Carriveau (2010) noted that most courses have three to five goals.
2. *General learning outcomes* (GLOs) are situated under goals and demonstrate how one may begin clarifying and breaking down overarching goals into more manageable units. At the same time, GLOs still include a level of complexity that makes them hard to capture concretely.
3. *Specific learning outcomes* (sLOs) are GLOs operationalized in a manner that allows focused assessment of components of the GLOs. Carriveau (2010) used lowercase as a reminder that the sLOs are part of the broader SLO plan. Figure 3.1 includes a sample format for conceptualizing these three levels of SLOs.

Breaking goals into GLOs and then into sLOs may also help counselor educators avoid creating kitchen-sink, Rubrik's cube like (Hatfield, 2009) outcomes that are overwhelming and impossible to assess. Consider the following SLO for a moment: "Students will develop, implement, and assess effectiveness of community-based prevention and intervention programs for high-risk youths." The previous statement is not one SLO. It is six smaller SLOs that perhaps link back to a GLO regarding program development:

- develop community-based prevention programs for high-risk youths,
- implement community-based prevention programs for high-risk youths,
- assess effectiveness of community-based prevention programs for high-risk youths,
- develop community-based intervention programs for high-risk youths,
- implement community-based intervention programs for high-risk youths, and
- assess effectiveness of community-based intervention programs for high-risk youths.

GOAL 1:	GLO 1.A: 　sLO 1.A.1: 　sLO 1.A.2: 　sLO 1.A.3:
	GLO 1.B: 　sLO 1.B.1: 　sLO 1.B.2:
	GLO 1.C: 　sLO 1.C.1: 　sLO 1.C.2: 　sLO 1.C.3: 　sLO 1.C.4:
GOAL 2:	GLO 2.A: 　sLO 2.A.1: 　sLO 2.A.2:
	GLO 2.B: 　sLO 2.B.1: 　sLO 2.B.2:
	GLO 2.C: 　sLO 2.C.1: 　sLO 2.C.2: 　sLO 1.C.3:

Figure 3.1
Goals, General Learning Outcomes (GLOs), and Specific Learning Outcomes (sLOs) Worksheet

Like outcomes developed with clients, SLOs at all levels should be clear, simple, measurable, and focused on the learner rather than the educator. Writers should also attend to ways of making SLOs observable. For example, one cannot observe the empathy that a candidate experiences internally. One can, however, observe the outward expression of empathy during an interaction with clients or in reflective writing assignments focused on empathy (we discuss dispositions more thoroughly in Chapter 9). Because simple structure becomes important in the assessment process, it is best if the SLO captures just one major learning domain: cognitive, affective, or behavioral. SLOs that include attention to more than one domain may be too complex to assess clearly. The goal, GLO, and sLO format, however, provides faculty members with options for articulating several aspects of an SLO. Finally, SLOs should be written at levels that represent developmental levels expected of students at the end of the course (for course-based SLOs) or academic program (for program-level SLOs).

The International Assembly for Collegiate Business Education (2014) developed a checklist for writing SLOs. We adapted the checklist slightly and include it below. Note the many ways in which strong SLOs parallel strong client goals and outcomes.

- The statements specify the level, criteria, or standards for the knowledge, skills, abilities, competencies, attitudes, or values that students are expected to be able to demonstrate.
- The statements include conditions under which students should be able to demonstrate their knowledge, skills, abilities, competencies, attitudes, or values.
- The statements are written using active verbs that specify definite, observable behaviors or performance levels.
- The statements are measurable.
- The intended SLOs are distinct and specific to the counseling program.
- The intended SLOs are aligned with the counseling program's mission and broad-based student learning goals.
- The statements specify (a) the areas/fields that will be the focus of assessment; (b) the knowledge, skills, abilities, competencies, attitudes, and values that students are expected to acquire in those areas/fields following completion of their programs of study; and (c) the depth of the knowledge, skills, abilities, competencies, attitudes, and values that students are expected to demonstrate.
- The intended SLOs are expressed in terms of the overall program and not individual courses.
- The statements are simple declarative statements that are capable of being assessed by a single assessment method—that is, they are expressed in ways that do not combine multiple intended outcomes into a single statement requiring the use of multiple assessment methods.
- The statements are expressed in ways that make them capable of being assessed by more than one assessment tool, instrument, or metric.
- The statements are expressed from the students' perspective and not in terms of what the counseling program will do, will provide, or intends to accomplish.
- It is possible to collect accurate and reliable assessment data for each intended learning outcome.
- The statements can be used to identify areas for changes and improvements.
- Considered together, the intended SLOs accurately reflect the key desired learning results for the counseling program.

Assessment experts often provide extensive lists of action verbs that educators can use when writing SLOs. Often, these verbs call attention to the category of SLO (cognitive, affective, behaviors) as well as the level of performance expected of students at that developmental level. More often than not, these verb lists are organized with attention to Bloom's (1956) *Taxonomy of Educational Objectives*. Numerous action lists and tutorials are available via a quick Internet search, and most college and university centers for teaching and learning include such lists on their websites. For some examples, see the Resources section at the end of this chapter.

The ways in which we communicate about SLOs set an important tone regarding our focus and expectations. Consider, for example, a program that has articulated an overarching goal statement that candidates can "provide mental health counseling and interdisciplinary advocacy services for clients at risk because of crisis, disaster, trauma, addiction, and/or co-occurring mental disorders." Clearly, the overarching goal is complex and is not written in a way that can be assessed. The program faculty members may divide the goal into GLOs with attention to utilizing evidence-based counseling approaches (CACREP 2016 Standard 5.F.3.U), conducting holistic assessments (CACREP 2016 Standard 5.F.3.T), and providing crisis and suicide intervention (CACREP 2016 Standards 2.F.5.k and 2.F.5.l). Each GLO may then be articulated into sLOs that program faculty members can assess more specifically. Consider the following sLOs that one might situate underneath the GLO regarding crisis and suicide intervention:

- List warning signs for suicide.
- Conceptualize a client at risk of suicide.
- Identify best practices regarding care for individuals at risk of suicide.
- Conduct a suicide risk assessment.
- Utilize best practices to ensure appropriate quality of care for individuals at risk of suicide.

The first three sLOs regarding suicide are cognitive in nature, and they may be assessed via a variety of methods, including several different types of assignments situated toward the end of a class. The first three sLOs may comprise important foundations for work with clients, but they do not tell us whether students are able to translate cognitive understanding into behaviors that they need to use to help clients at risk of suicide. The last two sLOs are more genuine and authentic in their connection to practice expectations and real-world meaning for students and clients alike. They are best assessed via simulations or performance in closely monitored field experiences. To ensure that the SLO assessment process has as much meaning as possible, counselor educators would be wise to gear SLO assessment procedures to these types of outcomes. After counselor educators have determined cognitive, affective, and behavioral SLOs that they wish students to develop over the course of their specific courses and overall programs, they are ready to begin developing a curriculum that aligns with overarching and specific goals for learning.

Mapping Curricula

Because few counselor educators will develop programs from scratch, educators are more likely to engage in a process of exploring how the curriculum aligns with overarching and specific goals for learning and making adjustments to curricula to best fit the needs of students. Whether used for assessment or strategic planning (Plaza, Draugalis, Slack, Skrepnek, & Sauer, 2007),

> curriculum mapping is concerned with what is taught (the content, the areas of expertise addressed, and the learning outcomes), how it is taught (the learning resources, the learning opportunities), when it is taught (the timetable, the curriculum sequence) and the measures used to determine whether the student has achieved the expected learning outcomes (assessment). (Harden, 2001, p. 123)

Curriculum mapping has roots in K–12 education, where it is used to help conceptualize and assess the curriculum as a whole. There are several books and software programs available regarding curriculum mapping in K–12 education (see Jacobs, 1997, 2005). More recently, faculty members in undergraduate, graduate, and professional programs have applied curriculum mapping to their processes (Deets, 2000; Harden, 2001; Plaza et al., 2007; Uchiyama & Radin, 2008).

There are two primary functions of curriculum maps: (1) to make the curriculum transparent to stakeholders and (2) to demonstrate connections or lack of connections within the program (Harden, 2001). Educators can use curriculum mapping to explore declared/ideal/aspirational curricula, examine taught/actual/delivered curricula, and identify curricula that students actually learn or take away (Harden, 2001; Plaza et al., 2007). In its most complex form, curriculum mapping involves attention to 10 major windows. Table 3.1 includes a summary of the windows and examples of applications for counselor educators.

A holistic curriculum mapping process involves generating a multidimensional view of the curriculum that reaches well beyond syllabi and course-related documents. As with most elements of assessment, the ability to seek and consider multiple sources of information adds richness to the experience that would be absent should one attend only to one source of information. For example, program administrators and faculty members may have a different understanding of broad and spe-

Table 3.1
Curriculum Mapping Windows

Window	Explanation for Counselor Education
Expected learning outcomes	Cognitive, affective, and behavioral outcomes of participating in counselor education programs; what students know or can do by the end of their programs
Curriculum content or areas of expertise covered	CACREP Standards, state certification or licensure standards, and faculty areas of expertise and emphasis; includes broad areas as well as nodes or units within areas (e.g., counseling theories with units including Person-Centered Theory, Individual Psychology, Choice Theory, Cognitive Theory); may be approximated through syllabus review
Student assessment	Ways in which student learning is assessed throughout all aspects of the program: course-based assessments, comprehensive examinations, field experiences, portfolios, theses/dissertations, and dispositions
Learning opportunities	Required courses, elective courses, cocurricular opportunities, field experiences
Learning location	Classrooms, clinics, field-based settings, online learning management systems
Learning resources	Libraries, clinics, learning management systems
Timetable	Chronological events within students' course of study (e.g., course sequencing, major gateways)
Staff	Core, affiliate, and adjunct faculty members; support staff; clinic personnel; graduate assistants; site supervisors; administrative leadership
Curriculum management	Program/departmental leadership, curriculum committees, other decision makers
Students	Personal and professional characteristics, status in program, evidence of learning

Note. From "AMEE Guide No. 21: Curriculum Mapping: A Tool for Transparent and Authentic Teaching and Learning" by R. M. Harden, 2001, *Medical Teacher, 23*, p. 127. Copyright 2001 by Taylor & Francis Group. Reprinted with permission. CACREP = Council for Accreditation of Counseling and Related Educational Programs.

cific aspects of the curriculum. Faculty members who tend to teach in isolated or highly specialized areas may understand one area well but may not understand broader interconnections among other aspects of the program. Students may tell a different story than faculty regarding their experiences in a program. Those who have engaged in curriculum mapping attest to its usefulness in moving beyond identification of SLOs to exploring how educators facilitate and later assess SLOs, improving coherence in programs and fostering greater collaboration and collegiality among faculty members (Koppang, 2004; Uchiyama & Radin, 2008).

A more intricate discussion of curriculum mapping methods is outside the scope of this book. Educators who wish to learn more about curriculum mapping will find several helpful resources at the end of this chapter. Specifically, Stiehl and Lewchuk (2008a) dedicated an entire book to helping university programs map their programs. Harden (2001) provided a practical look at curriculum mapping in a graduate professional program (medical education), including a multistep process ranging from assessing needs of stakeholders, to determining scope of the curriculum mapping task, to managing access to curriculum maps over time. He also addressed ways that various stakeholders may utilize curriculum maps, and he provided criteria for effective use of the maps. At the time of this printing, websites for the University of Hawai'i Manoa, Lehman College, and the University of Connecticut have provided a series of practical tools and templates for the curriculum mapping process (see the Resources section at the end of this chapter).

At the risk of oversimplifying what can be an incredibly complex process, we turn attention to practical considerations for mapping the counselor education curriculum on both course and program levels. We assume counselor educators who are engaging in this process have already identified (a) overarching and specific SLOs, (b) minimal content to be addressed in the curriculum, and (c) minimal experiences to be included in the curriculum.

Program faculty members will bring local perspectives and values to the development process; however, many SLOs, content, and experience priorities will align closely with already-established accreditation, licensure, and certification standards. For example, programs that are accredited by CACREP may come to the table with lists of minimal content requirements for the eight core curricular areas, lists of minimal content for accredited specialty areas, and an understanding that students will complete at least 100 hours of practicum and 600 hours of internship. That same program may be located in a state that requires a dedicated, 3-credit-hour addictions course for professional counseling licensure, and it may be staffed by faculty members who are committed to a social justice model for counseling above and beyond minimal requirements. These elements become nonnegotiable aspects of the curriculum development process.

If you have not yet identified SLOs, baseline content requirements, and baseline experience requirements, STOP HERE. Your curriculum mapping process will be more meaningful if you begin with the end in mind in terms of SLOs, and it will be much smoother if you begin with the end in mind in terms of nonnegotiable and desired elements. You may find the following questions helpful for establishing course and program parameters:

- What are our goals and SLOs for this specific course or program?
- How do these goals and SLOs fit into the overall curriculum?
- At a minimum, what course or program content is nonnegotiable? Have we considered
  –accreditation requirements?
  –licensure or certification requirements?
  –program, department, college, or university requirements?
  –linkage with SLOs?
- At a minimum, what course or program experience is nonnegotiable? Have we considered
  –accreditation requirements?
  –licensure or certification requirements?
  –program, department, college, or university requirements?
  –linkage with SLOs?
- Given our professional expertise, what course or program content above and beyond minimal content requirements would we like to see included in the learning experience?
- Given our professional expertise, what experiences above and beyond minimal experiences would we like to see included in the learning experience?

After one has an understanding of SLOs, content requirements, and experience requirements, it is time to begin the mapping process. As you will see in the curriculum mapping literature, there are many ways to do this. We present two methods that we believe to be most practical and straightforward: mapping from documents and starting from scratch. You may utilize both methods within specific courses or for programs as a whole.

One could identify SLOs, content, and experiences and utilize syllabi and curricular documents to create a matrix showing ways in which the current expressed curriculum aligns with the desired curriculum. Because faculty members may vary in level and quality of detail provided on syllabi and because not all syllabi represent what actually happens in the classroom, alignment of the ideal curriculum with existing syllabi alone is likely to fall flat and to give an incomplete picture. Rather, faculty members can use this matrix as a starting point for discussion regarding when, where, and how they address elements. They may also utilize this method to identify "orphan outcomes" (Hatfield, 2009), gaps in the curriculum, overlaps in the curriculum, and elements of the program not linked to SLOs or standards in meaningful ways.

When programs are considering substantial changes or wanting to challenge current paradigms, they may decide to start from scratch. In this case, they may represent elements of the programs on colored post-it notes (e.g., red for SLOs, orange for experiences, yellow for content, green for existing courses), cluster the elements, and examine the degree to which the clustered elements may be captured in new or existing courses or experiences. As with the first method, program faculty can examine orphan outcomes, gaps, overlaps, and unlinked or disconnected elements of the curriculum. Through the creative process, the faculty can then move toward creating a matrix in which they represent linkages between elements.

Although the original source is unclear, assessment experts tend to identify different levels of attention to SLOs in the matrix process: Introduced (I), Reinforced (R), and Mastery (M). Alternately, educators may identify levels of attention as Basic (B), Intermediate (I), or Advanced (A). These naming conventions allow faculty to attend to ways in which they revisit the most important elements of curriculum over time. For example, if an overarching program objective is "through a process of personal and professional reflection, identify a guiding theory of counseling that will serve as a foundation for counseling in the intended work setting," students may first hear about counseling theories in an introduction to theory course (I). They may revisit their beliefs and develop theory-specific skills in an advanced counseling skills course (R), and they may attend to theory again as part of the practicum experience (R). However, ultimate attention to guiding theory comes during internship (M), when students demonstrate alignment with theory through work with real clients.

In the following pages, we provide a series of worksheets and prompts that you may find helpful in the curriculum mapping and alignment process (see Figures 3.2, 3.3, and 3.4). You may also find these useful as you link your SLOs with your intended and actual curriculum. This may include attention to the overarching program-level curricula, or you could adapt the templates to map how one relates specific curricular standards and SLOs to specific lessons or activities within a course. Note that mapping specific standards and SLOs to specific courses meets portions of CACREP 2016 Standards 2.D and 2.F for documenting required SLOs and content areas on course syllabi and showing where content is covered in the curriculum for the overall program.

Although tedious at times, the curriculum mapping process will reveal a great deal about ways in which aspects of the program link together. The map may illustrate opportunities to reduce redundancies in programs (although educators may decide to retain redundancies for highly valued components), and it is likely to reveal opportunities to align or revise curriculum in intentional ways, including the need to develop new courses or revise existing courses, resituate sequence of courses, or collaborate across experiences. This is an interactive and iterative process. The strongest instructors consistently develop and revise curricula to meet the needs of learners, reflect the latest research, and approximate demands in the world of practice. Like many things, the curriculum map is dated the moment it is complete. Still, a strong curriculum map is a key foundation for a strong, integrated curriculum.

For each course or experience, indicate linkage of course with SLO as follows:

I = Introduced

R = Reinforced

M = Mastery (alternately, B = Basic, I = Intermediate, A = Advanced)

	SLO 1	SLO 2	SLO 3	SLO 4	SLO 5	SLO 6
Core Required Courses						
1.						
2.						
3.						
4.						
5.						
6.						
7.						
8.						
9.						
Clinical Mental Health Counseling Required Courses						
1.						
2.						
3.						
School Counseling Required Courses						
1.						
2.						
3.						
Marriage, Couple, and Family Counseling Required Courses						
1.						
2.						
3.						
Field Experiences						
1.						
2.						

Figure 3.2
Curriculum Map Template: Global Student Learning Outcomes (SLOs) by Course

For each course or experience, indicate linkage of course with content as follows:

I = Introduced

R = Reinforced

M = Mastery (alternately, B = Basic, I = Intermediate, A = Advanced)

	1. Professional and Ethics													2. Diversity								3. Development				
	a	b	c	d	e	f	g	h	i	j	k	l	m	a	b	c	d	e	f	g	h	a	b	c	d	e ...
Core Required Courses																										
1																										
2																										
3																										
4																										
5																										
6																										
7																										
8																										
9																										

	1. Professional and Ethics													2. Diversity								3. Development				
	a	b	c	d	e	f	g	h	i	j	k	l	m	a	b	c	d	e	f	g	h	a	b	c	d	e ...
Clinical Mental Health Counseling Required Courses																										
1																										
2																										
3																										

	1. Professional and Ethics													2. Diversity								3. Development				
	a	b	c	d	e	f	g	h	i	j	k	l	m	a	b	c	d	e	f	g	h	a	b	c	d	e ...
School Counseling Required Courses																										
1																										
2																										
3																										

	1. Professional and Ethics													2. Diversity								3. Development				
	a	b	c	d	e	f	g	h	i	j	k	l	m	a	b	c	d	e	f	g	h	a	b	c	d	e ...
Field Experiences																										
1																										
2																										

Figure 3.3
Curriculum Map Template:
Council for Accreditation of Counseling and Related Educational Programs Core Content by Course

In some ways, identifying meaningful SLOs is like identifying meaningful research questions (Barrio Minton & Gibson, 2012). After we know what we hope to know and why it is important, we can devise strategies for discovering that information. After programs have articulated goals, GLOs, and sLOS and have mapped content to the curriculum in intentional ways, it is time to craft the assessment plan to help discover just what students know and can do.

Crafting the Assessment Plan

In the remainder of this chapter, we discuss more general principles and strategies for building an assessment plan. After you understand the big picture, you will be best situated to explore assessment options and to construct evaluation measures—all skills that are explored in-depth in Part II of this book. CACREP 2016 Standards require that counselor education program administrators examine student knowing and skills "via multiple measures and over multiple points in time" (Section 4.F.2, p. 17) and do so in a way that includes attention to each core curricular domain and specialty area. In this way, assessment occurs on individual student levels as well as

	1. Professional and Ethics													2. Diversity								3. Development					
	a	b	c	d	e	f	g	h	i	j	k	l	m	a	b	c	d	e	f	g	h	a	b	c	d	e	...
SLO 1																											
SLO 2																											
SLO 3																											
SLO 4																											
SLO 5																											
SLO 6																											

Figure 3.4
Curriculum Map Template:
Council for Accreditation of Counseling and Related Educational Programs Core Content
by Student Learning Outcome (SLO)

overarching program levels. After SLOs are established and curricula are mapped, the next step is to determine how one will go about assessing student learning. This will include attention to broad considerations, such as the following:

- assessments used,
- placement of assessments in the curriculum,
- tools for rating or measuring performance on the assessment,
- personnel responsible for rating or measuring performance,
- procedures for aggregating and analyzing data,
- methods for making meaning of data on program and individual levels, and
- timeline.

SLO assessment experts and CACREP 2016 Standards are united in the expectation that assessment be both formative and summative. Across disciplines, students learn best when they have opportunities to practice skills and to engage in targeted feedback regarding skill development (Ambrose, Bridges, DiPietro, Lovett, & Norman, 2010). For both learning and assessment purposes, it makes sense to assess learning and to provide feedback at multiple points in time. From an assessment perspective, the most meaningful SLO data are genuine and authentic attempts to capture students' most complex, developed work (AACU, 2008). Together, these recommendations are consistent with the idea that complex programs involve assessments that are distributed throughout the curriculum and that are centralized at key capstones or gateways in the process (Stiehl & Lewchuk, 2008a).

Consider the previous example regarding the overarching program objective regarding developing a guiding theory of counseling. Students learned about theories in the introductory course, they revisited beliefs and developed theory-specific skills in an advanced skills course, and they implemented the theory during internship. The SLO is identified, and the curriculum is clearly linked. The next step is to add the formative and summative assessments of learning at multiple times and using multiple measures. At the beginning level, this may include a course-based examination focused on knowledge of theory and application to a hypothetical case. At the intermediate level, this may include a personal application paper in which a student explores resonance and beliefs more deeply and conceptualizes a practice client seen during the prepracticum experience. At the most advanced level, this may include a supervisor's observations of counseling over time and rating on final internship evaluation forms.

As with curriculum mapping, faculty members may work forward or backward in identifying assessments to link to SLOs. For example, faculty members could begin the process by taking inventory of assignments and assessments used throughout the program. This would include reviewing course syllabi for papers, examinations, projects, and demonstrations as well as considering broader evaluation tools including comprehensive examinations, portfolios, and field experience assessments. After generating a list of existing assessments, the group may examine the list to identify which activities are most authentic and advanced. Program faculty may find that they are already doing a great deal of assessment work, and creating the formal assessment plan may not be as foreboding as anticipated. At the same time, exclusive focus on current practices may lead to disjointed assessment plans and may create a barrier to more holistic and intentional plans.

SLO	
Standard(s)	
Associated courses or experiences	
Assessment type	☐ Course-based assessment ☐ Comprehensive examination ☐ Portfolio ☐ Field experience ☐ Thesis or dissertation
Assessment description	
Measure	
Indicator of success	
Placement	
Administered by	☐ Course instructor ☐ Advisor ☐ Committee
Evaluated by	☐ Course instructor ☐ Advisor ☐ Committee
Gateway	
Review procedures	

Figure 3.5
Assessment Development Worksheet

Note. SLO = Student Learning Outcome.

Faculty members can also work backward when creating assessment plans. In this case, they will start with the curriculum map, examine each SLO, and brainstorm how and where they wish to assess that SLO. Although this is starting from ground zero in some ways, this frees faculty members to think about assessment more holistically and may lead to more unified, focused assessment plans.

After the program faculty has decided what assessments to use, they are ready to consider more concrete aspects of the assessment plans. These include placement in the curriculum and procedures for implementing the plan. Figure 3.5 includes a worksheet to step through the decision-making process for each assessment activity, followed by two examples of the worksheet (see Figures 3.6 and 3.7). Figure 3.8 includes a template for an overarching assessment plan, followed by an example of the worksheet (see Figure 3.9). These tools will likely be most useful to you after reading Chapters 4–8.

SLO	Demonstrated mastery of core counseling knowledge necessary for licensure in state
Standard(s)	CACREP 2.F.1, 2.F.2, 2.F.3, 2.F.4, 2.F.5, 2.F.6, 2.F.7, 2.F.8
Associated courses or experiences	COUN 5100 Professional Orientation, COUN 5200 Multicultural Counseling, COUN 5300 Human Development in Counseling, COUN 5400 Career Counseling, COUN 5500 Essential Helping Skills, COUN 5510 Counseling Theory, COUN 5600 Group Counseling, COUN 5700 Assessment in Counseling, COUN 5800 Research and Program Evaluation in Counseling
Assessment type	☐ Course-based assessment ☑ Comprehensive examination ☐ Portfolio ☐ Field experience ☐ Thesis or dissertation
Assessment description	Comprehensive Professional Counseling Examination (CPCE) developed and administered by Center for Credentialing and Education (CCE)
Measure	Individualized CPCE score reports provided by CCE
Indicator of success	Scores ≥ 1 standard deviation below national mean for each of eight subscales
Placement	Upon enrollment in COUN 5910 Internship I
Administered by	☐ Course instructor ☐ Advisor ☑ Committee
Evaluated by	☐ Course instructor ☐ Advisor ☑ Committee
Gateway	Cleared to graduate upon successful completion
Review procedures	Individual data provided by Comprehensive Examination chair; aggregate data reviewed by full faculty each spring

Figure 3.6
Assessment Development Worksheet: Example 1

Note. SLO = Student Learning Outcome; CACREP = Council for Accreditation of Counseling and Related Educational Programs; COUN = Counseling.

SLO	Designs comprehensive developmental school counseling programs
Standard(s)	CACREP 5.G School Counseling 3
Associated courses or experiences	COUN 5100 Introduction to School Counseling, COUN 5120 Advanced School Counseling
Assessment type	☐ Course-based assessment ☐ Comprehensive examination ☑ Portfolio ☐ Field experience ☐ Thesis or dissertation
Assessment description	Students will develop a course-based portfolio illustrating ability to engage in practice of school counseling including attention to development, design, and administration of the comprehensive, developmental school counseling program
Measure	School Counseling Portfolio Rubric
Indicator of success	Meets expectations or exceeds expectations in at least 8 of 10 rubric areas; no more than two "Does Not Meet Expectations" ratings; overall mean rubric score ≥ 2.0
Placement	COUN 5910 Advanced School Counseling
Administered by	☑ Course instructor ☐ Advisor ☐ Committee
Evaluated by	☑ Course instructor ☐ Advisor ☐ Committee
Gateway	Cleared to register for COUN 5910 Practicum
Review procedures	Individual data reviewed by course instructor each semester; aggregate data presented to evaluation committee each spring

Figure 3.7
Assessment Development Worksheet: Example 2

Note. SLO = Student Learning Outcome; CACREP = Council for Accreditation of Counseling and Related Educational Programs; COUN = Counseling.

Working through these worksheets highlights the complexity of developing SLO assessment plans that capture multiple SLOs at multiple times and using multiple measures. Much of the professional literature is focused on assessing SLOs along large bodies of undergraduate students who may or may not complete cohesive programs. Although the concepts are the same, demands for developing comprehensive SLO assessment plans in graduate professional programs are different. Hatfield (2009) provided a comprehensive overview of considerations for evaluating program-level evaluation plans, and we adapted these recommendations into the following questions:

- What is a reasonable number of outcomes?
- Are the outcomes tied to the college mission/goals?
- Are the outcomes written in an appropriate format?
- Do faculty agree on the definition of the outcome?
- Are the outcomes supported by core courses?
- Does the plan rely on direct measures of student learning?
- Are the assessment methods appropriate to the outcomes?
- Is there a systematic approach to implementing the plan?
- What is the method for collecting and organizing data?
- How are faculty trained to use assessment tools?
- Do the assessment tools distinguish among levels of achievement?
- What happens to the data after having been collected?
- Have we used the data to improve learning and teaching?

SLO	Standard	Assessment	Measure	Success	Placement	Evaluation	Gateway

Figure 3.8
Assessment Plan Worksheet

Note. SLO = Student Learning Outcome.

SLO	Standard	Assessment	Measure	Success	Placement	Evaluation	Gateway
1—CK	2.F.1	CPCE—PO	Score report	≥ –1 *SD* of national mean	Internship	Committee	Cleared to graduate
1—CK	2.F.2	CPCE— Diversity	Score report	≥ –1 *SD* of national mean	Internship	Committee	Cleared to graduate
1—CK	2.F.3	CPCE— Development	Score report SC Rubric	≥ –1 *SD* of national mean	Internship	Committee	Cleared to graduate
2—CDSCP	5.G.C.3	SC Course Portfolio		≥ 2.0 overall	COUN 5120	Instructor	Register practicum

Figure 3.9
Assessment Plan Worksheet: Example

Note. SLO = Student Learning Outcome; CK = Core Knowledge; CPCE = Comprehensive Professional Counseling Examination; PO = Professional Orientation; CDSCP = Comprehensive Developmental School Counseling Program; SC = School Counseling; COUN = Counseling.

In this chapter, we have reviewed the process of identifying SLOs, discussed characteristics of strong SLOs, examined curriculum mapping procedures, and established criteria for developing assessment plans in this process. At this point, you should have the foundations you need to turn attention to technical aspects of developing assessment procedures and measures. We designed Part II of the text to do just that.

Resources

Adelman, C. (2015). *To imagine a verb: The language and syntax of learning outcomes statements* (Occasional Paper No. 24). Retrieved from http://learningoutcomesassessment.org/documents/Occasional_Paper_24.pdf

Carriveau, R. S. (2010). *Connecting the dots: Developing student learning outcomes and outcome based assessments.* Denton: University of North Texas.

Driscoll, A., & Wood, S. (2007). *Developing outcomes-based assessment for learner-centered education: A faculty introduction.* Sterling, VA: Stylus.

Harden, R. M. (2001). AMEE Guide No. 21: Curriculum mapping: A tool for transparent and authentic teaching and learning. *Medical Teacher, 23,* 123–137. doi:10.1080/01421590120036547

Hatfield, S. (2009). *Assessing your program-level assessment plan.* Manhattan, KS: IDEA Center.

Office of Academic Planning and Assessment. (2001a). *Course-based review and assessment: Methods for understanding student learning.* Retrieved from http://www.umass.edu/oapa/oapa/publications/online_handbooks/course_based.pdf

Office of Academic Planning and Assessment. (2001b). *Program-based review and assessment: Tools and techniques for program improvement.* Retrieved from http://www.umass.edu/oapa/oapa/publications/online_handbooks/program_based.pdf

Practical curriculum mapping examples:
- https://manoa.hawaii.edu/assessment/howto/mapping.htm
- http://www.lehman.edu/research/assessment/templates.php_
- http://assessment.uconn.edu/primer/mapping1.html

Stiehl, R., & Lewchuk, L. (2008a). *The assessment primer: Creating a flow of learning evidence.* Corvallis, OR: The Learning Organization.

Stiehl, R., & Lewchuk, L. (2008b). *The outcomes primer: Reconstructing the college curriculum* (3rd ed.). Corvallis, OR: The Learning Organization.

Part II
Selecting Assessments and Developing Measures

• • •

In Part I, we developed a broad-based foundation upon which counselor educators can develop SLO evaluation plans. After we understand the greater context of accountability assessment, articulate SLOs at the course and program levels, and align pedagogy to ensure appropriate attention to priorities, we are ready to turn attention to assessing student learning. In the chapters that follow, we focus on activities that counselor educators can use to assess student learning in courses and within programs. For clarity, we define *assessments* as stimuli or things students do that provide instructors and supervisors with the opportunity to evaluate SLOs. In the evaluation world, assessments are sometimes called *artifacts* as a reminder that these are the products of learning. Direct measures of student learning are not the only indicator of program quality, so we include attention to indirect measures of program quality as well. We conclude this unit with detailed exploration of measurement tools that faculty members use to assign numbers or meaning to assessments.

As discussed in the Part I introduction, we wrote this book with hopes of opening dialogue regarding unique and rigorous ways that educators may engage in the SLO evaluation process. For assessment to be meaningful, it must be unique and tailored to the specific nature of the course or the program. Although we provide a roadmap and several examples of what this process and its elements might look like, it is up to you to develop procedures that make sense for your students, your settings, and your priorities. Ideally, these procedures will also stimulate learning in a meaningful way.

> Faculty want more than a snapshot in time of student learning, which might be taken on a very bad day in the life of a particular student. Faculty who have been consulted about assessment for accountability are interested in using the papers, projects, exams, and simulated or actual professional practice opportunities they assign in the process of stimulating learning—both to assign grades to individual students and to demonstrate accountability by aggregating assessments across students in a class, courses in a major, and courses at an institution. (Banta, Griffin, Flateby, & Kahn, 2009, p. 6)

We cannot emphasize this point enough: Development of assessments for course and program outcomes is not a one-size-fits-all approach (AACU, 2008; Provezis, 2010; Urofsky, 2009). Rather, educators must consider the unique context in which learning occurs and overall placement of the SLO(s) in the curriculum. Contextual considerations include:

- unique learning outcomes,
- priority of the SLO for the program,
- size and stability of the faculty,
- size of the course or program,
- characteristics of students,
- program model (e.g., cohort, full-time, part-time, face-to-face, in person, placement of gateways, common core or distributed coursework),
- available resources (e.g., clinics, recording technology, learning management technology), time, and
- university or college priorities.

Consider the following programs taken from the authors' professional experiences:

- Program A has three master's-level, CACREP-accredited specialty areas and a CACREP-accredited doctoral program. At any given time, there are 300–350 students, 14 full-time faculty members, and 10 adjunct faculty members engaged in the program. Although some students attend full-time, most students are working adults who attend courses part-time and sequence courses on the basis of a constellation of needs. All students complete an on-campus practicum with state-of-the art learning equipment. The program is situated within a college that recently adopted an SLO evaluation system and hired two full-time staff members to administer the system.
- Program B has one master's-level, CACREP-accredited specialty area. At any given time, there are three full-time faculty members and 20 students dedicated to the program; occasionally, students enroll in coursework with affiliate faculty members in related departments, and students from other programs enroll in courses taught by core counseling faculty members. Students attend a full-time cohort model, and they complete all field experience in off-campus settings. The program does not have access to a formal SLO evaluation system.

It should be no surprise that the assessment activities adopted by the Program A faculty look appreciably different than those adopted by the Program B faculty. Closer examination would reveal that even the assessment activities within Program A vary widely; unlike the master's program, the doctoral program is a full-time, residential model in which all courses are taught by core faculty. Thus, the assessment methods for Program A's doctoral program are quite similar to the Program B's plans. Although some important SLOs are assessed via multiple means and at multiple points in time, other SLOs may be assessed just once via a less intensive process. When done with intention, this variation is normal and healthy in the SLO process.

AACU (2008) urged educators to focus on "students' authentic and complex performances in the context of their most advanced studies: research projects, community service projects, portfolios of student work, supervised internships, etc." (p. 9). This includes a need to move beyond one-shot testing or superficial exercises to understand deep meaning and true integration of skills necessary for success. Meyers and Nulty (2009) noted that quality curricula include authentic encounters in which educators

> provide students with teaching and learning materials, tasks and experiences which: (1) are authentic, real world and relevant; (2) are constructive, sequential and interlinked; (3) require students to use and engage with progressively higher order cognitive processes; (4) are all aligned with each other and the desired learning outcomes; and (5) provide challenge, interest and motivation to learn. (p. 567)

Similarly, Mueller (2014) identified five characteristics of authentic assessment, and he portrayed them on a continuum ranging from traditional to authentic. Within this framework, the best assessments of student learning involve opportunities for direct observations of students performing a real-life task—something quite different from historical testing perspectives. Consider the following characteristics of traditional and authentic assessment:

- *Traditional:* Selecting a response, contrived, recall/recognition, teacher-structured, indirect evidence
- *Authentic:* Performing a task, real-life, construction/application, student-centered, direct evidence

Stiehl and Lewchuk (2008b) provided five principles they believed presented "a way to achieve accountability without killing the spirit of learning" (p. 5). They include the following:

1. Effective learning assessment practices must reflect the fact that every student's journey is a different journey.
2. Observation of performance in the context of real work tasks provides the best evidence of intended outcomes.
3. Useful assessment is always embedded in the learning experience.
4. All measurement is approximation.
5. A broader understanding of assessment holds the key to student success.

These principles resonated with us, and we hope they will resonate with you. We encourage you to keep them in mind as you transition from envisioning your curriculum in an ideal way to assessing learning through more specific tasks.

The most frequently used program-level assessments used in higher education include portfolios, course-level assessments, rubrics, external judges, interviews (student, employer, and alumni), and surveys (employer, local, alumni, and national; Kuh & Ikenberry, 2009). Best practice involves focusing on a customized blend of direct and indirect assessments. *Direct assessments* include ways in which students create or enact products that become grist for the SLO evaluation mill. For example, papers, recorded counseling sessions, or examinations allow for direct assessment of student learning. *Indirect assessments* include self-reports of learning and course, instructor, or program satisfaction that provide educators with a sense of student experience without allowing for direct, measurable examination. Student and employer satisfaction surveys, teaching evaluations, and self-rated skills checklists serve as indirect assessments.

The best assessment plans involve assessments of SLOs in various ways and at various points in time. Ideally, these options tell a story and provide a snapshot of mastery. For example, skills assessment at the beginning of programs might be important for formative feedback and tracking, but most educators are much more concerned that students have mastered skills by the end of the program. It may be worth assessing high stakes SLOs, such as conducting suicide assessment and intervention, at several points in the curriculum—first in the classroom to determine students' readiness to perform basic tasks and later in authentic field experience settings as the need arises. At the same time, it would not be realistic to assume every internship student will have an opportunity to work with a client who is in need of suicide assessment and intervention. Similarly, educators might be more concerned about basic knowledge outcomes in more didactic courses (e.g., assessing working understanding of counseling theories in a theories course) but might find themselves shifting attention to integration of material in later experiences (e.g., assessing a student's ability to conceptualize a client from within the framework of a guiding theory during internship).

In practice, assessment may be formative or summative; CACREP 2016 Standards require attention to both formative and summative evaluations in counseling field experience (3.C). *Formative assessment* is the process by which educators provide ongoing, developmentally oriented feedback to students so that students and educators may customize their learning process in meaningful ways. Certainly, formative assessment is part of the requirement that the program faculty "systematically assess each student's progress throughout the program" (Standard 4.F, p. 16). Formative assessment tends to take place within course experiences and at important gateways within programs. In addition to informing learning, formative assessment can be important for due process considerations, especially if counselor educators are considering student remediation or dismissal.

Summative assessment involves examination of SLOs as a culminating snapshot. Ideally, complex, summative assessment tends to be less dynamic and presents higher stakes for students. For example, although educators may provide ongoing, formative feedback regarding essential counseling skill acquisition, the summative assessment may be an educator's final determination regarding the degree to which a student has demonstrated proficiency and is ready to proceed through the next gateway (e.g., course in a clinical sequence, graduation). Ideally, counselor educators will focus on summative assessments when it comes time to create SLO evaluation plans, thus including the most complex, authentic measures available. For example, program faculty members may provide students with midterm and final skills feedback over several semesters of clinical experience; however, the faculty members will use the final evaluation from the final semester of internship as the summative assessment of student learning. We recognize this may be challenging for some counselor educators who prefer to focus on implications and opportunities for growth even, and particularly, at the end of experience.

We expect counselor educators will draw from five primary SLO assessment activities when designing SLO evaluation plans:

1. Course-based assessments
2. Field experiences
3. Comprehensive examinations
4. Portfolios
5. Theses and dissertations

In Chapters 4–8, we focus attention on direct assessments of learning. For each category, we provide an overview of the assessment activity, identify benefits and drawbacks to the method, explore design considerations, and provide resources for further learning. In Chapter 9, we focus on assessment of student dispositions, and in Chapter 10, we include attention to indirect measures that are important for triangulating information as part of bigger picture understanding and planning (Barrio Minton & Gibson, 2012). Finally, Chapter 11 includes concrete attention to how counselor educators may begin to quantify evidence of learning outcomes via rubrics and observation tools. Part IV includes sample assessments and rubrics to demonstrate a range of creative assessment strategies. Educators must decide the degree to which they are relevant for their programs, courses, students, faculty members, and overall objectives.

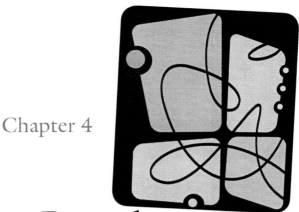

Chapter 4

Course-Based
Assessments

Course-based assessments (*CBAs*) are activities situated within courses that allow educators to assess students' attainment of knowledge, skills, or dispositions. These can be individual or group-based and include a wide range of activities, such as the following:

- objective (e.g., multiple choice, true/false) written examinations,
- subjective (e.g., essay, free response) written examinations,
- oral examinations,
- quizzes,
- homework assignments,
- papers,
- presentations,
- projects,
- skill observations,
- simulations or role-plays,
- service-learning engagements (see also Chapter 5),
- discussion board or blog participation,
- journals,
- in-class contributions, and
- course portfolios (see also Chapter 7).

Counselor educators and students are quite familiar with CBAs. We have completed hundreds or thousands of these types of assessments over the courses of our academic careers. Those who have been teaching for some time are quite used to identifying assignments and activities that serve dual purposes of facilitating and assessing learning. If you are reading this book as a way to enhance your assessment of SLOs for individual courses, all of your assessments are likely to be course-based. If you are creating a program-level assessment plan, you may decide to use CBAs as just one component of your larger assessment plan. In this chapter, we explore considerations for creating assessments on the individual course level. Regardless of your role, intentionality is critical when working with CBAs.

Intentionality in CBA

Just as counselor educators may engage in curriculum mapping within a course, we are hopeful that they also engage in intentional assessment planning within each course. Given the accountability context in higher education, many educators may already be expected to show how SLOs within a course link to broader objectives, including those specified by one's institution, state governing bodies, and independent accrediting agencies such as the Council for the Accreditation of Educator Preparation (CAEP; formerly the National Council for Accreditation of Teacher Education [NCATE]) and CACREP. Institutional policies may require or strongly encourage instructors to operationalize course objectives or learning outcomes and to indicate ways in which each SLO is assessed within the course. Table 4.1 includes an example of ways in which an instructor might link standards, SLOs, and assessments in a master's-level course in crisis and trauma counseling.

As you will likely notice in Table 4.1, crisis and trauma learning outcomes for this course are largely derived from CACREP 2016 Standards. At the same time, the instructor identifies several areas of focus that go beyond accreditation requirements. Learning outcomes associated with knowledge or more academic understanding are associated with the final examination. However, more applied or dynamic learning outcomes require a model session and critique, allowing students to begin trying on the specific content in a more complex, authentic manner.

Within a course, counselor educators should assess each SLO via at least one method. Counselor educators may choose to assess the most important SLOs at multiple points in time and by multiple means. For example, the first author routinely teaches courses in diagnosis and treatment planning for clinical mental health counseling (CMHC) students. In this course, she assesses an SLO related to CACREP 2016 Standard 5.C.2.d—"diagnostic process, including differential diagnosis and the use of diagnostic classification systems, including the *Diagnostic and Statistical Manual of Mental Disorders* (*DSM*) and the *International Classification of Diseases* (*ICD*)"—via weekly practice cases, a midterm examination, and a final examination. The SLO is simply too big to assess in one activity. However, she assesses the SLO regarding ability to conduct a biopsychosocial history (CACREP 2016 Standards 5.C.1.c and 5.C.3.a) via one project in which students conduct a mock interview with a peer and write a biopsychosocial history. She revisits the SLO for the final paper, part of which requires students to submit a biopsychosocial case study for a fictional client. This assessment plan allows for a combination of formative and summative assessments. For overarching program evaluation purposes, however, only data from the final case

Table 4.1
CACREP Standards, SLOs, and Assessment Matrices

CACREP Standard	SLO	Assessment
2.F.1.c	Understands counselors' roles and responsibilities as members of interdisciplinary community outreach and emergency management response teams	Final examination
2.F.3.g, 5.C.2.f, 5.D.2.h, 5.F.2.g	Identifies effects of crises, disasters, and other trauma-causing events on diverse individuals and families across the life span, including those with mental health diagnoses and disabilities	Final examination
	Applies crisis theories and models to scenarios relevant to anticipated work settings	Final examination
2.F.5.l	Applies suicide prevention models and strategies	Final examination
	Identifies ethical and legal considerations related to crisis and trauma counseling	Final examination
2.F.5.m	Conducts crisis intervention and PFA	Mock PFA session and critique
	Understands vicarious traumatization and strategies for managing	Self-care plan
2.F.7.c	Utilizes procedures for assessing risk of aggression or danger to others, self-inflicted harm, or suicide	Mock suicide crisis session and critique
2.F.7.d	Demonstrates skills for identifying and reporting abuse	Mock abuse crisis session and critique

Note. CACREP = Council for Accreditation of Counseling and Related Educational Programs; SLO = Student Learning Outcome; PFA = psychological first aid.

study are examined by the faculty as a whole. Just as program faculty may assign curricular items to specific courses or experiences, program faculty may also determine ways in which important SLOs are assessed within specific courses.

CBAs in Broader Program Evaluation

In the evaluation world, program-level CBAs may be situated in a course but are examined as evidence of overall program quality; these are often known as *key* or *signature assessments*. The assessments may be held steady across sections of a course and over periods of time to allow greater data collection regarding ways in which students meet SLOs within a program. In these instances, CBAs become part of the broader program-level SLO evaluation plan. These may include papers, projects, or examinations that are complex and designed to capture the most advanced learning in the course. CBAs are most appropriate for assessing knowledge or emerging skills outcomes and tend to be well-suited for assessment of up to a handful of SLOs. The lists below includes focused attention to benefits and drawbacks of CBAs.

Benefits of CBAs
Benefits of CBAs include the following:

- There is a specific location or home in the curriculum.
- There is a clear connection between everyday course business and assessment.
- Regular contact between instructors and students allows for ongoing communication regarding the activity, its purpose, and its role in evaluation.
- There is clear delegation of responsibility for evaluation and remediation.
- These types of assessment activities are most familiar to students.
- If well-designed, counselor educators can use CBAs to facilitate as well as assess learning.
- There is an opportunity to assess certain skills or situations that may not emerge during field experiences (e.g., psychological first aid, administering specific assessments, broader level program design and evaluation).
- Higher level examinations can facilitate greater knowledge of entry-level materials and deeper understanding of course materials overall (Jensen, McDaniel, Woodard, & Kummer, 2014).
- Practice with well-written objective examinations may help students prepare for standardized examinations.

Drawbacks of CBAs
Drawbacks of CBAs include the following:

- CBAs may not suit all instructors' philosophies of teaching or the learning theories to which they ascribe.
- CBAs may divert the focus of a course in a way that interferes with course rhythm.
- Faculty members may feel like they are "teaching to the test."
- CBAs may not be an appropriate summative snapshot of emerging skills or foundation knowledge covered at the beginning of the experience (e.g., essential counseling skills in the first course in the program vs. observation of essential counseling skills practicum or internship).
- There is limited opportunity to assess culminating skills or integration across areas.
- Faculty members may perceive and experience threat to academic freedom.
- Standardization across sections of the course may present logistical challenges.
- It is easy to write tests poorly, especially objective tests.
- Faculty members may struggle to evaluate students' work accurately, especially if they perceive evidence of SLO attainment as reflective of their teaching skills.
- Assessments may not approximate work demands in an authentic manner (e.g., students may be able to identify diagnoses based on a one-page description, but they may not demonstrate the same skills with a client who presents in a complex manner).

Design Considerations for CBAs

When designing CBAs, counselor educators need to attend to two key design considerations. First, faculty members should consider the role of the CBA in relation to the broader assessment plan and needs. This includes consideration of developmental sequencing within the program and impact on course load. Second, faculty members should design specific CBAs in ways that lend well to quality assessment. Some CBAs lend themselves to some SLOs more than others. For example, faculty members may use quizzes, examinations, and homework to assess acquisition of knowledge. Observations and simulations provide greater opportunities to assess skills.

Quality design will include attention to intersection of these two points. For example, a faculty member who is teaching a first-semester theories course may design an examination to assess student knowledge and basic application of key theories. This examination might be helpful for solidifying knowledge and informing student preparation for standardized comprehensive and licensure examinations. The faculty member might integrate some subjective examination questions that call for case example or illustration in ways that show higher order thinking. If faculty members are more concerned about higher level thinking, they might create a CBA in which students explore their guiding theory of counseling on the basis of counseling experience, literature regarding the theory, and personal reflection. Certainly, this assessment may be more meaningful, but it is not likely realistic for the first semester of study. Rather, the more complex guiding theory paper could be a culminating CBA in a more advanced course, such as advanced skills or practicum.

Key design considerations for CBAs include creation of opportunities to demonstrate authentic and complex learning (Meyers & Nulty, 2009). Because many courses may be didactic in nature, counselor educators will do well to consider the degree to which their CBAs approximate expectations within the world of practice in ways that are developmentally appropriate and meaningful for students. See below for a list of questions counselor educators may use to guide development of CBAs.

CBA development questions include the following:

- Which SLOs will we assess with this CBA?
- At what point(s) in the program do students take this course?
- To what degree does the existing curriculum match the CBA?
- What curricular adaptations are necessary to accommodate the CBA in a meaningful way?
- How much time will it take students to complete this CBA?
- Who will assess this CBA?
- How much time will it take evaluators to assess this CBA?
- What kind of feedback will students receive on their performance?
- What will happen when students do not demonstrate acceptable performance? Will just the first attempt count? Will students have opportunities for evolving attempts?

Strong CBAs will include careful attention to what, when, why, and how the CBA will be used in the greater program development plan. We could write volumes regarding design considerations for each major type. Such coverage goes well beyond the scope of this text. Still, you may find chapters on field experiences, comprehensive examinations, and portfolios helpful in thinking about how you may use adaptations of these as CBAs. Be sure to check out Part IV; the majority of the examples are designed for course-based use, thus illustrating the wide range of assessment opportunities within a single course.

Resources

Many teaching and learning centers provide technical assistance for creating examinations and other CBAs. You may find your college or university teaching and learning center to be an outstanding resource for thinking about assessment of learning. Although these centers tend to cater to those who teach large, undergraduate courses, they also include practical resources and provide consultation to instructors in more specialized areas. The following are our favorite resources regarding developing and using CBAs:

Authentic Assessment Toolbox: http://jfmueller.faculty.noctrl.edu/toolbox/index.htm

Spurlin, J. (n.d.). *Course-based assessment overview: Using student work from courses to assess program-level student learning outcomes.* Retrieved from https://assessment.dasa.ncsu.edu/wp-content/uploads/sites/53/2015/12/methods_course.pdf

Stasson, M. L., Doherty, K., & Poe, M. (2001). *Course-based review and assessment: Methods for understanding student learning.* Retrieved from http://www.umass.edu/oapa/oapa/publications/online_handbooks/course_based.pdf

Chapter 5

Field Experiences

Clinical preparation programs are ripe with opportunities to observe SLOs directly via student participation in field experiences. What better way to assess student ability to engage in the demands of the profession than by placement in situations in which they get to do what they have spent years preparing for. Each CACREP-accredited program requires a minimum of two semesters and 700 hours of field experience (100 practicum hours, 600 internship hours), and some students complete much more time in field experience. In helping professions, field experiences tend to be capstone clinical engagements in which students enroll after completing foundation coursework.

CACREP (2016) conceptualized practicum and internship as professional practice and noted that this culminating experience "provides for the application of theory and the development of counseling skills under supervision. These experiences will provide opportunities for students to counsel clients who represent the ethnic and demographic diversity of their community" (p. 13). Authentic in many ways, field experience assessments are not without challenges. The lists below include attention to benefits and drawbacks of field experience assessments.

Benefits of Field Experience Assessments

Benefits of field experience assessments include the following:

- Assuming appropriate placement, field experience is the most authentic of all assessment activities.
- Field experience assessments are well-suited for observing implementation of skills with clients.
- Capstone experience allows examination of culminating skills.
- Field experience assessments provide opportunity for multiple raters to engage in assessment (e.g., instructor, site supervisor).
- Field experience assessments may allow for broad-based impressions of student skill rather than single- or micro-level observations.
- Opportunities arise to collect supplemental assessments to be used in broader program evaluation (e.g., site supervisor ratings regarding quality of program, recommendations for improvement, student evaluation of site and site supervisor).
- Opportunities arise for vicarious learning and orientation to the world of practice through group supervision experience.

- Field experience assessments allow students to build their resume or vita needed for job searches and may lead to potential postgraduation placement (Burke & Snead, 2014).
- Field experience assessments allow students to evaluate fit and to build confidence in the field (Burke & Snead, 2014).
- Developmental process of placement allows for identification of areas for future growth and exploration (Burke & Snead, 2014).

Drawbacks of Field Experience Assessments

Drawbacks of field experience assessments include the following:

- Diversity of internship sites makes it difficult to standardize elements of the field experience (e.g., exclusive focus on certain populations, concerns, or services at some sites may make assessment of content-specific SLOs especially difficult).
- Multiple raters may have divergent expectations for types or levels of student performance (e.g., instructor would like to see more evidence of theoretical integration, site supervisor would like to see greater focus on client outcome data).
- Confidentiality and recording limitations may limit the degree to which faculty supervisors have true access to client interactions.
- Reviewing session recordings or engaging in live observation is time-intensive.
- Supervisors may struggle to balance broad-picture and individual-session perspectives.
- There is limited opportunity for assessment of knowledge-based SLOs.
- Students may not select recordings or present client concerns most illustrative of their counseling skills (e.g., instead focusing only on best performance).
- Students who know they are or will be observed may change in-session behaviors.
- Not all site supervisors are equally strong (Burke & Snead, 2014).
- Not all sites provide appropriate opportunities for experience (Burke & Snead, 2014).
- Field experiences are time-intensive to complete and to supervise (Burke & Snead, 2014).
- Evaluators may be tempted to treat internship as a "catch-all" for leftover or unassessed SLOs.

As we discuss next, counselor educators can use both the 2016 Standards (CACREP, 2016) and the *ACA Code of Ethics* (American Counseling Association [ACA], 2014) to guide development and assessment of quality field experiences within the program. This will include careful attention to remediation and due process built into assessment activities.

Design Considerations for Field Experience Assessments

It is difficult to discuss assessment of field experiences without considering best practices in counseling supervision. The *Best Practices in Clinical Supervision* (Association for Counselor Education and Supervision [ACES], 2011) include integrated attention to establishing goals and to evaluating learning throughout the clinical experience. Counselor educators who follow these best practice guidelines inherently develop field experiences that lend well to meaningful SLO assessment. If you have not done so recently, we encourage you to review the *Best Practices in Clinical Supervision* to see how they may inform formative and summative assessment of the field experience.

The CACREP 2016 Standards also provide concrete guidance regarding several minimal design considerations. These include the following:

- direct and indirect clock hour requirements for practicum and internship,
- individual and/or triadic supervision requirements (e.g., 1 hour weekly),
- group supervision requirements (e.g., 1.5 hours weekly with maximum ratio of 12:1),
- faculty supervisor qualifications (e.g., degree, experience, credentials, supervision expertise),
- student supervisor qualifications (e.g., student status, supervision preparation, supervision of supervision),
- site supervisor qualifications (e.g., degree, license, years of experience, supervision expertise, orientation to program),

- support between site and program (e.g., orientation, consultation, biweekly communication),
- observation (recording or live) capabilities,
- evaluation and documentation expectations, and
- supervision agreements or contracts.

The CACREP 2016 Standards include an expectation that students have opportunities to engage in a variety of professional counselor activities at a site. Naturally, these activities will include in-the-room counseling experience and should also include other professional responsibilities, including record keeping, outreach or education activities consistent with the site's mission, and staffing activities. Doing so will provide a roadmap for ensuring that field experiences provide authentic learning opportunities in developmentally appropriate ways.

Finally, the *ACA Code of Ethics* (ACA, 2014) includes several ethical standards that may contribute to quality field experience design. Of key concern is the reality that counseling supervisors have a "primary obligation" (Standard F.1, p. 12) to monitor client care and to ensure client welfare. ACA's (2014) standards also require that "supervisors document and provide supervisees with ongoing feedback regarding their performance and schedule periodic formal evaluative sessions throughout the supervisory relationship" (Standard F.6.a, p. 13). Consistent with the *Best Practices in Clinical Supervision* (ACES, 2011), the *ACA Code of Ethics* (ACA, 2014) attends to the dynamic process of field experiences in describing processes for gatekeeping and remediation of concern, including situations in which students must be dismissed from programs.

In addition to determining the basic elements of the experience (e.g., Who are the site supervisors? What are the sites? What are basic expectations for clinical performance?), design considerations need to balance formative and summative assessments in accordance with accreditation and ethical expectations. These assessments should be based on clear expectations for what skills should look like at various points in development. These should also include attention to the role of student reflection and insight in the process. For example, expectations for counseling practicum may be based on development of essential skills and emerging ability to conceptualize clients from the perspective of a guiding theory. Expectations for second semester internship may include higher level reflection and active engagement in intentional interventions. Both may include a reflective component in which students are asked to self-assess their level of skill and implications for next steps in their development.

Ideally, the field experience assessment plan includes integration of feedback from multiple parties and involves a balance of attention to session-specific and broader performance feedback. For example, one field experience assessment design may include the following elements:

- weekly hour logs and reflections used to monitor experiences and to identify areas of concern (faculty supervisor; formative assessment);
- weekly supervision sessions in which the student self-reports cases and explores recording or live observation of a session (site supervisor; formative assessment);
- biweekly submission of session recording, case conceptualization, and student self-evaluation (faculty supervisor; formative assessment);
- midterm meeting with site and faculty supervisor using the official field experience rating form (faculty and site supervisors; formative and summative assessment);
- final reflection paper regarding experience and growth as a counselor (faculty supervisor; summative assessment);
- development of a portfolio of other professional activities at the site (faculty supervisor; summative assessment); and
- final meeting with site and faculty supervisors using the official field experience rating form (faculty and site supervisors; summative assessment).

Evaluators must then decide which assessments count for overall program evaluation purposes. Although all of the above elements are an important part of the experience, the program faculty members may choose to enter only the culminating assessment form and the final portfolio as official SLO indicators. Later in this text, we provide sample forms and metrics for use with this assessment activity.

By carefully designing field experience activities and assessments, we can capture the most complex and authentic of student work. Because field experience includes several individuals beyond program students and faculty, intentionality is especially important. Although it is beyond the scope of this chapter, remediation and due process are essential components of the field experience process. Except in cases presenting egregious harm to clients or clear and intentional violation of ethical codes (McAdams & Foster, 2007), it is simply not appropriate for educators to say "skills not observed—dismissed." In Chapter 11, we attend to procedures for building evaluation forms. In Chapter 16, we address the intersection of SLO assessment and student review and retention. You can also find several sample frameworks for field experience assessment in Part IV.

Resources

Association for Counselor Education and Supervision. (2011). *Best practices in clinical supervision.* Retrieved from http://www.acesonline.net/sites/default/files/ACES-Best-Practices-in-clinical-supervision-document-FINAL.pdf

Hamlet, H. S., & Burnes, T. (2013). Professional School Counseling Internship: Developmental Assessment of Counseling Skills (CIDACS). *Counseling Outcome Research and Evaluation, 4,* 55–71. doi:10.1177/2150137812472196

Puckett, J. B., & Anderson, R. S. (2002). Assessing field experiences. *New Directions for Teaching and Learning, 91,* 53–60. doi:10.1002/tl.66

Shepherd, J. B., Britton, P. J., & Kress, V. E. (2008). Reliability and validity of the Professional Counseling Performance Evaluation. *Australian Journal of Guidance and Counselling, 18,* 219–232. doi:10.1375/ajgc.18.2.219

Chapter 6

Comprehensive Examinations

Comprehensive examinations provide opportunities for students to demonstrate culminating knowledge across a variety of areas. Sometimes called qualifying examinations or dubbed "comps," "quals," or "prelims," counselor educators can use these assessment tools as end-of-program rituals or as gateways to assess readiness to proceed to more advanced stages such as theses, dissertations, or field experiences. Counselor educators are likely to consider two primary types of comprehensive examinations as part of the overall SLO assessment plan: standardized examinations and local examinations.

In an examination of comprehensive and end-of-program assessments at the master's level, Baggerly and Osborn (2013) found that slightly more than one half of CACREP-accredited programs and one quarter of counselor education programs not accredited by CACREP required multiple-choice comprehensive examinations. Of those that used them, nearly two thirds of programs used the Counselor Preparation Comprehensive Examination (CPCE) offered by the National Board for Certified Counselors (NBCC) Center for Credentialing and Education (CCE); the remaining programs used multiple-choice examinations developed by program faculty. Similarly, 51% of CACREP-accredited programs, and 38% of non-CACREP accredited programs, required essay-style comprehensive examinations.

On the doctoral level, use of comprehensive examinations is standard practice across universities and disciplines and within counselor education programs (McAdams & Robertson, 2012; McAdams, Robertson, & Foster, 2013; Peterson, Bowman, Myer, & Maidl, 1992). Because experiences with standardized and local examinations tend to be so different, we attend separately to each type of comprehensive examination: standardized, local master's-level, and doctoral-level.

Standardized Comprehensive Examinations

Standardized examinations are examinations that are created, normed, validated, and often administered by outside bodies. These examinations are generally used for master's-level programs; there are no standardized examinations specific to doctoral-level counselor education and supervision programs.

CPCE

As noted previously, the CPCE is the most widely used comprehensive examination in the field. As of 2014, the CCE noted that the CPCE is used by more than 360 programs and provides programs with an objective measure of student knowledge in core curricular areas. Parallel to the National Counselor Examination (NCE) discussed below, the examination is designed to assess CACREP's (2009) eight core curricular areas:

1. Professional orientation and ethical practice
2. Social and cultural diversity
3. Human growth and development
4. Career development
5. Helping relationships
6. Group work
7. Assessment
8. Research and program evaluation

The examination tends to include 16–17 items for each core area and is administered during a half-day examination. At time of this printing, the CPCE costs $50.00 per student. Although NBCC controls the content of the examination, counseling programs are responsible for the following:

- deciding who is eligible to sit for the examination,
- administering the examination in accordance with CCE rules,
- determining criteria for passing specific areas and/or the examination as a whole, and
- stipulating remediation procedures for students who do not pass one area or the examination as a whole.

The CCE provides score reports for individual students as well as descriptive statistics on program and national levels. In this way, programs can use results for broader level evaluation of student and program performance as a whole on the core curricular areas. Although it is limited to assessment of knowledge and is fairly general in nature, we suspect that many programs will adopt the CPCE as one indicator that student learning has occurred in core curricular areas. Evaluators should note that the CPCE is reflective of academic achievement; in one study, undergraduate GPA, Graduate Record Examination (GRE)–Verbal Reasoning scores, and GRE–Quantitative Reasoning scores predicted 21% of the variance in CPCE total scores (Schmidt, Homeyer, & Walker, 2009).

NCE

The NBCC created the NCE, which is a standardized examination required for licensure in many states. On their website, NBCC notes that programs may not use the NCE as a comprehensive examination. NCE pass rates may serve as a supplemental measure or indicator for overall program evaluation, even if they cannot be part of the student-specific SLO assessment plan. However, both the CPCE and NCE cover the same areas and are often included in the same study guides. In the first author's experience, a CPCE pass criterion of one standard deviation below the national norm yielded first-attempt pass rates nearly identical to first-attempt pass rates for the NCE. Because of similar content structures between the NCE and CPCE, students who struggled with the CPCE also struggled with the NCE. This indicates that, in addition to providing a measure of student learning in core areas, the CPCE may provide practice experience for students, especially those who do not test well or who are concerned with the greater cost of the NCE.

State Certification Examinations

Counselor education programs may also utilize standardized state certification examinations as part of their SLO assessment plans. In some cases, students or candidates have access to state-required testing for counselor licensure or school counselor certification prior to graduation. For example, the State of Texas requires that the college or university endorse a school counselor candidate to take the TExES School Counselor examination prior to graduation. The purpose of the examination is to "assess whether an examinee has the requisite knowledge and skills that an entry-level educator in this field in Texas public schools must possess" (Texas Education Agency, 2012, p. 3). The examination has 100 multiple-choice items over three domains: Understanding Students; Planning and

Implementing the Developmental Guidance and Counseling Program; and Collaboration, Consultation, and Professionalism. The domains map to specific educational standards. Scores range from 100 to 300, with a passing score of 240. The state provides a testing manual, crosswalks demonstrating which standards are accessed within each domain, and specific score reports for each student. In this case, the specificity with which the state conducts the exam makes it possible for programs to use examination results as a measure of knowledge specific to the school counseling specialty area.

Design Considerations

As illustrated in the list below, there are several benefits and drawbacks to utilizing standardized examinations as a measure of student learning. When choosing to utilize standardized examinations, counselor education faculty should consider the degree to which the examination fits into the broader program framework as well as plans for remediating concerns identified through standardized assessment. In our experience, many counselor educators prefer to rely on more subjective assessments of learning throughout the program (e.g., looking to reflective journal responses in multicultural courses or examining demonstration videos in skills-based courses). Although most states require completion of standardized examinations for licensure, the need to complete them within the counselor education program may come as a jolt to students and faculty who have become accustomed to more subjective and process-oriented assessment. Counselor education faculty may need to consider how to prepare students for this reality without teaching to the test or sacrificing richness of CBAs. For example, the lead author visits with students in her multicultural counseling course regarding the types of questions that they might expect to see about social and cultural diversity on standardized exams. Although she does not grade them or dedicate class time to them, she sometimes places optional, automatically graded test bank quizzes on the course's learning management system.

Benefits of Standardized Examinations

Benefits of standardized examinations include the following:

- Standardized examinations are well-suited for broad assessment of knowledge and basic application.
- Objective and blind scoring by an outside entity decreases likelihood of bias for or against specific students.
- Format and expectations are likely familiar to graduate students (Burke & Snead, 2014).
- Standardized examinations free instructors and courses to focus on the learning—testing comes later.
- Test makers have invested attention to norming and validity considerations.
- Standardized examinations may be authentic in that they approximate or fulfill real-world requirements for licensure or certification.
- Proximity to licensure or certification requirements may facilitate student buy-in.
- Test reports may provide student feedback regarding major domains in need of attention.
- Test reports may provide program feedback regarding courses or experiences in which students perform well and struggle.
- Management by outside entities means little time or energy investment by faculty members (Burke & Snead, 2014).
- Examination itself is time-limited (Burke & Snead, 2014).
- Examinations allow for standardization across students and terms (Burke & Snead, 2014).
- Existing preparation manuals and resources may help students prepare.

Drawbacks of Standardized Examinations

Drawbacks of standardized examinations include the following:

- Standardized examinations do not assess counseling skills or potential for effectiveness as a counselor.
- Many programs may not utilize traditional testing formats throughout the curriculum.
- Some students do not test well, especially those with learning disabilities or for whom English is a second language.

- Test anxiety may hamper performance.
- Many standardized tests are known for testing bias for nondominant populations.
- Management by outside entities means loss of program control over content.
- Test reports yield general domain feedback rather than feedback on specific SLOs.
- Standardized examinations can be expensive.
- Nature of high-stakes examination makes students particularly vulnerable to off-days (e.g., illness, personal crisis).
- Students who are stretched thin with coursework and field experiences may struggle to prepare appropriately (Burke & Snead, 2014).
- Limited testing schedules may affect students' ability to graduate if they do not pass the first time.

Because standardized exams may not be associated with specific courses or aspects of the curricula, faculty will need to determine how to structure experiences so that students have the support they need to be successful in the endeavor. Faculty may decide whether to offer or endorse review sessions for students who reach this stage of their program. Students may be active participants in this process; for example, study groups may help mitigate anxiety associated with comprehensive examinations, particularly when professors mentor and support students through this process (Bartle & Bradwin, 2006). Similarly, Dipietro et al. (2010) described a scenario in which students in a course used wikis to engage in collaborative preparation for comprehensive examinations.

The next major design consideration for standardized assessments includes procedures for determining success on the examination and remediation opportunities for students who do not meet standards. Procedures for determining success vary among programs. In reference to the CPCE, this may include a percentage correct, distance from the national mean (e.g., no less than one standard deviation below the mean), and "faculty determination" (Baggerly & Osborn, 2013, p. 95). It is also possible that faculty members could decide to examine performance on specific domains rather than performance on the examination as a whole.

Faculty, then, must decide how to respond when students do not meet the standard. In their review of comprehensive examination procedures, Baggerly and Osborn (2013) found that programs allowed students to retake the examination up to a certain number of times, constructed action plans with students prior to retesting, or provided students with an alternate testing option (such as a different examination, essay-style examination, or oral examination). Although it is possible, Baggerly and Osborn reported that they did not encounter reports of students being dismissed from programs for not passing comprehensive examinations. Given the likely placement of standardized examinations at the end of the curricula, faculty must also consider life consequences for students who must wait months or more to retest prior to moving forward to graduation. For design consideration of prompts related to the use of standardized tests, see the list below.

Standardized Examination Development Questions

Standardized examination development questions to consider include the following:

- Which SLOs will we assess with this examination?
- To what degree does examination format and feedback allow for specific, focused assessment of SLOs?
- What evidence is provided for validity and reliability of the examination?
- To what degree does the examination approximate testing expectations for state licensure or certification?
- To what degree do existing curriculum and program emphases match examination content and foci?
- To what degree is the standardized testing format socially and culturally appropriate for the student body?
- What curricular adaptations are necessary to accommodate the standardized examination in a meaningful way?
- At what point in the program will students sit for this examination?
- How often will the examination be offered?
- How much time and effort will it take students to prepare for and complete this examination?

- What program support is necessary to support student success on this examination?
- How much time and effort will it take faculty to administer this examination?
- Who will determine standards for appropriate performance?
- What kinds of feedback will students receive on their performance?
- What will happen when students do not demonstrate acceptable performance? Remediation efforts? Retesting considerations? Appeal procedures? Time and financial cost to students?

Although the CPCE appears to be the single-most common comprehensive examination strategy for master's-level counseling programs, it is not the only option. In the following section, we attend to local master's-level comprehensive examinations.

Local Master's-Level Comprehensive Examinations

Local master's-level comprehensive examinations include examinations that are developed, administered, and scored by the counselor education faculty. In the study of master's comprehensive examinations discussed previously, Baggerly and Osborn (2013) found that 34.8% of programs utilized a program-developed, multiple-choice examination, and 47.1% of programs utilized a program-developed essay examination. Counselor educators may find broad variation and freedom in examination design. For example, the examinations may be objective and/or subjective, in-person and/or take-home, open- and/or closed-notes. They may be designed to assess knowledge only or call for deeper synthesis or application of material. They may be administered in large groups or on a case-by-case basis. They may be designed for the group as a whole or customized to interests or skills of individual students. Students may or may not be involved in the construction of the local comprehensive examination.

Design Considerations

Clarity of design and local examination process is critical to the success of the assessment activity (Baggerly & Osborn, 2013), and design considerations for standardized assessment also apply to local assessment. The primary strength of the local comprehensive examination is also its primary drawback. Although these examinations may be highly adaptable to unique strengths and foci of the counselor education program, they have the potential to be a high-stakes, low-validity activity, especially with regard to construction of multiple-choice items with which counselor educators may have had little preparation and experience. It is for this reason that we encourage counselor educators who desire an objective measure of core content knowledge to utilize a standardized assessment such as the CPCE when possible, thus freeing the local examination to focus on deeper levels of meaning and application available through essay and case-based responses that require students to construct responses in a more subjective manner. One caveat to this is for counselor education areas that may not be captured by a standardized exam, such as addictions; college student development; and marriage, couples, and family. Creating comprehensive exams in these areas can assess specific content and reflect program assessment processes (i.e., case study, exams) specifically. For a more complete listing of benefits and drawbacks of local examinations, refer to the list below.

Benefits of Local Examinations

Benefits of local examinations include the following:

- Like standardized examinations, local examinations may be well-suited for assessment of knowledge.
- Like standardized examinations, local examinations may utilize a format that is familiar and comfortable to students.
- Like standardized examinations, local examinations free instructors and courses to focus on the learning—testing comes later.
- Local examinations may be designed to address unique combinations of SLOs that exceed bounds of a single course.
- Local examinations may be customized to program-specific specialty areas or considerations.
- Constructed response items may allow for assessment of deeper knowledge and preliminary skill assessment.

- Faculty can tailor examination content to program foci.
- Faculty can tailor examination content to the unique needs and characteristics of the student body.
- Faculty can tailor the examination process to the unique program foci and student characteristics.
- Local examinations provide full control over logistics, such as timing and frequency of administration.
- Local examinations provide full control over the assessment and feedback procedures utilized.
- Objective or blind scoring may mitigate bias for or against specific students.

Drawbacks of Local Examinations

Drawbacks of local examinations include the following:

- Local examinations rarely assess counseling skills or potential for effectiveness as a counselor.
- Many programs may not utilize traditional testing formats throughout the curriculum.
- Some students do not test well, especially those with learning disabilities or for whom English is a second language.
- Developing, updating, and maintaining security for examinations with strong validity support takes time, effort, and experience.
- Faculty turnover or use of adjunct faculty members may result in disconnects between program curricula and content of examinations.
- Limited testing schedules may affect students' ability to graduate if they do not pass the first time.
- Nature of high-stakes examination makes students particularly vulnerable to off-days (e.g., illness, personal crisis).
- Students who are stretched thin with coursework and field experiences may struggle to prepare appropriately (Burke & Snead, 2014).
- If blind scoring is not utilized, examination may be subject to bias for or against specific students.

Counselor educators who wish to create local, multiple-choice or true–false examinations to assess knowledge should consider carefully the SLOs that they wish to assess with the examination and develop a test framework to use as a guide throughout the process. Although it is not inappropriate to utilize a single item to capture an SLO, one may develop a cluster of items that, taken together, assess understanding of a concept. There are several high-quality test construction resources available to the higher education community, and many university teaching and learning centers offer technical assistance with the process. Given the high stakes of this endeavor, we urge counselor educators who are working with this type of SLO assessment to seek consultation regarding construction of items, pilot the test with the student body, and engage in ongoing item analysis to continue to develop and refine the assessment tool. We include test construction resources at the end of this chapter.

Counselor educators may use open-ended or constructive response examinations to assess conceptual skills as well as knowledge. For example, a case-based examination could include several components that require students to engage in activities such as conceptualizing through lenses of human development and counseling theories, rendering diagnoses, constructing treatment plans, and identifying opportunities for advocacy. As with all other elements of testing, it is important that those who construct the assessment be clear about the SLOs that they wish to assess and ensure that they design prompts in ways that elicit desired content. Given the subjective nature of responses, program faculty will need to determine procedures for evaluating responses (e.g., use of rubrics, number and nature of reviewers). Faculty members do not need to confine local examinations to traditional testing blocks. Rather, local comprehensive examinations could involve take-home examinations, oral presentations or demonstrations, or papers in which students tie together material across a variety of areas. A comprehensive list of development questions regarding local examinations is included below.

Local Master's-Level Examination Development Questions

Local master's-level examination development questions to consider include the following:

- Which SLOs do we need to assess with this examination?
- What response format will be most appropriate for the SLO: objective, short-answer essay, expanded essay, multiple choice?

- What administration format will be most appropriate: in-person, take-home, open-notes, closed-notes, timed, untimed?
- What evidence do we have for validity and reliability of the examination?
- To what degree does examination approximate real-world expectations for knowledge and skills?
- To what degree do existing curriculum and program emphases match examination content and foci?
- To what degree is the testing format socially and culturally appropriate for the student body?
- What curricular adaptations are necessary to accommodate the examination in a meaningful way?
- How will program faculty ensure that those teaching courses, including adjunct instructors, remain aware of examination content relevant to their courses?
- At what point in the program will students sit for this examination?
- How often will the examination be offered? Will it be administered individually or in groups?
- How much time and effort will it take students to prepare for and complete this examination?
- What program support is necessary to support student success on this examination?
- How much time and effort will it take faculty to develop, administer, score, and analyze this examination and associated rubrics? Who will be responsible for these tasks?
- Who will be responsible for scoring examinations? Will scoring be individual, by independent committee, or by committee consensus? Will raters be blind to student identities?
- Who will determine standards for appropriate performance?
- What kinds of feedback will students receive on their performance?
- What will happen when students do not demonstrate acceptable performance? Remediation efforts? Retesting considerations? Appeal procedures? Time and financial cost to students?

Doctoral-Level Comprehensive Examinations

By definition, *doctoral-level comprehensive examinations* are local examinations. These examinations have long been used and discussed in the broader field and within counselor education. They tend to include both written and oral components (McAdams & Robertson, 2012). Perhaps best conceptualized as a final examination over one's entire body of coursework, the doctoral comprehensive examination often serves as a gateway between formal coursework and the dissertation, with students unable to proceed to dissertation until they have passed the examination.

The doctoral comprehensive examination has a long history in higher education and has been the subject of disdain and discussion for decades. For example, Eisenberg (1965) identified comprehensive examinations as a longstanding problem in psychology and asked whether there was a better way. More recently, S. Patton (2013) outlined controversy from the perspectives of students and faculty members and noted that graduate students were calling for change.

There is a small body of literature focused on doctoral-level comprehensive examinations in the counseling profession. Peterson et al. (1992) examined comprehensive examination practices among counselor education practices. Only 61% of programs had a written purpose for the examination; purposes included screening for minimum knowledge, provision of learning experience, assessment of writing skills, and use in program evaluation. At the time, theories and research were the most commonly tested areas, and few topic areas required examinees to demonstrate counseling competence. Program faculty members utilized a wide variety of practices when creating the exam, drawing from the faculty as a whole, charging to individual student committees, or charging to a general program examination committee. Most program faculty members utilized a 2-day format wherein examinees wrote for 4–8 hours per day. There was an expectation that advisors would assist students with preparation for the examination; however, few program faculty members provided students with reading lists, objectives, or sample questions. Examinations tended to be evaluated by a variety of individuals or committees, and feedback was provided to students at some time in the process. Peterson et al. cautioned counselor educators to be certain of their purpose in testing, to make objectives transparent to students, and to consider the role of anxiety in the process.

More recently, McAdams and Robertson (2012) explored the history of the interactive oral examination and articulated benefits and liabilities for examiners and examinees. For example, although oral examinations may allow more authentic, spontaneous, deep, and rich exploration of examinees' abilities to respond to the rigor of academic life, they may be viewed as highly subjective, secretive, culturally biased, antagonistic, and anxiety inducing. In a study of student experiences with the doctoral oral examination, McAdams et al. (2013) found that students reported the experience to be more challenging than the dissertation proposal and defense; however, they also noted that it was their first oral examination in the series of experiences. As a whole, the oral examination contributed to students' learning and served as a milestone, although some also noted that the process was uncomfortable or even harmful. These findings are consistent with those of Koltz, Odegard, Provost, Smith, and Kleist (2010), who utilized photovoice to capture a doctoral cohort's themes of self-doubt, pressure, industry, and motivation with regard to the comprehensive examination. McAdams and Robertson made a strong argument that the role of the educator will be subjective and ever-changing. Rather than work to eliminate subjectivity in the process, educators can heed suggestions to articulate purpose clearly, to be transparent about process and scoring procedures, and to prepare students throughout the curriculum.

Design Considerations

As illustrated in the list below, benefits and drawbacks of doctoral comprehensive examinations parallel those of master's comprehensive examinations.

Benefits of Doctoral-Level Comprehensive Examinations

Benefits of doctoral-level comprehensive examinations include the following:

- Doctoral-level comprehensive examinations allow for deep integration and synthesis across curricular areas.
- Doctoral-level comprehensive examinations serve as both practical and symbolic transition in curriculum.
- Rite of passage may have meaning for students (McAdams & Robertson, 2012).
- If conducted well, doctoral-level comprehensive examinations may be highly authentic for those who wish to enter academia (McAdams & Robertson, 2012).
- Doctoral-level comprehensive examinations may be customized to students' specialty interests or areas of expertise.
- Inclusion of blind or team review may increase objectivity.
- Oral examination may allow assessment of depth, authenticity of knowledge, oral communication, and mental stamina (McAdams & Robertson, 2012).
- If fostered well, preparation process may build a learning community.

Drawbacks of Doctoral-Level Comprehensive Examinations

Drawbacks of doctoral-level comprehensive examinations include the following:

- There is a long history of controversy and questioned relevance.
- The purpose of the examination is not always clearly identified (McAdams et al., 2013; Peterson et al., 1992).
- "Critics noted that oral evaluations are subjective, mysterious, and culturally biased at a time when greater objectivity, transparency, and cultural inclusion are preeminent educational values" (McAdams & Robertson, 2012, p. 179).
- Doctoral-level comprehensive examinations rarely include clinical performance (Peterson et al., 1992).
- Lack of blind review because of program size or process may increase subjectivity or bias.
- High-stakes test anxiety and unrealistic expectations may hamper performance, especially during timed examinations.
- Doctoral-level comprehensive examinations are time-intensive for students and faculty members (Burke & Snead, 2014).
- Location of examination outside of routine curriculum may limit amount of program attention or guidance available to students.

Regardless of design, it is critical that the faculty members are clear about purpose of the examination and are intentional in the design process (Baggerly & Osborn, 2013; McAdams & Robertson, 2012; McAdams et al., 2013). Design considerations for the doctoral-level comprehensive examination parallel those for master's-level standardized and local examinations and include considerations for both written and oral components.

When developing an overarching doctoral-level comprehensive examination, program faculty should agree on overarching purpose for the examination, content areas to be included, learning outcomes to be assessed, process for administering the examination, expectations for student performance, and procedures for responding to students who do not perform well on written and/or oral portions of the examination.

In response to concerns by colleagues, Loughead (1997) advised counselor educators to utilize Bloom's (1956) *Taxonomy of Educational Objectives* in the process of designing doctoral comprehensive examinations. She reminded faculty that curricula should set the stage by helping students go beyond initial demonstration of knowledge in CBAs, and she advised programs to communicate with students about the qualifying examination process—recommendations consistent with those of McAdams and Robertson (2012).

McAdams and Robertson (2012) provided a series of recommendations related to design and implementation of oral comprehensive examinations, including a need for program faculty to be explicit about purpose and importance of the examination and to be transparent about the examination process. They also recommended that counselor education program faculty members prepare students with regard to expected content, skills, and conduct related to the oral examination, and they provided examples of the ways in which program faculty members might go about providing this preparation as part of routine curricula. In particular, they included an oral viva rubric that counselor educators can use to assess students' oral examinations (see McAdams & Robertson, 2012, p. 189).

Doctoral-Level Comprehensive Examination Development Questions

You may find the following questions helpful for designing doctoral-level comprehensive examinations:

- What content areas and specific SLOs will be assessed with the examination?
- What is the overall purpose or goal of the examination?
- When will students take the comprehensive examination—after a certain number of credit hours? After all courses are completed? After a certain point in the last semester?
- Will students take the examination in groups or individually?
- How much time will students have to complete the examination—1 day, several days, 1 week, several weeks?
- Will students be able to access resources or notes during the examination?
- Who will write the examination questions—the faculty as a whole, a committee of faculty members, the student's doctoral committee, the student's major professor?
- What will be the student's role in the development of the questions?
- Will the student know of the nature and content of the questions prior to the examination?
- Will questions be held steady for the entire program or personalized for each student? Will the program faculty members utilize a testing bank or rotation of questions?
- If the program faculty members utilize personalized questions, how will they ensure consistent levels of rigor and equity in the process?
- Who will score student responses—the faculty as a whole, a committee of faculty members, the student's doctoral committee, the student's major professor?
- Will reviewers know the identity of the author?
- What metrics will the faculty use to evaluate responses?
- What is the relationship between written and oral examinations?
- How will the program faculty members provide student orientation, preparation, and support for the examination process?
- What will be the process for providing support, remediation, and due process for students who do not pass the written and/or oral portion of the examination?

Examples

The following examples are adapted from the authors' experiences at a range of CACREP-accredited programs, and they are designed to illustrate the variety of ways in which program faculty may utilize comprehensive examinations in the SLO assessment process:

- All master's students enrolled in the second semester of internship complete a local comprehensive examination consisting of approximately 100 multiple-choice questions and one long essay question. The essay question is tailored to a student's program of study (e.g., clinical mental health counseling, school counseling). Students who do not pass the examination on the first attempt must complete additional study before attempting a second examination in the same semester. If the student does not pass the examination, he or she cannot graduate as planned. A committee of faculty members scores all applications.
- By midpoint of internship, all master's students write a case study on an actual client. The case study format is designed by the program faculty and structured to reflect specific program learning objectives. Faculty members evaluate the written case study on criteria established prior to administration. After initial evaluation and feedback, students present video of the case in an oral defense of the written case study.
- After completing all required core coursework and enrolling in practicum, master's students are cleared to register to complete the CPCE. Program faculty members encourage students to take the CPCE at least one semester prior to planned graduation. Students must score no less than one standard deviation below the national mean to pass the exam. Students receive a score sheet in which performance on each of the eight core curricular areas is highlighted. Those who do not pass the examination may reattempt the exam during the subsequent semester.
- During the last half of the final semester of the master's program, students engage in a take-home comprehensive examination in which they craft a series of short papers in response to questions developed by the faculty as a whole. All students respond to the same questions. The student's advisor and one other faculty member complete rubrics for comprehensive examination papers.
- Doctoral students are eligible to complete comprehensive examinations in the final weeks of their required coursework. Each student's doctoral committee members write a series of eight examination questions covering designated areas of the curriculum (e.g., theory, career, group, appraisal) but do not inform the student regarding the specific content or nature of the question. Each morning and afternoon for three consecutive days, the student receives an envelope with the examination question and proceeds to write a response to be submitted at the end of a 3-hour writing period. Students are not allowed to access the Internet or to consult notes in the process. All members of the student's doctoral committee evaluate all items. At the beginning of the oral examination period, the student is allowed a designated period of time to address any process or content considerations he or she would like to address. Following the presentation, committee members examine the student as they desire.
- Doctoral students may choose to complete the comprehensive exam in the final 2 months of their coursework. Students choose a 48-hour period during which to complete a take-home comprehensive exam consisting of four questions written by their dissertation committee. They receive the questions at the beginning of the exam period and are able to make use of any relevant notes, books, or information. All four questions must be turned in by the end of the 48-hour period. The questions are evaluated by the dissertation committee. An oral exam follows, with committee members able to address questions about the written exam in further detail.
- Doctoral students are eligible to complete comprehensive examinations following the final semester of coursework. The examination includes four questions over four designated areas and is completed in a testing center over a period of 2 days. A doctoral examination committee constructs questions for each administration, and all students receive the same questions each semester. Students may utilize two pages of notes. Following completion of the examination, responses are blinded and sent to the faculty as a whole for grading. Students who receive ratings of "pass" or "conditional pass" by at least two of three raters may proceed to the oral

examination. The oral examination is conducted by the student's doctoral committee and includes primary focus on reviewer comments on the examination.

- Doctoral students are eligible to sit for comprehensive examinations following the final semester of coursework. The examination includes attention to four of the five primary areas of focus for doctoral programs, and program faculty members as a whole have agreed to SLOs to be assessed by each question. The student and doctoral committee members construct each question, taking care to ensure the question calls for the student to demonstrate associated SLOs. Six weeks prior to sitting for the examination, students submit a reading list and question summaries for committee approval. Students complete the examination at home and with open notes over the period of 1 month. After submission of the items, each item is evaluated by two committee members and one faculty member who is not on the student's dissertation committee. Students who receive two or more "proceed to orals" designations for each question proceed to the oral examination in which committee members focus on feedback to items, student reflection on the learning process, and implications for dissertation process. Students who do not receive "proceed to orals" ratings must complete individual items and remediation before sitting for the examination again.

As you can see, there may be great diversity in the nature of comprehensive examinations within a program. As with other assessment elements, counselor educators should select examination structures that most closely reflect the values and culture of the local program. We believe you will find the following resources helpful for examination development.

Resources

Baggerly, J., & Osborn, D. (2013). A survey of counselor education comprehensive exam types and procedures: Recommendations for clinical supervisors and counseling faculty. *The Clinical Supervisor, 32,* 90–104. doi:10.1080/07325223.2013.780933

Carriveau, R. S. (2010). *Connecting the dots: Developing student learning outcomes and outcome based assessments.* Denton: University of North Texas.

Cornell Center for Teaching Excellence. (n.d.). *Test construction manual.* Retrieved from http://www.cte.cornell.edu/documents/Test%20Construction%20Manual.pdf

Haladyna, T. M., & Rodriguez, M. C. (2013). *Developing and validating test items.* New York, NY: Routledge.

McAdams, C. R., & Robertson, D. L. (2012). An informed look at doctoral vivas (oral examinations) in the preparation of counselor educators. *Counselor Education and Supervision, 51,* 176–189.

Michigan State University Scoring Office. (n.d.). *Writing test items.* Retrieved from https://www.msu.edu/dept/soweb/writitem.html

National Board of Medical Examiners. (n.d.). *Constructing written test questions for the basic and clinical sciences* (3rd ed., Rev.). Retrieved from http://www.nbme.org/pdf/itemwriting_2003/2003iwgwhole.pdf

Secolsky, C., & Denison, D. B. (2012). *Handbook on measurement, assessment, and evaluation in higher education.* New York, NY: Routledge.

Chapter 7

Portfolios

"Portfolios embody an organized, purposeful, longitudinal collection of student work that tells a story of the student's efforts, progress, or achievement in a given area" (Swigonski, Ward, Mama, Rodgers, & Belicose, 2006, p. 813). Portfolios are one of the most common program assessment practices nationwide (Ewell et al., 2011)—approximately 20% of CACREP-accredited master's programs and 50% of nonaccredited master's programs use portfolios as part of their process (Baggerly & Osborn, 2013). Most simply, portfolios are a collection of artifacts that are organized around a common theme or purpose and that are tied together through intentional reflection (Swigonski et al., 2006).

Whether focused on a specific course, a series of courses or experiences, or the program as a whole, the portfolio can allow authentic assessment of individual students' performance while serving broader program evaluation and development needs (Banta et al., 2009; Meyer & Latham, 2008). Portfolios may be conceptualized as oriented toward demonstrating growth over time, showcasing culminating achievements, or evaluating specific activities and learning outcomes (Mueller, 2014). Portfolios serve a variety of purposes and provide an opportunity for formative and/or summative assessment of knowledge, skills, or dispositions. Composed of flexible and/or fixed components, portfolios may include attention to both direct (student artifacts and evidence) and indirect (student reflections or opinions) learning. Clear understanding and agreement regarding the purpose of the portfolio will be essential in determining what the portfolio should include and when and how the portfolio will be developed and assessed.

The portfolio has become a staple in K–12 education and teacher preparation, and the concept of a portfolio is not new to counselor education. Approximately two decades ago, Baltimore, Hickson, George, and Crutchfield (1996, p. 118) reviewed potential uses of portfolios in counselor education and suggested the following list of components that may be relevant for assessing learning and development among counseling students:

- A statement of goals, philosophy, counseling theory, and objectives
- Description of the process of improvement and self-evaluation of performance.
- Counseling-related activities outside the program
- Papers, written materials, and reflective feedback on assignments
- Reading journals and other material suggesting synthesis of material

- Group-related work
- Demonstration of basic counseling skills (e.g., empathy, listening)
- Demonstrations of advanced skills (e.g., confrontation, interpretation, crisis management)
- Items relating to areas of specialization and interest
- "Expert" feedback received from instructors and student responses
- Research including publications, proposals, and presentations
- Participation in professional activities (e.g., conferences, workshops)
- Reflection and evaluation of the portfolio process

Similarly, Carney, Cobia, and Shannon (1996) discussed the portfolio in evaluating overall competency of master's students and provided a sample portfolio mapped to the 1994 Standards (CACREP, 1994). More recently, social work educators developed a list of potential artifacts for inclusion in graduate and undergraduate clinical portfolios (Swigonski et al., 2006, p. 816); we list these artifacts below:

- introductory letter
- writing samples or drawings
- laboratory work
- plans or analyses
- videotapes and photographs of productions, presentations, or performances
- letters attesting to personal attributes or professional competencies
- lists of books read
- grade reports
- artifacts from out-of-school activities
- photographs of, or stories about, friends and family
- reflective statements
- goal statements
- self-assessment summaries of periodical articles as they relate to the course being taken
- outlines of lecture notes taken in class
- snapshots of teaching aids made to use in student teaching
- recordings of reports given in class
- video tapes
  –of committee work engaged in emphasizing cooperative learning within a committee
  –of interviews (role-play or with clients, with appropriate protection of confidentiality)
- self-evaluation of personal progress
- test results
- term papers
- self-monitoring, listing what has been learned well and what is left to learn
- journal and diary entries to indicate accomplishments and feelings
- electronic dialogues, links to references, and the interchanges of ideas in a chat room

Although most portfolios may focus on culmination or development of learning across areas, it is important to remember that faculty members may utilize a portfolio approach within specific courses and experiences. For example, the first author teaches a doctoral-level course in teaching in which students must create a course design portfolio that includes teaching a philosophy statement, syllabus, curriculum map, course assessment plan, sample lesson plans, recorded teaching demonstration, and paper illustrating the connections among portfolio components and literature regarding teaching and learning. Students also submit a reflective statement regarding their experience, growth, and development as counselor educators throughout the semester (see Part IV for this assignment and the corresponding rubric). Similarly, students in a professional school counseling course might begin to build a portfolio that demonstrates their approach to building and evaluating a comprehensive developmental school counseling program.

Professionals in the field may also benefit from the ability to document their development through the portfolio. James and Greenwalt (2001) proposed a working portfolio for professional counselors to use to document success and achievement. They advised professionals to include documentation including vita or resume, counseling coursework completed (e.g., syllabi, papers, tests), practicum and internship materials, postdegree supervision, work experience and artifacts, professional credentials, continuing education completed, presentations and publications, and professional service. By maintaining these documents over time, professionals will be able to track their progress, experiences, and competencies in a meaningful way. Because portfolios are so common in education settings, school counseling candidates may find themselves asked to provide portfolios of their work, and counselor educators may be asked to develop a teaching portfolio as part of the hiring or promotion and tenure process.

In addition to holding promise for documentation and assessment of growth in master's programs and among professional counselors, educators have explored potential uses of portfolios in doctoral education. Some have gone so far as to suggest that the portfolio presents a "legitimate alternative to the dissertation" in professional doctoral programs (Maxwell & Kupczyk-Romanczuk, 2009, p. 135). Thyer (2003) provided a strong description of a portfolio option for replacing doctoral comprehensive examinations in social work. The model included the specification of learning outcomes and the requirement that students select one or more artifacts (i.e., papers, manuscripts, presentations, policy manuals, demonstration sessions) that illustrated mastery of each learning outcome. To ensure clarity of match and reflection, Thyer also included the requirement for students to provide a cover page for each learning outcome explaining how the artifact(s) selected tied to the standard. The portfolio model involved intensive collaboration with doctoral committee members throughout the process; students disseminated initial work to their doctoral committee members, met with committee members individually for feedback, revised portfolios on the basis of faculty feedback, and were cleared to proceed to the oral comprehensive examinations after all committee members were satisfied with the learning product. The oral comprehensive examination included time for the student to present material, reflect on professional growth throughout the program, and respond to spontaneous questions regarding the learning objectives.

Although we are discussing portfolios in the context of assessing learning, portfolios may also hold promise for supporting student growth and development. Counselor educators explored the use of a course-based portfolio for developing multicultural counseling competencies and found that those who completed the portfolio condition demonstrated more multicultural awareness and skill on other assessments compared with those who focused on more traditional conceptualization (Coleman, Morris, & Norton, 2006). Wakimoto and Lewis (2014) studied graduate students' perceptions of portfolios and concluded that they viewed portfolios as constructive and useful in their development overall. Participants noted that the self-reflective component helped them gain insight on their development as professionals, and most participants found professional value in creating the product, especially when they had appropriate technical and developmental assistance for creating the portfolio.

As with other options for documenting and evaluating student learning, there are benefits and drawbacks to utilizing portfolios in SLO assessment. Although benefits are far-reaching because of the wide variety of portfolio options, drawbacks include questions related to time investment and appropriateness of structure. We summarized benefits and drawbacks in the lists below.

Benefits of Portfolios

Benefits to utilizing portfolios in SLO assessment include the following:

- Portfolios have promise for formative and summative assessment (Banta et al., 2009).
- Portfolios tell a story of development over time.
- Portfolios provide an authentic snapshot of work across the curriculum (Banta et al., 2009).
- Portfolios are amenable to integration with course and field experiences (Banta et al., 2009).
- Open-ended and flexible structure may capture creativity and diverse strengths.
- Students may find portfolios useful in the job search (Burke & Snead, 2014; Wakimoto & Lewis, 2014), especially for those in education settings.
- Portfolios teach professional self-reflection (Burke & Snead, 2014; Wakimoto & Lewis, 2014).
- Portfolios require students and faculty members to think broadly in terms of goals and objectives (Burke & Snead, 2014).
- Portfolios encourage synthesis of learning across courses and experiences (Burke & Snead, 2014).

- Portfolios involve less anxiety than high-stakes examinations (Burke & Snead, 2014).
- Portfolios include an opportunity to address student strengths and weaknesses (Burke & Snead, 2014).
- Portfolios are more time-efficient than theses (Burke & Snead, 2014).
- Portfolios are comprehensive, developmental, and growth-oriented (Carney et al., 1996).
- Portfolios may facilitate learning (Coleman et al., 2006).

Drawbacks to Portfolios

Drawbacks to utilizing portfolios in SLO assessment include the following:

- Portfolios contain wide variation in content (Burke & Snead, 2014).
- Portfolios are time-consuming for faculty and students alike (Burke & Snead, 2014; Carney et al., 1996).
- The structure may feel too rigid or open-ended for students (Burke & Snead, 2014).
- Evaluation may be subjective (Burke & Snead, 2014).
- Hard copy portfolios may require extensive time formatting and managing information.
- Electronic portfolios may require access to and skills with unfamiliar technology.
- Because portfolios are highly personalized, blind faculty review is not likely to be feasible.

Design Considerations

Individuals who wish to utilize portfolios for SLO assessment should start with focused exploration regarding the purpose of the portfolio. As with other SLO artifacts, it is critical that faculty members design requirements with the end in mind. This includes understanding the SLOs to be assessed, the assessment process (formative or summative), intended audience (faculty members, employers, others), and the role in student and program evaluation (Barrio Minton & Gibson, 2012). Given that portfolios often operate as comprehensive and culminating assessments of learning, Barrio Minton and Gibson (2012) recommended that program faculty members consider incorporating evidence of direct and indirect learning into the portfolio system.

When designing portfolios, faculty will do well to remember four key principles. First, the portfolio should be an intentional and focused product featuring materials selected to demonstrate objectives rather than a kitchen-sink approach to including documents. Unfocused portfolios may be too overwhelming and scattered to understand in a meaningful way. Second, the portfolio should allow balance of standardization and flexible creativity. Although most students will need direction to capture learning outcomes, the beauty of the portfolio lies, in part, in the ability of students to showcase diverse talents and accomplishments. Third, reflection is a critical component of the portfolio experience (Barrio Minton & Gibson, 2012; Carney et al., 1996; Graham & Megarry, 2005). Without reflection and integration, the portfolio loses meaning and power. Finally, students will likely require sustained, explicit communication and technical assistance to create meaningful products. Graduate students who completed portfolios noted the need for earlier contact or introduction regarding portfolio expectations in the program, more explicit instructions for completing the portfolio, and more consistency in expectation of format (Wakimoto & Lewis, 2014).

The *Authentic Assessment Toolbox* (Mueller, 2014) includes extensive attention to portfolio design components. In addition to stepping faculty members through the purposes of various portfolios, Mueller (2014) has included coverage of seven key design considerations: purpose, audience, content, process, management, communication, and evaluation. Under each, he has provided questions to consider and corresponding methods to utilize in the portfolio. The resource also includes a list of reflection prompts related to various types of educational goals. We expect you will find this resource invaluable in the portfolio design process.

In addition to reviewing considerations and design suggestions proposed by Mueller (2014), counselor educators may wish to consider using prompts in the list below to identify the purpose of the portfolio. After identifying the purpose of the portfolio, counselor educators can use later prompts to guide portfolio design and implementation considerations.

Design Considerations for Portfolios

Questions regarding design considerations for portfolios include the following:

- What SLOs will be assessed with this portfolio?
- Is the portfolio designed to be formative or summative?
- What are the best indicators for the SLOs? Papers? Presentations? Recorded sessions? Demonstrations? Curricula or learning materials developed? Feedback from site and university supervisors? Philosophy or reflection papers?
- What reflections or integrative statements should students complete?
- Should the portfolio include evaluations and feedback from others (e.g., graded papers and projects, final skills evaluations from site supervisors, observation feedback forms)?
- What do we wish to capture with the portfolio? Student development over time? Culmination of skills and knowledge at one time? Both?
- For whom is the portfolio designed? Faculty? Potential employers? Accreditors? All?
- How much structure, freedom, and flexibility will students require to optimize quality of product and data?

Implementation Considerations for Portfolios

Questions regarding implementation considerations for portfolios include the following:

- Where will this portfolio be placed in the curriculum? In a course? Field experience? Program as a whole?
- What specifically should go in the portfolio?
- Are elements of the portfolio required? Optional? Both?
- If the portfolio is not located within a course, who will help students understand requirements and expectations along the way?
- What course time or support is needed to help students complete the task meaningfully?
- What program time or support is needed to orient the students to portfolio requirements and formats?
- What advisor time or support is needed to maximize the portfolio experience?
- Will the portfolio be hard copy or electronic?
- If electronic, will students use a learning management system designated by the university (e.g., Blackboard, Tk20, LiveText; see Chapter 12), or will they be free to select their own documentation formats (e.g., individual Foliotek or Portfoliogen accounts)?
- What ethical concerns or considerations are present?
- If the portfolio involves supervisor feedback or client conceptualization, how will the program ensure security and confidentiality of information?
- When will the portfolio be assessed? At one specific program gateway (e.g., prior to field experience, at end of field experience, in capstone course)? At multiple gateways or points in time?
- Who will assess the portfolio? Course/experience instructor? Faculty advisor? Committee of faculty members? Faculty as a whole? Site supervisor? Peers?
- How will assessors provide feedback to students?
- What evaluation methods and documentation will faculty utilize? Rubrics or rating forms for the entire portfolio? Rubrics or rating forms for specific elements of the portfolio? Student self-reflection and rating?

Examples

Consider the following examples developed from the authors' and their colleagues' experiences at a range of CACREP-accredited counseling programs. As with many other elements of the SLO assessment process, these examples illustrate a variety of ways in which faculty members may utilize portfolios to support and assess student learning.

- A faculty member teaches the master's-level social and cultural diversity course during which she assesses students' growth toward multicultural counseling competence. She is particularly concerned with assessing CACREP 2016 Standards 2.F.2.c ("multicultural counseling competencies") and 2.F.2.d ("the impact of heritage, attitudes, beliefs, understandings, and acculturative experiences on an individual's view of others"). She develops a course portfolio in which students complete a series of activities, including the following: pre- and postassessments related to multicultural counseling competence, weekly reflection journals, a paper in which one's self as a cultural being is explored, and a series of experiential engagements designed to address a bias or growing edge. She provides students with developmentally oriented feedback throughout the semester and requires that students assemble materials into a portfolio as part of the final course project. The final project includes an expectation that students self-assess their growth toward competency, report overall growth throughout the semester, and identify implications for their future development.

- As part of a cumulative experience in a capstone school counseling course, a faculty member has students revisit key artifacts from earlier in their program, adjusting them to show mastery of school counseling practice-related standards (CACREP 2016 Standard 5.G.3) to fit their current perspectives as they prepare to enter the job market. After assessing individual artifacts, she guides students through a process of creating a portfolio to inform the job interview process. Portfolio elements include updated resume, revised philosophy of school counseling (an assignment from their first semester in the program), mission and vision statements for their ideal comprehensive school counseling program (CSCP), exemplars of guidance lessons and small group curricula that they have implemented, data collected from their internship sites to support programs implemented, evaluations from site and university supervisors, and an example of an ethical dilemma that they faced and their approach to resolving the situation. This portfolio allows the faculty to assess relevant student SLOs and requires students to attend to topics that will likely come up in a job interview. The instructor is solely responsible for evaluating the portfolio.

- School counseling master's students are required to begin a portfolio in the first school counseling course related to the role of the school counselor, elements of a CSCP, and the American School Counselor Association (ASCA) National Model. They continue to add to the portfolio during practicum and internship in planning, implementing, and evaluating school counseling interventions on the basis of school data. This demonstrates content knowledge and application of the use of data to provide evidence-based interventions to address academic, personal–social, and career-related objectives with students in K–12 settings.

- A doctoral-level program has a portfolio requirement to be completed in addition to doctoral comprehensive examinations and the dissertation. The portfolio requires that students engage in learning activities in each of the five core doctoral areas (CACREP, 2016): counseling, supervision, teaching, research and scholarship, and leadership and advocacy. The portfolio is composed of formal coursework completed and assessed throughout the curriculum (e.g., an integrated theory paper, a paper requiring integrated understanding of supervision frameworks and models, a teaching philosophy, a grant application, and a leadership philosophy paper), documented clinical experiences (e.g., final-hour logs and supervisor evaluations from internships related to counseling and supervision), artifacts from required teaching and supervisor engagements (e.g., feedback from students, learning materials developed), and optional materials tied to sLOs. In this way, the portfolio is both specified and flexible. Students preface each section with a reflective summary statement regarding their experiences and development over time; they conclude each area with a culminating paper on the topic. The program faculty members orient students to the portfolio requirements, documentation forms, and tips for success during the first required course in the program, and faculty members revisit these requirements at least once a year. Ultimately, students develop the portfolio in consultation with their major professors. Prior to the dissertation defense, students make the portfolio available electronically to all faculty members serving on their doctoral committee. At the dissertation defense, the committee and student discuss the portfolio. The committee fills out a rubric regarding student learning on each associated learning outcome, and the major professor enters the rubric into an electronic learning management tool.

These examples illustrate the varying scopes and purposes of portfolios in counselor education. We suspect that you will find the following resources helpful for considering the role of portfolios in your courses and programs.

Resources

Banta, T. W., Griffin, M., Flateby, T. L., & Kahn, S. (2009). *Three promising alternatives for assessing college students' knowledge and skills.* Retrieved from http://learningoutcomesassessment.org/documents/AlternativesforAssessment.pdf

James, S. H., & Greenwalt, B. C. (2001). Documenting success and achievement: Presentation and working portfolios for counselors. *Journal of Counseling & Development, 79,* 161–165. doi:10.1002/j.1556-6676.2001.tb01955.x

Meyer, B., & Latham, N. (2008). Implementing electronic portfolios: Benefits, challenges, and suggestions. *Educause Quarterly, 1,* 34–41.

Mueller, J. (2014). *Portfolios.* Retrieved from http://jfmueller.faculty.noctrl.edu/toolbox/portfolios.htm

Swan, G. (2009). Examining barriers in faculty adoption of an e-portfolio system. *Australasian Journal of Educational Technology, 25,* 627–644.

Thyer, B. A. (2003). A student portfolio approach to conducting doctoral social work comprehensive examinations. *Journal of Teaching in Social Work, 23,* 117–126. doi:10.1300/J067v23n03_10

Wetzel, K., & Strudler, N. (2005). The diffusion of electronic portfolios in teacher education: Next steps and recommendations from accomplished users. *Journal of Research on Technology in Education, 38,* 231–243.

Chapter 8

Theses and Dissertations

Of all the types of learning artifacts, many consider the dissertation to be the "ultimate educational product" (Lovitts, 2005, p. 18). A rite of passage focused on creation of knowledge, the thesis or dissertation process ensures that students demonstrate deep levels of knowledge regarding a specialty area, engage in meaningful research, and generate conclusions to help the field move forward. This process is closely connected to key purposes of doctoral programs as described in CACREP 2016 Standard 6.A.2:

> Doctoral programs (a) extend the knowledge base of the counseling profession in a climate of scholarly inquiry, (b) prepare students to inform professional practice by generating new knowledge for the profession, (c) support faculty and students in publishing and/or presenting the results of scholarly inquiry, and (d) equip students to assume positions of leadership in the profession and/or their area(s) of specialization.

More specifically, faculty members in programs that utilize a thesis or dissertation as a culminating educational artifact may find that the experience allows intimate opportunity to assess several learning outcomes related to research, including those focused on creating research questions, crafting designs, conducting analyses, writing for publication, engaging with the institutional review board, and ensuring ethical and culturally sensitive research practice (see CACREP 2016 Standard 6.B.4). Although completing the dissertation may require students to demonstrate knowledge and skill in several other areas that tie directly to CACREP (2016) SLOs, diversity in dissertation topics and methods makes it near impossible for programs to link other SLOs (e.g., knowledge of counseling theory, supervision models, pedagogical practices, or leadership and advocacy) to dissertations in a systemic manner.

An educational standard across disciplines and universities, the dissertation is perhaps the culminating learning product for doctoral programs. The dissertation process is an intense one that has yielded a degree of scholarly attention over the years. Blum (2010) described the dissertation as a "battleground of numerous emotional and developmental conflicts" (p. 74), noting that the process itself requires a substantial identity shift from student to producer of knowledge as individuals navigate dependency and autonomy. As with other elements of learning, those who researched the dissertation process found that student experiences were connected to several elements in the program environment: "students' research training, chair and student expectations, the chair–advisee relationship, interpersonal difficulties in the advising relationship, and social support" (Burkard et al., 2014, p. 20). Whereas strong collaborative relationships, academic foundations, and personal characteristics are amenable to positive dissertation experiences, deficiencies in preparation and difficult interpersonal relationships lend to negative dissertation experiences (Knox et al., 2011) and may be related to students' choices not to continue study at the all-but-dissertation stage.

Counselor education students seem to have similar experiences to doctoral students in other disciplines. In a qualitative study of counselor education student dissertation experiences, Flynn, Chasek, Harper, Murphy, and Jorgensen (2012) found that students discussed themes related to impact of environment, competing influences, personality traits, chair influence, committee function, and barriers to completion. Flynn et al. concluded that students in the dissertation process struggled to integrate overlapping and, at times, conflicting priorities related to interpersonal, intrapersonal, and professional processes in their lives. It is within this complex context that counselor educators will design dissertation structures, supports, and expectations.

"Theses and dissertations function as effective measuring tools to the degree that they are used with specificity and after agreement has been reached regarding what traits one proposes to isolate and measure" (Hamilton, Johnson, & Poudrier, 2010, p. 576). As with other types of student artifacts, theses and dissertations provide both benefits and drawbacks in the SLO assessment process.

Benefits of Theses and Dissertations

Benefits of theses and dissertations in the SLO assessment process include the following:

- Theses and dissertations are well-geared toward assessing deep learning regarding student specialty area.
- Theses and dissertations are tailored to assessment of research competency.
- Theses and dissertations provide authentic writing and research experience for those interested in academic settings (Burke & Snead, 2014).
- Theses and dissertations generate potential for publication (Burke & Snead, 2014).
- Theses and dissertations foster critical thinking skills (Burke & Snead, 2014).
- Independent nature of activity simulates self-management and responsibility necessary in many academic settings.
- Theses and dissertations are well-integrated into academic programs and traditions.
- Nature of doctoral committee provides natural source of assessors for the product.

Drawbacks of Theses and Dissertations

Drawbacks of theses and dissertations in the SLO assessment process include the following:

- Because dissertation topics vary widely, they do not allow for programwide assessment of SLOs beyond research and scholarship domains.
- Theses and dissertations do not correlate well to assessment of clinical, supervisory, or teaching SLOs.
- Varying nature of dissertation topics and designs limits the degree to which a large number of SLOs may be assessed in any given situation.
- Theses and dissertations are time-consuming for students and faculty alike (Burke & Snead, 2014).
- Theses and dissertations evoke anxiety and feelings of helplessness among students.
- Numerous students leave doctoral programs in all-but-dissertation status, perhaps because they are not prepared or interested to respond to the rigors of dissertation requirements.
- External factors may result in graduation delays and increased cost to students (Burke & Snead, 2014).
- Scholarly writing and research skills may not be relevant for the types of employment that students will seek (Burke & Snead, 2014).
- Quality of mentorship, product, and feedback may vary greatly among faculty members.

- Faculty members cannot include data for students who do not complete the program (Hamilton et al., 2010).
- Doctoral committee members may be too closely connected or invested in the dissertation process to serve as objective raters.

Design Considerations

Of key concern for the design process is awareness of the specific SLOs one can and cannot expect to assess across student dissertations in a program. Assume, for example, that five students graduate from a doctoral program each year. Two students complete a univariate design (part of CACREP 2016 Standard 6.B.4.b), one student completes a multivariate design (the other part of CACREP 2016 Standard 6.B.4.b), one student completes a phenomenological design (part of CACREP 2016 Standard 6.B.4.c), and one student completes a program evaluation (CACREP 2016 Standard 6.B.4.f). Because the students utilized different designs, the program faculty members can assess a lot about each individual student's understanding of one SLO, but they are limited in assessing student competency across the other standards. Similarly, the program faculty members might be able to assess different elements of standards depending on students' topic areas, but they will not be able to generate aggregate data about students' collective experiences or understanding of each SLO.

However, program faculty members could realistically assess all students' abilities related to generating research questions (CACREP 2016 Standard 6.B.4.g), professional writing (CACREP 2016 Standard 6.B.4.h), protections for human participants (CACREP 2016 Standard 6.B.4.j), and ethical considerations for research (CACREP 2016 Standard 6.B.4.l). The program faculty members may also be able to assess broader objectives, such as the ability to engage in scholarly dialogue or to understand the roles and responsibilities of doctoral-level counselor educators.

Hamilton et al. (2010) warned program faculty against using assessment of dissertation quality to generalize too broadly about program quality. Students' preexisting abilities greatly influence their quality of writing and research competence, and the nature of the faculty–student relationship influences the nature of the dissertation product developed over the program. In some cases, the product may more closely reflect the nature of faculty advising rather than the nature of student learning. Finally, there may be meaning in data from students who never make it to the dissertation proposal and defense; culminating assessments of learning at the dissertation level only take into consideration students who complete all requirements successfully.

Several scholars have provided guidance regarding ways in which faculty members can attend to the needs of students in the dissertation process. For example, Boote and Beile (2005) provided a convincing argument that students in education lack preparation and appropriate focus on the literature review. Because the literature review may be seen as "a necessary chore" (Boote & Beile, 2005, p. 5) rather than a meaningful part of the scholarly process, the authors suggested that students tend to struggle in this element of dissertation. They provided concrete suggestions for educators who are working with dissertation students, and they provided a rubric that faculty raters can use to provide feedback and to evaluate dissertation literature reviews (see Boote & Beile, 2005).

Just as students may struggle to integrate literature in a coherent, meaningful literature review, students may struggle to connect findings from the literature review into meaningful, literature-derived research questions. In a conceptual article, Fernando and Hulse-Killacky (2006) provided counselor educators and doctoral students with an inverted triangle method for helping to synthesize literature in a structured, logical manner. This included attention to methods for moving from general ideas about areas of interest and questions to a more focused understanding of the literature, which, in turn, leads to a specific, focused research question. In addition, they described use of research meetings and peer support as supportive elements in the scholarly community.

Recommendations specific to literature review and research question development are consistent with larger design considerations related to the dissertation process. Faculty members should keep aware of the need for active involvement, the need for balance of guidance and autonomy, and the impact of student isolation (Flynn et al., 2012). Flynn et al. (2012) suggested that programs build in supports, such as dissertation study groups and financial resources, for students. Such resources may be part of the formal or informal curricula and will help ensure that program processes map to culminating activities and evaluation methods (Boote & Beile, 2005; Hamilton et al., 2010).

Finally, design of the dissertation process may include attention to program and faculty expectations regarding dissertations. This may include development of explicit departmental policies and procedures to be held constant across students or perhaps less formal discussions of dissertation process and product expectations among faculty and student advisee pairs (Flynn et al., 2012; Hamilton et al., 2010; Knox et al., 2011). For example, whereas some universities are using a traditional, five-chapter dissertation (i.e., introduction, literature review, methodology, results, discussion), other programs are moving toward journal formatting in which students present the dissertation in a series of one or more journal articles ready for publication. Dissertation formatting expectations are likely to be linked to university, college, or department policies and may reflect local priorities and culture.

Thesis and dissertation development questions to consider include the following:

- Which SLOs do we wish to assess with this artifact?
- To what degree can we assess these SLOs across students, topics, and dissertation designs?
- To what degree are these SLOs related to learning in program as opposed to outside or pre-existing influence?
- To what degree does the thesis or dissertation process link to students' professional goals?
- What program supports are needed to ensure attention to the unique needs of our student body in the dissertation process?
- To what degree has the program, department, college, and/or university articulated expectations for dissertation quality and process?
- To what degree has the program articulated appropriate topics and methods for the dissertation?
- What are the minimal college and university requirements for dissertation format, length, and style? What will be the minimal program expectations for dissertation format, length, and style? To what degree should/will individual faculty members have authority to determine these elements with students?
- Who will evaluate the final dissertation product? Major professor? Committee members individually? Committee members collectively? Faculty as a whole? Outside reviewer?
- When will individuals evaluate the dissertation? At proposal (e.g., literature review, research questions, methodology)? At dissertation defense (e.g., total product)? Both times?
- What kinds of feedback will students receive on their performance?
- What will happen when students do not meet acceptable levels of performance?

Evaluation Considerations

Following completion of the dissertation, faculty members will need to determine how to assess the culminating product. This may include attention to who assesses (e.g., major professor, dissertation committee members individually, dissertation committee members as a whole, outside raters, faculty as a whole), when the product is assessed (e.g., prior to oral defense, at oral defense, after final edits), and how the product is assessed (e.g., via rubric or rating form). See the above bulleted list for questions to guide the use of the dissertation as a learning artifact.

Lovitts (2005) conducted an extensive study of 276 faculty members across 74 departments, 10 disciplines, and nine research universities. After recruiting expert participants who had a rich history of advising students related to dissertation, she set out to identify quality levels of the dissertation process. Published in *Academe* as "How to Grade a Dissertation" (a title to which she objected strongly), Lovitts identified a comprehensive list of quality indicators across aspects of the dissertation. She recommended that programs use these indicators to develop rubrics for evaluating dissertation quality, and she further suggested that faculty members make the rubrics public so that students and faculty members could refer to them throughout the dissertation development process. Although more focused on the individual process, Lovitts acknowledged the potential use of the resulting dissertation rubric in overall program evaluation, noting that committees may generate a consensus rubric at defense, outside raters could be asked to complete rubrics to ensure an additional level of objectivity, and programs could examine rubrics for patterns. The following lists include reprints of Lovitts's work regarding dissertation evaluation.

Dissertation Rubric Quality Indicators

Outstanding

- Is original and significant, ambitious, brilliant, clear, clever, coherent, compelling, concise, creative, elegant, engaging, exciting, interesting, insightful, persuasive, sophisticated, surprising, and thoughtful
- Is very well written and organized
- Is synthetic and interdisciplinary
- Connects components in a seamless way
- Exhibits mature, independent thinking
- Has a point of view and a strong, confident, independent, and authoritative voice
- Asks new questions or addresses an important question or problem
- Clearly states the problem and why it is important
- Displays a deep understanding of a massive amount of complicated literature
- Exhibits command and authority over the material
- Argument is focused, logical, rigorous, and sustained
- Is theoretically sophisticated and shows a deep understanding of theory
- Has a brilliant research design
- Uses or develops new tools, methods, approaches, or types of analyses
- Is thoroughly researched
- Has rich data from multiple sources
- Analysis is comprehensive, complete, sophisticated, and convincing
- Results are significant
- Conclusion ties the whole thing together
- Is publishable in top-tier journals
- Is of interest to a larger community and changes the way people think
- Pushes the discipline's boundaries and opens new areas for research

Very Good

- Is solid
- Is well written and organized
- Has some original ideas, insights, and observations, but is less original, significant, ambitious, interesting, and exciting than the outstanding category
- Has a good question or problem that tends to be small and traditional
- Is the next step in a research program (good normal science)
- Shows understanding and mastery of the subject matter
- Has a strong, comprehensive, and coherent argument
- Includes well-executed research
- Demonstrates technical competence
- Uses appropriate (standard) theory, methods, and techniques
- Obtains solid, expected results or answers
- Misses opportunities to completely explore interesting issues and connections
- Makes a modest contribution to the field but does not open it up

Acceptable

- Is workmanlike
- Demonstrates technical competence
- Shows the ability to do research
- Is not very original or significant
- Is not interesting, exciting, or surprising
- Displays little creativity, imagination, or insight
- Writing is pedestrian and plodding
- Has a weak structure and organization
- Is narrow in scope
- Has a question or problem that is not exciting—is often highly derivative or an extension of the advisor's work
- Displays a narrow understanding of the field
- Reviews the literature adequately—knows the literature but is not critical of it or does not discuss what is important

- Can sustain an argument, but the argument is not imaginative, complex, or convincing
- Demonstrates understanding of theory at a simple level, and theory is minimally to competently applied to the problem
- Uses standard methods
- Has an unsophisticated analysis—does not explore all possibilities and misses connections
- Has predictable results that are not exciting
- Makes a small contribution

Unacceptable

- Is poorly written
- Has spelling and grammatical errors
- Has a sloppy presentation
- Contains errors or mistakes
- Plagiarizes or deliberately misreads or misuses sources
- Does not understand basic concepts, processes, or conventions of the discipline
- Lacks careful thoughts
- Looks at a question or problem that is trivial, weak, unoriginal, or already solved
- Does not understand or misses relevant literature
- Has a weak, inconsistent, self-contradictory, unconvincing, or invalid argument
- Does not handle theory well, or theory is missing or wrong
- Relies on inappropriate or incorrect methods
- Has data that are flawed, wrong, false, fudged, or misinterpreted
- Has wrong, inappropriate, incoherent, or confused analysis
- Includes results that are obvious, already known, unexplained, on misinterpreted
- Has unsupported or exaggerated interpretation
- Does not make a contribution

Note. From "How to Grade a Dissertation," by B. E. Lovitts, 2005, *Academe, 91,* p. 20. Copyright 2005 by the American Association of University Professors. Reprinted with permission.

Dimensions of Dissertation Components

Component 1: Introduction

The introduction

- Includes a problem statement
- Makes clear the research question to be addressed
- Describes the motivation for the study
- Describes the context in which the question arises
- Summarizes the dissertation's findings
- Discusses the importance of the findings
- Provides a roadmap for readers

Component 2: Literature Review

The review

- Is comprehensive and up to date
- Shows a command of the literature
- Contextualizes the problem
- Includes a discussion of the literature that is selective, synthetic, analytical, and thematic

Component 3: Theory

The theory that is applied or developed

- Is appropriate
- Is logically interpreted
- Is well understood
- Aligns with the question at hand

In addition, the author shows comprehension of the theory's

- Strengths
- Limitations

Component 4: Methods

The methods applied or developed are

- Appropriate
- Described in detail
- In alignment with the question addressed and the theory used

In addition, the author demonstrates

- An understanding of the methods' advantages and disadvantages
- How to use the methods

Component 5: Results or Analysis

The analysis
- Is appropriate
- Aligns with the question and hypotheses raised
- Shows sophistication
- Is iterative

In addition, the amount and quality of data or information are

- Sufficient
- Well presented
- Intelligently interpreted

The author also cogently expresses

- The insights gained from the study
- The study's limitations

Component 6: Discussion or Conclusion

The conclusion

- Summarizes the findings
- Provides perspective on them
- Refers back to the introduction
- Ties everything together
- Discusses the study's strengths and weaknesses
- Discusses implications and applications for the discipline
- Discusses future directions for research

Note. From "How to Grade a Dissertation," by B. E. Lovitts, 2005, *Academe, 91*, p. 22. Copyright 2005 by the American Association of University Professors. Reprinted with permission.

Resources

As with other elements of the assessment design process, it is essential that counselor educators have a clear understanding of the purpose of the dissertation, expectations for dissertation scope and quality, and ways in which the evaluation of dissertation work links to the understanding of students' progress and quality of the program overall. We believe that you will find the following resources helpful in conceptualizing dissertations as a culminating assessment product for a doctoral program.

Boote, D. N., & Beile, P. (2005). Scholars before researchers: On the centrality of the dissertation literature review in research preparation. *Educational Researcher, 34,* 3–15. doi:10.3102/0013189X034006003

Borders, L. D., Wester, K. L., Granello, D. H., Chang, C. Y., Hays, D. G., Pepperell, J., & Spurgeon, S. L. (2012). Association for Counselor Education and Supervision guidelines for research mentorship: Development and implementation. *Counselor Education and Supervision, 51,* 162–175. doi:10.1002/j.1556-6978.2012.00012.x

Lovitts, B. E. (2005). How to grade a dissertation. *Academe, 91,* 18–23.

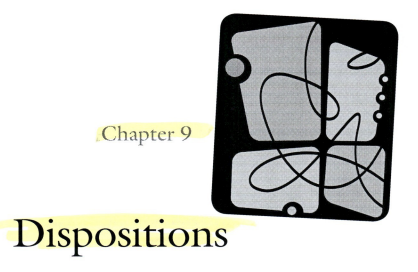

Chapter 9

Dispositions

Simply put, a *disposition* is a "prevailing tendency, mood, or inclination"; "temperamental makeup"; or "the tendency of something to act in a certain manner under given circumstances" ("Disposition," n.d.). Both innate and learned, there is little doubt that counselor dispositions play a critical role in effectiveness, ability to promote well-being, and potential to cause harm. Indeed, the preamble to the *ACA Code of Ethics* (ACA, 2014) includes overt attention to professional values and dispositions:

> Professional values are an important way of living out an ethical commitment. The following are core professional values of the counseling profession:
>
> 1. enhancing human development throughout the life span;
> 2. honoring diversity and embracing a multicultural approach in support of the worth, dignity, potential, and uniqueness of people within their social and cultural contexts;
> 3. promoting social justice;
> 4. safeguarding the integrity of the counselor–client relationship; and
> 5. practicing in a competent and ethical manner. (p. 3)

Throughout the majority of this text, we focused attention to evidence of student learning in terms of knowledge and skills. We would be remiss if we did not include discussion of dispositions as part of the evaluation process.

In this chapter, we attend to the task of defining and operationalizing dispositions, and we situate this definition in the context of current accreditation, ethics, and competency statements. Although disposition assessment is relatively young to the field, we provide an overview of some best practices related to assessment of dispositions. We conclude this chapter with resources to help you operationalize dispositions relevant to your program and integrate them into your systematic, developmental assessment plan.

Professional Counseling Dispositions

Assessment of dispositions is an ongoing component of accreditation requirements for educators, school psychologists, and social workers (Spurgeon, Gibbons, & Cochran, 2012). In many ways,

CAEP (previously NCATE) has led the way on integration of disposition into educator preparation standards. NCATE (2014) defined *professional dispositions* as

> professional attitudes, values, and beliefs demonstrated through both verbal and non-verbal behaviors as educators interact with students, families, colleagues, and communities. These positive behaviors support student learning and development. NCATE expects institutions to assess professional dispositions based on observable behaviors in educational settings. The two professional dispositions that NCATE expects institutions to assess are *fairness* and the belief that all students can learn. Based on their mission and conceptual framework, professional education units can identify, define, and operationalize additional professional dispositions.

Although some may believe that dispositions are not as reliable or meaningful as direct observations of knowledge and skill, Dollarhide (2013) made a strong argument for integration of dispositions and underlying values in counselor education, noting that values lie at the heart of the counseling process. She provided evidence of values underlying even the most behavioral of ethical standards. Winterowd, Adams, Miville, and Mintz (2009) also argued that dispositions underlie one's ability and willingness to enact a skill:

> A disposition, if clearly identified, can be a more accurate standard for addressing competence than the standard of mastery because if a behavior is seen with enough frequency across enough situations, indicating one's disposition to use a skill, then not only can mastery be safely assumed, but also the appropriate application of the skill can be ensured. Dispositions are useful for conceptualizing virtues in that they are a profession's operational definition of the virtues most relevant to that profession . . . Conversely, a disposition might thwart effective learning in a trainee who is being defensive when offered a suggestion by a supervisor and is indicative of the "vice" of closed-mindedness. In short, dispositions may lead toward effective or noneffective professional behaviors. (p. 678)

Certainly, one can make the argument that the professional attitudes, values, and beliefs of professional counselors play a crucial role in their effectiveness with clients. In meta-analyses regarding counseling outcomes, researchers have consistently found that common factors in the relationship account for better counseling outcomes than specific therapeutic techniques or models (M. J. Lambert & Barley, 2001). Notably, less tangible ways of being become central in building therapeutic relationships.

The *ACA Code of Ethics* (ACA, 2014) includes overt and sustained attention to counselor attitudes, values, and dispositions as the cornerstone to ethical counseling practice. This infusion of dispositions is so profound and sustained that it is difficult to separate dispositions from ethical practice. For example, Section A includes attention to trust as a cornerstone of the counseling relationship and specifies that counselors should engage in personal exploration regarding the impact of their beliefs and values on the counseling relationship. Standard A.4.b requires that counselors refrain from imposing personal values on clients—a process that requires dispositions regarding awareness and ability to manage power. Section B.1.a includes more specific attention to awareness and sensitivity regarding cultural considerations.

The CACREP 2016 Standards also include attention to counselor dispositions, and competency documents such as the Multicultural Counseling Competencies (Arredondo et al., 1996) and the Spirituality Competencies (Association for Spiritual, Ethical, and Religious Values in Counseling, 2009) include heavy attention to less tangible dispositions. Although attention to dispositions was implied in previous standard iterations, the CACREP 2016 Standards are the first to include overt attention to dispositions, noting attention to professional dispositions as integral. The following list includes an overview of CACREP 2016 Standards involving assessment of dispositions.

CACREP 2016 Standards Relevant to Dispositions

- Entry-level admission decision recommendations are made by the academic unit's selection committee and include consideration of each applicant's (1) relevance of career goals, (2) aptitude for graduate level study, (3) potential success in forming effective counseling relationships, and (4) respect for cultural differences (Standard 1.L).
- The impact of heritage, attitudes, beliefs, understandings, and acculturative experiences on an individual's views of others (Standard 2.F.2.d).
- Counselor characteristics and behaviors that influence the counseling process (Standard 2.F.5.f).

- The counselor education program faculty demonstrate the use of the following to evaluate program objectives: (1) aggregate student assessment data that address student knowledge, skills, and professional dispositions; (2) demographic and other characteristics of applicants, students, and graduates; and (3) data from systematic follow-up studies of graduates, site supervisors, and employers of program graduates (Standard 4.B).
- The counselor education program faculty systematically assesses each student's professional dispositions throughout the program. The assessment process includes the following: (1) identification of key professional dispositions, (2) measurement of student professional dispositions over multiple points in time, and (3) review or analysis of data (Standard 4.G).
- Doctoral program admission criteria include (a) academic aptitude for doctoral-level study; (b) previous professional experience; (c) fitness for the profession, including self-awareness and emotional stability; (d) oral and written communication skills; (e) cultural sensitivity and awareness; and (f) potential for scholarship, professional leadership, and advocacy (Standard 6.A.3).

Note. From *2016 Standards*, by the Council for Accreditation of Counseling and Related Educational Programs, 2016. Copyright 2016 by the Council for Accreditation of Counseling and Related Educational Programs. Reprinted with permission.

Both academic and nonacademic characteristics rise to the surface when considering important skills and qualities for counselor education students (Swank & Smith-Adcock, 2014). As we review in Chapter 16, intrapersonal and interpersonal dispositions are the most often identified concerns leading to remediation of counseling students (Brown, 2013; Henderson & Dufrene, 2012). In the next section, we review some best practice guidelines for moving toward integrated assessment of student dispositions.

Best Practices

Assessment of dispositions presents unique challenges to counselor educators because dispositions and values tend to be less tangible than knowledge and skills (Dollarhide, 2013). As discussed previously, the *ACA Code of Ethics* (ACA, 2014) and some competency documents provide a starting place for identifying dispositions, but our profession has not yet articulated and embraced a clear set of standards of conduct (Homrich, Delorenzi, Bloom, & Godbee, 2014). Homrich et al. (2014) argued convincingly that

> gatekeepers in the profession of counseling, psychology, social work, and marriage and family therapy would benefit from a set of clearly defined, observable, and measurable criteria for trainee behavior that are widely agreed upon and uniformly acknowledged as minimal expectations across clinical disciplines. (p. 129)

In turn, they used a rigorous identification process to articulate three sets of minimal behaviors expected of graduate counseling students. These included attention to professional behaviors, interpersonal behaviors, and intrapersonal behaviors, with extensive attention to operationalized dispositions. These operationalized dispositions provide a strong foundation upon which counselor educators can build.

Screening for dispositions begins during the admissions process in which counselor educators are responsible for considering candidates' potential for success, with particular attention to dispositions (CACREP, 2016). Swank and Smith-Adcock (2014) reviewed admissions procedures of CACREP-accredited counselor education programs and found that a strong majority of master's programs used personal statements and interviews as part of the admissions process, presumably in attempts to understand candidate dispositions and fit with the program and profession. Further, they recommended that programs consider utilizing established measures for disposition assessment as early as the admissions process (Swank & Smith-Adcock, 2014).

Best practice will include multimodal disposition assessment including attention to dispositions throughout coursework, in clinical experiences, and as part of ongoing student review and retention procedures (Spurgeon et al., 2012; Winterowd et al., 2009). Transparent communication regarding expectations and reasons for those expectations will assist with student integration and understanding throughout the program (V. A. Foster & McAdams, 2009; Spurgeon et al., 2012; Winterowd et al., 2009), especially when counselor educators work attention of dispositions into course learning outcomes (Dollarhide, 2013; Winterowd et al., 2009).

"Affective measures of learning refer to the attempt to capture authentic learning in terms of values, attitudes, and learning dispositions" (Dollarhide, 2013, p. 223). Dollarhide (2013) attended to this process within the context of a social and cultural diversity course, noting that there are five stages of learning related to the affective/values domain: receiving a value, responding to the learning, valuing, organization, and characterization by a value or value complex. She provided explicit guidance for linking educational objectives to pedagogical methodology and assessment elements within a course structure. Counselor educators may find this resource helpful in considering how to build overt, concrete attention to dispositions into the entire SLO process. For example, counselor educators might write learning outcomes specific to openness and cultural sensitivity and learning outcomes for a multicultural course. Ability to receive and integrate feedback may become an SLO for a practicum or internship course.

Although literature regarding disposition assessment is relatively sparse in counselor education, we identified several clear, best practice themes. These include the need to

- clearly articulate dispositions of interest;
- link dispositions of interest to professional counseling literature, ethical codes, and expert opinion;
- operationalize dispositions as concretely as possible;
- communicate with students regarding dispositions and their definitions; and
- link dispositions to admissions assessments, overarching program assessments, and course-based learning outcomes.

In the next section, we overview two published examples of the disposition assessment process. You may find these illustrations particularly helpful in identifying, articulating, and planning for assessment of dispositions in your counselor education program.

Examples

Spurgeon et al. (2012) published an intensive case study example of one counselor education program's process for creating personal dispositions. This included reviewing existing dispositions in other professional programs, making faculty values overt, gathering input from stakeholders, and reflecting on insights from student review and retention procedures. Through this process, they developed a series of five personal dispositions and corresponding operational definitions, as illustrated in the following list of dispositions and operational definitions (Spurgeon et al., 2012, p. 103):

- *Commitment*—Investment in learning; development of counselor identity; advocacy; professional excellence; civic engagement; collaboration; scholar/practitioner; interpersonal competence
- *Openness*—Openness to ideas, learning, and change; openness to giving and receiving feedback; openness to growth; openness to others; openness to self-development
- *Respect*—Perceives and honors diversity; appropriate self-care; adherence to the wellness philosophy
- *Integrity*—Personal responsibility; personal and professional maturity; honesty; courage; congruence
- *Self-awareness*—Integrity; humility; self-reflection and exploration of self; understanding of place in history

After operationalizing the dispositions, the counselor education faculty integrated dispositions into its website, handbooks, syllabi, and clinical evaluation forms, thus ensuring students were aware of expectations and the program had a systematic method for assessing them (Spurgeon et al., 2012). Students involved in this process reported that they understood and appreciated systematic integration of dispositions throughout the program, and initial mixed methods responses indicated that the process helped shape their program in meaningful ways (Gibbons, Cochran, Spurgeon, & Diambra, 2013). Counselor educators who have not yet developed a disposition assessment practice may find this article especially helpful for developing and operationalizing their own dispositions.

In another exemplar piece, Winterowd et al. (2009, pp. 680–683) operationalized values in the *Counseling Psychology Model Training Values Statement Addressing Diversity* (Council of Counseling Psychology Training Programs, 2006) into a total of nine virtues that were embedded in a standard document and were placed on a rating scale. These virtues included being respectful; being inclusive; being collaborative and cooperative; being open; being inquisitive, self-aware, and introspective; being culturally aware; being socially just; professional growth; and self-improvement. Counselor educators may find this rating scale and discussion of process helpful for operationalizing their own values and virtues into measurable dispositions.

Attention to dispositions is now a central task of counselor educators. This will require that counselor educators operationalize dispositions, link them to the curriculum in intentional ways, and build intentional opportunities for assessment. You may find the following resources helpful for this process.

Resources

Brown, M. (2013). A content analysis of problematic behavior in counselor education programs. *Counselor Education and Supervision, 52,* 179–192. doi:10.1002/j.1556-6978.2013.00036.x

Dollarhide, C. T. (2013). Using a values-based taxonomy in counselor education. *Counseling and Values, 58,* 221–236. doi:10.1002/j.2161-007X.2013.00035.x

Homrich, A. M., Delorenzi, L. D., Bloom, Z. D., & Godbee, B. (2014). Making the case for standards of conduct in clinical training. *Counselor Education and Supervision, 53,* 126–144. doi:10.1002/j.1556-6978.2014.00053.x

Spurgeon, S. L., Gibbons, M. M., & Cochran, J. L. (2012). Creating personal dispositions for a professional counseling program. *Counseling and Values, 57,* 96–109.

Swank, J. M., & Smith-Adcock, S. (2014). Gatekeeping during admissions: A survey of counselor education programs. *Counselor Education and Supervision, 53,* 47–61. doi:10.1002/j.1556-6978.2014.00048.x

University of North Carolina at Charlotte. (n.d.). *Professional dispositions plan and information.* Retrieved from http://education.uncc.edu/resources/professional-dispositions-plan-and-information

University of Texas at San Antonio. (n.d.). *Fitness to Practice forms.* Retrieved from http://education.utsa.edu/counseling/fitness_to_practice/

Winterowd, C. L., Adams, E. M., Miville, M. L., & Mintz, L. B. (2009). Operationalizing, instilling, and assessing counseling psychology training values related to diversity in academic programs. *The Counseling Psychologist, 37,* 676–704. doi:10.1177/0011000009331936

Chapter 10

Indirect Measures

To this point, we have focused on assessing what students know and can do through their participation in courses and culminating experiences, such as internship, portfolios, comprehensive examinations, and theses or dissertations. We also attended to how student dispositions may affect enactment of knowledge and skills. These elements are at the heart of the SLO evaluation plan. Strong program evaluation plans also include indirect measures of learning and the learning environment. Although indirect measures alone are not sufficient for SLO outcomes (Hatfield, 2009), information gleaned from indirect measures provide important information regarding the learning context and possibilities for course and program improvement.

In this chapter, we define and provide several examples of indirect measures of learning as part of the greater program evaluation process. Next, we provide concrete guidance for identifying and developing indirect measures. We close the chapter with several resources for further study.

Indirect Measures in Context

Suskie (2009) conceptualized two primary types of indirect measures: those related to student learning and those related to learning processes. Indirect measures of student learning include course and assignment grades, nature and percentage of graduate placement, alumni perceptions of career, student and alumni perceptions of learning, course-focused evaluations, and student productivity and honors. Indirect measures of learning environment include program media and syllabi, reports of student–faculty interaction, and nature of course methods and assignments. Suskie claimed that indirect measures of program evaluation included possible reactions or student satisfaction indicators of their program experience. If dissatisfied with their experiences, students may have not learned what was intended for them to learn. However, this does not give an adequate picture of learning outcomes. In essence, satisfaction or dissatisfaction clouds the picture.

National studies of program assessment practices revealed common use of indirect assessments in program evaluation. At the university level, more than 80% of universities used national student surveys, more than 60% used alumni surveys, more than 60% used locally developed surveys, and just less than one half used employer surveys (Kuh et al., 2014). At the program level, nearly half of programs used locally developed surveys, one third surveyed alumni, one fifth surveyed employers, and one fifth conducted student interviews or focus groups (Ewell et al., 2011).

Prior to the CACREP 2009 Standards, counselor education programs focused on answering the question of "how well is the program faculty doing their job of admitting, educating, and graduating counselors-in-training (CITs)?" This information was gathered from different sources at different times, including perceptions of current students, students at program completion, and alumni.

Indirect Measures of Focus in the CACREP 2016 Standards

A tradition of indirect assessment continues in the CACREP 2016 Standards, and the following list includes indirect measures that will be included in any program evaluation plan:

- Program graduate follow-up studies (Standard 4.B.3)
- Site supervisor follow-up studies (Standard 4.B.3)
- Employer follow-up studies (Standard 4.B.3)
- Number of graduates (Standard 4.E.1)
- Pass rates on credentialing examinations (Standard 4.E.2)
- Completion rates (Standard 4.E.3)
- Job placement rates (Standard 4.E.4)
- Student evaluation of faculty teaching (Standard 4.J)
- Student evaluation of site supervisors (Standard 4.K)

Alumni and employer surveys are often central indirect measures. "Alumni and employer surveys have the advantage of ranking high in believability and utility for both formative, faculty-driven assessment purposes as well as for summative evaluations at the system or state level" (Hoey & Gardner, 1999, p. 43). This is particularly powerful when programs triangulate results with other data from the program evaluation process. Whereas direct measures of SLOs may be summative in nature, indirect measures may help educators determine why learning is or is not occurring (Suskie, 2009). For this reason, counselor education programs must consider indirect measures of student learning alongside direct evidence of SLOs (Urofsky & Bobby, 2012).

It is important to understand strengths, limitations, and interactions among direct and indirect measures. For example, students and alumni may not be reliable informants regarding their knowledge and skills (Heath, DeHoek, & Locatelli, 2012; Weldy & Turnipseed, 2010), especially when they may be unaware of what they do not know (Kruger & Dunning, 1999). In one case, Master of Social Work students with lower levels of directly observed competencies self-reported higher levels of knowledge and skill on indirect assessments; this was in direct contrast to more accurate reporting by peers with higher levels of competence (Calderon, 2013). Additionally, informants' ability to recall information may change as time passes, and their perceptions of satisfaction and dissatisfaction with the program and university may morph as they navigate different elements of the program and life after graduation.

"Retention, graduation, and placement rates and the like are also important outcomes, but they don't tell us exactly what students have and haven't learned" (Suskie, 2009, p. 22). There are several mitigating factors that can influence these indicators. For example, economic downturns affect the availability of paid counseling positions in the world of work; in this case, even highly competent graduates may struggle to find employment in the months following graduation. This could lead to lower than usual placement rates, graduate dissatisfaction, and difficulty securing meaningful data from employers. When using these types of data in program evaluation, one should be sure to provide enough context that users can draw appropriate conclusions about program outcomes.

Design Considerations

Counselor educators will choose from a variety of indirect measures when constructing program evaluation plans. Given the context of university accountability expectations, we suspect that counselor educators will most likely find themselves considering three primary types of indirect assessments: follow-up studies, graduate performance data, and instructor and supervisor evaluation. In this section, we outline key design considerations for each major area.

Formal Follow-Up Studies

CACREP 2016 Standard 4.B requires that counselor education programs conduct systematic studies of program graduates, employers, and site supervisors. Most literature focuses on alumni studies, although many of these principles can be extended to studies of site supervisors and alumni employers.

Alumni Studies

Cabrera, Weerts, and Zulick (2005) identified three main approaches to alumni surveys: alumni outcomes approach, engagement and competencies approach, and alumni giving approach. The alumni outcomes approach includes attention to characteristics and satisfaction with the institution as well as engagements and employment since graduation. In counselor education, this may include questions regarding students' perceptions of faculty, advising, and program support. Alumni may reflect on program or institutional supports that they accessed during their time as students (e.g., participation in Chi Sigma Iota, engagement in a mentor program). Alumni may also report their current employment status, salary, licenses and certifications, engagement in the professional counseling community, and satisfaction with the world of work. In all, responses may help program faculty members paint a picture regarding their alumni's engagements, current accomplishments, and connections with the program. They may also inform understanding regarding where alumni go and what they do following graduation.

The engagement and competencies approach to alumni surveys includes a focus on student characteristics and experiences in the program as well as alumni perceptions of competencies attained in the program and used since graduation (Cabrera et al., 2005). This may include participants' perceptions of the importance of knowledge or skills for work in the field together with the degree to which graduates attained the knowledge or skills (Hoey & Gardner, 1999). In this type of alumni survey, counselor education programs may articulate a series of program objectives or SLOs for which they have alumni rate the importance of the competency in their current position and rate the degree to which the program prepared them for that competency. Depending on the nature of the items and sample size, programs may be able to conduct more sophisticated analyses regarding discrepancies in scores, trends for specific groups of alumni, and relationships with other aspects of program experiences or quality (see Hoey & Gardner, 1999).

Finally, some alumni surveys are focused on understanding willingness and ability to support the institution via donations; these often include questions geared at helping institutions identify potential donors (Cabrera et al., 2005). In our experience, the alumni giving approach is most often situated at the university or college level. Although counselor education programs may have an alumni donor base, it is not likely that they will be completing these types of surveys as part of program evaluation.

Those who use alumni surveys should clearly articulate the purposes and contexts of the surveys so that decision makers can gather the information most important to their goals. For counselor education, we suspect that program faculty members are most interested in a combination of the alumni outcomes approach and the engagement and competencies approach. We encourage faculty members to go about designing and implementing alumni studies as they would more rigorous investigations; this will include attention to the connection among evaluation question, survey design, sampling, and data analysis.

Reflection Prompts for Alumni Studies

The following list of questions may be helpful in considering the design of alumni studies:

- What are our overarching program objectives?
- What do we already know about our progress toward these objectives?
- What do we need to know to round out our understanding of these objectives?
- What do we need to know to satisfy accrediting bodies and administrators?
- Do alumni participate in any other type of data collection effort within the department, college, or university? If so, how can we ensure that this survey produces unique information?
- What type of data do we need to answer our questions? Qualitative? Quantitative? Mixed? Written? Oral?
- How can we ensure the validity of our methods?

- What is our sampling plan? How many responses do we need to make sense of data in a meaningful way?
- What is the best way to reach our alumni? Mail? E-mail? Phone? In person?
- At what point will alumni be best suited to provide the information that we need to know? How does the nature of our questions influence our plan for data collection?
- How much time will it take alumni to provide the information that we need?
- What are the most appropriate methods for analyzing alumni data? Do we have adequate sample size and resources for analyzing data?
- What ethical protections or safeguards are necessary when collecting information from alumni?
- How will we connect overall themes and findings in light of the overarching evaluation plan?
- Would we like to be able to compare information over time? If so, how does that inform plans for updating and revising the survey?

Response rate and response accuracy are of particular concern for alumni follow-up studies. A moderate-sized counselor education program may only graduate several dozen students a year, and alumni response rates of 10%–15% seem to be fairly common. This presents a substantial challenge for gathering meaningful information. Possible reasons for low response rates include survey fatigue, the mobile nature of the student population, lack of accurate contact information, volume of university contacts and postgraduation requests, and spam or junk filters. Although data suggest that limited response rates on alumni surveys do not necessarily mean that results will not be representative (A. D. Lambert & Miller, 2014), program faculty members may wish to think through creative solutions for reaching their constituents. This may include visiting with students prior to graduation regarding upcoming survey requests, collecting nonuniversity e-mail addresses and contact information during the final internship course, maintaining alumni communications (e.g., newsletter, listservs, Facebook groups), and conducting web searches to locate individuals who do not respond to mail or e-mail invitations. These activities will assist in both alumni follow-up studies and formal program performance efforts. The following is a sample alumni survey.

Sample Alumni Survey

What year did you graduate from the Counselor Education program at the University?

From which counselor education specialty area did you receive your degree (i.e., school, clinical mental health, marriage, couples, and family counseling)?

What is your current professional position (i.e., licensed professional counselor, professional school counselor)?

What is your primary work setting if employed? If working in a school setting, please describe the setting (i.e., elementary, middle, high, postsecondary).

What do you see as the major strengths of your counselor education program at the University?

What do you see as the major areas in need of improvement for your counselor education program at the University?

PROFESSIONAL DISPOSITIONS: Please choose from the following responses to select the response that best describes the preparation you received in your counselor education program for each of the following areas of professional knowledge and skills.

A = Excellent   B = Good   C = Fair   D = Poor   E = Did not receive any preparation

_____ Appreciating the roles and responsibilities of the profession
_____ Understanding professional and ethical standards in your area of expertise

LEARNING ENVIRONMENT: Please choose from the following responses to select the response that best describes the preparation you received in your counselor education program for each of the following areas of professional knowledge and skills.

A = Excellent   B = Good   C = Fair   D = Poor   E = Did not receive any preparation

_____ Creating an environment that encourages the academic growth of all students
_____ Creating an environment that encourages the personal growth of all students
_____ Creating an environment that encourages the social growth of all students

_____ Creating an environment that encourages the career growth of all students

_____ Creating an environment where all students can be successful

_____ Creating an environment where diversity is celebrated

ASSESSMENT AND REFLECTIVE PRACTICE: Please use the following responses to select the response that best describes the preparation you received in your counselor education program for each of the following areas of professional knowledge and skills.

A = Excellent   B = Good   C = Fair   D = Poor   E = Did not receive any preparation

_____ Evaluating overall program effectiveness

_____ Assessing student/client needs

_____ Assessing student academic outcomes

_____ Assessing student/client personal/social outcomes

_____ Assessing student/client career outcomes

_____ Using assessment results to inform and adjust practice

_____ Using current research to inform practice

_____ Using critical thinking skills to inform practice

_____ Engaging in reflective practice

_____ Collaborating professionally with colleagues and other relevant individuals

_____ How would you describe the overall professional preparation you received in your counselor education program?

For the professional practice areas where you feel underprepared, please provide more information about how the counselor education program faculty could better address that particular area.

What other topics/experiences would you like to see in the curriculum?

Please provide any additional feedback you have on the program:

Site Supervisor Studies

Because all students complete a series of field experiences as a part of the counselor education program, counselor education program members have the unique opportunity to gather data from individuals who are intimately aware of the knowledge and skills with which students are leaving the programs. Site supervisors are well-positioned to discuss how well student competencies align with current demands in the world of practice. In addition to completing formal assessment of student learning during field experiences, counselor education program members can look to site supervisors to provide other information regarding program strengths and opportunities.

As with alumni studies, there are a variety of methods by which program members can collect data from site supervisors. For example, counselor education program members could include an anonymous quantitative or qualitative survey focused on program elements in each student's evaluation materials. Alternately, all faculty members could ask a brief series of interview questions during each site visit. Faculty members could identify key informants who are well-acquainted with program students to participate in longer interviews in face-to-face, phone, or videoconference format. Finally, the program faculty could assemble an advisory panel of site supervisors across settings to provide focus-group data to the program on an ongoing basis.

As with alumni studies, program members should first determine what they need to know from site supervisors and then construct a systematic plan for accessing this information. Ideally, the information collected will complement and supplement direct measures of student learning and indirect measures of alumni experiences and satisfaction. You may find the questions in the Reflection Prompts for Alumni Studies section helpful for framing the approach to site supervisor studies.

Employer Studies

Finally, accreditation CACREP 2016 Standards require that programs engage in formal study of graduate employers. In some ways, program members may find striking parallels between design considerations and types of questions for site supervisors and alumni employers. Those designing these assessments, however, should consider two unique elements. First, access to program employers will most likely come directly through alumni; the ability to reach program employers is directly related to the ability to reach program alumni. Ongoing connections with alumni and timely outreach to determine the specific nature of placement will be important for developing a database of employers for inclusion in follow-up studies. Second, program employers are not likely to have the same degree of ties, allegiance to a program, or direct information about performance as site supervisors who have daily contact with students.

Program faculty members may wish to consider how program employers can provide unique information and perspectives beyond that of alumni and immediate site supervisors. For example, program employers may have a unique sense of graduates' long-range performance as well as more immediate directions in the field that may affect program focus or operation. As with site supervisors, program faculty members may consider whether questions for program employers may be best answered through written surveys, brief phone interviews, advisory panels, or focus groups. In this case, an advisory panel or a focus group of individuals associated with school districts or community agencies that have hired multiple program graduates may provide the richest source of information for programs. As with site supervisor studies, the information collected should complement and supplement direct and other indirect measures. You might find the questions in the Reflection Prompts for Alumni Studies section helpful for framing the approach to employer studies.

Graduate Performance Data

Consistent with a number of regulatory expectations, CACREP 2016 Standard 4.E requires that programs make public graduate performance data, including pass rates on credentialing examinations, program completion rates, and job placement rates. Program members should include both direct and indirect indicators of graduate performance data. Testing agencies and credentialing bodies often make program pass rates available to the program faculty members directly. For example, the State of Texas provides each counselor education program with aggregate data regarding NCE pass rates for their students, and the Texas State Board for Educator Certification provides program faculty members with pass rates and score data for graduates who sat for the state certification examination. Programs in which the Graduate School Administration of the NCE is utilized will receive more detailed reporting of graduates' performance on each of the NCE scales and subscales. These data will be more accurate and complete than requesting that alumni self-report their examination pass rates and scores as part of a follow-up study.

Similarly, program faculty members will need to report program completion rates. Completion rates are of particular interest to institutional effectiveness staff and are a common metric for attention throughout the university context. Completion rates should be based on official university data and may include a proportion of matriculated students who completed the program in the optimal amount of time (e.g., 3 or 4 years) as well as the maximum amount of time (e.g., 6 years to degree plan expiration).

Several accrediting bodies are interested in understanding the 180-day job placement rate for graduates. In small programs, program faculty may have close enough contact with alumni to be able to report and track specific employment status of graduates. In other programs, the program faculty will need to determine a means for following up with graduates to collect these data and may do so as part of an initial alumni follow-up. Program faculty members will need to work together to define what they mean by 180-day job placement rates. This may include gathering contextual information from graduates to understand reasons for nonplacement; in general, individuals who remove themselves from the job market for family, health, or academic reasons are not counted in this rate. The following is an example of an alumni employment survey.

Sample Alumni Employment Survey

We would like to know what alumni are up to. The next few questions will help us know more about your life events since graduation.

Which licenses or certifications have you obtained since graduation?
- ☐ None
- ☐ LPC [Licensed Professional Counselor]–Intern
- ☐ NCC [National Certified Counselor]
- ☐ Certified School Counselor
- ☐ Other (please specify): _____

Are you employed?
- ☐ Yes, I am employed in a position directly related to my training at University
- ☐ Yes, I am employed in a position somewhat related to my training at University
- ☐ Yes, but I am not employed in the counseling field
- ☐ No, but I'm actively seeking employment
- ☐ No, and I'm not actively seeking employment
- ☐ Other (please specify): _____

If yes to employment . . .
Congratulations! Please tell us about your position(s).
Position: _____
Employer Name (e.g., Agency, School, City): _____
City: _____ State: _____

Are you seeking advanced training or another graduate degree?
- ☐ Yes
- ☐ No

If yes to advanced training or degree . . .
Congratulations! Please tell us a bit about your area of study.
Program: _____
University: _____

Although CACREP 2016 Standard 4.E does not require reporting at this level, programs may wish to collect additional information regarding the nature of job placement to include the nature of work, full- or part-time status, salary, and other details that may provide a richer context for understanding graduates' experiences.

Instructor and Supervisor Evaluation

Students should also have regular opportunity to evaluate faculty instructors (CACREP 2016 Standard 4.J) and site supervisors (CACREP 2016 Standard 4.K). In most cases, the university, college, and/or department will have a standardized procedure for gathering student opinions of faculty instruction. This procedure may include a uniform assessment for all members of the faculty or may allow program faculty members to shape the nature of the assessment to areas of focus for the unit. Certainly, instructors of intimate, graduate-level clinical courses may desire different feedback than instructors of sections of undergraduate introductory courses serving several hundreds of students.

If the counselor education program members deem the existing student evaluations appropriate, the program simply needs to be in compliance with existing procedures. In the event that the university, college, or larger department procedure does not adequately capture elements of teaching effectiveness that are most important to counselor educators, the program faculty members may wish to advocate for a supplemental evaluation of instructional effectiveness. Generally open-ended in nature, this may allow faculty members to collect richer or more targeted information regarding their students' experiences. As with other student opinions of teaching effectiveness, the program faculty members should take care to develop the instrument with intentionality and to ensure student privacy and safety in providing feedback. This will likely include confidential administration of the questionnaire, compilation by an individual who is not the faculty member, and delayed release of results until after student grades and evaluations have been processed for the semester.

The CACREP 2016 Standards require that students also have regular opportunities to evaluate supervisors. Unlike evaluation of faculty teaching, this may require that program faculty members develop an instrument or format for students to provide feedback regarding their experience with faculty and site supervisors. As with other locally developed instruments, this instrument should be developed with attention to utility and practicality. Whereas faculty members in one program may develop a rating instrument based on the *Best Practices in Clinical Supervision* (ACES, 2011) guidelines, faculty members in another program may develop a questionnaire asking supervisees to respond to several open-ended questions regarding the nature of their supervisory relationships. Program faculty members will need to consider opportunities for collecting information and providing feedback to supervisors in ways that promote safety for the supervisee. This is particularly important given that a supervisor may serve only a few students during any given semester, and a supervisee may depend on the supervisor to serve as a reference in job or doctoral program searches. In some commercial learning management programs, anonymous surveys are allowed to be attached to student internship binders or to be submitted through a course portal.

Although the process of faculty and site supervisor evaluations is generally considered private and developmental, it is important to consider these points of feedback for overall program development. As with formal teaching evaluations, the department or program chair may review copies of all student evaluations of faculty supervisors. When students express concerns regarding faculty member performance, the relevant party may work with the faculty member to develop more effective teaching or supervision strategies. In some cases, program faculty and administration may also use these data to inform personnel decisions. In the case of site supervisor feedback, the department chair or internship coordinator may review copies of student evaluation for themes. If the supervisor is employed within the program, results may be shared and development may be supported much like in evaluation of teaching. If the supervisor is located in practicum or internship sites, program faculty members may provide thematic feedback, increase consultation opportunities, develop more advanced supervision training, or, ultimately, decide whether to direct students to or away from the sites.

Conclusion

In this chapter, we identified several indirect measures of program quality and student learning. Supplemental data from students, alumni, site supervisors, and program employers may illuminate program strengths and opportunities for growth. These data go beyond direct measures of learning to help us understand how and why students are learning in the program. In addition, examination of student completion rates, pass rates on certification examinations, and employability of graduates provide faculty members with important contextual information regarding their students' experiences before and after the program. You may find the following resources helpful in further developing indirect program evaluation measures.

Resources

Cabrera, A., Weerts, D., & Zulick, B. (2005). Making an impact with alumni surveys. *New Directions for Institutional Research, 126,* 5–17. doi:10.1002/ir.144

Calderon, O. (2013). Direct and indirect measures of learning outcomes in an MSW program: What do we actually measure? *Journal of Social Work Education, 49,* 408–419. doi:10.1080/104377 97.2013.796767

Developing a Survey Instrument [Rutgers webpage]: http://njaes.rutgers.edu/evaluation/resources/survey-instrument.asp

Hoey, J. J., & Gardner, D. C. (1999). Using surveys of alumni and their employers to improve an institution. *New Directions for Institutional Research, 101,* 43–59.

Lambert, A. D., & Miller, A. L. (2014). Lower response rates on alumni surveys might not mean lower response representativeness. *Educational Research Quarterly, 37,* 38–51.

Puerzer, R. J., & Rooney, D. M. (2002). The alumni survey as an effective assessment tool for small engineering programs. *Journal of Engineering Education, 91,* 109–116.

Taylor-Powell, E. (1998). *Questionnaire design: Asking questions with a purpose.* Retrieved from http://learningstore.uwex.edu/Assets/pdfs/G3658-02.pdf

Chapter 11

Creating Measures

In previous chapters, we included attention to a wide variety of CBAs, field experience activities, and capstone requirements that call on students to demonstrate their knowledge or skills (Suskie, 2009). To this point, we have focused on creating opportunities to see what students know or can do, but we have not yet focused on how we measure degree of performance demonstrated through those activities. Rubrics and observation forms are evaluation measures that are used across training programs in counselor education, teacher education, and special education, and rubrics and rating forms are growing in popularity across higher education settings (Kuh et al., 2014). These measures include the expectations of student skills performance as well as the criteria for evaluating those skills.

In this chapter, we provide a comprehensive review of types and uses of rubrics in evaluation SLOs. Specifically, the construction of rubrics is outlined as to the purpose of the rubric (i.e., scoring/grading or describing performance). The construction of observation/rating scales and their uses are examined, and reliability and validity considerations for collecting meaningful data are offered.

Rubrics

Grading rubrics are among the most objective methods to assess knowledge and skills. A grading rubric is a scoring guide for the specific assignment, but it can also be a document that specifies "the expectations for assignments by listing the criteria and describing levels of quality from excellent to poor" (Reddy & Andrade, 2010, p. 435). Because the nature of a rubric is to introduce structure and organization in applying scoring criteria and standards to assignments, faculty can be resistant to using them (Reddy & Andrade, 2010; Suskie, 2009). Faculty members may think that a structure is being imposed on them, attempting to change how they are teaching. Yes, the rubric is more structured, but there is freedom in constructing rubric formats as long as they serve the desired purpose. According to Andrade (2005), rubrics help faculty members clarify and communicate learning goals to students. They guide expectations and feedback on students' progress toward attaining these goals. Organizing these goals in a rubric can lead to a more efficient grading and feedback system and may benefit students by helping them understand levels of performance expected of them as part of the course experiences (Ambrose et al., 2010).

Prior to creating a rubric for an assignment, faculty members may wish to consider the following questions (Allen, 2004; Huba & Freed, 1999; Stevens & Levi, 2005):

- Why was the assignment created? (Examining the purpose of the assignment)
- Has this assignment or something similar been given before? (Familiarity with expectations for student performance on assignment and grading/scoring experience)
- How is the assignment connected with other assignments and the course content/instruction as a whole? (Examining the meaningfulness of the assignment)
- When the assignment is completed successfully, what skills/knowledge/dispositions will the student have demonstrated? (Intentionality of building skills/knowledge/dispositions with a CACREP Standards foundation)
- What is the assigned task in the assignment? (Skills/knowledge/dispositions are associated through theory and/or evidence with the task content/behavior)
- What is the evidence to the learned/demonstrated skill/knowledge/disposition? (Delineating the assignment artifact that is associated with the assignment, such as paper, presentation, videotape counseling session, etc.)
- What are the highest and worst expectations for a student's performance on the assignment? (Guides the grading/scoring within the parameters of the criteria and standards)

Counselor educators have to determine the purpose of the rubrics that they use for assessing learning on CBAs, field experiences, comprehensive examinations, dissertations, and portfolios. If the assignment is a key assessment to evaluate SLOs, then one of the main purposes of the rubric is to integrate performance parameters that reflect knowledge and skill standards. Typically, when rubrics are used for this purpose, they include three essential components: evaluation criteria, quality definitions, and a scoring strategy (Popham, as cited in Reddy & Andrade, 2010).

Evaluation Criteria

Evaluation criteria include indicators required for the student to perform or demonstrate and that reflect content or skills (Parke, 2001; Reddy, 2007). These indicators are the specific parameters of the assignment that are required of the students. Essentially, this area of the rubric is where the dimensions of the task or performance are described. When using the rubric for course-embedded SLO evaluations, faculty members should link accreditation standards applicable to the course and the assessment to each indicator (Barrio Minton & Gibson, 2012). This may include delineating core curricular standards and specific specialty area standards as articulated in the CACREP 2016 Standards.

Delineation of standards often involves breaking down SLOs into component parts and operationalizing them in a way that can be more readily assessed. For example, Table 11.1 contains an example of a rubric designed to assess suicide assessment (CACREP 2016 Standard 2.F.7.c), and the "Criterion" column includes the evaluation criteria. For this assessment, there are five criteria to evaluate how well students can perform a suicide assessment, which include the following: Asks "the question," essential skills, risk formulation, protective factors, and history and warning signs. Performing these skills and assessing this information are indicators that the CIT has demonstrated the ability to conduct a suicide risk assessment in this specific situation.

A few helpful hints in creating the evaluation criteria include the following:

- Break down the parts of the task/assignment in simple and direct terms. Vague language and ambiguous meaning are confusing for student and educator.
- Specify skills, knowledge, and/or dispositions required in the task. This provides a clear picture of the required information that needs to be demonstrated.
- Remember that each dimension of the task may represent a different type of analysis. Some dimensions of the task may be related to specific CACREP Standards; other dimensions may be related to program-specific SLOs.

How well students demonstrate and apply their knowledge and skills are described in the quality definitions of the rubric that are delineated in the performance levels of the scoring strategy.

Table 11.1
Suicide Assessment Rubric Example

Criterion	Quality Definitions for Knowledge and Skills		
	3 = Exceeds	2 = Meets	1 = Does Not Meet
Asks "the question"	Student asks about suicide clearly and directly.	Student asks about suicide directly.	Student does not ask about suicide clearly and directly.
Essential skills	Masterful use of essential counseling skills, including appropriate questions and reflections throughout session. Student uses basic counseling skills in a way that greatly enhances suicide assessment and intervention. Student provides supportive place to explore ideation.	Draws from some essential counseling skills but shows overuse, underuse, or inappropriate use of these skills occasionally. Still, use of foundation skills enhances suicide assessment and intervention. Student provides somewhat of a supportive space for client to explore ideation.	Unable to use essential counseling skills, including appropriate questions and reflections, in a way that promotes session flow and outcome. Student fails to provide a supportive place or to integrate essential skills with demands of suicide assessment.
Risk formulation	Student supports the client's courage to disclose while eliciting details necessary for risk formulation, including plan, means, method, and intent.	Mechanics of suicide assessment are appropriate (e.g., eliciting details necessary for risk formulation); however, relational aspects or flow of questioning needs attention at times.	Suicide assessment is missing key elements, such as means, method, plan, and intent.
Protective factors	Student elicits protective factors, deterrents, and reasons for living.	Student shows at least some attention to protective factors, deterrents, and reasons for living.	Student does not sufficiently attend to protective factors, deterrents, and reasons for living.
History and warning signs	Assessment includes clear attention to suicide history (see American Association of Suicidology, 2003).	Assessment includes some attention to suicide history (see American Association of Suicidology, 2003).	Student does not attend to suicide history (see American Association of Suicidology, 2003).

Scoring Strategy

When creating the scoring strategy for a rubric, Suskie (2009) recommended using at least three but no more than five performance levels. When there are multiple performance levels, users may find it more difficult to differentiate between knowledge or skills at each level. This can decrease reliability of ratings. However, too few performance level choices may result in rating inflation. For example, the majority of a practicum class may score in the "Exceeds Expectations" range for their counseling skills ratings. This may be due to rating scales that are too restrictive. In choosing between too few options, raters may use extraneous factors and not clinical observation to make a difficult choice between two ratings (Lumley, 2002). In this case, raters could also give the student the benefit of the doubt and rate him or her higher than actual skills observed.

There are a wide variety of ways to name performance levels. Consider the following sample descriptors of performance levels:

- Above Expectation, At Expectation, Below Expectation
- Below Target, Target, Exceeds Target
- Does Not Meet Expectations, Meets Expectations, Exceeds Expectations
- Excellent, Good, Fair, Poor
- Highly Integrated, Aware, Emerging, Unexamined
- Pass, Fail
- Satisfactory, Unsatisfactory
- Target, Acceptable, Beginning, Does Not Exhibit
- Target, Acceptable, Developing, Unacceptable
- Target, Acceptable, Unacceptable
- Target, Average, Beginning
- Target, Acceptable, Needs Development, Unacceptable
- Target, Met 3 (Very Good), Met 2 (Adequate), Met 1 (Minimal), Not Met

The sample rubric (see Table 11.1) includes three performance levels (i.e., Exceeds Expectations, Meets Expectations, and Does Not Meet Expectations) for each criterion. Hence, students receive a rating or score for each evaluation criterion (e.g., 3 = Exceeds, 2 = Meets, 1 = Does Not Meet). This rating can be a performance level label, grade points for the assignment, or both. In this rubric, different knowledge and skills are being assessed for each evaluation criterion, although they are all linked to the same standards. The counselor education faculty may choose to save these data by each content or skill indicator being evaluated, which would provide five different scores (e.g., one for each criterion). This is called an *analytical rubric*.

For some assignments, the rubric (called a *holistic rubric*) may be assessing performance or knowledge related to only one global standard. For example, an assignment for doctoral students may require them to write a reflection paper on leadership in counselor education. The entire assignment may be related to only one standard but could be evaluated on different evaluation criteria (i.e., Exceeds Expectations, Meets, Does Not Meet).

The total score on a rubric may or may not correspond to the grade points for the assignment in the course. In the case of the suicide assessment demonstration, the assignment may be worth a total of 15 points in the class. Faculty can also create descriptive rubrics that include descriptions of the performance that are assigned a specific rating without weights assigned to each criterion depending on the knowledge or skills being assessed. In the case of suicide assessment, this is a necessary skill to obtain and can be intimidating for the students to demonstrate initially. With a descriptive rubric that evaluates the skills without assigning a grade, this may decrease the intensity inherent in performing this skill. It still allows performance levels for the criterion component, and standards can still be assessed, recorded, and managed. After one has determined evaluation criteria and scoring procedures, it is time to operationalize criteria into quality definitions.

Quality Definitions

For students to understand specific expectations for their performance, a detailed description or quality definition is provided that delineates what is expected at a particular level of achievement (Reddy, 2007). For each of the evaluation criteria described previously, there is a continuum of quality definitions.

How will counselor educators know whether the student understands and is able to perform the content representative of a specific standard? How will the student demonstrate a skill that illustrates each specific standard? Quality definitions allow counselor educators to evaluate student knowledge and skills that exceed, meet, or do not meet expectations according to the evaluation criteria. They also help faculty be consistent in evaluating student performance across time, students, and assignments.

Stevens and Levi (2005) suggested that one should start by creating definitions of the highest and lowest levels of performance (i.e., "Exceeds"). Consider the following for writing this first definition:

- What are the specific characteristics, skills, or behaviors for the attribute of the criteria being assessed?
- What are some common mistakes in performance of this attribute that you do not want to see?
- How would you describe above average, average, and below average performance for the observable attribute?

After the performance levels have been defined at the extreme endpoints, faculty can define the middle levels of performance. In Table 11.1, the quality definitions for each evaluation criteria are found in the columns labeled "Exceeds," "Meets," and "Does Not Meet."

For the evaluation criterion "Asks 'the question'" in Table 11.1, the quality definition for "Exceeds" indicates that the student needs to "Ask about suicide clearly and directly." The words "clearly and directly" are key to this definition and may mean that the student says to the client, "Are you thinking about killing yourself?" In the "Meets" column, the quality definition indicates that the student "Asks about suicide directly." Note that this definition contains only the word "directly" and may indicate that the student says to the client, "Are you thinking of hurting yourself?" In this case, the student is attempting to find out whether the client is going to harm him- or herself but does not ask the question about "killing yourself" clearly. For the quality definition of "Does Not Meet," the student "Does not ask about suicide clearly and directly." The student, in this case, would not assess for suicide or harm. For each criterion listed as part of the evaluation criteria, students receive ratings on their performance of this assessment as it meets the quality definition. Not surprisingly, quality definitions across performance levels on observation forms are also needed. Although counselor education programs have a history of utilizing observation and rating forms more frequently than rubrics, the effectiveness of these measures in assessing SLOs needs more attention.

Observation or Rating Forms

Observation or rating forms are used frequently in counselor education programs for the purpose of evaluating students' performance in field experiences. At the doctoral level, observation forms may be used to evaluate students' clinical skills in advanced practicum or their teaching and supervision skills in internships. Creating an effective observation form is similar to creating a rubric and requires that counselor educators include specific criteria to be assessed, quality definitions, and an overall scoring strategy (Barrio Minton & Gibson, 2012). One of the main differences is that faculty may be using the observation form to evaluate knowledge and skills demonstrated over a specific period of time (e.g., practicum or internship) rather than evaluating one specific task or assignment. The rating form may also differ from a rubric in that quality definitions are not always operationalized.

Consider the following observation rating form that is used in a doctoral-level advanced practicum course. This form can be used as part of the doctoral student's final evaluation after the site supervisor has observed and supervised him or her throughout the semester. On the basis of these observations, the site supervisor would complete the form. The evaluation criterion in this example includes Items 1–6 on the form. The quality definitions are applied to all items and are not written to be specific to the evaluation criterion, so the student will be rated as "Exceeds," "Meets," or "Does Not Meet Expectation" on the basis of the quality definitions provided at the top of the form.

Advanced Practicum Observation Rating Form

Please rate (circle) the advanced practicum student according to the following scale based on the different areas of his/her professional development.

NA = Not able to observe
1 = Does Not Meet Expectations (Attribute/skill/behavior is not implemented or is used inappropriately.)
2 = Meets Expectations (Attribute/skill/behavior is used appropriately and consistently.)
3 = Exceeds Expectations (Attribute/skill/behavior is highly developed and consistently performed.)

CACREP 2016 Doctoral Standard: B.1.b-f

COUNSELING SKILLS AND PROCESS

1. Genuine interest in	NA	1 2 3
2. Ability to understand the client's point of view	NA	1 2 3
3. Ability to relate to diverse clients	NA	1 2 3
4. Ability to establish and maintain rapport	NA	1 2 3
5. Ability to assess and have insight into client's problems	NA	1 2 3
6. Demonstrates effective helping skills (paraphrasing, feeling reflection, summarizing, effective probing, etc.)	NA	1 2 3

This form of rating guide is considered more holistic (Suskie, 2009). Using holistic ratings may not be as reliable because the interpretation of the criteria and quality definition for performance is influenced by the subjectivity of the rater or supervisor. To address this problem, counselor education program faculty can provide raters with training on the observation form or incorporate more specific directions for use on the observation form. Finally, the overall scoring strategy for the form may include the average or median rating assigned, sum of all scores, or overall holistic impression. The program faculty should determine whether the mean, median, or sum is more appropriate for the purpose of the specific observation. As with rubrics, the student's rating would be linked to the specific CACREP Standard(s) being assessed with the observation form.

Process Considerations

If determining what measures to use in assessing and evaluating SLOs reminds you of choosing instrumentation to be included in research studies, you are on the right track. Much thought and consideration should be given to both the process of evaluation and the specific measurement tools used for evaluation of individualized instruction, group instruction, programmatic decisions and documentation, and institutional accreditation processes. An effective design, understanding, and competent use of measures are important, as the results need to be credible and trustworthy (Jonsson & Svingby, 2007).

In terms of direct measurement of SLOs, rubrics are considered the "mainstay of outcomes-based assessment" (Reddy, 2007, p. 8). There are many advantages of using rubrics in evaluation because they

- help clarify vague instructional goals;
- help students understand instructor expectations for assignments;
- help students self-improve;
- inspire better student performance;
- make scoring an assignment easier, faster, unbiased, consistent, and more accurate;
- improve feedback to students; and
- improve feedback to faculty and staff (Andrade, 2005; Suskie, 2009).

Used appropriately, students receive grades based on identified criteria, and they also receive specific feedback that encourages reflection. When used for evaluation of SLOs, rubrics demonstrate how the counselor education curriculum, student learning and performance, and CACREP Standards are linked. However, this is based on the use of reliable and valid rubrics.

Reliability

One of the major concerns with rubric use is the reliability and validity of the specific measure (Jonsson & Svingby, 2007; Reddy, 2007). In using rubrics, *scoring* or *rater reliability* refers to the "consistency of scores that are assigned by two independent raters and that are assigned by the same rater at different points in time" (Reddy, 2007, p. 12). Although a rubric may be used by one instructor only, there should be consistency in the scores or ratings that this instructor assigns if the performance is the same. If two or more raters are using a rubric to rate specific SLOs, programs will need to train raters on use of the rubric. For example, if a program employs doctoral students to assess suicide assessment demonstration videotapes, those individuals will need to be trained to understand the criterion and the behaviors expected at each of the performance levels. Responsible faculty members may rate and discuss videotapes with doctoral students until they obtain some level of consistent rating percentage. In the majority of research on rater consensus, 70% agreement is not exceeded (Jonsson & Svingby, 2007). Determining whether this level of consensus is acceptable depends on what the rubric is assessing and the stakes of the assessment. Is it for classroom use, clinical use, or large-scale outcomes use? What impact will performance on the rubric have on the students' standing or progress in the program? Of course, the higher stakes for the assessment, the more important it is that program faculty members use rigorous validity measures.

Moskal and Leydens (2000) suggested the following questions to evaluate the clarity of a rubric and, in turn, to boost interrater and intrarater reliability:

1. Are scoring categories well defined?
2. Are the differences between the score categories clear?
3. Would two independent raters arrive at the same score for a given response on the basis of the scoring rubric?
4. Are the scoring criteria behaving the same across different populations of students?
5. Are the scoring criteria implicit or explicit (are the students aware of the criteria prior to performing)?

When creating a rubric, counselor educators should consider several factors that can affect interrater reliability. Topic-specific rubrics tend to produce more consistent scores (Marzano, 2002). When all students perform the same task and the scoring procedures are well-defined, reliability will most likely be high (Brennan, as cited in Jonsson & Svingby, 2007). If students are allowed to choose their own topics or design their own projects, reliability will be lower. For the suicide assessment demonstration (see Table 11.1), there may be high levels of reliability because of the specificity of the topic and behaviors expected as explained by the rubric. However, oral presentations for a different assignment may produce lower levels of reliability because of the variability in content and performance style.

The number of raters, amount of training, and performance levels needing to be rated affect interrater reliability for a rubric (Jonsson & Svingby, 2007). If raters are provided appropriate training in scoring the rubric, reliability estimates will be stronger. However, high levels of reliability are difficult to obtain as the number of raters to score a rubric is increased beyond two (Marzano, 2002). This effect on reliability occurs also when the number of levels of performance increases (Williams & Rink, 2003). The suicide assessment demonstration rubric would require less training of raters if the performance levels included only "Meets" or "Does Not Meet." Because there are three performance levels (i.e., including "Exceeds"), more training of raters to differentiate between the levels is needed.

Counselor education faculty members need to pay careful attention to performance levels used in rubrics. Although there is more freedom for faculty members to create their own type and number of performance levels for course-based rubrics, the program as a whole may benefit from using a common metric with at least the same scoring strategies and number of performance levels (e.g., 0 = Does Not Meet Expectations, 1 = Meets Expectations, 2 = Exceeds Expectations; Barrio Minton & Gibson, 2012). If there is a large number of faculty in the program, a common metric will provide some level of consistency. A common metric will also control for reliability if some of the SLOs are assessed collectively (i.e., ratings from both site and faculty practicum and internship supervisors). Finally, when the same scoring strategy is used across SLO measures, including rubrics, analyzing and making meaning of the data are less complex compared with the use of rubrics with different performance levels and scoring strategies. For example, if a score of 1 always means "Meets Expectations," faculty members will be able to interpret measures of central tendency across different assignments and rating forms.

Validity

Validity of the rubric is as important as its reliability. Is the rubric measuring what it has been created to measure? Validity of the rubric depends on how the specific assessment is created and how clearly performance expectations are articulated (Moskal & Leydens, 2000). In a rubric, this information is found in the evaluation criteria and quality definitions for each performance level. In the suicide assessment demonstration, several objectives are present, including content knowledge about suicide assessment and skills performance of the assessment. It is a simulation performance-based assessment to determine whether CITs will be able to conduct a suicide assessment in a different situation and setting. Therefore, there are both content and criterion-related evidence of validity to be considered. If there are extraneous elements not related to the purpose of the evaluation being measured and scored, validity may be compromised. The following list includes questions intended to examine each type of validity for rubrics:

Content
1. Do the evaluation criteria address any extraneous content?
2. Do the evaluation criteria of the scoring rubric address all aspects of the intended content?
3. Is there any content addressed in the task that should be evaluated through the rubric, but is not?

Construct
1. Are all of the important facets of the intended construct evaluated through the scoring criteria?
2. Is any of the evaluation criteria irrelevant to the construct of interest?

Criterion
1. How do the scoring criteria reflect competencies that would suggest success on future or related performances?
2. What are the important components of the future or related performance that may be evaluated through the use of the assessment instrument?
3. How do the scoring criteria measure the important components of the future or related performance?
4. Are there any facets of the future or related performance that are not reflected in the scoring criteria?

Note. From "Scoring Rubric Development: Validity and Reliability," by B. M. Moskal and J. A. Leydens, 2000, *Practical Assessment, Research & Evaluation, 7,* Table 1. Copyright 2000 by http://PAREonline.net/getvn.asp?v=7&n=10. Reprinted with permission.

There may be consequential evidence of validity that occurs when examining the consequences of uses of the assessment results (Moskal & Leydens, 2000). For example, if using the rubric affects the instruction of the counselor educator for better or worse, this becomes a consequence of the use of the rubric and affects the consequential evidence of validity (Jonsson & Svingby, 2007). This is a result of a factor not related to the original purpose of the rubric and may aid in identifying possible alternative interpretations of the results (American Educational Research Association, American Psychological Association [APA], & National Council on Measurement in Education, 1999).

The remaining question is, how do counselor educators design a rubric to measure the objectives they need to measure? Research on this topic indicates that the language used in rubrics needs to be appropriate, clear, and representative of the knowledge or skills being measured (Reddy & Andrade, 2010). Knowledge of where the CITs are developmentally in their programs; vocabulary, knowledge, and skills they possess based on curriculum structure; and objectives and expectations based on the current course or clinical experience will clarify language that will be used in the measure. Descriptive criteria and quality definitions will leave little room for misinterpretation in knowledge and skills that are expected.

Resources

Association of American Colleges and Universities. (2008). *Civic engagement VALUE rubric.* Retrieved from http://www.in.gov/che/files/All_VALUE_Rubrics.pdf

Buck Institute for Education. (2012). *Rubric for rubrics.* Retrieved from http://bie.org/object/document/rubric_for_rubrics

DePaul University. (n.d.). *Rubrics.* Retrieved from http://teachingcommons.depaul.edu/Feedback_Grading/rubrics.html

iRubric [rubric design and assessment system webpage]: http://www.rcampus.com/indexrubric.cfm

Jonsson, A., & Svingby, G. (2007). The use of scoring rubrics: Reliability, validity and educational consequences. *Educational Research Review, 2,* 130–144.

Marzano, R. J. (2002). A comparison of selected methods of scoring classroom assessments. *Applied Measurement in Evaluation, 15,* 249–267.

Moskal, B. M., & Leydens, J. A. (2000). Scoring rubric development: Validity and reliability. *Practical Assessment, Research & Evaluation, 7,* Article 10.

Reddy, Y. M., & Andrade, H. (2010). A review of rubric use in higher education. *Assessment and Evaluation in Higher Education, 35,* 435–448. doi:10.1080/0260293090286859

RubiStar: http://rubistar.4teachers.org/index.php

University of Connecticut. (n.d.). *How to create rubrics.* Retrieved from http://assessment.uconn.edu/docs/How_to_Create_Rubrics.pdf

Part III
Moving Forward

•••

To this point, we have explored the purpose of SLO assessment and the role of SLO assessment in the greater program evaluation process. We have also included guidelines and considerations for constructing a wide variety of assignments and activities that will allow you to better understand what students know and are able to do as a result of their experiences within the program. The role of indirect measures, dispositions, and rubrics in the evaluation process has also been considered.

These design steps are at the heart of a high-quality and meaningful SLO assessment plan. However, designing quality measures alone is not sufficient for quality assessment practice. Too often, educators invest energy up front in the process only to neglect the critical next step in the process: doing something with the data to inform continuous improvement practices. In the next major section of this book, we discuss administrative processes and decisions that will help you to collect and manage data (Chapter 12), analyze data (Chapter 13), report data (Chapter 14), and make meaning of data for program improvement (Chapter 15), student support (Chapter 16), and scholarly endeavors (Chapter 17).

Chapter 12

Collecting and Managing Data

The design and implementation of program evaluation requires as much consideration as the research study. Unlike a research study, however, there is no end point or final product. Program evaluation continues and is maintained with improvements being implemented along the way. These improvements can only be informed by data that have been collected, analyzed, and considered by the faculty. To make this a more efficient and effective process, faculty members should collect and organize data systematically for analyses (Hatfield, 2009). Some questions to consider in this process include the following:

1. When will specific components (i.e., SLOs; dispositions; candidate, graduate, and alumni surveys) be collected within the context of the candidate's program?
2. What is the timing of this process?
3. Who will collect data?
4. How will data be collected?
5. Where will data be stored?
6. Will commercial and/or noncommercial SLO evaluation software be utilized?
7. What data analyses need to be conducted?
8. What results will be reported?
9. To whom will results be reported?
10. What will program faculty do with the results?

In this chapter, we explore Questions 1–6 as they pertain to program evaluation for accreditation purposes. We address remaining questions in chapters to come.

Elements of Data Collection and Management

Prior to implementation of the 2009 CACREP Standards, counselor education programs collected more general data regarding program effectiveness (CACREP, 2001). Most data were collected through indirect measures and did not focus on specific SLOs. Because evaluating SLOs has become an integral part of the evaluation process for CACREP-accredited programs, the amount of data that programs must collect and manage has grown exponentially. For example, there are 34

Standards in the school counseling area (CACREP, 2016). Does this mean that there needs to be 34 different measures? Not necessarily, but there should be multiple measures gathered at multiple points of the program that are used to evaluate students' knowledge and/or skills reflective of the domains (Foundations, Contextual Dimensions, and Practice) of both core and specialty area Standards. Collecting this information can be complex, and the management of the data can become unwieldy if not planned appropriately. In creating a data management plan, faculty members will need to examine resources, physical collection of data, and artifact characteristics.

For the program evaluation process to be successful, faculty support, commitment, and participation are key (Peach, Mukherjee, & Hornyak, 2007). Financial resources, human resources, and technical resources are three of the most important resources to consider in program evaluation. According to Kelley, Tong, and Choi (2010), adequate funding needs to be allocated to various assessment activities. These include training faculty regarding program assessment and evaluation, investing in an assessment management system (AMS) or electronic portfolio system, budgeting for data collection and analysis support personnel, and paying accreditation maintenance and reaccreditation fees.

Financial resources are important but are not recommended in lieu of a foundation of good human resources. For counselor education programs, human resources will include faculty, program administrative support, school or college administrative support, and technical support. Support from the college or school administration may be solicited to change the assessment culture among program faculty. Forms of this support may include additional training on developing SLOs or AMSs, release time from college or school committee obligations to focus on program evaluation, or additional administrative assistance to organize and implement the program evaluation process. When appropriate support for increased workload is provided, faculty members may find themselves experiencing less resistance (Kelley et al., 2010).

Part of the time-commitment factor comes from learning how to collect, store, and manage information electronically. If the counselor education program uses a college- or school-created data system, technical support may not be necessary because personnel in those departments can enter raw data. However, some data may be collected via computerized or electronic survey formats that will need to be created and disseminated to specific groups, such as alumni and site supervisors. Support for qualitative and quantitative data analyses should also be considered as both technical and human resources.

AMSs

Resources available for assessment and evaluation of higher education programs vary because of numerous factors. The size of the program, department, college, school, or university may dictate the amount and type of resources provided (Barrio Minton & Gibson, 2012). Smaller programs with fewer counseling specialty areas may determine that manual artifact and data collection meets their programs' needs.

As discussed earlier in parts of this book, faculty members may use several assessment activities and rating forms to assess student learning and dispositions throughout their programs. The data collected in these measures need to be collected, analyzed, and maintained to make meaning of program effectiveness. Each program faculty must determine where and how this information is stored. In the next sections, we offer considerations for handling these data via manual assessment systems not connected to larger databases outside of the program and commercial assessment systems that are connected to database systems within the college or university.

Manual Data Management

There are several factors that can contribute to a program utilizing manual assessment management. In this procedure, faculty members may collect electronic and hard copy measures (i.e., rubrics, rating sheets) and organize them to look at individual, cohort, or course-based segments of student outcomes.

We have received feedback from various counselor education program members who are entering data via Qualtrics or who are using Excel, Access, and SPSS databases to input and analyze data. Although not sophisticated, these systems provide faculty with a starting point for understanding their data and connect them to program outcomes. For smaller programs that tend to use focused data collection measures, manual data management may be perfectly appropriate. For example, program faculty may enter data in Excel spreadsheets or statistical software programs so they may access, aggregate, and disaggregate data in the systematic review process. To do so, program faculty must delineate the data repository by asking questions such as the following:

- Where do all of the data go?
- How long do they stay?
- What happens before, during, and after data are received in that place?

Repositories can include program-based databases. For example, a learning management system—such as Blackboard, Moodle, or Desire2Learn—may provide a platform for students to submit course or program artifacts. Designated course instructors and program faculty will be responsible for measures associated with the students' submissions and exporting data to more global databases that allow for analyses.

Our hopes are that a culture of assessment will be created and maintained to support faculty with existing skills in managing a data collection system and to entice other faculty in developing an interest in this area. In addition to intrinsic interest and motivation in this area, counselor education programs and departments could count this as service activities and release these faculty members from additional service responsibilities or award these additional support for continuing professional development.

Finally, manual assessment management needs to be reevaluated continuously. Does this still work to meet the needs and priorities of the program? Is the faculty able to continue to manage this process in this form? If the counselor education program has several counseling areas (e.g., school, clinical mental health), has several adjunct faculty, includes satellite campuses, or has large student populations, collecting and managing data may be too complex and cumbersome to handle with an in-house database. A commercial electronic AMS may need to be utilized for this situation.

Commercial Electronic Assessment Management

Commercial electronic AMSs are electronic systems used by educators to collect and manage SLO data (Oakleaf, Belanger, & Graham, 2013). Some of these systems are also known as electronic assessment portfolio systems because they can also archive student work as examples of learning products or artifacts (Meyer & Latham, 2008). Strudler and Wetzel (2005) reported that one of the main impetuses for transitioning to the use of electronic portfolios in higher education was to address "NCATE requirements for documenting teacher candidates' attainment of standards" (p. 419). The attractiveness of this type of system is that it seems to be an all-in-one system that can link accreditation standards to SLOs, aid in analyzing and reporting data, and organize and store student artifacts.

If the counselor education program faculty is considering utilizing an electronic AMS, it will want to answer several questions:

1. *What Are the Needs of the Program?*
   If an existing in-house program will provide the information required for the program evaluation, there is no need to purchase an AMS. Some counselor education programs have in-house support personnel who have created systems in existing word processing or data analysis software systems that are adequate. With these systems, the faculty members may need to use more time for analyses to make the results meaningful for their program. For example, the in-house system may not be able to report information based on disaggregated data or data organized by different variables (i.e., demographic). Therefore, faculty or staff would need to complete this process manually.

2. *What Is the Assessment Ability of the System?*
   The main purpose for purchasing a commercial AMS is to support counselor education faculty members in their program evaluation efforts. Some systems are more appropriate for offering summative assessments (i.e., end of program findings) rather than formative assessments (i.e., tracking learning, behaviors, and skills throughout the program; Oakleaf et al., 2013). Summative assessment may be more appropriate for only measuring program effectiveness, whereas formative assessment could allow for ongoing measurement of SLOs and other measures of program effectiveness. Additionally, if the AMS allows for the integration of direct measures (i.e., rubrics, observational ratings) and accreditation or other standards, then SLOs can be mapped in the program curriculum and can be reported.

3. *What Is the Storage Capability of the System? What Will It Hold, How Much Will It Hold, and for How Long Will It Hold It?*
   Each AMS has its own unique capabilities for storage. One consideration is how well the system integrates with existing institutional data management tools and sources (RiCharde, 2009). For example, admission data may be collected through the graduate school offices for counselor education programs via an electronic database. This information may be exported to a commercial AMS to be used in counselor education program evaluation, but access may be "dependent on permissions set by assessment management system administrators" (Oakleaf et al., 2013, p. 99). Second, an environmental-friendly or "green" consideration is to select an AMS that can hold student artifacts and large amounts of data. If this option is chosen, the data are stored on an external server supported by the AMS. Many of these systems also include faculty portfolio capabilities that allow faculty members to create and maintain their own online portfolios, websites, and scholarly artifacts. Finally, storage capability includes the length of time that the information will be available in the AMS. This will be determined by the commercial system and should be discussed among counselor education faculty, school or college administrators, and the system provider.

4. *What Are System Capabilities for Managing, Analyzing, and Reporting Data?*
   Beyond collection and storing capabilities, knowing how data are managed, analyzed, and reported is important to counselor education programs. Counselor education program members need to demonstrate how they are using program evaluation and SLO data to make decisions about program modifications (CACREP, 2016). To do this, they examine aggregated and disaggregated data closely. Prior to the CACREP 2009 Standards, program evaluation summary data were the primary focus. Counselor education program members could simply report demographic data and disaggregate standardized licensure exam scores, graduation rates, and employment results by these demographics.

   The addition of SLO evaluation has made the process more complex and time-consuming. Program-level aggregate and disaggregate data can also be maintained. Individual-level and program-level data can be analyzed together and used to inform modifications and improvements to the counselor education program. The way in which data are entered, analyzed, and retrieved for reporting may be customized to the specific counselor education program depending on what is allowed by the AMS. Additionally, data may be able to be exported to analysis software systems to allow more customized data analysis. For example, program faculty may be interested in examining SLO data for a cohort of students about to enter practicum. The AMS may or may not be able to code for specific cohort, but when the data is exported to SPSS, faculty members could code the specific students in the cohort and run the analysis.

5. *What Are the Expectations of the Faculty in Using the AMS?*
   As discussed previously, faculty members do not readily give up their time. If faculty members perceive learning an AMS as unimportant or as something that will take time away from an already hectic schedule, they may resist the process (Suskie, 2009). If one-time training and continuing support will be provided, faculty members may present with less resistance and more acceptance. Counselor educators should consider how much interaction with the system will be required of faculty and students. For example, students required to submit papers and videos for grading and evaluation will need faculty who are comfortable retrieving, scoring, and returning these items in the system. In addition to day-to-day interactions, all assignments, rubrics, rating forms, and surveys must first be configured within the system before they can be used for data collection and management. Program staff should determine whether individual faculty members, designated faculty leads, or administrative support personnel should be responsible for these tasks. Faculty members who support using a commercial AMS may be willing to offer informal support to staff who feel less comfortable using the system.

6. *Technology Support, Ease of Use, and Security*
   One of the major stumbling blocks to acquiring an AMS may be the amount of support available for using the system. Although costs associated with the system are always a consideration, on-site and off-site support are needed when using an AMS (Oakleaf et al., 2013; Suskie, 2009). Supports for training and technology-related purposes should be part of the budget for the system. Program faculty need to investigate how much training will be required to

implement and maintain the system. RiCharde (2009) suggested that program faculty "select a data-management tool with the least sophisticated user in mind" (p. 13), whether it is for outcomes assessment or program review. The majority of commercial vendors offer training support as part of management system costs, but the level and type of customer service vary (Oakleaf et al., 2013).

Technology support for the AMS may be managed off-site by the vendor. This means that the vendor has physical maintenance and support of a web-based system. When considering a system, the capabilities of existing technology at the program-level need to match the requirements of the commercial assessment system. Additional technology concerns with the AMS may stem from issues with access, modification, and document confidentiality. For counselor education programs, there may be ethical considerations regarding the types of student artifacts that are submitted through the AMS. For example, counseling simulation videos between students may be appropriate for upload within the system, but actual client sessions are most likely inappropriate for upload. The security of the server, who has access to documents, and the length of time that information is saved in the system are topics to be explored at the program level and with vendors. Finally, the program needs to investigate what kind of support is needed from information technology (IT) staff to use and maintain the technology at the college or university (Suskie, 2009). At a minimum, IT staff need to be aware of the system and what supports the vendor provides. Housing the system on-campus may lend more control but will require more involvement and resources from IT staff.

7. *What Are the Costs?*
It may be surprising that this question comes at the end of the list when it is usually asked first by administrators holding the purse strings. Make no mistake: A AMS is a major purchase and commitment. If money is available to make a purchase, counselor educators should conduct a cost–benefit analysis. There may be one-time costs or student subscription costs that may not be integrated into the budget every year, but support may be required as a cost. What will the AMS provide the program? Will it address all of the assessment and evaluation needs of the program? Are there direct benefits to students, faculty, and administrators? These are questions that should be explored prior to making a decision.

Faculty can look in two areas to determine which vendors to approach. First, if the college or university has implemented a commercial AMS for university wide accreditation needs, the counselor education program faculty may be able to use this system for their own specific evaluation needs. Keep in mind that this may require technology support to customize for counselor education. Second, counselor educators can ask their colleagues who are using AMSs at other colleges and universities the following questions (list adapted from Suskie, 2009):

- Which vendors are they using?
- How much were initial costs versus annual fees?
- Where is the system housed (i.e., site or web-based)?
- How secure is the server where data are stored?
- Are faculty and staff using it? If so, how?
- If faculty are not using it, who is and how?
- Is the technology user-friendly?
- How much training and support do the faculty require in using the system?
- How much training and support do the students require in using the system?
- Does the system interface with other technologies on campus? If so, which ones?
- What are the technology and/or software requirements?
- How much on-site IT staff support does the system require?

After faculty members narrow down the list of possible vendors, program members should invite them to provide online or in-person demonstrations of their products. Vendors should be available to answer questions from faculty, staff, and administrators. On the basis of customization features, on-site versus web-based access, and level of support, initial and annual costs will vary by vendor. Budgets in higher education are typically wrapped in departmental, school, college, and/or university politics. Generally, faculty who involve college/university administrators early in the decision-making process will meet with less resistance when advocating for their choice of system.

Process Considerations

Program faculty members must consider advantages and challenges of both manual and commercial AMSs. Earlier in the chapter, considerations were discussed between using noncommercial versus commercial AMSs. Some commercial AMSs you may wish to consider include the following:

- Chalk & Wire,
- Desire2Learn (Brightspace),
- Digication,
- Foliotek,
- Learning Objects,
- Longsight,
- Mahara,
- rCampus, and
- Symplicity.

Oakleaf et al. (2013) developed a comprehensive comparison of commercial AMS components. Available via open access, the chart provides potential consumers with information on some of the aspects discussed in this chapter. These characteristics are listed next.

AMS Characteristics

Assessment Ability

- Supports summative assessments
- Supports formative assessments
- Supports course-level grading
- Supports student evaluations of courses, faculty, etc.
- Supports building of rubrics
- Supports application of rubrics
- Links standards to outcomes, rubrics, etc.

Outcomes Alignment

- Links/aligns outcomes used within individual units, departments, programs, divisions, etc.
- Generates curriculum maps
- Links/aligns outcomes used across different units, departments, programs, divisions, etc.
- Links/aligns outcomes other than learning outcome (strategic, research, grant, development, admissions, student affairs, library, etc.)

Repository Capacity

- Serves as a repository for assessment evidence/data
- Stores assessment documentation
- Supports submission of student-created products/projects
- Supports assessment of student-created products/projects
- Integrates new and existing evidence/data sources
- Includes faculty productivity evidence/data

Data Management

- Segments evidence/data for detailed analysis
- Incorporates statistical analysis of evidence/data
- Supports customization of terminology/naming conventions to match institutional culture/procedures
- Maintains a record of assessment progress
- Captures student-level evidence/data
- Collects/tracks program-level assessment evidence/data

System Integration

- Integrates budgetary systems into assessment processes
- Integrates strategic planning into assessment processes

- Integrates evidence/data from student information systems
- Integrates evidence/data from learning management systems
- Supports student-level portfolios
- Supports institutional (faculty, staff) assessment of student-level portfolios
- Supports assignment of assessment tasks/responsibilities/duties
- Allows for role-based or unit-based (department, school, etc.) permissions to be set for individual users

Support Services

- Provides hosting service
- Provides institutional-hosting option
- Provides consulting/training services
- Provides customer service support

Internal Reporting Accreditation Reporting

- Generates assessment reports suitable for internal purposes (e.g., strategic planning, program review, annual reports)
- Enables participation of staff, faculty, and administrators institution wide
- Documents progress toward institutional level priorities, goals, missions, outcomes
- Supports specific accreditation organization's requirements (e.g., CAEP [Council for the Accreditation of Educator Preparation], SACS [Southern Association of Colleges and Schools], etc.)
- Includes accreditation and program review templates
- Generates assessment reports suitable for external purposes (e.g., program or institutional accreditation documents)

Action Taking

- Supports "closing the loop" processes (decision-making, action-taking)
- Supports reporting of assessment evidence/data and results to stakeholders
- Generates assessment plans
- Generates "action" plans, "to do" lists, and/or status reports

Note. From "Choosing and Using Assessment Management Systems: What Librarians Need to Know," by M. Oakleaf, J. Belanger, and C. Graham, 2013, *Proceedings of the ACRL 15th National Conference*, Appendix A, pp. 102–104. Copyright 2013 by the Association of College and Research Libraries. Reprinted with permission.

There are several advantages to using an AMS in evaluating counselor education programs. After the system is implemented, collecting, organizing, managing, analyzing, and reporting data are more economical, efficient, and useful (Oakleaf et al., 2013; RiCharde, 2009). Tracking progress and SLOs of individual students in specific cohorts and courses allows counselor educators to make modifications immediately rather than learning about general issues at the end of a student's program. Tracking and discussing these data will encourage counselor educators to be more intentional about teaching and learning aspects of their role. For example, data on a faculty member's assignment may indicate need for modification to the assignment, rubric, or instruction related to the topic of interest. This aspect of the system may help counselor educators make sense of comments and concerns reported on student evaluations of teaching at the end of the course. Standardized reporting and data collection can also provide consistency in course expectations for adjunct faculty or doctoral teaching assistants.

For accreditation purposes, commercial AMSs meet the obvious need for program evaluation and measuring SLOs. However, some of these systems will also act as a repository for student artifacts that are requested in accreditation visits. This will allow faculty to pull student artifacts and feedback, field experience forms, or portfolio examples of student work. Faculty members may find it helpful to compare student artifacts across time as they work to decipher the impact of assignments or program modifications.

A major concern of using an AMS is faculty buy-in (Oakleaf et al., 2013; Suskie, 2009). Some faculty will not believe that a new system is any more effective than an existing system or no system at all. Faculty members may be concerned about their own ability to use the system and may hesitate to learn more technological aspects of program evaluation.

A second issue is related to the financial and human resource costs associated with a system. In a recent survey distributed on the Counselor Education and Supervision Listserv, few listserv members responded to a question about AMS use with counselor education programs. Of those that responded, the majority indicated that on-site AMS personnel support at the college or school level was needed to set up, manage, and assist program faculty with data collection, analysis, management, and reporting. This was perceived as a direct effect of the type of AMS chosen as well as the relative needs of the program.

Purchasing an AMS specifically for the counselor education program may be cost-prohibitive. If the system is based on a remote or web-based server, this will mean less work for the local IT staff (RiCharde, 2009) because the vendor is responsible for upgrades, back-ups, security, and crashes. However, during the initial selection process, counselor educators should consider who owns the data, how data are secured, and how data will integrate with other local databases. With this type of system, there is a reliance on the vendor's support to address concerns that may result in response delays.

Finally, it is important to consider how a system can be used at the course level. Many AMSs can interface with learning management systems (e.g., Blackboard, Moodle, Sakai) to coordinate assignment submissions, store student artifacts, assess assignments, and analyze results. For activities that require inputs from sources outside of the university (i.e., practicum or internship site supervisors), AMSs can coordinate observation forms and evaluations to occur automatically at preplanned times in the term. The information obtained is automatically integrated into the assessment system for analyses.

Regardless of how a program faculty decides to collect and manage data, there are several factors to consider. The level of complexity to the process is relative to needs of the program, faculty, and students. However, financial and technical personnel support from the university is needed for successful program and student evaluation.

Resources

Centers for Disease Control and Prevention [Data collection and analysis webpage]: http://www.cdc.gov/healthyyouth/evaluation/data.htm

National Institute for Learning Outcomes Assessment. (2012, June). *What to consider when selecting an assessment management system.* Retrieved from https://illinois.edu/blog/view/915/75817

Pell Institute and Pathways to College Network. (2015). *Collect data.* Retrieved from http://toolkit.pellinstitute.org/evaluation-guide/collect-data/

University of Kansas, Work Group for Community Health and Development. (2014). Section 5: Collecting and analyzing data. In *Community Tool Box* (Chapter 37, Operations in Evaluating Community Interventions). Retrieved from http://ctb.ku.edu/en/table-of-contents/evaluate/evaluate-community-interventions/collect-analyze-data/main

Chapter 13

Analyzing Data

After the assessment plan has been created, measures have been developed and implemented, and data have been collected, it is time to analyze data. Before rushing to choose from statistical analyses, faculty members should revisit the purpose for collecting data. That purpose may include a combination of meeting systematic program evaluation requirements, evaluating SLOs, and exploring specific needs of individual programs. If counselor education program faculty members conduct data analyses and report findings based solely on CACREP requirements, the bigger picture of program evaluation is lost. Data analysis should help program faculty members determine what is going well and what needs extra attention while being transparent in the process.

Appropriate data analysis will provide a better understanding of data and will help faculty members summarize data into meaningful pieces of information that can guide adjustments that may need to occur in program curricula. Unfortunately, this process has received negative attention because there are false impressions that complex statistical analyses need to be conducted. This is not necessarily true. Typically, data analysis for program evaluation involves descriptive statistics such as frequencies, means, and percentages. In some cases, inferential statistics—such as within- and between-groups comparisons—may be warranted. Before doing any statistics, it is important to examine the type and amount of data collected.

In this chapter, we discuss how to examine data after having been collected and before any analyses occur. The type of data collected will reflect the purpose of the program evaluation and will direct the statistical analyses to be conducted. We offer several practical applications and considerations of analyzing program data.

Examining the Data

The measures used in data collection are included in the program's assessment plan. Creating those measures requires considerable planning, as they are based on program needs, demographics, and standards. Before analyzing collected data, there are several steps that faculty members need to take. First, faculty should review the data visually for outliers and possible mistakes (Office of Planning and Institutional Effectiveness, 2014). For example, if an SLO for a standard that most students were expected to "Meet Expectations" or "Exceed Expectations" has an unanticipated number of students assessed at a "Does Not Meet Expectations" level, this may signal a problem. That problem may lie with the measure, the assignment, instruction of the material assessed, faculty use of the measure, outside events, or a combination of factors. A second example may be an alumni survey question with an added or missing word that alters the meaning for participants. If not detected before data analysis, this type of clerical error can cause erroneous interpretation of the data. Regardless of the reason, faculty members should closely examine unanticipated results prior to data analysis and interpretation.

A second step is to consider missing data or "missingness." There are social and natural reasons for missing data, such as attrition of students, sickness, refusal to complete a survey, or technical issues with data collection. These may be legitimate reasons for missing data, and the missing data may appear to occur at random. However, data may not be missing randomly. For example, one might notice that data are missing for specific students, cohorts, or evaluators. If there are patterns of missing data, program faculty will need to determine how to interpret and respond to the meaning of this pattern. In cases of nonrandom missing data, data that are present may need to be interpreted with caution because the representativeness of the data is in question.

Next, faculty members need to remind themselves of the purpose and rationale for collecting the specific data. The type of data collected determines statistical procedures that are appropriate for the analysis. For quantitative data, counselor educators should choose statistics that fit the type of data collected and that also meet program needs (Office of Planning and Institutional Effectiveness, 2014). For example, are the data in categorical or numerical formats? Categorical data are a type of nominal data that are "based on groupings or categories for the evaluation of student performance" (Office of Planning and Institutional Effectiveness, 2014, p. 19). If using a rubric to measure SLOs, the performance levels represent different categories. For example, categorical data for performance levels of "Does Not Meet Expectations," "Meets Expectations," and "Exceeds Expectations" would inform faculty how many students perform specific criteria for each of those categories. This type of data does not provide any other information beyond the number of students performing at the specified level. However, numerical data may provide more specific information. Numerical data may be based on scales that measure student performance or ratings on perceived learning. For example, a 5-point Likert scale may be used in an alumni survey that assesses the graduate's perception of what he or she perceived were the strengths and weaknesses of the counselor education program. This Likert scale could have the following numerical values attached to descriptors for each item: 1 = *not at all*, 2 = *occasionally*, 3 = *somewhat*, 4 = *usually*, 5 = *always*. For either specific survey questions (e.g., faculty members were knowledgeable) or for the entire survey (e.g., satisfaction with graduate school program), numerical data could include basic descriptive statistics (e.g., mean, median, mode).

Direct and indirect measures utilized in the evaluation of the program and SLOs can generate either categorical or numerical data. Using the counselor education and supervision doctoral program rubric for a presentation assignment as an example, we illustrate categorical and numerical data gathered for a direct measure (see Table 13.1). For this assignment, several SLOs tied to CACREP Standards are being measured. The possible performance levels achieved for each criterion include "Not Met," "Met," or "Exceeds." The doctoral student's performance on each of the criteria can be categorized in these categories. If there are six doctoral students in the class during the 2015–2016 academic year, categorical results may indicate that for doctoral CACREP 2016 Standard 6.B.1.a, five of the six doctoral students performed at the "Exceeds" level, and one of the six performed at the "Met" level. Because there is a range of points assigned for each performance level, the overall presentation can also be scored on a numerical scale. For example, the six doctoral students could have an average performance of 5.25 points for doctoral CACREP 2016 Standard 6.B.1.a and an average performance of 26 points overall on the entire assignment. The numerical data on this assignment will provide faculty with more specific information on performance than the categorical data. At the same time, sample size is so small that it would not be appropriate to perform inferential statistics on the data.

Similar to direct measures, categorical and numerical data can be obtained from indirect measures such as site supervisor evaluations of the program and alumni surveys. The following example includes sample questions for a practicum site supervisor that would result in categorical data.

Table 13.1
Sample Counselor Education Doctoral Program Assignment Rubric

Component and Corresponding Standard	Unmet (0–2 Points)	Met (3–4 Points)	Exceeds (5–6 Points)
Presents a 20–30 minute video of a current client in advanced practicum. Provides a typed case study format for all classmates and instructor.	Session is less than 20 minutes, and/or no case study is provided.	Session is 20–30 minutes in length, and case study is provided.	Session is 20–30 minutes in length, student prepares audience to watch for specific events and interactions within the session, student asks for specific supervision needs, and case study is provided and is comprehensive in the categories included.
Provides review of the basic propositions, tenets, and interventions of the theory from chosen paradigm. Provides one-page handout to the class and instructor (CACREP 2016 Standard 6.B.1.a).	Review does not include all items required, and/or a one-page handout is not provided.	Review includes all required items, one-page handout is provided, and at least five peer-refereed references are included in the review.	Review is comprehensive of the required items, one-page handout is specific, and references are in correct APA Style format.
Discusses and demonstrates applicability of chosen theory in the counseling session. Includes whether and how the theory was utilized or could be utilized with the case client in comparison with one other counseling theory (approved by the instructor). Highlights strengths and weaknesses, theoretical efficacy, applicability to multicultural populations, and ethical and legal considerations within the given paradigm (CACREP 2016 Standards 6.B.1.b, 6.B.1.c, 6.B.1.f).	Student does not include discussion of chosen theory applicability to the case client, and/or no strengths/weaknesses, theoretical efficacy, applicability to multicultural populations, or legal/ethical implications are discussed.	Student uses some of the chosen theory "language" in applying it to case client and provides some information (inconsistently) on strengths/weaknesses, theoretical efficacy, applicability to multicultural populations, or legal/ethical implications.	Student uses theoretical "language" consistently when discussing the applicability of the theory to the case client and provides a comprehensive overview of strengths/weaknesses, theoretical efficacy, applicability to multicultural populations, and legal/ethical implications.
Discusses multiple methods for evaluating counseling effectiveness with the case client (CACREP 2016 Standard 6.B.1.e).	No method of evaluating counseling effectiveness was discussed.	A method of evaluating counseling effectiveness was discussed but not in relation to student's counseling work with the case client.	Two or more methods of evaluating counseling effectiveness were discussed, and examples were provided; if appropriate, references were provided.
Demonstrates ability to apply a personal counseling orientation based on theory and a specific counseling paradigm (CACREP 2016 Standard 6.B.1.b).	Student does not apply a personal counseling orientation in the client session.	Student applies a personal counseling orientation based on a specific theory but not related to the chosen paradigm.	Student applies a personal counseling orientation based on the specific theory of the chosen counseling paradigm and is able to articulate this orientation clearly.
Final disposition	Unmet (0–10 points)	Met (11–20 points)	Exceeds (21–30 points)

Note. CACREP = Council for Accreditation of Counseling and Related Educational Programs; APA = American Psychological Association.

Sample Site Supervisor Evaluation of the Program

Please evaluate the educational program of the University Counselor Education program on the basis of your experience of master's degree students completing their practicum/internship requirement. Use the following scale to compare this student's preparation with other master's degree students who are completing their practicum/internship requirement.

1 = Very Poor   2 = Poor   3 = Average   4 = Above Average   5 = Excellent

_____ Student's overall education preparation?
_____ Student's clinical skills ability?

_____ Student's ethical behavior?
_____ Student's theoretical knowledge?
_____ Student's administrative skills?
_____ Student's ability to recognize professional limitations and seek supervision when appropriate?
_____ Supervisor's perception of support from University Faculty and Staff?

Strengths of the Program: (please list/write): _____

Suggestions for Program Improvement: (please list/write): _____

This measure is based on the site supervisor's perception of the university's counselor education; however, the person completing the rating infers program quality based on interactions with one or two students. In essence, it is an indirect measure of the effectiveness of the program in preparing students because it does not provide information on how or how well students performed this skill.

For numerical data to be collected on indirect measures, a range of ratings is usually included for the person who is completing the rating or survey form. The following Alumni Survey is an example of how numerical data can be collected on indirect measures. In this survey, a 4-point Likert scale is used to assess how graduates perceive elements of their educational experience. Results from this survey could provide descriptive results, including measures of central tendency (e.g., mean, median, and mode) as well as variance (e.g., standard deviation). For example, 10 graduates in May 2012 who complete the survey could indicate a mean rating of 3.5 for the quality of teaching (Item 2). The numerical results provide more specific information in quantifying graduates' perceptions of their graduate program experience.

Alumni Survey

Please rate the following items on the following scale:

1 = Strongly Disagree   2 = Disagree   3 = Agree   4 = Strongly Agree

_____ Overall, the courses in the counselor education program were challenging.
_____ Overall, the quality of the teaching was high.
_____ Overall, faculty members were well prepared for classes.
_____ My knowledge of given topics in counseling was strengthened through the assignments required in courses.
_____ The clinical experiences required in the counselor education program provided a solid foundation that prepared me for my career as a professional counselor.

Please provide additional input on ways to improve your degree program.

What things did you find most useful in your degree program? _____

What did you find as the most effective aspects of your training?_____

What recommendations do you have for changes in the program? _____

What did you find as the least effective aspects of your training? _____

The examples of measures included in this chapter demonstrate the range of responses and types of data that can be collected. Intentionality in planning these measures allows program faculty members to utilize data analyses that inform their program and SLO planning.

Analyzing Data

After faculty members have determined the type of data to be collected, they can turn attention to data analysis. We first focus on quantitative data analysis and then follow-up with a discussion about qualitative data analysis. Examples of each are provided.

When the focus is on SLOs, the typical analysis of data involves counts and percentages. For program evaluation, percentages include a numerical description of a proportion of the total number of individuals achieving or responding in a specific category (Whiston, 2013). Program members may also set performance indicators to define a measure of change for the results in the program. These indicators should be linked with overall program goals and priorities. In one example, the alumni survey may have indicated that the research courses needed to be strengthened. A program may determine that at least 90% of students will receive "Meets Expectations" or "Exceeds Expectations" for specific research standards. If 23 of 25 counselor education master's degree students achieved an "Exceeds" for a specific criterion on research, this would mean that 92% achieved an "Exceeds" for this learning outcome and have exceeded the set performance indicator. This example includes both the count and percentage for the categorical data obtained for this specific measure.

The alumni survey example above may yield counts and percentages for consideration. For example, 13 of 20 graduates who completed the survey selected 3 (*Agree*), and seven graduates selected 4 (*Strongly Agree*) on Item 3 ("Faculty members were well prepared for class"). The counts are 13 and 7, respectively for *Agree* and *Strongly Agree*. Percentages would indicate that 13 of 20 (65%) of graduates agreed, and 7 or 20 (35%) strongly agreed that faculty members were well prepared for class; no graduate disagreed with this statement. The counts demonstrate how many individuals were involved in the activity, and the percentage is the rate of the individual's success of the programmed outcome.

You may also wish to calculate descriptive and inferential statistics. The *mean* (average), *median* (middle value in an ascending list of scores), and *mode* (most frequent score) can provide a way to report and discuss results (Whiston, 2013). Additionally, these metrics can help faculty members make comparisons between and among groups of students (i.e., across specialty areas, courses, or cohorts). Counselor educators may be interested in determining whether there are any statistically significant differences or findings using inferential statistics (e.g., *t* tests, analyses of variance), especially when examining disaggregated data.

Up to this point, we have provided examples of aggregated data that apply to the whole population of students. Program faculty members may also be interested in analyzing results and outcomes by specific characteristics (disaggregated data; Meyer & Latham, 2008; Wetzel & Strudler, 2005). Provided there is a large enough sample size, program faculty members can separate data on the basis of cohort, specialty area, gender, ethnicity, age, or other student characteristics. In many cases, sample sizes will be too small to use inferential statistics in a meaningful way. However, program members may want to compare scores on standardized tests before and after a curricular change or clinical rating form changes after implementing new approaches to an advanced skills prepracticum or practicum.

Another helpful statistic is the *standard deviation* (the average distance of scores or ratings from the mean; Whiston, 2013). Standard deviations inform program faculty about the variability of responses, which could have significant implications about the measure, instruction, students, and the overall program. Small standard deviations indicate little variability in students' performance or ratings. This may indicate a large degree of agreement regarding experiences or skills. At the same time, a small standard deviation on rubric scores or clinical effectiveness rating forms may indicate that the current system is not adequate at distinguishing among different levels of performance. Conversely, large standard deviations indicate greater variability. Determining what constitutes small or large standard deviations will depend on the response scale used in the measure. Using the sample alumni survey, the response scale is a 4-point Likert scale. If the standard deviation for Item 2 was 0.50, this would be considered small because there are only 1-point differences between responses. If the standard deviation was 2.00, the standard deviation would indicate that there was a lot of variability among responders. Because Item 2 is about the quality of teaching, a large standard deviation may indicate concerns with variability in faculty quality, faculty turnover, or curricular changes. On rubrics or rating forms, a large standard deviation may indicate great variability in student performance or lack of interrater agreement on use of the form.

It is also important that program members consider quantitative data in the context of qualitative program evaluation data. As discussed in earlier chapters, program members can acquire data through interviews, observations, and written documents such as surveys. If interviews are conducted with students, site supervisors, or employers, data should be analyzed appropriately for rich and more meaningful data. This may be a more appropriate format for programs with smaller numbers of students to gain meaningful results from quantitative analyses. To encourage discussion and help control for bias, the program faculty will likely want to conduct a task analysis of open-ended responses by a team of faculty members.

Because of the nature of program evaluation, there may be an assumption that deductive analysis based on the program's Logic Model should occur and involve analyzing data according to the model. However, data that emerge that do not fit the model should be examined carefully to determine whether nonmodel aspects of the program are emerging in the data (M. Q. Patton, 2003). Program faculty and staff should be equipped to conduct content analysis or coding for categories and themes when appropriate for the type of data obtained. Caution should be used in overinterpreting one comment when no other response is similar to it.

Process Considerations

In addition to deciding how to analyze data, faculty members should consider timing of data analysis. First, faculty members determine the data collection schedule. Considerations include attention to questions such as the following:

- When are site supervisor, employer, alumni, and graduating student surveys collected?
- Should this information be analyzed at the time of collection or at some later time? Why or why not?
- Are SLO measurement data analyzed immediately?
- Do the program faculty and staff wait and analyze all of the outcomes once a year? Twice a year?

When data are analyzed depends on the needs of each individual program. Large programs that utilize many adjunct faculty or site supervisors may want to analyze data several times a year as a way of assessing perceptions about quality of instruction or supervision. However, a dedicated process once a year may allow more depth of attention to themes and findings across areas.

Counselor education program faculty and staff should assess the support within their department, school, or college for data analysis. If an AMS has been employed to collect and manage data, there may be data analysis tools built into the system or a method to export the data to data analysis software. A college or university assessment or accreditation office may collaborate with the program to create an assessment plan including a collaborative data analysis schedule. If program members will be the ones to conduct data analyses, faculty members may wish to advocate for course release, monetary compensation, or professional development in exchange for extensive services. The responsibility of data analysis is a commitment of both time and expertise, so this should be recognized as going beyond the fair-share responsibilities typical of program faculty.

One final reminder is that data analysis should not wait for a self-study or other external demand. Program evaluation should be continuous and systematic, and there must be "evidence of the use of program evaluation data to inform program modifications" (CACREP 2016 Standard 4.C). Between accrediting body and local reviews, annual reporting and sharing of results based on data-driven decisions are required. If the program is in the process of accreditation, the bottom line is that these processes have to be completed. Why wait for a self-study to reap the benefits of your program evaluation? Data analyses of this information will inform improvements that need to occur, including what needs to be revised, added to, or deleted from the counselor education program. In essence, the program faculty members will be working more efficiently with program improvements, leaving more time for their own professional projects.

Resources

Centers for Disease Control and Prevention. (2009a, April). Analyzing qualitative data for evaluation. *Evaluation Briefs, 19,* 1–2. Retrieved from http://www.cdc.gov/healthyyouth/evaluation/pdf/brief19.pdf

Centers for Disease Control and Prevention. (2009b, July). Analyzing quantitative data for evaluation. *Evaluation Briefs, 20,* 1–2. Retrieved from http://www.cdc.gov/healthyyouth/evaluation/pdf/brief20.pdf

Leahy, J. (2004). Using excel for analyzing survey questionnaires. *Program Development & Evaluation* (G3658-14). Retrieved from http://learningstore.uwex.edu/Assets/pdfs/G3658-14.pdf

Patton, M. Q. (2003). *Qualitative evaluation checklist.* Retrieved from https://cyfernetsearch.org/sites/default/files/Patton,%202003.pdf

Pell Institute and Pathways to College Network. (2015). *Analyze quantitative data*. Retrieved from http://toolkit.pellinstitute.org/evaluation-guide/analyze/analyze-quantitative-data/

Taylor-Powell, E., & Renner, M. (2003). Analyzing qualitative data. *Program Development & Evaluation* (G3658-12). Retrieved from http://learningstore.uwex.edu/Assets/pdfs/G3658-12.pdf

University of Kansas, Work Group for Community Health and Development. (2014). Section 5: Collecting and analyzing data. In *Community Tool Box* (Chapter 37, Operations in Evaluating Community Interventions). Retrieved from http://ctb.ku.edu/en/table-of-contents/evaluate/evaluate-community-interventions/collect-analyze-data/main

U.S. Department of Housing and Urban Development, Office of Policy Development and Research. (n.d.). *Program evaluation and analysis: A technical guide for state and local governments*. Retrieved from https://www.bja.gov/evaluation/guide/documents/documentb.html

Chapter 14

Reporting Data

Data reporting is one of the final parts of the program evaluation process; however, how results are shared deserves as much consideration as all of the other elements of program evaluation. According to CACREP (2016), formative and summative program evaluation results are disseminated annually to stakeholders by accredited programs. Different stakeholders will have different needs and expectations related to what they need to see reported (and how it is reported) as part of the program and SLO evaluation process. In this chapter, we attend to reporting results of program evaluation and course assessments. Because elements within this section of the chapter are specific, we integrate attention to process considerations in each section.

Sharing Results

Who?

Results of data analysis should first be explored with the counselor education faculty members involved in the data collection process. This provides an opportunity for individual faculty members to present data that they have collected within their classes and to provide additional insight on contextual factors and trends influencing results. Specific specialty area faculty (i.e., clinical mental health counseling, school counseling, counselor education and supervision) may want to meet separately to discuss SLO results. Faculty members could begin initial planning sessions to address concerns based on the results or plan to meet with stakeholders who may help to explain findings and who will aid in program modifications.

Stakeholders for counselor education programs are individuals, higher education offices, clinical sites, and other institutions that may be affected by the program results and any modifications made to the program. Examples of stakeholders include the following:

- students enrolled in the counselor education program;
- alumni;
- employers of graduates;
- advisory boards;
- colleagues in the current institution (i.e., college and university administrators; core, adjunct, and affiliate faculty members; staff members); and
- colleagues at other institutions, including practicum and internship clinical sites.

Results should be shared and discussed with relevant stakeholders before the program faculty members make final recommendations on how the results will be interpreted and used. For example, faculty may want to meet with specialty area advisory boards before making decisions about possible curriculum and clinical changes to the program. In addition, meeting with affiliate faculty members outside of the program who teach counselor education students may provide insight and impetus for changes in courses not directed by counselor education faculty. Although program faculty should not require current students to meet to discuss assessment findings because of power differentials in the faculty–student relationship, faculty members may find voluntary focus groups or anonymous student feedback mechanisms helpful for contextualizing findings and recommendations.

What?

Counselor educators have an ethical responsibility to disseminate assessment results in an accurate and responsible manner (ACA, 2014). Consideration should be given to "who is the audience and what do they need to know to make conclusions about the assessment process and its results" (Jonson, 2006, p. 65). When determining what specific information should be shared, counselor educators should consider the what, how, and why of the assessment process as well as the specific nature of the results. For example, only aggregated results should be reported to specific audiences to maintain the confidentiality of students (Suskie, 2009). If there are only five male students in a program with 80 students total, results based on disaggregated data by gender may be too revealing if shared with the current student population. This information may be more appropriate for faculty discussions only.

A second consideration is to understand the audience and their needs (Suskie, 2009). What are their priorities in hearing in these results? Will they be making any decisions on the basis of these results? What questions do they need to answer with these results? The following is a list of audience questions that may be helpful in determining what information to share. The list only addresses questions that individual faculty members, the faculty as a whole, campus leaders, and accreditors may ask themselves or program representatives about the program evaluation results. However, students, site supervisors, and advisory board members may have additional questions about the results that should be considered. Alumni may be interested in the program's efforts, which may have an impact on their contributions to support the program or department.

Audience Questions

Individual Counselor Education Faculty Member

Questions that an individual counselor education faculty member should consider include the following:

- Are the students learning information in the courses that I teach or supervise that will help them be successful as professional counselors?
- Are students demonstrating skills that are consistent with professional counselors?
- Where are students having difficulty learning and demonstrating skills?
- What can be improved in the individual courses or with my teaching strategies that can address issues with knowledge and skill development?

Counselor Education Program Faculty and Staff

Questions that counselor education program faculty and staff should consider include the following:

- Are students learning the most important things about being a professional counselor in our program?
- Are students demonstrating knowledge and skills that will help them be successful as a professional counselor?
- Are there any improvements in our students' learning and/or skills?
- Did program changes result in any student learning improvements?
- What are the roadblocks to student learning and/or ability to demonstrate counseling skills?
- What can we change in our counselor education program to help students learn knowledge and skills?
- Do our students need additional resources and/or technologies to achieve identified outcomes? If so, how do we advocate for these?

Higher Education/Campus Leadership

Questions that higher education/campus leadership should consider include the following:

- Was the counselor education program effective in achieving its program goals? SLOs?
- Are these goals aligned with their accrediting body (CACREP)?
- Is the program working efficiently with current resources and technologies?
- Are the faculty utilizing the most effective and efficient pedagogical and clinical practices to help students achieve?
- Do the counselor education program members need any additional resources and/or technologies to be more effective in attaining their goals?
- Should we support any proposed changes? If so, how and which ones?

Accreditors

Questions that accreditors should consider include the following:

- Has this counselor education program demonstrated continuous, systematic evaluation? If so, how?
- What program modifications were implemented, how were they assessed, and what were the results?
- Did students demonstrate knowledge and skills according to CACREP Standards? How?
- What are the perceptions of counselor education graduates, site supervisors, and graduate employers about the effectiveness of the program in attaining their goals?
- What program modifications are needed on the basis of the current data analysis?
- Are the current counselor education program resources adequate for meeting goals effectively?

For individual courses, faculty can be systematic in reporting course assessment results, or subsets of courses may be reported on a rotating basis. These results can include data on the grade distribution, SLOs collected, modifications made to the course, and results of modifications after implementation. This information feeds into the annual program evaluation report and demonstrated systematic program evaluation and assessment of SLOs.

When reported, results need to be focused and clear, with positive results highlighted (Suskie, 2009). Although it is tempting to focus on the less positive or troublesome areas and skip over the positive results, we encourage program faculty to focus on this explicitly. Highlighting positive results helps demonstrate what faculty members are doing well, which is evidence of their overall effectiveness. There have been too many cases of needing to provide a rationale for keeping or hiring faculty in higher education. Providing evidence of success indicates that the program has good resources for what it is doing well.

Attending to things we do too well gives us little room for using assessment results to inform program changes in a meaningful way. Consistently meeting or exceeding targets indicates an opportunity to shift aspirations and is a hallmark of a continuous improvement cycle. With that said, less positive results still need to be addressed. Counselor educators may be able to offer some explanation for these results as they are offered. This is appropriate, especially if a possible plan to address these concerns has been formulated. Identifying opportunities for further growth and remediating problem areas and concerns are some of the main purposes of program evaluation. Using results to improve the program as well as student learning is the impetus for assessing these areas. Program faculty should avoid blaming one individual, course, or program component for the program not being effective. Program evaluation should not be punitive or set up the faculty to not work collaboratively and effectively in addressing the concerns revealed through the evaluation.

How?

Results can be shared in multiple formats, including verbal presentations, written reports, and electronic reports and visuals. Program faculty members should first determine the most effective method of conveying program evaluation results on the basis of their stakeholders' needs. Results should be published in a format that is accessible to the program's stakeholders. The main objective in disseminating the data is for recipients to absorb the results and to construct personal meaning from it, rather than discarding the information (Suskie, 2009).

For individual course assessment results, a simple written report (see the example at the end of this chapter) can be generated to include the following:

- header (course number and title, section number if applicable, academic term),
- course catalog description,
- grade distribution,
- modifications made to the course (substantive changes and the source of improvement, such as an action plan, meeting minutes),
- SLOs based on course assignments (include specific course with evaluation criteria [i.e., rubric, rating form] and reported outcomes from the evaluation),
- student feedback (specific to course elements, not course instruction),
- instructor reflection (brief narrative reflection on effectiveness of instruction, course structure and assessments, and circumstances that may have affected the outcomes), and
- course improvement plans (brief outline of activities to improve course).

Initially, the course assessment report may appear to be excessive to program faculty members. However, it can be reframed as an effort to organize the systematic evaluation processes that are required in the program's assessment plan. These reports not only provide organized data ready for review and modifications but also offer a pipeline of data required in the annual program evaluation report.

When an annual written report is generated for the program results, faculty members may want to consider using tables and graphs to consider key findings. Tables and graphs can convey data in a succinct manner and can make comparisons easier to see (Suskie, 2009). Statistical software programs and AMSs that include software to create graphics from data can generate graphs and tables from data sets. For example, one might use simple pie or bar charts to convey percentages and/or frequency counts related to demographic data.

Aggregated and disaggregated data can be reported in tables with specific components explained to highlight outcomes that may be a result of program changes to address a specific concern from previous program evaluations. For example, a program may focus attention on improvement of NCE scores during one academic year. Table 14.1 illustrates difference in scores on the basis of specialty area type (i.e., CMHC; school counseling; and marriage, couple, and family counseling [MCFC]), gender, and year of administration.

As is illustrated in the table, there is a difference in the years following the 2012–2013 academic year. It appears that something occurred to affect the scores in a positive direction for all student groups. If the program faculty implemented an intervention to increase NCE scores, it appears that it may have been effective. However, this table includes results that provide additional information. It appears that female students perform better on the exam than male students. Additionally, students in the CMHC and MCFC programs perform better than the school counseling students. Are these results of concern to the program faculty? They may be, and the program may implement assessments to gather more information or interventions to address this issue. For this table and these results, the faculty may conduct additional statistical analysis to determine whether differences are statistically and practically significant and to make a decision as to whether those differences are significant for

Table 14.1
Sample of National Counselor Examination Score Results by Academic Year

Variable	2011–2012	2012–2013	2013–2014	2014–2015
Average of all students	110	108	123	135
Gender				
Men	107	103	122	132
Women	114	110	125	139
Specialty area				
CMHC	113	111	125	139
School	109	105	119	129
MCFC	111	110	123	135

Note. CMHC = clinical mental health counselor; MCFC = marriage, couple, and family counseling.

the program. Those statistics can also be reported with the table. Displaying data visually also makes interpretation easier for those who do not have a general understanding of statistical terminology.

The purpose of the program summary report is to document that program evaluation is part of counselor education culture. The report can be used as a tool to highlight any program modifications (on the basis of data) that have been implemented with the results of those modifications. It should include data from the following:

- alumni surveys,
- site supervisor program evaluations,
- program completion rates,
- licensure/certification pass rates,
- SLO attainment for each specialty area,
- employer surveys, and
- job placement rates.

Components of an annual program evaluation summary report may include the following:

1. *Time frame*: This component is defined as the time period of the program evaluation (e.g., 2015–2016).
2. *Evaluation methodology*: This component is a description of what data were collected and how they were collected. Example data sources include the following: formal graduating student and follow-up studies (e.g., master's program graduates, doctoral program graduates, master's and doctoral program graduates' employers, program evaluation by internship site supervisors).
3. *Key evaluation findings*: Program level results should be separated (master's program findings are reported first; doctoral program findings are reported last). This information can include the following: national licensure examination/certification results, state licensure/certification exam results, internship evaluations, graduating students' survey results, site supervisor program evaluation results, and alumni survey results. This information can also be disaggregated by specialty area. Faculty members may find it helpful to use tables, charts, and graphs to display large amounts of data quickly and to highlight specific findings and outcomes.
4. *Key modifications to programs (master's separated from doctoral)*: Key changes based on specific data are reported in this section. These may include attention to structure, content, or process of curriculum; faculty assignment; advising procedures; and field experiences placements and support.
5. *Recommendations*: These recommendations are based on the findings and modifications. Program faculty may propose recommendations for program and evaluation processes and needed program modifications. In using the data to assess the program evaluation process as well as to make program modifications, faculty members achieve the essence of continuous program evaluation. More information on using data for program purposes is provided in Chapter 15.

When reporting the results of evaluations, questions that help to identify the specific elements pertaining to SLOs include the following:

1. What are the outcome measures? How was student learning measured (direct or indirect measures)?
2. What was the performance standard for the measure? What were acceptable levels of student performance? How was this defined?
3. What data were collected and with whom? The student population should be described (e.g., first-year students, school CITs).
4. What were the data analysis and the results? How many students achieved and exceeded acceptable levels of performance?
5. What do these results mean for the program? Should there be any modifications to the program, course, and so forth on the basis of these results?
6. What are program strengths on the basis of these SLOs?
7. What are the recommendations to the program on the basis of the SLOs?

It may not be effective to report all SLOs individually in a program evaluation report. Saturating faculty and other stakeholders with too much data may not allow for other important findings to be absorbed and acted on in a constructive manner. It is important to highlight results in which learning outcomes are supported in the curriculum and those that result in changes being implemented for improvement. Keep in mind that all results should be answering the questions designed to specifically address the objectives of the program evaluation. In addition, the following groups must be notified when the report is available: current students, program faculty, institutional administrators, and cooperating agency personnel (e.g., site supervisors, alumni employers, site/agency administrators; CACREP, 2016). An example of a program annual report that could be included on an institution's website in accordance with CACREP requirements is provided next.

Counselor Education University: 2015 Systematic Program Evaluation Summary

In accordance with Council for Accreditation of Counseling and Related Educational Programs (CACREP) Standards, the Counselor Education University Counselor Education Program conducts systematic program evaluation activities, including the following:

Program review: curricular review, advisory council feedback, National Counselor Examination (NCE) pass rates, Praxis exam scores, and student performance and grade profiles across courses.

Formal graduating student and follow-up studies (Master of Science [MS] program graduates, MS program graduates' employers, doctoral program graduates, and doctoral program graduates' employers).

During the 2014–2015 academic year, the counselor education program student population self-reported on the following demographic variables:

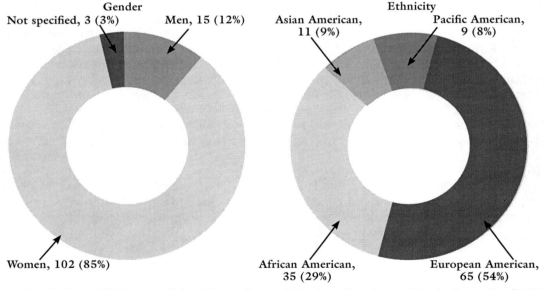

Evaluation Findings: MS Program (School Counseling and Marriage, Couples, and Family Counseling [MCFC])

- 95% (n = 20 of 21) of the MS students who sat for the NCE administered by the Counselor Education University between Fall 2014 and Spring 2015 passed the NCE.
- 100% (n = 16 of 16) of the MS students who sat for the NTE Praxis examination in School Counseling and Guidance between Fall 2014 and Spring 2015 passed the Praxis (M = 680.85; South Carolina School Guidance required score = 550).
- Formal follow-up studies of graduates from Fall 2014 to Spring 2015 (n = 3 of 30; 10%) were conducted by the Counselor Education University College of Education to assess professional growth and activity:
    - 100% of respondents were currently employed as counselors.
    - 33% of respondents reported attending a professional conference; 66% reported reading professional journals; and 33% reported holding a local, state, regional, national, or international professional organization office or engaging in committee work.
    - MS graduates reported that group work, self-assessments, and presentations were the most helpful part of the program.

- In addition to the follow-up studies of graduates from Fall 2014 to Spring 2015 conducted by the College of Education, the Counselor Education program also conducted follow-up studies of graduates (n = 10 of 20) in the specific areas of school counseling and MCFC. Using a Likert scale of 1–5 (1 = *strongly disagree*, 2 = *disagree*, 3 = *neutral*, 4 = *agree*, 5 = *strongly agree*), the following results were obtained:
  –Graduates reported they agreed to strongly agreed (M = 4.52) that they were very happy with the academic and clinical education they received at Counselor Education University.
  –Graduates reported responses of neutral to agreed (M = 3.81) that the entire program of academic and clinical education provided a solid foundation for a professional career in clinical, educational, agency, or governmental settings.
  –Graduates reported they agreed to strongly agreed (M = 4.71) that the expectations of the site supervisors and Counselor Education faculty were clear, reasonable, and appropriate for field experience courses.

- For the MCFC graduates (n = 15 of 18), the following results were reported:
  –Graduates reported they agreed (M = 4) that there was quality supervision offered by faculty members for practicum and internship.
  –Graduates reported they agreed to strongly agreed (M = 4.33) that there was quality supervision offered by other supervisors (including site supervisors) for practicum and internship.
  –Graduates reported they agreed to strongly agreed (M = 4.33) they would recommend the Counselor Education University MCFC program to others interested in preparation to work as a MCFC.
  –Graduates reported that strengths of the program included providing a systemic framework for helping families, knowledge/experience of certain faculty, prepracticum experiences, individual supervision, and focus on self as a therapist.
  –Recommendations from alumni included the following: larger and more diverse faculty with LPC (licensed professional counselor)/LMFT (licensed marriage and family therapist) credentials, greater focus on the licensing process, increasing network opportunities for jobs/extern positions after graduation, strengthen human sexuality and diagnosis training, and more aid in practicum and internship placements.
  –Although employers of graduates were sent surveys, none were returned during this time period.

- For the school counseling graduates (n = 15 of 17), the following results were reported:
  –Graduates reported they agreed (M = 4) that there was quality supervision offered by faculty members for practicum and internship.
  –Graduates reported they agreed to strongly agreed (M = 4.57) that there was quality supervision offered by other supervisors (including site supervisors) for practicum and internship.
  –Graduates agreed to strongly agreed (M = 4.42) they would recommend the Counselor Education University School Counseling MS program to others interested in preparation to work as a professional school counselor.
  –Graduates reported that strengths of the program included the following: knowledgeable faculty, excellent site supervisors for internship, and comprehensive school counseling curriculum.
  –Recommendations from alumni included the following: offer a classroom management course, require special education coursework, strengthen prepracticum clinical experiences, reexamine site placement decision-making process, and reevaluate the inclusion of specific courses in the curriculum.
  –Although employers of graduates were sent surveys, none were returned during this time period.

MS Program Graduates and Employment

- During 2014–2015, 24 students completed the MS degree in School Counseling, and 14 students completed the MS degree in MCFC. Of the graduates, 35 of 42 students became employed as counselors or in counseling-related positions immediately following graduation.
- MS Counselor Education student learning outcome (SLO) results from all key assignments and measures of SLOs were reviewed for students enrolled currently in the school and MCFC programs. Most standards were being met, with the exception of two specific core research standards.

Key Modifications: MS Program

Because most individuals who participated in the formal follow-up studies completed study in the program under the CACREP 2009 Standards, alumni feedback was integral in modifying our program to meet or exceed the CACREP 2016 Standards. Key modifications include the following:

- Created a new course entitled "Sexuality Counseling" to meet the standards and needs of the MCFC students.
- Met with educational foundations faculty responsible for research coursework to assist in providing course content and assessment for two research standards not being met with existing curricula.
- Included additional research content and assessment measures in practicum requirements.

Evaluation Findings: PhD Program (Counselor Education and Supervision)

Formal follow-up studies of graduates from Fall 2014 to Spring 2016 (n = 5 of 6) were conducted by the Counselor Education University College of Education to assess professional growth and activity:

- Three respondents indicated that they were employed as counselors, and two were employed as counselor educators.
- Respondents reported attending professional conferences; reading professional journals; and holding local, state, regional, national, or international professional organization offices or engaging in committee work.
- Respondents reported that the part-time, evening schedule of the program was most helpful because they worked full-time.
- Graduates recommended that faculty help/assist with placement/leads for employment, provide better assistance with letter of recommendation, and work with students better on providing education classes that could lead to administration/certification.

In addition to the follow-up studies of graduates from Fall 2014 to Spring 2015 conducted by the College of Education, the Counselor Education program also conducted follow-up studies of graduates (n = 3 of 4) in the specific area of Counselor Education and Supervision. Using a 5-point Likert scale (1 = *strongly disagree*, 2 = *disagree*, 3 = *neutral*, 4 = *agree*, 5 = *strongly agree*), the following results were obtained:

- Graduates reported they agreed to strongly agreed (M = 4.66) that they were very happy with the academic and clinical education they received at Counselor Education.
- Graduates reported they agreed to strongly agreed (M = 4.66) that the entire program of academic and clinical education provided a solid foundation for a professional career in private practice, higher education, agency, or governmental settings.
- Graduates reported they agreed to strongly agreed (M = 5) that the faculty committee that guided their dissertation was competent, supportive, and reasonably accessible to them during the entire process of the research.
- Graduates reported they agreed to strongly agreed (M = 4.66) that there was quality individual supervision or feedback on courses after the first teaching experience was complete.
- Graduates reported that program strengths included the following: competent and supportive faculty, strong clinical and teaching preparation, evening courses available, and clinical lab for videotaped practice sessions.
- Graduates recommended the following: create an on-site clinic to enhance counseling research, provide more opportunities for students to practice qualitative research, require students to coauthor articles with faculty members, and participate in submission process for journals.
- Although employers of graduates were sent surveys, none were returned during this time period.

PhD Counselor Education SLO Results

Results from all key assignments and measures of SLOs were reviewed for students enrolled currently in the counselor education and supervision doctoral program. The third area of internship (3 of 5 areas need to be included in the program) was not included.

PhD Program Graduates and Employment

During 2014–2015, eight students completed the PhD degree in Counselor Education and Supervision. Of the graduates, three of eight students became employed as full-time counselor educators, three students continued in counselor positions, and two students continued counseling practice and began work as adjunct professors in counselor education.

Key Modifications: PhD Program

Because most individuals who participated in the formal follow-up studies completed study in the program under the CACREP 2009 Standards, alumni feedback was integral in modifying our program to meet or exceed the CACREP 2016 Standards. Key modifications include the following:

- Created biannual comprehensive written exam administration dates with a single set of questions for each administration for consistency and logistical management purposes.
- Doctoral advisees utilized the EDCE 855 (1 credit hour) internships for doctoral students to assist in research and to learn about research methodology and publication processes.

In conclusion, data reporting is a time to summarize the achievements of the program and to acknowledge how the goal of the program is continuous improvement through the modifications being planned and implemented. It is a comprehensive process with much planning and revision taking place. Reporting these processes and results allows for program faculty to be transparent, which can result in positive consequences to include better student recruitment; program resources; and local, state, and national reputation. Finally, it demonstrates good counselor education evidence-based practices in pedagogy, supervision, and research.

Resources

Boyd, H. H. (2002). Quick tips: Basics of good evaluation reporting. *Program Development & Evaluation*. Retrieved from http://www.uwex.edu/ces/4h/evaluation/documents/Tipsheet14.pdf

Centers for Disease Control and Prevention, National Center for Chronic Disease Prevention and Health Promotion. (2013). *Developing an effective evaluation report: Setting the course for effective program evaluation*. Retrieved from http://www.cdc.gov/eval/materials/Developing-An-Effective-Evaluation-Report_TAG508.pdf

Estell, J. K. (2006). *Streamlining the assessment process with the Faculty Course Assessment Report*. Retrieved from http://secedha.ece.ufl.edu/meetings/2006/Estelle.pdf

Jankowski, N. A., & Provezis, S. J. (2011). *Making student learning evidence transparent: The state of the art*. Retrieved from http://www.learningoutcomeassessment.org/documents/transparencyofevidence.pdf

Office of Academic Planning and Assessment. (2001). *Program-based review and assessment: Tools and techniques for program improvement*. Retrieved from http://www.umass.edu/oapa/oapa/publications/online_handbooks/program_based.pdf

Chapter 15

Using Data to Enhance Programs

As discussed in Chapter 14, data reporting leads to the next logical step of applying the results to program planning and revision. Although all aspects of the program evaluation and the SLO assessment process can have an impact on students, overall programming decisions are directly affected by the evaluation results. In this chapter, we focus on how counselor educators can use these data to inform program-level decisions.

Planning and revision of counselor education programs based on program evaluation data are healthy practices. In essence, it promotes growth of the program and the development of faculty, students, staff, community, and future clients. Accreditation and ethical standards (e.g., ACA, 2014; CACREP, 2016) are in place to delineate why and how this should occur in counselor education programs. In this chapter, we discuss the best role of SLO evaluation in informing program curricular and policy modifications consistent with CACREP 2016 Standard 4.C: "counselor education program faculty provide evidence of the use of program evaluation data to inform program modifications." Practical steps for documenting, planning, and implementing changes based on program data are offered. The chapter wraps up with suggestions for using program data to modify existing evaluation plans.

Informing Program Curricular and Policy Modifications

Accountability across higher education programs, departments, schools, colleges, and universities has increased significantly in the past several decades (Ewell et al., 2011). Proving quality and effectiveness has higher education professionals learning how to utilize direct and indirect measures in their program evaluation efforts. Current program evaluation practice goes beyond documentation of simple participation in program evaluation activities to demonstration of how programs use program evaluation data to guide daily operations. "Closing the loop" or using the data for program improvement is the goal in program evaluation, and it is the most neglected part of the evaluation process.

How programs and institutions have utilized program evaluation and SLO data has varied. In a survey of randomly selected higher education programs from a pool of regionally accredited, undergraduate degree-granting, 2- and 4-year public, private, and for-profit U.S. institutions, programs most commonly used (74%) program evaluation data for program review (Ewell et al., 2011). Additional but less frequent uses than for program review included the following: improving instruction, fulfilling accreditation requirements, improving curriculum, informing planning, evaluating programs, supporting budgets, and evaluating faculty. Although these were used similarly in accredited and nonaccredited programs, accredited programs engaged in these activities 20% more frequently than nonaccredited programs.

At the program level, data are used to make curriculum changes and to enhance pedagogy (Ewell et al., 2011). Administrative offices use data to support budgets and to evaluate faculty. For administrative personnel and higher education program faculty, there are major concerns regarding program evaluation and how data are used. Level of assessment activity is among the highest in programs associated with education (including counselor education); not surprising, 90% of education programs reported using data for program review.

The question remains: How well are programs using assessment and evaluation data to elevate their programs. The National Institute for Learning Outcomes Assessment conducted a study of nine cases of program data use to address this question (Baker, Jankowski, Provezis, & Kinzie, 2012). Many of the institutions represented in the case studies created a culture of assessment on campus, which promoted a meaning-making attitude and commitment in how evaluation data were used. At the program level best practices in using data that reflected student learning for program- and classroom-level improvement included the following:

- setting faculty priorities;
- securing resources for professional development;
- improving student support services;
- revising curriculum, courses, and assignments;
- informing program reviews/departmental self-studies;
- aligning curriculum; and
- improving program outcomes (Baker et al., 2012, p. 10).

Although these are the most reported uses of data, program faculty may prioritize student and faculty development, constituent group program involvement, and supports/awards for innovative ideas and results. The process of prioritizing involves a careful examination of both data and evaluation process.

Practical Steps for Using Data for Program Improvement

What are the specifics to using data? There are various ways to utilize the data collected for program improvement, and effective use requires intentionality on the part of the program faculty. Blaich and Wise (2011) suggested five steps for effective use of data for higher education institutions. These are not listed in sequential order but can be used in line with the program needs. These steps include data auditing, developing a clear focus, communicating outcomes, requesting resources, and seeking student input and feedback.

Data Auditing

Data auditing involves listing all assessment data that are collected and any that are in the plan to collect. Faculty members collect data to help them reflect on "what students *bring* to college, what they *experience* in college, and what they *learn* in college" (Blaich & Wise, 2011, p. 13). Program members consider standardized tests (e.g., Miller Analogies Test and GRE scores) and summative achievement data (e.g., GPAs) along with what SLOs that can be used in the existing information systems. If data are not available, there may be a need to create or access this information. For counselor education programs, examining the whole picture of data for the program and for student learning is key to this data audit.

One example of this is to consider preadmission data. Typically, college and university graduate school admission offices assist in collecting paper artifacts such as transcripts, standardized test scores, letters of recommendation (that may or may not include ratings), and essays. Program members may also collect interviewer ratings/observations during on-site interviews or interactions. Together, these pieces of preadmission data may inform the program faculty about possible candidates and program assessment practices. Program faculty may ask questions such as "How does this part of program evaluation connect with the other aspects?" and "What is not known that needs to be known for program evaluation?" For example, counselor education programs may have an application rating form (e.g., point ranges for GRE/Miller Analogies Test score ranges, GPAs, and reference letters) for determining who is accepted. However, the program faculty are concerned that they are not getting a good handle on student dispositions before they are admitted. They want to implement an interview process with admissions and have determined that they need an interviewer rating form that can be compared across individual faculty member ratings. Once admitted, these ratings can also be compared with dispositional ratings that are conducted during the student's matriculation in the program to determine whether the interview rating is reliable. Putting these different aspects of program data and collection into the context of the whole program will help faculty determine the priorities for program improvement.

Developing a Clear Focus

The second step in using data effectively for program improvement is to develop a clear focus on program improvement by narrowing the focus to no more than three priorities or outcomes for the year (Blaich & Wise, 2011). With a lot of data available, program personnel are apt to become overwhelmed with what the data are and are not telling them about program effectiveness. Because of the multiple options for program improvement and revision that may evolve from these data, program priorities should be focused.

Focusing on priorities continues to be part of the continuous, systematic review, and it necessitates intentionality in the steps for program improvement. Program faculty members should review the mission and goals of the program and purposes for their assessment and evaluation plan to determine improvement implementation for the current year. For example, the counselor education program members may be conducting an annual review of students, but the only data sources are grades. The program has no indication of how students would evaluate themselves or be evaluated on dispositions. Hence, faculty may decide to create a method of assessing dispositions systemically during the course of a student's matriculation in the program. Consequently, this may affect the review and remediation process in the next year.

If data from SLOs and standardized program measures (e.g., NCE results) indicate that students are weak in specific areas, program faculty may examine those areas to determine opportunities for improvement. This may be an indication of possible weak course content, instruction, or professional identity that needs to be addressed. Priorities on improving performance on the NCE and improving student–faculty relationships may emerge from this information. These data can also inform strategies for adding full-time faculty members. In essence, the focus on outcomes related to the data should address the faculty's program goals and priorities.

Communicating Outcomes

As mentioned previously, a culture of assessment and evaluation needs to be part of the program, school/college, and university. If this is in place, the third step of communication about outcomes is a naturally occurring component of the culture. Blaich and Wise (2011) suggested that program faculty begin conversations about program evaluation, data, and outcomes prior to any data being reported. Program objectives

(1) reflect current knowledge and projected needs concerning counseling practice in a multicultural and pluralistic society; (2) reflect input from all persons involved in the conduct of the program, including counselor education program faculty, current and former students, and personnel in cooperating agencies; (3) address student learning; and (4) are written so they can be evaluated. (CACREP 2016 Standard 2.B)

Typically, program faculty members convene advisory boards for specialty areas to revise program objectives. Discussion regarding program priorities, current data, and planned intervention and evaluation efforts can be part of these discussions. Asking "what if" questions (e.g., What if the results do not come back as expected?) in these discussions could promote alternative recommendations when the faculty members review data and make decisions about changes. Counselor education program faculty members are encouraged to also have these conversations at the department, school/college, and university levels to gauge the supports offered and needed for planning and implementing changes. These conversations build a foundation and offer a precursor to resource requests.

Requesting Resources

We hope that any reader who has implemented a program assessment and evaluation plan has been offered resources by higher administrators to do this. These resources are typically needed: software (for data analysis), personnel support (for typing reports and gathering information), and release time for coordinating the process and writing reports. What is the common theme of all of these activities? These resources are provided for implementing the plan and not using the data. What resources will be needed to use the data? Unfortunately, we cannot answer this question specifically. Of course, we offer several questions to review to answer the resource question:

- What resources are needed to fulfill the program's objectives?
- What resources are needed to meet with current students, alumni, and participating agencies to gain feedback on anticipated and real outcome data?
- What resources are available now, and what is needed if anticipated outcomes are realized?
- What resources are needed to revise program objectives?
- What resources are needed if anticipated outcomes are not realized?
- Where will resources be requested (person/office)?
- What are the consequences (i.e., for students, faculty, staff, department, school/college, university, community, participating agencies) if resources are not obtained?

Program faculty members are encouraged to answer these comprehensively by writing a resource request plan to submit to institutional leaders to anticipate any surprises or concerns that will require a rationale for resources. Some program faculty may require outside consultants as resources for program evaluation plans, which requires advanced planning and financial resources that may extend to institutional budgets related to these purposes.

Seeking Student Input and Feedback

One additional step to using program data effectively is having informal conversations with current and former students. This may seem like an extension of the community outcomes steps, but it is less about "what if" and more of "what about." For example, what about the admissions process is effective and not effective? What about the comprehensive exam is appropriate and not appropriate to assess student learning? What about feedback provided in clinical sequence helps students to build or not build skills over time?

Although student input and feedback are important, program members should also keep aware of ethical guidelines and power differentials during this evaluation step. For example, current students may or may not feel comfortable discussing the admission requirements or sharing elements of the program that have been difficult for them. These discussions should not become part of a course or program requirement but should be presented as an opportunity to help improve the program. Information gained from these discussions can help connect the dots between program components and outcome data. Essentially, evaluation data may make more sense after these discussions are held so appropriate improvements can be made.

With these steps, program faculty members need to remember to pace their use of data. According to Blaich and Wise (2011), it may take programs 3–4 years to understand, plan, and act on one to two learning outcomes from program evaluation data. The process takes considerable patience and forethought to implement objectives that fit programs effectively and comprehensively.

For counselor education, this is a more recent process and requirement for our programs. However, best practices in assessment and evaluation should not be deficits because they have been core training components of our programs as well as part of the role of researcher in our identities. The evolving primary concern from writing this book is the paucity of literature and research in program evaluation that are offered in professional counseling journals and books. As a profession, this can be

addressed at the program and profession-at-large levels. At the program level, best practice should always include consistent evaluation of the program evaluation process. Program evaluation is a dynamic process with people, policies, and standards always changing. The old adage of "if it's not broke, don't fix it" does not apply to the process, and program faculty members are encouraged to engage in continuous evaluation of program evaluation. For the profession, counseling practitioners and educators are encouraged to engage in program evaluation and to document these processes and/or results to submit for publication in counseling publications. Less of a reliance on other disciplines in program evaluation needs to evolve within the counseling profession. Until we have developed sufficient resources in this area, several good resources on the use of program evaluation data are offered at the end of this chapter.

Resources

Baker, G. R., Jankowski, N. A., Provezis, S., & Kinzie, J. (2012). *Using assessment results: Promising practices of institutions that do it well.* Retrieved from http://www.learningoutcomesassessment.org/documents/CrossCase_FINAL.pdf

Berrett, D. (2014, January 21). Colleges measure learning in more ways, but seldom share results. *The Chronicle of Higher Education.* Retrieved from http://chronicle.com/article/Colleges-Measure-Learning-in/144117/?cid=at&utm_source=at&utm_medium=en

Blaich, C., & Wise, K. (2011). *From gathering to using assessment results: Lessons from the Wabash National Study.* Retrieved from http://learningoutcomesassessment.org/documents/Wabash_001.pdf

Chapter 16

Using Data to Support Individual Student Development

The SLO assessment process offers powerful opportunities to learn about what students know and can do as a result of their participation in counselor education programs. This process allows opportunity to examine and improve program quality and processes as a whole, and it also offers unique opportunities to provide customized support to individual students as they develop knowledge and skills needed to be effective in the world of practice.

The *ACA Code of Ethics* (ACA, 2014) and the *2016 Standards* (CACREP, 2016) are clear regarding counselor educators' responsibilities for articulating competencies expected of students, assessing competencies in a planful manner, and engaging in remediation processes to support student development and to guide those who do not have strong potential for success in the profession to more appropriately matched fields of study. Because these processes are so important, we include the following list of specific accreditation and ethical standards relevant to individual student support.

CACREP 2016 Standards Relevant to
Individual Student Support

The CACREP 2016 Standards that are relevant to individual student support include the following (emphasis added):

- Before or at the beginning of the first term of enrollment in the academic unit, the program provides a new student orientation during which a program handbook is disseminated and discussed, students' *ethical and professional obligations and personal growth expectations* as counselors-in-training are explained, and eligibility for licensure/certification is reviewed (Standard 1.M).
- The student handbook includes the (1) mission statement of the academic unit and program objectives; (2) information about professional counseling organizations, opportunities for professional involvement, and activities appropriate for students; (3) matriculation requirements; (4) *expectations of students*; (5) academic appeal policy; (6) written endorsement policy explaining the procedures for recommending students for credentialing and employment; and (7) *policy for student retention, remediation, and dismissal from the program* (Standard 1.N).
- Counselor education programs have and follow a policy for student retention, remediation, and dismissal from the program consistent with institutional due process policies and with the counseling profession's ethical codes and standards (Standard 1.O).
- *Formative and summative evaluations* of the student's counseling performance and ability to integrate and apply knowledge are conducted as part of the student's practicum and internship (Standard 3.C).

- The counselor education program faculty systematically assesses each student's progress throughout the program by examining student learning in relation to a combination of knowledge and skills. The assessment process includes the following: (1) identification of key performance indicators of student learning in each of the eight core areas and in each student's respective specialty area(s) (for doctoral programs, each of the five doctoral core areas), (2) measurement of student learning conducted via multiple measures and over multiple points in time, and (3) review or analysis of data (Standard 4.F).
- The counselor education program faculty systematically assesses each student's professional dispositions throughout the program. The assessment process includes the following: (1) identification of key professional dispositions, (2) measurement of student professional dispositions over multiple points in time, and (3) review or analysis of data (Standard 4.G).
- The counselor education program faculty has a systematic process in place for the use of individual student assessment data in relation to retention, remediation, and dismissal (Standard 4.H).

ACA (2014) Ethical Standards Relevant to Individual Student Support

The ACA (2014) ethical standards that are relevant to individual student support include the following (emphasis added):

- Supervisors document and provide supervisees with *ongoing feedback regarding their performance* and schedule periodic *formal evaluative sessions* throughout the supervisory relationship (Standard F.6.a).
- Through initial and ongoing evaluation, supervisors are aware of supervisee limitations that might impede performance. Supervisors *assist supervisees in securing remedial assistance when needed*. They *recommend dismissal* from training programs, applied counseling settings, and state or voluntary professional credentialing processes when those supervisees are unable to demonstrate that they can provide competent professional services to a range of diverse clients. Supervisors seek *consultation and document their decisions to dismiss or refer supervisees for assistance*. They ensure that supervisees are aware of options available to them to address such decisions (Standard F.6.b).
- Counselor educators recognize that program orientation is a developmental process that begins following students' initial contact with the counselor education program and continues throughout the educational and clinical training of students. Counselor education faculty provide prospective and current students with information about the counselor education program's expectations, including:
  1. the values and ethical principles of the profession;
  2. the type and level of skill and knowledge acquisition required for successful completion of the training;
  3. technology requirements;
  4. program training goals, objectives, and mission, and subject matter to be covered;
  5. *bases for evaluation*;
  6. training components that encourage self-growth or self-disclosure as part of the training process;
  7. the type of supervision settings and requirements of the sites for required clinical field experiences;
  8. *student and supervisor evaluation and dismissal policies and procedures*; and
  9. up-to-date employment prospects for graduates (Standard F.8.a).
- Counselor educators may *require students to address* any personal concerns that have the potential to affect professional competency (Standard F.8.d).
- Counselor educators clearly state to students, prior to and throughout the training program, the *levels of competency expected, appraisal methods, and timing of evaluations* for both didactic and clinical competencies. Counselor educators provide students with ongoing feedback regarding their performance throughout the training program (Standard F.9.a).
- Counselor educators, *through ongoing evaluation, are aware of and address the inability of some students to achieve counseling competencies*. Counselor educators do the following:
  1. assist students in securing remedial assistance when needed,
  2. seek professional consultation and document their decision to dismiss or refer students for assistance, and
  3. ensure that students have recourse in a timely manner to address decisions requiring them to seek assistance or to dismiss them and provide students with due process according to institutional policies and procedures (Standard F.9.b).
- If students request counseling, or if counseling services are suggested as part of a remediation process, counselor educators assist students in identifying appropriate services (Standard F.9.c).

In this chapter, we discuss best practices for student review and retention, and we identify opportunities for using data to determine whether students are progressing as expected. We end the chapter with discussion of remediation and gatekeeping opportunities and provision of key resources. Throughout the chapter, we offer some discussion prompts and practical tips for ensuring strong support of students throughout the SLO evaluation process.

Best Practices in Student Review

Both the *2016 Standards* (CACREP, 2016) and the *ACA Code of Ethics* (ACA, 2014) are clear that counselor educators and supervisors are responsible for articulating expectations of students, providing students with formative feedback regarding their progress in the program, and creating summative evaluations at the end of major courses or curricular experiences. Both bodies also identify the need for programs to focus attention on a range of behaviors, including academic performance, clinical skills, and dispositions congruent with those of effective professional counselors. In earlier chapters, we provided extensive attention to methods of assessing academic and clinical learning, and Chapter 9 includes attention to procedures for assessing less tangible dispositions or characteristics.

By engaging in ongoing assessment of SLOs and dispositions, counselor educators will have rich sources of data regarding student performance across the curriculum. In this section, we attend to considerations for constructing a meaningful student review process.

The SLO articulation and curriculum mapping process discussed earlier in this book will guide counselor educators through the process of developing and articulating expectations for student performance. By publishing this information on the program webpage, in student handbooks, and in course syllabi, counselor educators are transparent about standards on which students will be evaluated. Ideally, this communication occurs at multiple times and via multiple communication venues so students have ready access to the material and can make sense of it at times and in ways that fit their developmental needs (V. A. Foster & McAdams, 2009; Pease-Carter & Barrio Minton, 2012).

Counselor education programs must next determine when they will assess student development and performance. This includes, but is not limited to, timing or placement of assessment activities in the curriculum. For example, the program faculty may decide to utilize CBAs as a primary means of assessment. In this case, the course instructor may be responsible for evaluating student learning through the use of rubrics. He or she may have a course policy that requires a certain level of performance on the assessment to earn a passing grade in the course. The faculty may also adopt a policy that students who do not meet SLOs on course-based key assessments be required to do additional work before moving on from the course, even if they earn a passing score overall. At the same time, relying solely on CBA feedback and course grades without ever attending to the bigger picture of student development short-circuits a rich opportunity to support more holistic student learning.

Methods for developmental assessment will be as rich and varied as counselor education programs. Some programs may task the systematic developmental assessment process to the faculty as a whole, others may appoint a student development committee, and still others may task a student-specific advisory committee with reviewing progress and providing feedback. This assessment may be calendar-based or milestone-based. In a calendar-based assessment, reviews are conducted at one time each year, at the end of each semester, or on a rolling basis. A gateway-based assessment includes reviews triggered at designated course or program transitions. For example, the program members may review all students who have reached a certain number of completed credit hours each semester, or the faculty may build review into certain gateway or transition courses. Prerequisite clinical courses, application processes for practicum and internship, and applications for comprehensive examinations or dissertations provide natural points for reviewing overall student progress and readiness to progress in the program.

As with development of the SLO assessment plan as a whole, it is critical that faculty members tailor these decisions to the unique characteristics of their programs. What is practical and efficient for a faculty of five in a full-time cohort program with few or no adjunct instructors will be quite different than what is practical and efficient for a faculty of 20 in a part-time, student-paced program with equally as many adjunct instructors. Similarly, program administrators who require applications, gateway interviews or performances, or advising checks at certain points may find themselves better able to integrate advisor-led systematic review processes compared with program administrators who are more dispersed in their operations.

The third requirement is that the program has a plan for how the assessment will occur. If you have reached this point in the book, you have already walked through the process of specifying procedures for assessing student learning in core curricular areas, field experiences, and capstone activities such as comprehensive examinations and dissertations; you have also considered procedures by which you will attend to assessment of candidate dispositions. At this stage, then, one simply needs to pull together the assessment activities that will be used and the broader level considerations of responsible parties and timing of assessment.

Next, programs must specify measures used to assess "key performance indicators of student learning" (CACREP 2016 Standard 4.F) and "key professional dispositions" (CACREP 2016 Standard 4.G). If you followed the process of identifying assessments and creating related measures earlier in this book, this element should flow naturally from your planning process. However, it will be helpful to determine the broader process of review format. In a gateway system, for example, the program faculty may decide to focus attention on three major SLOs and may connect those SLOs with the CBAs, and they may document via a systematic review form or document kept in student files. The program members may also decide to send an official letter noting the status of the review and including attention to faculty commendations as well as suggestions for continued growth. In smaller or more intimate programs, the program faculty may utilize advising rituals as a way of pulling together assessments from a variety of sources and making overall decisions about student progress. For example, a doctoral program may include focused student review and feedback at the end of each academic year, with comprehensive examinations, and at the dissertation proposal. Whatever the format, the program members will specify what will be reviewed and how those materials will be documented.

Next, programs will indicate procedures for "review of analysis of data" (CACREP 2016 Standards 4.F and 4.G). As with previous items, the process of specifying assessments and measures to be used flows naturally to the decision about how to analyze and use data. Inherent in this step is the need to specify level of performance expected and possibility of using data to facilitate development even before formal, systematic reviews. Again, steps used here will depend on individual program considerations including format and housing of data. Program members with centralized AMSs may have ready access to individual-level reports. Program members without these systems will need to design procedures for tracking individual-level data for consideration.

Finally, programs must articulate processes for student retention and remediation. Faculty members who identify concerns with academic, personal, or clinical progress are responsible for calling attention to these concerns and working with students to promote growth toward competency. Ideally, such a process is conducted in a transparent, open manner (Foster, Leppma, & Hutchinson, 2014; Foster & McAdams, 2009). Because there is a considerable body of literature on best practices in remediation and gatekeeping, we address this consideration in the next section.

Best Practices in Remediation and Gatekeeping

Several counseling scholars have attended to the importance of strong performance assessment procedures in identifying and supporting students who struggle with counseling knowledge or skills or who demonstrate problematic behaviors. As is illustrated throughout the *2016 Standards* (CACREP, 2016) and the *ACA Code of Ethics* (ACA, 2014), counselor educators have ethical and legal responsibilities to identify problematic behaviors and dispositions and to support students in remediating concerns or exiting the program when students are unable or unwilling to develop the knowledge, skills, or dispositions needed for success in the profession. This process begins prior to admission and continues until a student has graduated, withdraws, or is dismissed from a program (Ziomek-Daigle & Christensen, 2010).

In a systematic content analysis of existing literature, Henderson and Dufrene (2012) found eight primary themes regarding behaviors associated with remediation: ethical behaviors, symptoms of a mental health diagnosis, intrinsic characteristics, counseling skills, feedback, self-reflective abilities, personal difficulties, and procedural compliance. Such themes are consistent with a more direct study of gatekeeping practices in counselor education (Li, Trusty, Lampe, & Lin, 2008; Ziomek-Daigle & Christensen, 2010) and professional psychology (Vacha-Haase, Davenport, & Kerewsky, 2004) programs.

It is noteworthy that so many of these elements requiring remediation are focused on overall student dispositions. In many cases, SLO rubrics may focus more on knowledge and skills than on dispositions, thus creating a gap in the assessment process. Assuming dispositions are important to the counselor education program (and we believe they are), counselor education program members would do well to articulate dispositions as part of overall program expectations. Brown (2013) recently found that approximately one third of counselor education programs utilized assessment instruments to assess problematic behaviors. She found common domains across assessment tools, including attention to dispositions such as responsibility, competence, maturity, and integrity. Use of such assessment tools is another way of making expectations transparent.

Certainly, remediation situations are high-stakes and tend to evoke strong emotions in students and counselor educators alike. Thankfully, strong remediation begins with strong assessment (McAdams & Foster, 2007). McAdams and Foster (2007) provided counselor educators with a guide to just and fair remediation. In particular, they noted the need for remediation plans to meet three specific requirements:

- *Substantive due process*—this includes the need for students to have relevant, comparable plans that are not overly restrictive and that are developed with corrective intent rather than punishment or discipline in mind.
- *Procedural due process*—this includes the need for clear expectations in advance, supervision and support through the process, regular progress evaluation, and thorough documentation.
- *Fundamental fairness*—this includes the need to attend to accessibility of requirements for students as well as adaptability to unique needs and identities of students.

Consistent with the idea of fundamental fairness, reflective awareness is especially important when cultural factors may be at play in educators' assessment of problematic behaviors and students' responses to their learning environments (Goodrich & Shin, 2013).

Counselor educators who identify problematic behaviors or performance deficiencies develop clear, concrete, fair, focused, and responsible plans for helping students develop the behaviors necessary for success in the program and the profession. Henderson and Dufrene (2011) criticized the literature for being focused on dismissal procedures after remediation rather than on remediation as a process itself. They identified several literature-based suggestions for remediation and suggested that potential interventions include attention to supports such as the following:

- personal counseling,
- increased faculty contact,
- increased supervision,
- repetition of academic or clinical coursework,
- removal from clinical work,
- additional assignments,
- additional coursework,
- leave of absence, and
- workshops or continuing education.

These methods for remediation were highly consistent with those found in other studies regarding remediation processes, especially as it related to use of personal counseling as a frequent intervention (Vacha-Haase et al., 2004; Ziomek-Daigle & Christensen, 2010).

Several scholars have provided concrete guidance for developing strong remediation plans. For example, Kress and Protivnak (2009) provided a Professional Development Plan template and guidelines for identification of problematic behaviors, identification of remediation activities, formative feedback, student involvement in the process, signatures as an important part of the process, specified timelines, specified rights to appeal, and provisions for immediate dismissal. These findings are consistent with those of other counseling scholars (e.g., Bhat, 2005; McAdams & Foster, 2007; Wilkerson, 2006). Figure 16.1 includes a sample professional development plan that you may find helpful for documenting concerns and remediation activities. In addition, the resource list at the end of this chapter includes weblinks to several program webpages and handbooks that we found particularly helpful in navigating the student development process.

Student Name: _____ Date: _____

For you to continue to progress toward receiving your counseling degree at (insert name of program), the counseling faculty is collectively requiring that you engage in the following behaviors that relate to the competencies addressed within our program's retention policy.

Competency Area A: _____

1.

2.

3.

Competency Area B: _____

1.

2.

3.

To successfully engage in the aforementioned behaviors, the student will

1.

2.

3.

I understand and agree to the conditions of this document. Any breach of this agreement constitutes grounds for being removed from the counseling program. I understand that I can appeal this plan prior to signing the agreement/plan. I understand and agree to all of the conditions of this document. If I do not follow through on completing all of the tasks outlined in this contract within 1 year, I understand that I will be terminated from the counseling program. I also understand the program's retention policy and am clear that there are certain behaviors that, if violated, will supersede this agreement and may result in immediate removal from the program (e.g., ethics violations).

_____   _____
Date   Student

_____   _____
Date   Faculty Representative

Figure 16.1
Sample Professional Development Plan

Note. From "Professional Development Plans to Remedy Problematic Counseling Student Behaviors," by V. E. Kress and J. J. Protivnak, 2009, *Counselor Education and Supervision, 48,* pp. 165–166. Copyright 2009 by the American Counseling Association. Reprinted with permission.

Resources

Brown, M. (2013). A content analysis of problematic behavior in counselor education programs. *Counselor Education and Supervision, 52,* 179–192. doi:10.1002/j.1556-6978.2013.00036.x

Foster, V. A., & McAdams, C. R., III. (2009). A framework for creating a climate of transparency for professional performance assessment: Fostering student investment in gatekeeping. *Counselor Education and Supervision, 48,* 271–285. doi:10.1002/j.1556-6978.2009.tb00080.x

Goodrich, K. M., & Shin, R. Q. (2013). A culturally responsive intervention for addressing problematic behaviors in counseling students. *Counselor Education and Supervision, 52,* 43–55. doi:10.1002/j.1556-6978.2013.00027.x

Henderson, K. L., & Dufrene, R. L. (2011). Student remediation: Practical considerations for counselor educators and supervisors. From *VISTAS Online.* Retrieved from http://www.counseling.org/resources/library/vistas/2011-v-online/Article_45.pdf

Henderson, K. L., & Dufrene, R. L. (2012). Student behaviors associated with remediation: A content analysis. *Counseling Outcome Research and Evaluation, 3,* 48–60. doi:10.1177/2150137812437364

Kress, V. E., & Protivnak, J. J. (2009). Professional development plans to remedy problematic counseling student behaviors. *Counselor Education and Supervision, 48,* 154–167.

McAdams, C. R., & Foster, V. A. (2007). A guide to just and fair remediation of performance deficiencies. *Counselor Education and Supervision, 47,* 2–13.

University of North Texas, College of Education [website to download exemplar policies and forms; see Master's Student Handbook]: http://www.coe.unt.edu/counseling-and-higher-education/resources/counseling-resources

University of Texas at San Antonio, College of Education and Human Development [website to download exemplar policies and forms]: http://education.utsa.edu/counseling/fitness_to_practice/

Ziomek-Daigle, J., & Christensen, T. M. (2010). An emergent theory of gatekeeping practices in counselor education. *Journal of Counseling & Development, 88,* 407–415. doi:10.1002/j.1556-6678.2010.tb00040.x

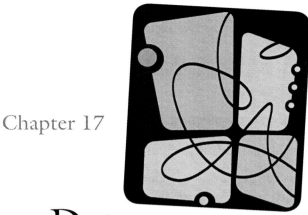

Chapter 17

Using Data
in the SoTL

As mentioned in Chapters 15 and 16, the process of developing and implementing SLOs has benefits beyond immediate, local assessment of what our students are learning. In this final chapter, we urge our readers to take the next step in this process—generating and publishing instructional research.

Accreditation standards mandating evaluation of SLOs provide unique opportunities to take an additional step and to generate instructional research, contributing to the literature on counselor education. The SoTL was initially conceptualized by Boyer (1990) in *Scholarship Reconsidered*. Over time, the Carnegie Foundation identified SoTL as "problem posing about an issue of teaching or learning, study of the problem through methods appropriate to the disciplinary epistemologies, applications of results to practice, communication of results, self-reflection, and peer review" (Cambridge, 2001 as cited in McKinney, 2004, p. 2), or, more simply, the "systematic reflection on teaching and learning made public" (McKinney, 2007, p. 157). Performing instructional research and publishing on the SoTL are logical next steps in building connections between teaching methods and our students' (and, potentially, their future clients') outcomes.

In a recent study of the teaching and learning-related publications in ACA journals, only about 10% of teaching-related articles in counselor education included formal evaluation of SLOs, and rigor of research designs and analyses varied widely (Barrio Minton, Wachter Morris, & Yaites, 2014). With the shift of accreditation bodies to documenting SLOs, counselor educators have an opportunity to use those same SLOs to examine instructional practice.

Requirements to collect SLO data, however, do not guarantee that research will be rigorous or helpful in moving the profession forward. Much like the more traditional scholarship of discovery, SoTL needs to be well-designed. In our experience reading SoTL both within and outside counselor education, publications sometimes appear less rigorous, in part because they may have been designed as an afterthought. Faculty members may realize that a teaching method was powerful, and they want to share that experience. They may not, however, examine the concepts that might have contributed to its power at the same level of depth and theoretical grounding as they would a traditional research study. Similarly, they may focus on student perceptions or reports of satisfaction with the learning experience rather on overt knowledge and skills students gained as a result of the method. Through careful consideration and application of appropriate research design, we have the opportunity to elevate our teaching by examining it thoughtfully, using the data that we are already collecting.

The CACREP 2009 Standards implemented new foci for counselor education around the successful facilitation and assessment of student learning. This trend continued in the 2016 Standards and is reflective of the requirements of other accreditation bodies (e.g., NCATE/CAEP) that would affect both universities and the colleges and schools that house counselor education programs. At the doctoral level, the 2009 Standards outlined basic knowledge and skills related to preparation for and engagement with teaching. The 2016 Standards have increased their specificity and clarity around a few aspects of teaching, including attention to adult development and learning, online instruction, gatekeeping, assessment of learning, and mentoring. This provides counselor educators and doctoral students with the opportunity to think critically about how to assess the methods that we use to train practitioners and future counselor educators.

To train counselors well, we need to be able to understand and explain how we assess student learning. We all benefit when results of well-designed SoTL are disseminated so that we can learn from each other. It is time for teaching-related scholarship to expand beyond discussion of teaching strategies, individual insights, and student enjoyment to a more grounded scholarly discussion, ideally, with direct evidence of learning.

Challenges and Considerations in Conducting Instructional Research

Conducting instructional research for SoTL is a parallel process to conducting research for more traditional scholarship. The primary difference seems to be not in the process itself but in the attention we pay to the details of setting up and conducting sound studies. This challenge is not limited to counselor education and may be linked to how we think about ourselves as teachers and researchers. Performing rigorous instructional research means melding one's identity as a teacher and a researcher, building intentional assignments while also considering research design and data collection.

First, when we are describing instructional research, we are explicitly moving beyond just a description of a technique. Although there is room for a thorough discussion of a technique, even one without initial outcome data, there needs to be a rationale for that particular technique. What is the rationale that can be built from not only the counseling literature but also from theories of adult learning? If this is an innovative technique that is a significant departure from learning theories, what is the rationale for why it could be successful? Demonstrating intentionality in our teaching techniques and grounding them in the substantial learning-related research will help us highlight why we think that our classroom methods work.

Second, as with any research study, the purpose of the study and the research questions need to be explicitly stated and operationalized. This will mean attending to these factors prior to engaging in the teaching activity. All too often, it seems that the SoTL-related papers in our field are based on excitement about how well something worked and a desire to share that with others. If you anticipate that an assignment or class activity might generate good learning outcomes, preplanning can go a long way toward helping construct sound instructional research to evaluate whether it was effective. This also means moving beyond questions that solely focus on satisfaction, enjoyment, or personal meaning to incorporate measurements of knowledge and skill acquisition.

With clearly operationalized variables and research questions, selecting an appropriate sample will also be easier. It makes sense that initial evaluations of techniques and teaching approaches might take place in a single program or single classroom. With planning, however, there is increased ability to collaborate across programs or to use multiple measurements to increase generalizability or to reduce threats to validity.

Faculty members who engage in SoTL and utilize quantitative designs should select instruments that are validated and psychometrically sound or utilize instrument design protocols to construct surveys. Training outside raters to assess learning products could also provide an additional way to assess learning while minimizing potential instructor bias. Looking at course sequencing and concurrent work with clients in field experiences might also open up opportunities to explore immediate course impact as well the relationship of learning to clinical work, client outcomes, and depth and breadth of learning in subsequent courses.

With prior planning, the possibility also exists to select alternate designs to the traditional quantitative survey response. For example, single-subject, mixed-methods, and qualitative designs might lend themselves well to examining learning that occurs in the classroom. Of particular relevance is determining the proper design prior to data collection. Qualitative methods differ widely and should be given adequate care and consideration in determining the best method to address the research questions. In addition, with qualitative methods, it is particularly important to recognize potential researcher–instructor isolation and to use safeguards to minimize bias and conflict of interest. For specific considerations and challenges for qualitative and quantitative designs, see Table 17.1.

What we urge counselor educators who hope to contribute to SoTL is to approach instructional research like any other research project. Start with a good research question. Choose the methodology that is best tailored to answer that question. Identify your source(s) of data. Limit threats to internal and external validity. Analyze data using appropriate statistics. Critically reflect on the data analyses to better understand potential implications for teaching, research, and practice. In doing so, you will be strengthening your own teaching practice (and research skills) and meaningfully contributing to the body of knowledge available to counselor educators and our sister professions.

Table 17.1
Challenges and Considerations in Instructional Research

Type of Design	Challenges	Considerations
Qualitative	Designs overly general or not named	Determine design and analysis prior to data collection
	Researcher/instructor isolation	Incorporate safeguards to minimize conflicts of interest and researcher/instructor bias
	Depth and breadth of data collected	Consider learning artifacts and ways of measuring aspects of student growth beyond personal reflection
	Focus on personal reflection rather than skill or knowledge acquisition	Specify RQs and appropriate analyses in advance
Quantitative	Designs overly general or not named	Clarify ways to minimize coercion or instructor bias
	Researcher/instructor isolation	Use resources and analyses geared to small sample sizes
	Excessive attention to descriptive statistics	Consider series of single-subject explorations
	Lack of power	Conduct a priori power analyses to determine appropriate sample size
	Lack of attention to effect size	Analyze results for effect size
	Limited match between RQs and analysis	Match design and instrumentation to possible analyses
	Limitations rarely owned	Discuss limitations frankly

Note. RQs = research questions.

Part IV
Applications
• • •

Let's be honest. Have you read this book, or did you just come here surfing for assignment ideas? If you do not yet have a firm understanding of SLO evaluation, *go back now*. Make sure you understand *what* and *why* you are doing and why it is so important to be intentional rather than just piece assignments together. Then, come back and dive in.

Okay, that said, by now you have thoroughly explored all of the elements of the SLO assessment process. We hope that you have been thinking of opportunities to apply these principles within your own courses, field experiences, and programs as a whole. The remainder of this book includes edited chapters in which counselor educators discuss key considerations for assessing learning in each of the CACREP core curricular and specialty areas. We selected authors who were known for their work related to the core and specialty areas. We asked two things: to tie their work directly to the CACREP 2016 Standards and to show us a richness of options for addressing the tasks at hand.

We provide these chapters to you as a starting point for exploration rather than a recipe approach or a single-stop shop. We hope you will look to the examples after first considering the big picture of what you want to know for your unique program. Then, with intentionality, creativity, and local context that only you can bring to your process, perhaps you will find the following exemplars helpful for approaching your tasks. Feel free to adapt the assignments and corresponding rubrics in ways that work for you.

— *Carrie A. Wachter Morris, Casey A. Barrio Minton, and Donna M. Gibson*

Chapter 18

Professional Counseling Orientation and Ethical Practice

Margaret R. Lamar and Tyler M. Kimbel

Professional Counseling Orientation and Ethical Practice is the first core curricular area listed in the CACREP 2016 Standards under Section 2: Professional Counseling Identity, and this is for good reason. The content within this core area should be taught early and often throughout counselor education programs to help CITs establish a solid foundation of knowledge upon which they can build their professional identity and clinical skills. Students enrolled in entry-level (i.e., master's-level) counseling programs begin developing a strong understanding of who professional counselors are through orientation processes at the beginning of their programs (Gibson, Dollarhide, & Moss, 2010). Additionally, counseling students should be able to recognize and articulate the importance of professional identity in the current context of the evolving counseling profession and what it means to have a unified counselor identity first, clarified by their chosen specialty area second. It is also essential for counselor educators to help CITs develop, in addition to knowledge and skills, attitudes and beliefs that strengthen professional identity (Owens & Neale-McFall, 2014). Orientative endeavors further help students obtain perspectives about the nature of counselors' work, how counseling fits into the broader landscape of helping professions, and also what kind of professional future they might expect before spending valuable time and resources completing a graduate program (Granello & Hazler, 1998). The instruction of ethical practice goes hand-in-hand with laying the introductory, foundational groundwork of professional counseling orientation in that it provides students with the knowledge and skills necessary to become competent and ethical practitioners who are able to meet the health, safety, and welfare needs of the public that they serve within the arena of their chosen specialty area.

Content standards within the professional counseling orientation and ethical practice core curricular area provide opportunities for student learning related to the rich history of the counseling profession (CACREP 2016 Standard 2.F.1.a), the multiple roles and functions of professional counselors (CACREP 2016 Standards 2.F.1.b, 2.F.1.c, 2.F.1.d), and the ethical responsibility counselors have to their clients (CACREP 2016 Standard 2.F.1.i). Student learning that occurs within this core area truly sets the stage for student learning to expand throughout the seven other core areas, as the topics related to orientation and ethics are essential in facilitating the development of professional identity in beginning counselors. As counselor educators assess SLOs in this area, it is pertinent to go beyond assessment of basic knowledge and to examine student comprehension of factors that define the counseling profession, counselor identity, counselor development, and current issues in counseling. This helps students jump-start their journeys to becoming professional counselors by acclimating them to the profession and by fostering an early adoption of a professional counseling identity. Subsequently, assessing student learning related to ethical practice is key to ensuring that CITs understand the role of their professional ethical code in not only guiding counseling practice but also in helping differentiate counselors from other mental health professionals. It is crucial for counselor educators to make certain that students know their professional code of ethics and how to apply this knowledge to their day-to-day work with clients. A significant aspect of knowing how to utilize ethical applications is the requirement that one knows how to identify ethical dilemmas, a skill that should also be included in assessing SLOs related to this core area.

The following suggested assignments were carefully developed to enhance student learning and assessment of SLOs related to material covered in the core area of professional counseling orientation and ethical practice. The Professional Development Planning Portfolio assignment is designed to be a starting point for counseling students to be able to identify and begin taking ownership of a professional counselor identity. The portfolio will help students initiate a professional development plan that they can follow and expand on as they matriculate through their graduate programs. This assignment also introduces students to the real-world life of counselors and addresses other important topics such as self-care plans, active engagement within the counseling profession, and knowledge about licensure/certification processes. The Exploring Counseling and Related Mental Health Professions assignment is intended to help students deepen their understanding of the professional identity of counselors and to be able to clearly differentiate counseling from the other mental health professions. Finally, the Ethics Group Project is designed to increase students' ability to identify ethical dilemmas and work through them by applying an ethical decision-making model. Through this activity, students should be able to demonstrate their capacity for resolving ethically challenging situations in an appropriate and professional manner.

Professional Development Planning Portfolio

SLOs assessed: CACREP 2016 Standards 2.F.1.b, 2.F.1.c, 2.F.1.d, 2.F.1.e, 2.F.1.f, 2.F.1.g, 2.F.1.k

Throughout the semester/quarter, you will work on compiling a portfolio with multiple components addressing various areas of your professional development. The purpose of this portfolio is to design a professional development plan that will continue to evolve throughout your professional career. This will be a living document that continues to develop beyond this class. Do not view these professional developments as complete but rather as a jumping off point to developing your professional identity throughout this program and your career as a counselor.

Self-Care Plan (Standard 2.F.1.l)

Counselor impairment is a major issue for many counselors. Using a self-care plan is an important tool to promote your own wellness and to provide the best care for your clients. You should develop a self-care plan to maintain your wellness as a counselor. This list should be things you can do (or already do) on a regular basis to keep you healthy. The goal is for counselors to consistently engage in these behaviors, not just look to them when they are feeling impaired. Include two to three appropriate activities or behaviors in each of the following categories on the basis of Myers and Sweeney's (2008) Essential Self model of wellness: creative, coping, social, essential, and physical.

You can draw inspiration from any of the readings, your classmates, the self-care assessment, or your own imagination. This list should continue to evolve; it is not final.

Counselor Licensure/Certification Requirements (Standard 2.F.1.g)

Write a short overview of the licensure or certification requirements for becoming a professional counselor in your state on the basis of the professional credential you anticipate seeking after graduation (e.g., licensed professional counselor, licensed/certified school counselor, licensed marriage and family therapist). List the requirements for the state in which you plan to reside and practice. Cite the website or resource where you found your information. Most U.S. states have a website devoted to the governing authority for counselor licensure (e.g., licensure board). The

ACA website has links for licensed professional counselor licensure information by state; the ASCA website has links for school counselor licensure/certification by state. For students outside the United States, a government website should have the information you need. In your overview, be sure to include the following items: licensure title for professional counselors (e.g., licensed professional counselor, licensed mental health counselor, licensed marriage and family therapist), education requirements, supervised practice/experiential requirements, examination(s) required, application process, and any other requirements that one would need to fulfill to obtain licensure as a professional counselor in your state.

Continuing Education and Licensure Maintenance (Standard 2.F.1.g)

Write a short overview of continuing education and other licensure status maintenance requirements for your state or the state in which you plan to reside and practice. Cite the website or resource where you found your information. Along with the above requirements, find and list three resources for obtaining continuing education.

Professional Engagement (Standard 2.F.1.f)

Remaining engaged in professional organizations is an important aspect of developing your professional counselor identity. Write an overview of three professional counseling organizations you are interested in joining. In your overview, include the following items: name of the organization, area of counseling the organization represents, how to become a member, membership benefits, current news or events, opportunities for professional development, and ways to get involved in the organization. Cite the organization's website. You may include national, international, regional, state, or local counseling organizations.

Counseling Specialty Area Development (Standard 2.F.1.a)

In addition to having a professional counselor identity, many counselors also have an identity related to a chosen specialty area. Research two counseling specialty areas you may be interested in pursuing (e.g., addiction, career, clinical mental health, clinical rehabilitation, college counseling and student affairs, marriage, couple and family, school). Include the following items for each specialty area you identify: a brief history (e.g., how did this area come to be a part of professional counseling?), the populations counselors may work with, typical workplace settings, professional organizations, required education, and available licensure or certifications.

A Day in the Life: Learning From Counselors (Standards 2.F.1.b, 2.F.1.c)

The purpose of this assignment is for you to deepen your understanding of counseling from someone who has experience in the field. Find a practicing counselor to interview about his or her work. It is recommended that you look for someone working in a specialty area or with a population in which you are interested. Make an appointment and prepare questions ahead of time. Talk to him or her about his or her typical work day, professional interests, challenges, how he or she works or interacts with related helping professionals, professional identity, population/specialty area, and any other topic that you would like to address. Keep your interview around 30–45 minutes. Write a three- to four-page paper and include the following items: background information on the counselor you interviewed (e.g., work setting, years of experience, licenses or certifications), highlights from your interview, and personal reflections on what you learned about the profession and your identity as a counselor.

Professional Advocacy Proposal (Standards 2.F.1.d, 2.F.1.e)

For this proposal, design an advocacy project that promotes the counseling profession. In your proposal, include the following items: the purpose of your advocacy project, who you hope to reach through your advocacy efforts, a description of the activities related to the project, anticipated outcomes, and how you believe this project will promote the counseling profession. Discuss your rationale for the area of advocacy you have chosen, using support from the literature. Table 18.1 includes the rubric associated with this assignment.

Table 18.1
Professional Development Planning Portfolio Rubric

Criterion (CACREP Standard)	Does Not Meet Expectations	Meets Expectations	Exceeds Expectations
Self-care plan (2.F.1.l)	Plan is missing one or more categories from the wellness model, lacks a sufficient number of self-care activities within one or more categories, or contains inappropriate activities; plan does not demonstrate understanding of counselor wellness or self-care.	Plan includes appropriate self-care activities in all categories; each category includes two to three relevant activities; most activities are clearly described; plan demonstrates a basic understanding of counselor wellness and self-care.	Plan goes above and beyond the number of appropriate self-care activities required in each category; activities are described clearly and comprehensively; plan demonstrates an exceptional understanding of counselor wellness and holistic self-care.
Counselor licensure or certification requirements (2.F.1.g)	Overview is missing one or more items, lacks sufficient detail in two or more areas, is missing appropriate citation, or contains blatant incorrect information; overview does not demonstrate a basic understanding of professional licensure or certification process and requirements.	Overview includes appropriate description of all items; most items are clearly described; overview demonstrates a basic understanding of professional licensure or certification process and requirements.	Overview goes above and beyond in providing details for each item required; descriptions are clear and comprehensive; overview demonstrates an exceptional understanding of professional licensure or certification process and requirements.
Continuing education and licensure maintenance (2.F.1.g)	Overview is missing one or more items, missing appropriate citations, or contains blatantly incorrect information; overview does not demonstrate a basic understanding of continuing education resources and/or licensure maintenance requirements.	Overview includes appropriate description of requirements and education resources; overview demonstrates a basic understanding of continuing education resources and licensure maintenance requirements.	Overview goes above and beyond in providing details for requirements and education resources; overview demonstrates an exceptional understanding of continuing education resources and licensure maintenance requirements.
Professional engagement (2.F.1.f)	Overview is missing one or more items, lacks sufficient details in two or more items, is missing appropriate citations, or contains blatantly incorrect information; overview does not demonstrate a basic understanding of professional counseling organizations and related opportunities for engagement.	Overview includes appropriate description of all items; most items are clearly described; overview demonstrates a basic understanding of professional counseling organizations and related opportunities for engagement.	Overview goes above and beyond in providing details for each item required; descriptions are clear and comprehensive; overview demonstrates an exceptional understanding of professional counseling organizations and related opportunities for engagement.
Counseling specialty area development (2.F.1.a)	Overview is missing one or more items, lacks sufficient details in two or more items, is missing appropriate citations, or contains blatantly incorrect information; overview does not demonstrate a basic understanding of at least two counseling specialty areas.	Overview includes appropriate description of all items; most items are clearly described; overview demonstrates a basic understanding of at least two counseling specialty areas.	Overview goes above and beyond in providing details for each item required; descriptions are clear and comprehensive; overview demonstrates an exceptional understanding of at least two counseling specialty areas.
A day in the life: Learning from counselors (2.F.1.b, 2.F.1.c)	Overview is missing one or more items, lacks sufficient details in two or more items, is missing appropriate citations, or contains blatantly incorrect information; overview does not demonstrate a basic understanding of roles, responsibilities, and functions of professional counselors.	Overview includes appropriate description of all items; most items are clearly described; overview demonstrates a basic understanding of roles, responsibilities, and functions of professional counselors.	Overview goes above and beyond in providing details for each item required, descriptions are clear and comprehensive; overview demonstrates an exceptional understanding of roles, responsibilities, and functions of professional counselors.

(Continued)

Table 18.1 (*Continued*)
Professional Development Planning Portfolio Rubric

Criterion (CACREP Standard)	Does Not Meet Expectations	Meets Expectations	Exceeds Expectations
Professional advocacy proposal (2.F.1.d, 2.F.1.e)	Proposal is missing one or more items, lacks sufficient details in two or more items, is missing appropriate support from the literature, or contains blatantly incorrect information; proposal does not demonstrate a basic understanding of professional advocacy.	Proposal includes appropriate description of a relevant advocacy project and includes appropriate support from the literature, and most items are clearly described; proposal demonstrates a basic understanding of professional advocacy.	Proposal goes above and beyond in providing details for each item required; ideas are fully supported with current and relevant literature; descriptions are clear and comprehensive; proposal demonstrates an exceptional understanding of professional advocacy.

Note. CACREP = Council for Accreditation of Counseling and Related Educational Programs.

Exploring Counseling and Related Mental Health Professions

SLOs assessed: CACREP 2016 Standards 2.F.1.b, 2.F.1.f, 2.F.1.g, 2.F.1.i

This assignment is focused on helping you learn about the professional identity, scope of practice, professional organizations, licensure requirements, ethical codes, and day-to-day functions of counselors and related mental health professionals.

Create a table comparing the following mental health professions. This table should include the following roles: professional counselors, marriage and family therapists, clinical social workers, addictions counselors, psychologists, and psychiatrists.

For each of the professionals listed above, include the following items in the table you create:

- Primary functions, day-to-day work tasks, officially recognized scope of practice, and common workplace settings for each type of professional
- Primary professional organizations, such as credentialing bodies or professional membership associations to which these professionals typically belong
- Available licensure or certification titles for each mental health professional
- Professional code of ethics/code of conduct followed by each mental health professional

The table you develop should present each item for all professionals in a clear and succinct manner. After your table is complete, write a two- to three-page reflection paper about the information you included in your mental health professions table. In your reflection paper, respond to the following questions: How are the other mental health professions similar to the counseling profession? How are they different? What contextual factors contribute to these similarities and differences? Table 18.2 includes the rubric associated with this assignment.

Ethics Group Project

SLO assessed: CACREP 2016 Standard 2.F.1.i

The purpose of this assignment is to develop your ethical decision-making skills and work with others to solve a counseling agency ethical dilemma. Students will be put into groups to work collaboratively as if they were professional counselors working at the same agency. You and the rest of your team will create a vignette with at least two ethical issues, chosen from the list below, and turn it in to the instructor. Your team will then be given a vignette created by another team.

Ethical issues can be chosen from the list below. (We will draw to determine which team gets to choose first. Each team will choose one topic during the first round, and then we will reverse the team order to choose your second issue. Each issue can only be chosen by one team.)

Table18.2
Exploring Counseling and Related Mental Health Professions Rubric

Use the following key to assess each item in the rubric below:

2 = *Exceeds expectations*. Table goes above and beyond in providing accurate details for each item across all professionals; all item descriptions are clear and succinct, yet comprehensive in nature.

1 = *Meets expectations*. Table is complete; includes accurate information for each item across all professionals; most item descriptions are clear and succinct.

0 = *Does not meet expectations*. Table is missing one or more items, multiple item descriptions include inaccurate information, and/or the table is blatantly insufficient.

Add up scores across each row to calculate a total row score; then sum the total row scores to determine a combined total score (highest combined total score possible = 60). Use the following ranges to determine the degree to which the overall learning outcomes have been met.

Total Scores: 46–60 = *Exceeds expectations*; 30–45 = *Meets expectations*; 29 and below = *Does not meet expectations*

1. Table 2.F.1.b. Knowledge of primary professional functions

Professional Counselors	☐ 2	☐ 1	☐ 0
Marriage and Family Therapists	☐ 2	☐ 1	☐ 0
Clinical Social Workers	☐ 2	☐ 1	☐ 0
Addiction Counselors	☐ 2	☐ 1	☐ 0
Psychologists	☐ 2	☐ 1	☐ 0
Psychiatrists	☐ 2	☐ 1	☐ 0

Total row score _____

2. Table 2.F.1.f. Knowledge of professional organizations

Professional Counselors	☐ 2	☐ 1	☐ 0
Marriage and Family Therapists	☐ 2	☐ 1	☐ 0
Clinical Social Workers	☐ 2	☐ 1	☐ 0
Addiction Counselors	☐ 2	☐ 1	☐ 0
Psychologists	☐ 2	☐ 1	☐ 0
Psychiatrists	☐ 2	☐ 1	☐ 0

Total row score _____

3. Table 2.F.1.g. Knowledge of available licensure or certification titles

Professional Counselors	☐ 2	☐ 1	☐ 0
Marriage and Family Therapists	☐ 2	☐ 1	☐ 0
Clinical Social Workers	☐ 2	☐ 1	☐ 0
Addiction Counselors	☐ 2	☐ 1	☐ 0
Psychologists	☐ 2	☐ 1	☐ 0
Psychiatrists	☐ 2	☐ 1	☐ 0

Total row score _____

4. Table 2.F.1.i. Knowledge of appropriate ethical codes

Professional Counselors	☐ 2	☐ 1	☐ 0
Marriage and Family Therapists	☐ 2	☐ 1	☐ 0
Clinical Social Workers	☐ 2	☐ 1	☐ 0
Addiction Counselors	☐ 2	☐ 1	☐ 0
Psychologists	☐ 2	☐ 1	☐ 0
Psychiatrists	☐ 2	☐ 1	☐ 0

Total row score _____

5. *Reflection Paper:* Ability to identify, understand, and synthesize the similarities and differences between counseling and related mental health professions. (This item total score is multiplied by 6 to determine the total row score for the reflection paper.)

Professional Counselors	☐ 2	☐ 1	☐ 0
Marriage and Family Therapists	☐ 2	☐ 1	☐ 0
Clinical Social Workers	☐ 2	☐ 1	☐ 0
Addiction Counselors	☐ 2	☐ 1	☐ 0
Psychologists	☐ 2	☐ 1	☐ 0
Psychiatrists	☐ 2	☐ 1	☐ 0

Total row score _____ × 6 = _____

Combined Total Score: _____ *Check one:* ☐ 29 and below (does not meet expectations)
☐ 30–45 (meets expectations)
☐ 46–60 (exceeds expectations)

- Supervision
- Multiple relationships
- Boundary violations
- Counselor impairment
- Client dependence
- Value conflict
- Multicultural issues
- Informed consent
- Record keeping
- Online counseling
- Technology in counseling
- Children and adolescents
- Unethical behavior by a colleague
- Confidentiality
- Sexual attraction
- Competence
- Couple and family
- Groups
- Gifts
- Bartering

Your team will use an ethical decision-making model to approach the ethical dilemmas presented. You will orally present your case to the class, outlining the issues of concern, discussing potential courses of action and their implications, highlighting current research supporting the steps your team took, and presenting the final decision(s) you made. Table 18.3 includes the rubric associated with this assignment.

Table 18.3
Ethics Group Project Rubric

Criterion (CACREP Standard)	Does Not Meet Expectations	Meets Expectations	Exceeds Expectations
Ethics group project/ presentation (2.F.1.i)	Presentation is missing components of or does not utilize an ethical decision-making model; does not identify one or more ethical issues present in vignette; presentation lacks sufficient details in outlining a resolution for ethical issues; resolution includes inappropriate course of action; ethical codes are not cited for ethical issues; lacks support from the literature for ethical decisions; presentation does not demonstrate a basic ability to identify ethical dilemmas or to apply an ethical decision-making model.	Presentation appropriately utilizes an ethical decision-making model; sufficiently identifies ethical issues present in vignette; presentation provides sufficient details in outlining a resolution for ethical issues; resolution includes appropriate course of action; ethical codes are cited in outlining a resolution for ethical dilemmas; resolution includes appropriate support from the literature; presentation demonstrates a basic ability to identify ethical dilemmas and to apply an ethical decision-making model to resolve ethical issues.	Presentation goes above and beyond in applying an ethical decision-making model within a cultural context; identifies more than two potential ethical issues present in vignette; descriptions of ethical decision-making processes are clear and comprehensive; ethical codes are appropriately cited in the resolution for ethical dilemmas; an ethical course of action is chosen and clearly described; presentation demonstrates an exceptional ability to identify ethical dilemmas or to apply an ethical decision-making model to resolve ethical issues.

Note. CACREP = Council for Accreditation of Counseling and Related Educational Programs.

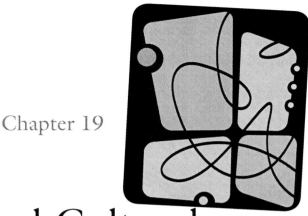

Chapter 19

Social and Cultural Diversity

C. Peeper McDonald and Catherine Y. Chang

It is well known that the study of social and cultural diversity is a mainstay of the counseling profession and is growing more relevant as the population of clients and students we serve as professionals, educators, and supervisors grows more diverse (Hanna & Cardona, 2012; Rockquemore, Brunsma, & Delgado, 2009). As a result of this growing social and cultural diversity, the fourth force in counseling known as multiculturalism is an important area of focus that must be infused in all areas of counselor training and deserves more attention related to expanding the repertoire of techniques used in multicultural counseling and training (Hanna & Cardona, 2012; Pedersen, 1991). The counseling profession is adamant about the study and integration of social and cultural diversity as it relates to counselor training and as a result is treated as a core competency and standards for counselor education programs.

As the counseling profession embraces multiculturalism, it is imperative that counselor educators meet expectations for accountability in teaching CITs about social and cultural diversity. The counselor education literature points to an assessment of students' knowledge, skills, and attitudes in any content area; however, the attainment of minimum competencies related to social and cultural diversity can be difficult to evaluate in students (Arredondo et al., 1996). Learning about social and cultural diversity requires students to look inwardly at who they are as cultural beings and to gain awareness of ways in which they affect others for the ultimate goal of understanding how this may have an impact on the counseling relationship. For many students, this process can be difficult and often makes them feel vulnerable.

In response to the complex yet rewarding task of teaching and evaluating students in the area of social and cultural diversity, in this chapter we provide three activities and rubrics to assess learning in the CACREP (2016) common core competencies related to social and cultural diversity. The first activity is a worksheet that requires students to articulate and discuss what cultural groups they are members of, to identify the privileges they receive as a result of being members of these particular groups, and to reflect on how being members in a privileged group(s) affects their work with diverse clients. The second assignment is a photo-journaling activity that asks students to use photographs and reflective writing as media to discuss who students are in relation to others, client populations that may be difficult to work with and how students envision overcoming this, and how who they are as human beings affects their overall work with clients. The final project is a summative examination of a particular diverse population, the history and current contexts of that population, and reflection of the student's initial and current responses toward members of that population.

Membership Has Its Privileges
(Chang, Gnilka, & O'Hara, 2014)

SLOs assessed: CACREP 2016 Standards 2.F.2.d, 2.F.2.h

White privilege can be defined as an invisible knapsack of unearned assets that can be used to cash in each day for advantages not given to those who do not fit this mold (McIntosh, 1989). Memberships in various cultural groups also can be associated with certain privileges. In this four-part activity, students are first asked to name specific cultural groups with which they identify and to list privileges associated with that group. Then, they are asked to generate examples of how the privileges that they experience affect others who do not belong to this same group. After participants spend time listing and personally reflecting upon the cultural groups with which they share membership and the accompanying privileges they receive, facilitators hold a group discussion regarding how this activity fosters students' understanding of self and culturally diverse clients in addition to what role students play as future counselors in eliminating biases, prejudices, and processes of intentional and unintentional oppression and discrimination on the basis of these privileges. After completion of the discussion, students are asked to reflect on the activity in a three- to four-page paper in which they name specific cultural groups with which they identify, list privileges associated with each group, and reflect on the following prompts:

- How might the privileges I experience affect others who do not belong to this same group?
- How does membership in a privileged group affect my work with clients who do not share the same privilege(s)?

Table 19.1 includes the rubric associated with this assignment.

Photo-Journal (Adapted From Orr & Smith, 2013)

SLOs assessed: CACREP 2016 Standards 2.F.2.a, 2.F.2.b, 2.F.2.h

This activity is designed to be used as a cumulative experience across the span of a semester. Participants will create photographs that represent/embody an expression of who the students

Table 19.1
Membership Has Its Privileges Rubric

Criterion (CACREP Standard)	Does Not Meet Expectations	Meets Expectations	Exceeds Expectations
The impact of heritage, attitudes, beliefs, understandings, and acculturative experiences on an individual's view of others (2.F.2.d)	Demonstrates minimal knowledge of attitudes and beliefs about privilege and thoughtfulness related to how privileges affect culturally diverse clients.	Demonstrates acceptable knowledge of attitudes and beliefs about privilege and is able to contribute to the discussion related to how privileges affect culturally diverse clients.	Demonstrates exceptional knowledge of attitudes and beliefs about privilege and is able to substantially contribute to the group's learning related to how privileges affect culturally diverse clients.
The effects of power and privilege for counselors and clients (2.F.2.e)	Demonstrates minimal awareness of the effects of power and privilege for counselors and clients.	Demonstrates acceptable awareness of the effects of power and privilege for counselors and clients and is able to contribute to the discussion related to how privilege affects relationships with clients who do not belong in the same group.	Demonstrates exceptional awareness of the effects of power and privilege for counselors and clients and is able to substantially contribute to the discussion related to how privilege affects relationships with clients who do not belong in the same group.
Strategies for identifying and eliminating barriers, prejudices, and processes of intentional and unintentional oppression and discrimination (2.F.2.h)	Demonstrates minimal understanding of personal role in eliminating biases, prejudices, and processes of intentional and unintentional oppression and discrimination as it specifically relates to privilege.	Demonstrates acceptable understanding and is able to contribute to a discussion about personal role in eliminating biases/prejudices and intentional and unintentional oppression related to privilege.	Demonstrates exceptional understanding and is able to substantially contribute to a discussion about privilege and personal role in eliminating biases/prejudices and intentional and unintentional oppression.

Note. CACREP = Council for Accreditation of Counseling and Related Educational Programs.

are in addition to photographs that represent a client population that they envision will be difficult for them to work with. Each student will type a brief journal entry reflection (minimum one paragraph and maximum one double-spaced typed page) to accompany each photograph. Facilitators are encouraged to promote confidentiality of the photo-journals while also encouraging group discussions about the experience. The photo-journal reflection(s) will respond to the following prompts:

1. Who am I? (In what cultural groups do I feel I have membership?) Why did I choose this photograph to represent me?
2. Of the cultural groups with which I identify, which of these have privilege in society, and how have I experienced that privilege?
3. In what ways does the photograph fall short of representing me? What identities do I hold that may not be visible? How have I experienced mislabeling because of this? How might I have mislabeled others on the basis of appearance?
4. How does my photograph speak to multicultural and pluralistic trends, including characteristics and concerns within and among diverse groups nationally and internationally?
5. With what types of clients am I most concerned about working and why? What can I do to overcome the fear and anxiety related to working with this client population?
6. A bias I keep hidden is . . .
7. How does this photo-journal contribute to my development and understanding of theories of multicultural counseling, identity development, and social justice?
8. What oppression and prejudice has this client population historically faced?
9. What did you learn about yourself and others from this assignment?

Table 19.2 includes the rubric associated with this assignment.

Table 19.2
Photo-Journal Rubric

Criterion (CACREP Standard)	Does Not Meet Expectations	Meets Expectations	Exceeds Expectations
Multicultural and pluralistic characteristics within and among diverse groups nationally and internationally (2.F.2.a)	Demonstrates minimal knowledge of multicultural and pluralistic trends, including characteristics and concerns within and among diverse groups as presented in content of photo-journal.	Demonstrates acceptable knowledge of multicultural and pluralistic trends, including characteristics and concerns within and among diverse groups as presented in content of photo-journal, and is able to contribute to the discussion about the photo-journal.	Demonstrates exceptional knowledge of multicultural and pluralistic trends, including characteristics and concerns within and among diverse groups as presented in content of photo-journal, and is able to substantially contribute to the group's learning related to the discussion about the photo-journal.
Theories and models of multicultural counseling, cultural identity development, and social justice and advocacy (2.F.2.b)	Demonstrates minimal knowledge of theories of multicultural counseling, cultural identity development, and social justice and advocacy as presented in content of photo-journal.	Demonstrates acceptable knowledge of theories of multicultural counseling, identity development, and social justice and advocacy as presented in content of photo-journal and students' contributions to the group discussion.	Demonstrates exceptional knowledge of theories of multicultural counseling, identity development, and social justice and advocacy as presented in content of photo-journal and students' substantial contributions to the group discussion.
Strategies for identifying and eliminating barriers, prejudices, and processes of intentional and unintentional oppression and discrimination (2.F.2.h)	Demonstrates minimal understanding of personal strategies in eliminating biases, prejudices, and processes of intentional and unintentional oppression and discrimination as they specifically relate to the photo-journal.	Demonstrates acceptable understanding and is able to contribute to a discussion about personal role in eliminating biases/prejudices and intentional and unintentional oppression related to the process of photo-journaling.	Demonstrates exceptional understanding and is able to substantially contribute to a discussion about photo-journaling and personal role in eliminating biases/prejudices and intentional and unintentional oppression.

Note. CACREP = Council for Accreditation of Counseling and Related Educational Programs.

Crash Course in Another Way of Being
(Adapted From Wachter, 2007)

SLOs assessed: CACREP 2016 Standards 2.F.2.a, 2.F.2.b, 2.F.2.h

For this project, students will identify a group of individuals with whom they might have difficulty working. Once identified, students will be asked to design and implement a plan to build knowledge and understanding of the identified group. This is an assignment that is meant to be comprehensive in nature and requires several weeks of self-reflection, research, planning, and implementation. *This is NOT something that can be left until the last minute.*

To complete this project successfully, students must do the following:

- Identify a group that they lack knowledge about or have encountered challenges with empathy and/or understanding.
- Analyze the dominant or other relevant culture's historical record of oppression, prejudice, or bias toward that group.
- Analyze current popular culture messages (e.g., TV and other media representations) about that group.
- Analyze current themes and trends affecting the identified group.
- Be proactive in procuring an opportunity to directly involve yourself in interviewing, interacting with, and actively hearing and understanding the experiences of at least one member of the identified group. Ideally, this would involve multiple members, with students taking the part of a learner—truly listening and hearing those perspectives and engaging in a positive dialogue and interaction.
- Complete a 10- to 15-page paper on the experience.

The paper will consist of the following:

- Reasons why the identified group was chosen by the individual student (i.e., what are your identified challenges?).
- A synopsis of historical and/or systematic oppression.
- Examples of popular media content and themes.
- A brief synopsis of the experiential activities you were involved in.
- Where the individual(s) you interacted with might fit in the relevant identity models. In the absence of an identity model specific to that group, what parallels can you illuminate? This should include examples from your interaction, citations, and so forth to explain how you reached these conclusions.
- An analysis of your feelings, reactions, and cognitions in regard to your own identity development. Where are you in terms of your development as a cultural being?
- Any impact this activity might have had on you.
- Your overall reflections on your growth and challenges as a cultural human being.

Table 19.3 includes the rubric associated with this assignment.

Table 19.3
Crash Course in Another Way of Being Rubric

Criterion (CACREP Standard)	Does Not Meet Expectations	Meets Expectations	Exceeds Expectations
Personal insight and reflection	Demonstrates minimal attention to reflective components of paper. Any reflection is cursory and surface-level.	Demonstrates acceptable attention to reflective components of paper. Identifies personal biases and discusses his or her personal reflections in context of identity development.	Demonstrates great thought and attention to reflective components of paper. Personal biases are owned and confronted in paper. Reflections on growth and challenges include concrete plans, goals, or details.
Multicultural and pluralistic characteristics within and among diverse groups nationally and internationally (2.F.2.a)	Demonstrates minimal knowledge of multicultural and pluralistic trends, including characteristics and concerns within and among diverse groups as presented in content of paper.	Demonstrates acceptable knowledge of multicultural and pluralistic trends, including characteristics and concerns within and among diverse groups as presented in content of paper, with special emphasis given to student's self-reflection and synthesis of learning.	Demonstrates exceptional knowledge of multicultural and pluralistic trends, including characteristics and concerns within and among diverse groups as presented in content of paper, with special emphasis given to student's self-reflection, synthesis of learning, and impact of learning on future counseling outcomes.
Theories and models of multicultural counseling, cultural identity development, and social justice and advocacy (2.F.2.b)	Demonstrates minimal knowledge of theories of multicultural counseling, cultural identity development, and social justice and advocacy as presented in content of paper.	Demonstrates acceptable knowledge of theories of multicultural counseling, identity development, and social justice and advocacy as presented in content of paper, specifically with regard to student's understanding of identified group.	Demonstrates exceptional knowledge of theories of multicultural counseling, identity development, and social justice and advocacy as presented in content of paper, specifically with regard to student's understanding of identified group and how this understanding affects the student as a future counselor.
Strategies for identifying and eliminating barriers, prejudices, and processes of intentional and unintentional oppression and discrimination (2.F.2.h)	Demonstrates minimal understanding of personal strategies in eliminating biases, prejudices, and processes of intentional and unintentional oppression and discrimination as it specifically relates to the student's identified group, demonstrated within the content of paper.	Demonstrates acceptable understanding and is able to contribute to a discussion about personal role in eliminating biases/prejudices and intentional and unintentional oppression related to the student's identified group, with special regard given to meaningful self-reflection, demonstrated within the content of paper.	Demonstrates exceptional understanding and is able to substantially contribute to a discussion about photojournal and personal role in eliminating biases/prejudices and intentional and unintentional oppression related to the student's identified group, with special regard given to meaningful self-reflection, and the way in which the student plans to become an agent of change, demonstrated within the content of paper.
Quality of writing	Persistent difficulty with writing results in difficulty conveying meaning. Difficulty may include two or more of the following: focus, logic, organization, style, grammar, or APA Style.	Occasional difficulty with writing, but meaning is clear overall. Difficulty may include one or more of the following: focus, logic, organization, style, grammar, or APA Style.	Exceptional, precise quality of writing. Excels in the following areas: focus, logic, organization, style, grammar, and APA Style.

Note. CACREP = Council for Accreditation of Counseling and Related Educational Programs; APA = American Psychological Association.

Chapter 20

Human Growth
and Development

Laura M. Gonzalez and Maria Adele Paredes

*This chapter is dedicated to Dr. Jane E. Myers in recognition of her advocacy
for human development and wellness in the counseling profession.*

• • •

The counseling profession has sought to maintain a core value of promoting human development, growth, and wellness. Indeed, this is part of what differentiates us from similar helping professions that are more focused on treating psychopathology or remediating social contexts (Vacc & Loesch, 2000). From our professional beginnings in vocational development to our present focus on promoting strengths and maintaining wellness, counselors have worked to enhance development for clients in all phases of the life span and across all functional areas (e.g., cognitive, social, emotional, identity, moral, physical, and psychological development; Vacc & Loesch, 2000). Thus, the study of human development focuses on our evolving capabilities and needs across several domains, as contrasted with a focus on symptoms of illness or medical and psychological diagnoses. The counseling literature is vast in which a developmental framework is used, addressing topics such as spiritual growth, addictions, career assessment, consultation in schools, family therapy, and cross-cultural counseling. Thus, counseling curricula incorporate human development as a topic in many places. In addition to the core Human Development course that is often taught, material focused on development can be present in other courses (e.g., career, multicultural, helping skills, group, assessment) and specialty areas (e.g., child, youth, adolescent, adult, geriatric, couple and family, school, and college counseling).

The CACREP 2016 Standards focus on normative development across the life span, encompassing issues of learning, personality, neurobiology, social systems, environmental context, and individual characteristics. The standards also encourage attention to crises, disasters, trauma, addiction, and other stressors that can affect development. Finally, counselors also are encouraged to identify strategies to promote resilient responses and to support wellness across the life span. For programs that include coursework on psychopathology and diagnostic categories, the developmental perspective can provide a helpful counterpoint. Both normative and problematic development can be conceptualized by shifting from an individual diagnostic perspective to a case formulation perspective (Ivey, Ivey, Myers, & Sweeney, 2005; Zalaquett, Fuerth, Stein, Ivey, & Ivey, 2008). In other words, the mental health symptoms being described by clients can be understood developmentally as responses or efforts to cope with the challenges or barriers present in the environment (Ivey & Ivey, 2005).

The thoughts, behaviors, and feelings of clients may be dysfunctional in the current context of their lives but are not necessarily pathological (Zalaquett et al., 2008).

Developmental counseling and therapy (Ivey, 1986) provide one way for instructors and students to make the connection from developmental theory to practice. Thus, following the framework of developmental counseling and therapy, CITs can take a view of clients' psychosocial stressors interacting with their biological, family, cultural, and social contexts that is more consistent with our core values. The developmental counseling assessment interview allows counselors to identify which information processing modalities a client is utilizing to describe the presenting problem, and which modalities may be underutilized or blocked in that specific situation. Thus, an intervention to promote healthy development and wellness could focus on building strengths and promoting increased development in one of the blocked modalities, allowing clients to experience new ways of constructing meaning or solving problems in their lives. Such an intervention also takes environment into consideration, thus addressing contextual stressors, such as poverty or discrimination, in a way that does not pathologize the person experiencing them but focuses on removing barriers and blocks to healthy development.

The assignments and activities that are shared in this chapter are drawn from different courses to model the scope and variety that is possible in addressing development in counseling. However, we encourage readers to use these models creatively and adaptively. For example, the case conceptualization activity in the developmental interview assignment could be expanded to compare and contrast a *DSM* diagnostic approach to the client narrative with a developmental counseling approach to the case. To model a greater range of diversity in identities and experiences, one could also include a video case study to represent contextual considerations that complement those already present in the classroom.

Similarly, the digital media project could be adapted by asking students to observe or interact with younger children, youths, or adults. Instructors could also narrow the focus to the most relevant types of development (e.g., cognitive, social, emotional, identity, psychological) or keep the scope broad to highlight the independent progress that individuals can make across developmental areas. Students could be encouraged to consider not only why an individual might be progressing more rapidly in cognitive rather than social development but also what types of counseling interventions could provide support in the needed areas.

Finally, the developmental transitions paper can be narrowed or broadened depending on the class in which it is used. In shifting the age range of developmental transitions under consideration, instructors could deepen class discussion about markers of optimal health and wellness across the life span, and they could elicit conversation about the types of typical barriers/crises/stressors than can be experienced in each age range as well as the types of supports or resources to support resilient responses that might be appropriate given the clients' developmental range. The description of this assignment was modified from a syllabus (MHS 6423–Counseling Adolescents) that had been shared on the ACA–ACES syllabus clearinghouse.

Developmental Interview

SLOs assessed: CACREP 2016 Standards 2.F.3.a, 2.F.3.b, 2.F.3.c, 2.F.3.e

Using Tamase's (1989) Introspective Developmental Counseling (IDC) protocol (see the Appendix in Ivey et al., 2005), conduct an interview with a fellow classmate. Sessions are to be conducted in the clinic and videotaped, and the sessions will be supervised as part of the course practicum. You will be a client for one session and a counselor for one session. Sessions are 50–60 minutes.

Prepare a three-page summary paper (in APA Style) briefly describing the individual (one paragraph; half-page maximum), the IDC interview (one paragraph, half-page maximum), and significant learning (2.50 pages) based on developmental theory. Learning must be related to at least three different developmental theories or issues covered in class. References are required to document the theory choices, which should include both a brief statement about the nature of the theory and an example or examples from the interview to support the theory. An assessment of cognitive style will be included in the interview summary. The paper should end with a concluding paragraph (half page) exploring the usefulness of the IDC interview questions, in whole or in part, with future clients. Tables 20.1, 20.2, and 20.3 include the rubric associated with this and the following assignments.

Table 20.1
Developmental Interview Rubric

Criterion	Does Not Meet Expectations	Meets Expectations	Exceeds Expectations
Participation in practicum sessions to elicit client narrative	Student did not complete client or counselor portion of practicum interview.	Student completed both portions of practicum interview but at a surface level that does not allow for insights about human development to emerge (either as counselor or client).	Student completed both portions of practicum interview and showed diligent effort both in conducting the protocol thoroughly and in sharing genuine details from client point of view.
Processing of IDC protocol from counselor perspective	Interview summary paper contains little description of client narrative, contains no insight or significant learning about the style of the client, or lacks depth and insight. As a practical counseling exercise, the student does not demonstrate skill.	Interview summary paper contains the required sections and content from the client narrative at a basic level. However, insights and descriptions are not detailed or fully articulated. As a practical counseling exercise, the student demonstrates adequate skill.	Interview summary paper contains the required sections and generates new and important meaning in description of the client narrative. Insights are offered with detail and clarity. As a practical counseling exercise, the student demonstrates high levels of skill.
Developmental theory across life span, including personality, learning style and environmental factors	Paper does not show foundation in any developmental theory.	Student does refer to developmental theory but does not show mastery of assumptions and details. Student shows a baseline understanding of human development theory.	Student shows full breadth and depth of use of developmental theory. Student shows deep understanding and insight regarding human development.
Written expression	Written expression shows difficulty in one or more of the following: focus, logic, organization, style, grammar, or APA Style.	Written expression conveys meaning of author most of the time, with occasional difficulty in focus, logic, organization, style, grammar, or APA Style.	Written expression is fluent, clear, expressive, and precise. No problems noted in focus, logic, organization, style, grammar, or APA Style.

Note. IDC = Introspective Developmental Counseling; APA = American Psychological Association.

Using Digital Storytelling to Describe the Development of Individuals in Context

SLOs assessed: CACREP 2016 Standards 2.F.3.e, 2.F.3.f, 2.F.3.g, 2.F.3.i

Working together in small groups, students will do the following:

- Identify a population that you would like to know more about.
- Review the scholarly literature to understand how mental health challenges or wellness issues have been described for your population or what theories have been used to frame their development. Write a brief literature review paper for your group, which describes the articles you found and then integrates that information to create a picture of what is known and what is still to be learned about the developmental strengths and challenges of individuals in this population. The paper should be three to four pages and in APA Style.
- Find a way to start a direct line of communication with that population (e.g., through an organization, a support office, a contact in the community, a social media site). Be sure to provide an informed consent form so individuals know that anything they share with you will be used in your final presentation in our class but not shared beyond class. (Note: this assignment was originally implemented to study college student populations, so ethical considerations should be discussed if translating it to populations with the potential for greater stressors or mental health diagnoses.)
- Invite approximately 8–10 individuals in this population to share three photographs or images with you, addressing the following:
    - What is it like to be a part of this group and live in this community?
    - What are some stressors or barriers you experience as a member of this group as you try to achieve your personal, social, academic, or career goals?

–What would achieving success or wellness look like for you? What helps you be resilient in the face of challenges?
- Find a way to listen to them as they tell you about the image that they chose and how it answers the question (e.g., individual appointments, a group meeting, a public forum, a web-based option).
- Keep a reflection log about how this experience is changing your ideas about individuals in this population.
- Create a presentation that will be shared during our last two classes. These can include, but are not limited to, PPT or Prezi, audio/video files, or media "walls." Think *digital storytelling* to help your classmates understand what it is like to be in these individuals' shoes.

In the final class presentation, you are to provide the following:

1. A brief description of the population you have selected (e.g., size, demographic, cultural, social, educational characteristics—on the basis of your literature review) (15 minutes).
2. The digital storytelling project—individuals describing their experiences or needs in their own words (15–20 minutes).
3. Description of counseling-based services that could be created/strengthened to address those needs (15 minutes).
4. Reflection on how your perceptions of the population were changed by engaging in this process—can be drawn from your journal entries (10 minutes).

Table 20.2
Digital Storytelling Rubric

Category and Criterion	Does Not Meet Expectations	Meets Expectations	Exceeds Expectations
Written content			
Individual, biological, neurological, physiological, systemic, spiritual, and environmental factors that affect human development, functioning, and behavior	In literature review, student does not reference theory, and cited work is reported only at a factual level, not thoughtfully integrated. Student does not convey the main developmental issues for this population.	In literature review, student includes a theoretical framework and makes some connection among the studies cited. Student is able to convey a basic picture of the developmental issues for this population.	In literature review, student does an exemplary job of utilizing theory and integrating cited studies into a coherent whole. Student conveys a detailed and thoughtful picture of the chosen population and their development.
Effects of crises, stressors, and other trauma-causing events on diverse individuals across the life span	Student does not convey the pertinent contextual considerations or stressors for this population.	Student conveys a basic picture of the pertinent contextual considerations or stressors for this population.	Student conveys a complete picture of the pertinent contextual considerations or stressors for this population.
Ethical and culturally relevant strategies for promoting resilience and optimum development and wellness across the life span	Student does not convey the pertinent strategies or resources that could address needs or promote healthy development for this population.	Student conveys a basic picture of the pertinent strategies or resources that could address needs or promote healthy development for this population.	Student conveys a complete picture of the pertinent strategies or resources that could address needs or promote healthy development for this population.
Verbal presentation			
Use of digital media, including creativity and style	Visual images are sparse and not integrated into a digital story of the students who were interviewed. Creativity and style are minimal.	Visual images are sufficient in number to represent the perspectives of the students who were interviewed. Images are integrated to tell the students' stories. Creativity and style are moderate.	Visual images are vivid and provide a clear and convincing digital story of the students who were interviewed. The overall digital project is fully integrated, with the images providing extra detail in support of the narrative. Creativity and style are excellent.
Presentation style	Team member reflections on learning and creativity in presentation style are minimal. Presentation does not sum up to a holistic and coherent view of the population.	Team member reflections on learning and creativity in presentation style are adequate. Presentation creates a coherent view of the population at a basic level.	Team member reflections on learning and creativity in presentation style are excellent. Presentation creates a holistic and compelling portrait of the population.
Focus/organization	Verbal and digital media presentations are not focused, logical, or compelling.	Verbal and digital media presentations are only moderately successful at being focused, logical, or compelling.	Verbal and digital media presentations are fully successful at being focused, logical, and compelling.

Developmental Transitions Paper

SLOs assessed: CACREP 2016 Standards 2.F.3.a, 2.F.3.e, 2.F.3.f, 2.F.3.i

Students will investigate and be prepared to discuss developmental issues facing individuals during transitional periods. Examples could include but are not limited to the following:

- Transition from preschool activities to elementary school
- Transition from high school to work or college
- Transition from late adolescent roles to early adult roles
- Transition from working roles (e.g., career, family responsibilities) to retiring from working roles

Students will select one of the four developmental transition periods listed in the above bulleted list and will write a six- to eight-page paper. Students will provide a context for the paper/discussion by describing the assigned transition period. Be sure to include what changes individuals can expect with regard to their cognitive/learning, social, emotional, and physical development during these transitions. You will also want to include tips and resources for parents, life partners, or peers who are interacting with individuals at this stage. Finally, include a description of counseling interventions that can support the transition. Prepare a one-page outline to be shared in class. The paper should conform to APA Style guidelines, which can be found in the *Publication Manual of the American Psychological Association* (6th ed.; APA, 2010).

Table 20.3
Developmental Transitions Rubric

Category	Does Not Meet Expectations	Meets Expectations	Exceeds Expectations
Theories of development and transition periods across the life span	Description of the developmental periods and/or the transition between them is not fully accurate.	Components of the developmental periods and transitions are present and accurate but with minimal details or elaboration.	Developmental periods and transitions are fully accurate and described with eloquence and detail.
Individual, biological, neurological, physiological, systemic, spiritual, and environmental factors that affect human development, functioning, and behavior	Student only includes one of the types of development (e.g., cognitive/learning, social, emotional, physical).	Two or three of the types of development are included with sufficient attention to detail, or more than three types are listed but with minimal to no explanation.	Multiple types of development are included, with detailed description of expected changes in those areas.
Implications for promoting resilience and optimum development (e.g., counseling practice)	Only one practical implications section is included (e.g., tips for parents or counseling interventions), and few to no examples are provided to illustrate.	Both practical implications sections are included (parents/peers and counseling interventions), but amount of detail shared stays at a basic level.	Both implications sections are included, and the student shows clear ability to move from theory to application by describing clearly how to support individuals experiencing these developmental transitions.
Quality of writing	Paper does not follow APA Style, is not clearly and logically written, and does not include a one-page outline.	Paper adheres to APA Style with a few errors, conveys its meaning at a basic level of clarity, and includes a one-page outline with minimal details.	Paper adheres to APA Style with no errors; conveys its meaning fluently, logically, and persuasively; and includes a full one-page outline.

Note. APA = American Psychological Association.

Chapter 21

Career Counseling
and Development

Marie F. Shoffner

Studies of the training and supervision of career counselors or counseling students in career classes are relatively sparse, with a "marked lack of empirical or theoretical scholarship on what constitutes the most effective approaches to training career counselors" (Ladany & O'Shaughnessy, 2014, p. 375). In a 10-year review of articles related to professional counseling, Barrio Minton et al. (2014) found only four on teaching career counseling. Until recently, there has also been relatively little literature addressing ways to assess learning in career courses. However, the conceptual literature on career counseling contains a solid body of work on helping CITs learn to use career assessments (e.g., Osborn, 2009) and using activities designed to make career counseling and development courses more engaging, relevant, and connected to other master's-level content and to students' own career development (e.g., ACES & National Career Development Association [NCDA], 2000; Ladany & O'Shaughnessy, 2014; Osborn, 2009; Pope & Minor, 2000).

Students often see the core content area of career counseling and development as irrelevant (Ladany & O'Shaughnessy, 2014; Lara, Kline, & Paulson, 2011; Toman, 2012). Before beginning the career class, many hold misconceptions about and negativity toward career counseling (Lara et al., 2011). They see the course as irrelevant and lacking in clinical applicability (Ladany & O'Shaughnessy, 2014). Ladany and O'Shaughnessy (2014) used the term *enthusiasm gap* to describe students' low interest in and negative attitudes (Lara et al., 2011) toward career counseling.

However, the world of work is an important aspect of all clients' lives, and an understanding of career development and its role in optimal human wellness is crucial to ethical practice. Recognizing this, our accrediting bodies and professional organizations still view career counseling as essential to the training of counselors (Lara et al., 2011), even though many career practitioners and counselor educators agree that it has become marginalized (e.g., Ladany & O'Shaughnessy, 2014; Lara et al., 2011; Toman, 2012).

Unless a program offers the career counseling specialty, most master's-level students take one career counseling and development course during their counseling program (Lara et al., 2011). This course, therefore, is often instrumental in its influence on students' interest in and attitudes about career counseling. The activities incorporated into the course, the attitudes of the faculty members teaching the course, and peers' derisive or enthusiastic comments do much to influence students' subsequent attitudes (Lara et al., 2011).

In their research, Lara et al. (2011) found that when students integrated and synthesized career content and concepts with their own life experiences and journey or with the career journey of clients, they appreciated the importance of career-focused interventions and career development. They further found that practice with peers or with clients was related to more positive attitudes. However, these students did not feel competent in the actual practice of career counseling (Lara et al., 2011).

Toman (2012) suggested that "creating an environment where students appreciate learning and appreciate the uniqueness of their own career stories is one way to influence their interest in the field of career development and counseling" (p. 188). In addition, connecting career development to other counseling concepts challenges the belief that career counseling is on the fringes of counselor education (Lara et al., 2011). Both of these suggestions are in line with the recommendations made by ACES and NCDA (2000).

In this section, I delineate two assignments and one on-going set of simulation experiences to help master's-level students develop an understanding of career theories and assessments, develop an understanding of their own career development in terms of theories and assessments, and develop skills in career counseling and the interpretation of formal and informal career assessments. The first activity is designed to develop the counseling skills of master's-level students who have already completed a course in basic counseling skills and a course in counseling theories. The second activity is an assignment focused on the self-assessment of the student's individual career journey. The final activity is an interventions portfolio (or online notebook) that includes specific interventions for career counseling and development for a specific population.

Career Counseling and Assessment Simulations

SLOs assessed: CACREP 2016 Standards 2.F.4.e, 2.F.4.i

In-class counseling simulations are designed to ascertain student skills in assessing key career development factors, including abilities, interests, values, and personality (Standard 2.F.4.e) and to assess student competency in using assessment tools and techniques for career planning and decision making (Standard 2.F.4.i).

All students will complete various career-related appraisals as part of this course and will subsequently participate in counseling simulations with classmates during class time for the following assessments: Career Genogram, Career Lifeline, Self-Directed Search, Strong Interest Inventory, Values Sort/Ranking, Myers Briggs Type Indicator (MBTI), and Life Story. Advanced doctoral students and the instructor will evaluate your performance. Tables 21.1 and 21.2 include the rubrics associated with these assignments.

Table 21.1
Career Counseling and Assessment Simulation Rubric

Criterion (CACREP Standard)	Does Not Meet Expectations	Meets Expectations	Exceeds Expectations
Exhibits skills in the use of strategies for assessing abilities, interests, values, personality, and other factors that contribute to career development (2.F.4.e)	Does not actively participate in completing assessments and simulating the client role or the counselor role. Does not attempt to address guidelines for counseling suggested by instructor or doctoral students. Does not make adjustments in counseling on the basis of feedback.	Actively participates in completing assessments and simulating the client role and the counselor role. Attempts to address guidelines suggested by instructor. Makes adjustments in counseling on the basis of feedback. Makes some growth in counseling and assessment skills.	Actively participates in completing assessments and simulating the client role and the counselor role. Attempts to address guidelines suggested by instructor. Makes adjustments in counseling on the basis of feedback. Generalizes feedback across multiple counseling sessions. Exhibits considerable and consistent growth in counseling and assessment skills.
Exhibits competency in identifying and using assessment tools and techniques relevant to career planning and decision making (2.F.4.i)	Does not appropriately use assessment tools or does not use counseling techniques relevant to career exploration, planning, and decision making.	Appropriately uses most assessment tools and uses counseling techniques relevant to career exploration, planning, and decision making, as delineated by instructor, most of the time.	Appropriately uses all assessment tools and uses counseling techniques relevant to career exploration, planning, and decision making, as delineated by instructor, almost all of the time. Consistently grows in use of assessment tools and techniques over the course of the semester.

Note. CACREP = Council for Accreditation of Counseling and Related Educational Programs.

Table 21.2
Career Journey Self-Assessment Rubric (200 points)

Criterion (CACREP Standard)	Does Not Meet Expectations	Meets Expectations	Exceeds Expectations
Adheres to APA Style, proper grammar, correct spelling and punctuation	Does not adhere to APA Style or often uses incorrect grammar, spelling, and/or punctuation (0–17 points).	In major ways, adheres to APA Style; almost always uses correct grammar, spelling, and punctuation (17–18 points).	Always adheres to APA Style; always uses correct grammar, spelling, and punctuation (18.5–20 points).
Exhibits understanding about the purpose and use of the three primary assessments (Strong Interest Inventory, MBTI, Values assessment) (2.F.4.e, 2.F.4.i)	Does not discuss the Strong Interest Inventory, the MBTI, or Values assessment, or does not include detailed results of these three assessments, or does not address the meaning (relevance) of those results in personal career journey (0–29.5 points).	Discusses the Strong Interest Inventory, the MBTI, and the Values assessment, including basic information about the purpose of each assessment. Presents detailed, relevant results and the meaning (relevance) of those results in personal career journey (30–32.5 points).	Discusses the Strong Interest Inventory, the MBTI, and the Values assessment, including basic information about the purpose, structure, use, and properties of each. Presents relevant results and the detailed meaning (relevance) of those results in personal career journey (32.5–35 points).
Exhibits understanding about the purpose and use of additional assessments (Genogram, Career Lifeline, Self-Directed Search, Life Story) (2.F.4.e, 2.F.4.i)	Does not discuss any additional assessments or does not include the results of additional assessments, or does not address the meaning of those results (0–29.5 points).	Discusses most additional assessments, including basic information about the purpose of included assessments. Presents relevant results of these assessments. Does not include the meaning (relevance) of those results in personal career journey (30–32.5 points).	Discusses all additional assessments, including basic information about the purpose, structure, use, and properties of the assessments. Presents relevant results of these assessments. Includes the meaning (relevance) of those results in personal career journey (32.5–35 points).
Exhibits knowledge and understanding about theories and models of career development, counseling, and decision making (2.F.4.a)	Does not address any theories or models of career development or incorrectly presents theories or models (0–29.5 points).	Correctly presents at least two theories/models of career development and relates them to personal career journey. Correctly connects these theories/models to the three primary assessments (Strong Interest Inventory, MBTI, and Values assessment) and to personal career journey (30–32.5 points).	Correctly presents at least three theories/models of career development and relates them to personal career journey in some detail. Correctly connects these theories/models to the three primary assessments, to other in-class assessments, and to personal career journey (32.5–35 points).
Exhibits knowledge about the interrelationships among work, family, and other life roles and factors (2.F.4.b)	Does not address the interrelationships among work, family, life roles, or other factors (including culture or diversity), or does not relate these to career theories/models, or does not connect these to any assessments (0–29.5 points).	Correctly addresses the interrelationships between work and family, including early career experiences (ages 0–10 years), family influence, life roles, and culture, and relates these to two theories/models. Connects these to several assessments (30–32.5 points).	Correctly addresses the interrelationships between work and family, including early career experiences (ages 0–10 years), family influence, life roles, and culture, and relates these to three theories/models. Connects these to most covered assessments (32.5–35 points).
Exhibits knowledge and skills for identifying and utilizing career, avocational, educational, occupational, and labor market information resources, technology, and information systems (2.F.4.c), available through the Internet, computer-based guidance systems, and printed materials	Does not address the interplay of career, avocational, educational, occupational, or labor market information or trends related to personal career journey (0–17 points).	Addresses the interplay of career, avocational, educational, and occupational or labor market information/trends as they relate to personal career journey (17–18 points).	Addresses the interplay of career, avocational, educational, and occupational or labor market information/trends as they relate to personal career journey. Connects this to assessments and to interrelationships among work, family, and other life roles (18.5–20 points).
Demonstrates understanding of approaches for assessing the conditions of the work environment on clients' overall life experiences (2.F.4.d)	Does not address personal experience of the conditions of work environment(s) and their influence on overall life experiences (0–17 points).	Addresses personal experience of the conditions of work environment(s) and their influence on overall life experiences (17–18 points).	Addresses personal experience of the conditions of work environment(s) and their influence on overall life experiences. Connects this to career theories/models (18.5–20 points).
Total point span	0–169	171–184	185.5–200

Note. CACREP = Council for Accreditation of Counseling and Related Educational Programs; APA = American Psychological Association; MBTI = Myers Briggs Type Indicator.

Career Journey Self-Assessment

SLOs assessed: CACREP 2016 Standards 2.F.4.a, 2.F.4.b, 2.F.4.c, 2.F.4.d

Students will complete several formal and informal career assessments during the semester, and they also will participate in counseling simulations based on the assessments. These assessments are used to facilitate understanding of career development and the career counseling process. They are also used to facilitate self-awareness, growth, and critical thinking about career development. All career assessment and simulation experiences during the semester form the basis (the data) for this assignment.

In this paper, students should discuss the properties of the Self-Directed Search, the Strong Interest Inventory, the Skills Confidence Inventory (part of the Strong Interest Inventory), and the MBTI, and they should present a detailed discussion of their results. Students must include the implications of these results for their personal career development.

Students should also include additional information gained from all other assessments used during the course. In the paper, students should discuss how these formal and informal assessments describe their career journey, including the journey to this counseling program.

Career Counseling and Development Interventions Portfolio

SLOs assessed: CACREP 2016 Standards 2.F.4c, 2.F.4.f, 2.F.4.g, 2.F.4.h, 2.F.4.j

Students will prepare a set of career development interventions for use at an elementary, middle, or high school, college, or mental health setting (choose one level). Together, these interventions will form an online portfolio. The notebook should be organized in the following format:

    I. Introduction
   II. Websites
  III. Guidance or Programming Lesson Plan
  IV. Presentation Lesson Plan
   V. Group Counseling Lesson Plans (six sessions)
  VI. References

In the Introduction, students should include the pertinent developmental career issues and needs, overall career development goals/objectives, and general strategies for their population. This introduction should also describe the pertinent cultural factors affecting the specific audience for whom the interventions are intended.

The websites should focus on the chosen client population, and at least one website should include Interest Inventories or Ability/Skill Inventories, a second website should include Occupations Databases or Occupational Information, and a third website should include Career-Related Activities (for the students). Other websites might include Job Search websites, Career-Related Activities websites (for the clients, not for parents, teachers, instructors, or others). All listed websites should include the URL as a direct link to the website (no cut-and-paste to website but a direct link), a critique of the website using NCDA's guidelines (all criteria) for evaluating websites, and a brief (one paragraph) statement of how the website would be used by counselors and clients (or a group of clients) as part of a career-related intervention. All websites must be directly accessible.

The remaining interventions include the following: one classroom guidance lesson plan (for K–12 students) or programming lesson plan (for college or university students or for a specific population addressed by mental health counselors); one parent, teacher, significant other, mental health service professionals, or college instructor experience in lesson plan format (e.g., a presentation to parents on career-related activities to use with elementary school students, a 1-hour in-service for teachers on ways to integrate career-related activities into the curriculum, programming for college advisors related to typical college student career development, a presentation for group home resident counselors on ways to address client career development); and an overview and six sessions for a group counseling experience (i.e., in six separate lesson plans) focused on career development.

Each or these interventions must be described so that it can be performed by other counselors (professional school counselors, college/university professionals, or mental health counselors). Therefore, each intervention should include goals, objectives, methods, materials, and evaluation for that specific activity.

Interventions should be individual creations or adaptations, and they should represent integration and synthesis of best interventions for the chosen age group. No intervention is to be copied directly from the Internet, the text, or from any other printed or online sources. Students are encouraged to do additional research. For example, the *Professional School Counselor*, the *Journal of College Counseling*, and *The Career Development Quarterly* contain articles that can form the basis for an intervention. Students must cite and reference all sources (in APA Style). Table 21.3 includes the rubric associated with this assignment.

Table 21.3
Career Counseling and Development Interventions Portfolio Rubric (100 points)

Criterion (CACREP Standard)	Does Not Meet Expectations	Meets Expectations	Exceeds Expectations
Sections of intervention notebook	One or more sections are not included, or a table of contents is not included, or sections are not clearly separate and delineated or adequately marked. Access is unclear. Notebook is not user friendly (0–17.5 points).	All sections of the notebook are included, and there is a table of contents. Notebook is user friendly. Some sections are not clearly delineated in separate sections or are not adequately marked. Sections are not easily accessible, or access is unclear (18–18.5 points).	All sections of the notebook are included and are clearly delineated in separate and marked sections. Each section is easily accessible, and access is clear. A clear and inclusive table of contents is included and is directly related to section access. The notebook is user friendly (19–20 points).
Lesson plans	Lesson plans are not included for all relevant sections. Lesson plans do not include all components or are not designed on the basis of the provided template. Sections of more than one of the lesson plans are not logically consistent, or more than one of the lesson plans includes objectives that are ambiguous or not measurable. More than two lesson plans are not clear enough or complete enough to be implemented by a reader (0–17.5 points).	Lesson plans are included for all relevant sections. Lesson plans include all components and are designed on the basis of the provided template. Sections of one of the lesson plans are not logically consistent, or one of the lesson plans includes objectives that are ambiguous or not measurable. One or two lesson plans are not clear enough or complete enough to be implemented by a reader (18–18.5 points).	Lesson plans are included for all relevant sections. Lesson plans include all components and are designed on the basis of the provided template. All sections of the lesson plans are logically consistent (e.g., objectives and evaluation are obviously and clearly connected). All objectives are unambiguous and measurable. All lesson plans are clear and complete and can be implemented by a reader (19–20 points).
Websites (2.F.4.c)	All six sections are not included, or more than one of the websites is not described. There are no in-depth website descriptions (0–17.5 points).	All six sections are included. One or two of the websites do not include descriptions. The required numbers of websites do not include a more in-depth description, or the description is inadequate (18–18.5 points).	All six sections are included. Four (for groups of two) or six (for larger groups) of the required website sections include website descriptions. Two or three (depending on group size) of the websites include a more in-depth description, including use of website with clientele (K–12 or postsecondary students) (19–20 points).
Exhibits knowledge of strategies for career development program planning, organization, implementation, administration, and evaluation (2.F.4.f)	Introduction does not clearly depict an understanding of how the interventions fit within a career development program. More than two lesson plan evaluations are unclear or are not connected to overall career development for the relevant population (0–7.5 points).	Introduction depicts clear understanding of how the interventions fit within a career development program. One or two lesson plan evaluations are unclear or not connected to overall career development for the relevant population (8–8.5 points).	Introduction depicts clear understanding of how the interventions fit within a career development program. Evaluations included in lesson plans are clear and connected to overall career development for the relevant population (9–10 points).
Exhibits knowledge of strategies for advocating for diverse clients' career and educational development and employment opportunities in a global economy (2.F.4.g)	Neither the introduction or lesson plans refer to ways of addressing diverse students, or do so only in a broad way. More than two website choices or descriptions do not show clear connection to educational development and employment opportunities relevant to the population (0–7.5 points).	Introduction and lesson plans refer to the ways of addressing diverse students but are unclear or ambiguous. One or two website choices or descriptions do not show clear connection to educational development and employment opportunities relevant to the population (8–8.5 points).	Introduction and lesson plans include clear unambiguous reference to the ways of addressing diverse students. Website inclusion and descriptions show clear connection to educational development and employment opportunities relevant to the population (9–10 points).

(Continued)

Table 21.3 (*Continued*)
Career Counseling and Development Interventions Portfolio Rubric (100 points)

Criterion (CACREP Standard)	Does Not Meet Expectations	Meets Expectations	Exceeds Expectations
Exhibits knowledge of strategies for facilitating client skill development for career, educational, and lifework planning and management (2.F.4.h)	Introduction and lesson plans do not include strategies for developing skills related to career development and lifework planning, or the addressed skills are not clearly related to the population or are developmentally inappropriate (0–7.5 points).	Introduction or lesson plans include strategies (programmatic or specifically intervention-based) for developing skills related to career development and lifework planning, but some are not developmentally appropriate (8–8.5 points).	Introduction or lesson plans include strategies (programmatic or specifically intervention-based) for developing skills related to career development and lifework planning (9–10 points).
Exhibits knowledge of ethical and culturally relevant strategies for addressing career development (2.F.4.j)	Neither the introduction nor any of the lesson plans include culturally relevant strategies for addressing career development or include unethical practice or strategies (0–7.5 points).	Introduction and lesson plans indicate clear ethical and culturally relevant strategies for addressing career development, but strategies are not integrated and connected from the introduction into the specific lesson plans (8–8.5 points).	Introduction and lesson plans indicate clear ethical and culturally relevant strategies for addressing career development, and strategies are integrated and connected from the introduction into the specific lesson plans (9–10 points).

Note. CACREP = Council for Accreditation of Counseling and Related Educational Programs.

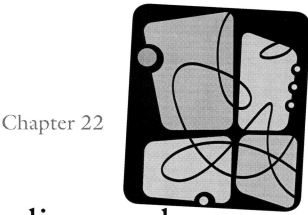

Chapter 22

Counseling and Helping Relationships

Jacqueline M. Swank, M. Kristina DePue, and Jonathan H. Ohrt

Helping Relationships is one of the eight common core curricular areas (Standard 2.F.5) for master's-level counseling programs identified in the CACREP 2016 Standards and encompasses 14 unique components ranging from theories and models of counseling to community resources for helping. Counselor educators infuse the vast content in this core area within the master's-level curriculum throughout various knowledge and skill-based courses. Additionally, the components of the Helping Relationships area is integrated within SLO domains for each of the six master's-level program specialty areas. Although each of these components is crucial in counselor preparation, it is not feasible to address each of them within this chapter. Therefore, we have selected five components that we emphasize in this chapter: (a) counselor characteristics and behaviors (Standard 2.F.5.f); (b) interview, counseling, and case conceptualization skills (Standard 2.F.5.g); (c) personal model of counseling (Standard 2.F.5.n); (d) consultation theories, models, and strategies (Standard 2.F.5.c); and (e) community-based resources (Standard 2.F.5.k).

Basic counseling skills, along with the dispositions and behaviors of the counselor, are foundational competency areas of Helping Relationships. Additionally, as gatekeepers for the counseling profession, counselor educators have the legal and ethical responsibility to measure students' counseling competencies (ACA, 2014; CACREP, 2009; Lambie, Mullen, Swank, & Blount, 2015; Swank & Lambie, 2012; Swank, Lambie, & Witta, 2012). Although researchers have discussed the assessment of counseling skills for several decades, it was not until recently that scholars developed a comprehensive assessment (Counseling Competencies Scale [CCS]; Swank et al., 2012) to assess counseling competencies in the areas of counseling skills, dispositions, and behaviors. In addition, researchers have acknowledged the use of the CCS to measure SLOs (Swank & Lambie, 2012). Therefore, we describe an activity that requires students to demonstrate counseling competencies in the area of counseling skills, and we also present a revised version of the CCS (Counselor Competencies Scale—Revised [CCS–R]; Lambie et al., 2015) that is used to assess counseling skills, dispositions, and behaviors.

A counselor's theoretical orientation provides a foundation for interacting with clients. Therefore, counseling theories are a crucial component of Helping Relationships. Understanding counseling theories and identifying a theoretical orientation that is congruent with the individual are complex, developmental processes. Counselor educators need to continually expose students to activities focused on understanding and reflecting on theories throughout the preparation process to optimize learning (Spruill & Benshoff, 2000). Thus, we describe an activity to help students conceptualize and reflect on the development of their theoretical orientation.

Finally, "consultation is a helping relationship in which human service professionals work with individuals and/or groups in a variety of settings (such as agencies, schools, and businesses) to help them work more effectively" (Dougherty, 2005, p. 1). School counselors provide consultation within the scope of delivering a comprehensive, developmental school counseling program (ASCA, 2012). Community counselors may also provide consultation services to parents, teachers, and other stakeholders. In a review of 18 studies, Guli (2005) found that parent consultation was an effective method for changing school-related behaviors. Thus, it is crucial for counseling students to develop an understanding of the consultation process. Therefore, we describe an activity that assesses students' knowledge and skill in describing the selection and implementation of a consultation model.

Counseling Session Analysis

SLO assessed: CACREP 2016 Standard 2.5.F

This assignment is used within a counseling skills course. The counseling session is conducted between two students enrolled in the course. Students are encouraged to discuss a real concern during the session.

Conduct a 50-minute recorded individual counseling session with your partner and complete the following three components of the analysis:

1. Review the session and transcribe a 10-minute section of the session that does not include the first or last 10 minutes. Provide a brief paragraph to introduce the client and use a table to organize the transcript that includes three columns: (1) what was said verbatim; (2) what skill was used (counselor's responses only); and (3) what you did and why, or what you could have done differently (counselor's responses only; method used by Young, 2012).
2. Write a two- to four-page self-assessment of your session (include the client's presenting problem, include how you would work with the client in future sessions, include your strengths and challenges during the session [list at least two of each], and reflect on what it was like to conduct a counseling session).
3. Evaluate your counseling skills by completing the CCS–R, Part 1: Counseling Skills and Therapeutic Conditions.

CCS–R

The CCS–R is used by the counselor education/supervisor to assess the student's counseling skills in reviewing his or her tape and transcription. The self-assessment, reflection, and critique are used in supervision with the student.

The CCS–R assesses counselors' and trainees' skills development and professional competencies. Additionally, the CCS–R provides counselors and trainees with direct feedback regarding (a) their demonstrated ability to apply counseling skills, (b) their demonstrated ability to facilitate therapeutic conditions, and (c) their counseling dispositions (dominant qualities) and behaviors, which offers the counselors and trainees practical areas for improvement to support their development as effective and ethical professional counselors.

Scales Evaluation Guidelines

Exceeds Expectations/Demonstrates Competencies (5) = the counselor or trainee demonstrates strong (i.e., exceeding the expectations of a beginning professional counselor) knowledge, skills, and dispositions in the specified counseling skill(s), ability to facilitate therapeutic conditions, and professional disposition(s) and behavior(s).

Meets Expectations/Demonstrates Competencies (4) = the counselor or trainee demonstrates consistent and proficient knowledge, skills, and dispositions in the specified counseling skill(s), ability to facilitate therapeutic conditions, and professional disposition(s) and behavior(s). A beginning professional counselor should be at the "Demonstrates Competencies" level at the conclusion of his or her practicum and/or internship.

Near Expectations/Developing Toward Competencies (3) = the counselor or trainee demonstrates inconsistent and limited knowledge, skills, and dispositions in the specified counseling skill(s), ability to facilitate therapeutic conditions, and professional disposition(s) and behavior(s).

Below Expectations/Insufficient/Unacceptable (2) = the counselor or trainee demonstrates limited or no evidence of the knowledge, skills, and dispositions in the specified counseling skill(s), ability to facilitate therapeutic conditions, and professional disposition(s) and behavior(s).

Harmful (1) = the counselor or trainee demonstrates harmful use of knowledge, skills, and dispositions in the specified counseling skill(s), ability to facilitate therapeutic conditions, and professional disposition(s) and behavior(s).

Directions: Evaluate the counselor's or trainee's counseling skills, ability to facilitate therapeutic conditions, and professional dispositions and behaviors per rubric evaluation descriptions, and record rating in the "score" column on the left.

Note. From "The Counseling Competencies Scale: Validation and Refinement," by G. W. Lambie, P. R. Mullen, J. M. Swank, and A. Blount, 2015. Copyright 2015 by Glenn W. Lambie. Contact Glenn W. Lambie (Glenn.Lambie@ucf.edu) at the University of Central Florida Counselor Education Program regarding use. Reprinted with permission.

CACREP 2016 Common Core Standards Relating to the CCS–R

- Strategies for personal and professional self-evaluation and implications for practice (Section II, Standard 1.k).
- Self-care strategies appropriate to the counselor role (Section II, Standard 1.l).
- Multicultural counseling competencies (Section II, Standard 2.c).
- A general framework for understanding differing abilities and strategies for differentiated interventions (Section II, Standard 3.h).
- Ethical and culturally relevant strategies for establishing and maintaining in-person and technology-assisted relationships (Section II, Standard 5.d).
- Counselor characteristics and behaviors that influence the counseling processes (Section II, Standard 5.f).
- Essential interviewing, counseling, and case conceptualization skills (Section II, Standard 5.g).
- Developmentally relevant counseling treatment or intervention plans (Section II, Standard 5.h).
- Processes for aiding students in developing a personal model of counseling (Section II, Standard 5.n).
- The counselor education program faculty has a systematic process in place for the use of individual student assessment data in relation to retention, remediation, and dismissal (Section 4, Standard H).
- Professional practice, which includes practicum and internship, provides for the application of theory and the development of counseling skills under supervision. These experiences will provide opportunities for students to counsel clients who represent the ethnic and demographic diversity of their community (Section III, Professional Practice).
- Entry-level professional practice and practicum (Section III, Professional Practice).

  A. Students are covered by individual professional counseling liability insurance policies while enrolled in practicum and internship.

  B. Supervision of practicum students includes program-appropriate audio/video recordings and/or live supervision of students' interactions with clients.

  C. Formative and summative evaluations of the student's counseling performance and ability to integrate and apply knowledge are conducted as part of the student's practicum.

  F. Students must complete supervised counseling practicum experiences that total a minimum of 100 clock hours over a full academic term that is a minimum of 10 weeks.

  G. Practicum students must complete at least 40 clock hours of direct service with actual clients that contributes to the development of counseling skills.

  H. Practicum students have weekly interaction with supervisors that averages 1 hour per week of individual and/or triadic supervision throughout the practicum by (1) a counselor education program faculty member, (2) a student supervisor who is under the supervision of a counselor education program faculty member, or (3) a site supervisor who is working in consultation on a regular schedule with a counselor education program faculty member in accordance with the supervision agreement

  I. Practicum students participate in an average of 1.50 hours per week of group supervision on a regular schedule throughout the practicum. Group supervision must be provided by a counselor education program faculty member or a student supervisor who is under the supervision of a counselor education program faculty member.

Table 22.1 includes the rubric associated with counseling skills and therapeutic conditions, and Table 22.2 includes the rubric associated with counseling dispositions and behaviors.

Integrative Counseling Theories Paper

SLOs assessed: CACREP 2016 Standards 2.F.5.a, 2.F.5.n

You will be asked to write a paper based on your counseling theory, which includes, but is not limited to, the following:

- the philosophical paradigm or view of human nature,
- the function and role of the counselor,
- the client's function or role,
- the goals or outcomes of the counseling process,
- techniques and methods you would use,
- multicultural considerations,
- strengths and limitations of the approach, and
- discussion of how the theory fits with your worldview.

You are required to use at least five peer-reviewed counseling articles to support your statements. You may also choose to cite your textbook; however, this is in addition to the five required counseling articles. The paper must be a minimum of 8 and a maximum of 12 pages including the cover page and reference pages. Papers should be consistent with APA Style guidelines, including an appropriate title page, headings, margins, and spacing (no abstract is necessary). Table 22.3 includes the rubric associated with this assignment.

Consultation Model

SLOs assessed: CACREP 2016 Standards 2.F.5.c, 2.F.5.j

Describe, on the basis of professional literature, a practical consultation model to use when working with parents, teachers, or other mental health professionals. Within the discussion, include references to consultation theories and address (a) consultation stages, (b) cultural considerations, (c) consultation goal setting, and (d) how you will evaluate consultation effectiveness. Next, construct a case study of a hypothetical consultee who brings a client case to you. Create an outline for the consultation following your consultation model. Describe the format and interventions you will use. Identify five community-based resources with brief descriptions that may be of assistance to the client with whom the consultee is working. Papers should be consistent with APA Style guidelines, including an appropriate title page, headings, margins, and spacing (no abstract is necessary). Table 22.4 includes the rubric associated with this assignment.

Table 22.1
Part 1: Counseling Skills and Therapeutic Conditions

Number and Primary Counseling Skill(s)	Specific Skill	5	4	3	2	1
1.A Nonverbal skills ___ score	Includes body position, eye contact, posture, distance from client, voice tone, rate of speech, use of silence, and so forth (attuned to the emotional state and cultural norms of the clients)	Demonstrates effective nonverbal communication skills, conveying connectedness and empathy (85%)	Demonstrates effective nonverbal communication skills (for the majority of counseling sessions; 70%)	Demonstrates inconsistency in his or her nonverbal communication skills	Demonstrates limited nonverbal communication skills	Demonstrates poor nonverbal communication skills, such as ignoring client and/or giving judgmental looks
1.B Encouragers ___ score	Includes minimal encouragers and door openers such as "Tell me more about . . ." and "Hmm"	Demonstrates appropriate use of encouragers, which supports development of a therapeutic relationship (85%)	Demonstrates appropriate use of encouragers, which supports development of a therapeutic relationship (for the majority of counseling sessions; 70%)	Demonstrates inconsistency in his or her use of appropriate encouragers	Demonstrates limited ability to use appropriate encouragers	Demonstrates poor ability to use appropriate encouragers, such as using skills in a judgmental manner
1.C Questions ___ score	Use of appropriate open and closed questioning (e.g., avoidance of double questions)	Demonstrates appropriate use of open- and closed-ended questioning, with an emphasis on open-ended question (85%)	Demonstrates appropriate use of open- and close-ended questions (for the majority of counseling sessions; 70%)	Demonstrates inconsistency in using open-ended questions and may use closed questions for prolonged periods	Demonstrates limited ability to use open-ended questions with restricted effectiveness	Demonstrates poor ability to use open-ended questions, such as questions that tend to confuse clients or restrict the counseling process
1.D Reflecting: Paraphrasing ___ score	Basic reflection of content—paraphrasing (with couples and families, paraphrasing the different clients' multiple perspectives)	Demonstrates appropriate use of paraphrasing as a primary therapeutic approach (85%)	Demonstrates appropriate use of paraphrasing (for the majority of counseling sessions; 70%)	Demonstrates paraphrasing inconsistently and inaccurately or mechanical or parroted responses	Demonstrates limited proficiency in paraphrasing or is often inaccurate	Demonstrates poor ability to paraphrase, such as being judgmental and/or dismissive
1.E Reflecting: Reflection of feelings ___ score	Reflection of feelings (with couples and families, reflection of each clients' feelings)	Demonstrates appropriate use of reflection of feelings as a primary approach (85%)	Demonstrates appropriate use of reflection of feelings (for the majority of counseling sessions; 70%)	Demonstrates reflection of feelings inconsistently and is not matching the client	Demonstrates limited proficiency in reflecting feelings and/or is often inaccurate	Demonstrates poor ability to reflective feelings, such as being judgmental and/or dismissive
1.F Reflecting: Summarizing ___ score	Summarizing content, feelings, behaviors, and future plans (with couples and families, summarizing relational patterns of interaction)	Demonstrates consistent ability to use summarization to include content, feelings, behaviors, and future plans (85%)	Demonstrates ability to appropriately use summarization to include content, feelings, behaviors, and future plans (for the majority of counseling sessions; 70%)	Demonstrates inconsistent and inaccurate ability to use summarization	Demonstrates limited ability to use summarization (e.g., summary suggests counselor does not understand clients or is overly focused on content rather than process)	Demonstrates poor ability to summarize, such as being judgmental and/or dismissive
1.G Advanced reflection (Meaning) ___ score	Advanced reflection of meaning, including values and core beliefs (taking counseling to a deeper level)	Demonstrates consistent use of advanced reflection and promotes discussions of greater depth during counseling sessions (85%)	Demonstrates ability to appropriately use advanced reflection, supporting increased exploration in session (for the majority of counseling sessions; 70%)	Demonstrates inconsistent and inaccurate ability to use advanced reflection; counseling sessions appear superficial	Demonstrates limited ability to use advanced reflection and/or switches topics in counseling often	Demonstrates poor ability to use advance reflection, such as being judgmental and/or dismissive

(Continued)

Table 22.1 (*Continued*)
Part 1: Counseling Skills and Therapeutic Conditions

Number and Primary Counseling Skill(s)	Specific Skill	5	4	3	2	1
1.H Confrontation ___ score	Counselor challenges clients to recognize and evaluate inconsistencies	Demonstrates the ability to challenge clients through verbalizing inconsistencies and discrepancies in the clients' words and/or actions in a supportive fashion; balance of challenge and support (85%)	Demonstrates the ability to challenge clients through verbalizing inconsistencies and discrepancies in the clients' words and/or actions in a supportive fashion (can confront, but hesitant), or this action was not needed; therefore, appropriately not used (for the majority of counseling sessions; 70%)	Demonstrates inconsistent ability to challenge clients through verbalizing inconsistencies and discrepancies in clients' words and/or actions in a supportive fashion; used minimally/missed opportunity	Demonstrates limited ability to challenge clients through verbalizing discrepancies in the client's words and/or actions in a supportive and caring fashion, and/or skill is lacking	Demonstrates poor ability to use confrontation, such as degrading client or being harsh, judgmental, and/or aggressive
1.I Goal setting ___ score	Counselor collaborates with clients to establish realistic, appropriate, and attainable therapeutic goals (with couples and families, supports clients in establishing common therapeutic goals)	Demonstrates consistent ability to establish collaborative and appropriate therapeutic goals with clients (85%)	Demonstrates ability to establish collaborative and appropriate therapeutic goals with client (for the majority of counseling sessions; 70%)	Demonstrates inconsistent ability to establish collaborative and appropriate therapeutic goals with clients	Demonstrates limited ability to establish collaborative, appropriate therapeutic goals with clients	Demonstrates poor ability to develop collaborative therapeutic goals, such as identifying unattainable goals, and agreeing with goals that may be harmful to the clients
1.J Focus of counseling ___ score	Counselor focuses (or refocuses) clients on their therapeutic goals (i.e., purposeful counseling)	Demonstrates consistent ability to focus and/or refocus counseling on clients' goal attainment (85%)	Demonstrates ability to focus and/or refocus counseling on clients' goal attainment (for the majority of counseling sessions; 70%)	Demonstrates inconsistent ability to focus and/or refocus counseling on clients' therapeutic goal attainment	Demonstrates limited ability to focus and/or refocus counseling on clients' therapeutic goal attainment	Demonstrates poor ability to maintain focus in counseling, such as moving focus away from clients' goals
1.K Facilitate therapeutic environment: Empathy and caring ___ score	Expresses accurate empathy and care; counselor is "present" and open to clients (includes immediacy and concreteness)	Demonstrates consistent ability to be empathic and uses appropriate responses (85%)	Demonstrates ability to be empathic and uses appropriate responses (for the majority of counseling sessions; 70%)	Demonstrates inconsistent ability to be empathic and/or use appropriate responses	Demonstrates limited ability to be empathic and/or uses appropriate responses	Demonstrates poor ability to be empathic and caring, such as creating an unsafe space for clients
1.L Facilitate therapeutic environment: Respect and compassion ___ score	Counselor expresses appropriate respect and compassion for clients	Demonstrates consistent ability to be respectful, accepting, and compassionate with clients (85%)	Demonstrates ability to be respectful, accepting, and compassionate with clients (for the majority of counseling sessions; 70%)	Demonstrates inconsistent ability to be respectful, accepting, and compassionate with clients	Demonstrates limited ability to be respectful, accepting, and/or compassionate with clients	Demonstrates poor ability to be respectful and compassionate with clients, such as having conditional respect

___ *Total* (out of a possible 60 points)

Note. Council for Accreditation of Counseling and Related Educational Programs (CACREP) 2016 Specialty Standards represented in Table 22.1 include Clinical Mental Health Counseling (techniques and interventions for prevention and treatment of a broad range of mental health issues; Section 3: Professional Practice, Standard B); Marriage, Couple, and Family Counseling (techniques and interventions of marriage, couple, and family counseling; Section 3: Professional Practice, Standard C); and School Counseling (techniques of personal/social counseling in school settings; Section 3: Professional Practice, Standard F). Specific Skill = Specific counseling skills and therapeutic conditions descriptors; 5 = Exceeds expectations/demonstrates competencies; 4 = Meets expectations/demonstrates competencies; 3 = Near expectations/developing toward competencies; 2 = Below expectations/unacceptable; 1 = Harmful.

Table 22.2
Part 2: Counseling Dispositions and Behaviors

Number and Primary Counseling Disp.	Specific Skill	5	4	3	2	1
2.A Professional ethics ____ score	Adheres to the ethical guidelines of ACA, ASCA, IAMFC, APA, and NBCC; including practices within competencies	Demonstrates consistent and advanced (i.e., exploration and deliberation) ethical behavior and judgments	Demonstrates consistent ethical behavior and judgments	Demonstrates ethical behavior and judgments but on a concrete level with a basic ethical decision-making process	Demonstrates limited ethical behavior and judgment and a limited ethical decision-making process	Demonstrates poor ethical behavior and judgment, such as violating the ethical codes and/or makes poor decisions
2.B Professional behavior ____ score	Behaves in a professional manner toward supervisors, peers, and clients (e.g., emotional regulation); is respectful and appreciative to the culture of colleagues and is able to effectively collaborate with others	Demonstrates consistent and advanced respectfulness and thoughtfulness, and is appropriate within all professional interactions	Demonstrates consistent respectfulness and thoughtfulness, and is appropriate within all professional interactions	Demonstrates inconsistent respectfulness and thoughtfulness, and is appropriate within professional interactions	Demonstrates limited respectfulness and thoughtfulness and acts inappropriately within some professional interactions	Demonstrates poor professional behavior, such as repeatedly being disrespectful of others and/or impeding the professional atmosphere of the counseling setting/course
2.C Professional and personal boundaries ____ score	Maintains appropriate boundaries with supervisors, peers, and clients	Demonstrates consistent and strong appropriate boundaries with supervisors, peers, and clients	Demonstrates consistent, appropriate boundaries with supervisors, peers, and clients	Demonstrates appropriate boundaries inconsistently with supervisors, peers, and clients	Demonstrates inappropriate boundaries with supervisors, peers, and clients	Demonstrates poor boundaries with supervisors, peers, and clients, such as engaging in dual relationships
2.D Knowledge and adherence to site and course policies ____ score	Demonstrates an understanding and appreciation for all counseling site and course policies and procedures	Demonstrates consistent adherence to all counseling site and course policies and procedures, including strong attendance and engagement	Demonstrates adherence to most counseling site and course policies and procedures, including strong attendance and engagement	Demonstrates inconsistent adherence to counseling site and course policies and procedures, including attendance and engagement	Demonstrates limited adherence to counseling site and course policies and procedures, including attendance and engagement	Demonstrates poor adherence to counseling site and course policies, such as failing to adhere to policies after discussing with supervisor/instructor
2.E Record keeping and task completion ____ score	Completes all weekly record keeping and tasks correctly and promptly (e.g., case notes, psychosocial reports, treatment plans, supervisory report)	Completes all required record keeping, documentation, and assigned tasks in a through, timely, and comprehensive fashion	Completes all required record keeping, documentation, and tasks in a competent and timely fashion	Completes all required record keeping, documentation, and tasks but in an inconsistent and questionable fashion	Completes required record keeping, documentation, and tasks inconsistently and in a poor fashion	Fails to complete paperwork and/or tasks by specified deadline
2.F Multicultural competence in counseling relationship ____ score	Demonstrates respect for culture (e.g., race, ethnicity, gender, spirituality, religion, sexual orientation, disability, social class) and awareness of and responsiveness to ways in which culture interacts with the counseling relationship	Demonstrates consistent and advanced multicultural competencies (knowledge, self-awareness, appreciation, and skills) in interactions with clients	Demonstrates multicultural competencies (knowledge, self-awareness, appreciation, and skills) in interactions with clients	Demonstrates inconsistent multicultural competencies (knowledge, self-awareness, appreciation, and skills) in interactions with clients	Demonstrates limited multicultural competencies (knowledge, self-awareness, appreciation, and skills) in interactions with clients	Demonstrates poor multicultural competencies, such as being disrespectful, dismissive, and defensive regarding the significance of culture in the counseling relationship

(Continued)

Table 22.2 (*Continued*)
Part 2: Counseling Dispositions and Behaviors

Number and Primary Counseling Disp.	Specific Skill	5	4	3	2	1
2.G Emotional stability and self-control ____ score	Demonstrates self-awareness and emotional stability (i.e., congruence between mood and affect) and self-control (i.e., impulse control) in relationships with clients	Demonstrates consistent emotional stability and appropriateness in interpersonal interactions with clients	Demonstrates emotional stability and appropriateness in interpersonal interactions with clients	Demonstrates inconsistent emotional stability and appropriateness in interpersonal interactions with clients	Demonstrates limited emotional stability and appropriateness in interpersonal interactions with clients	Demonstrates poor emotional stability and appropriateness in interpersonal interactions with client, such as having high levels of emotional reactants with clients
2.H Motivated to learn and grow/Initiative ____ score	Demonstrates engagement in learning and development of his or her counseling competencies	Demonstrates consistent and strong engagement in promoting his or her professional and personal growth and development	Demonstrates consistent engagement in promoting his or her professional and personal growth and development	Demonstrates inconsistent engagement in promoting his or her professional and personal growth and development	Demonstrates limited engagement in promoting his or her professional and personal growth and development	Demonstrates poor engagement in promoting his or her professional and personal growth and development, such as expressing lack of appreciation for profession and/or apathy to learning
2.I Openness to feedback ____ score	Responds nondefensively and alters behavior in accordance with supervisory and/or instructor feedback	Demonstrates consistent and strong openness to supervisory and/or instructor feedback and implements suggested changes	Demonstrates consistent openness to supervisory and/or instructor feedback and implements suggested changes	Demonstrates openness to supervisory and/or instructor feedback, however, does not implement suggested changes	Demonstrates a lack of openness to supervisory and/or instructor feedback and does not implement suggested changes	Demonstrates no openness to supervisory and/or instructor feedback and is defensive and/or dismissive when given feedback
2.J Flexibility and adaptability ____ score	Demonstrates ability to adapt to changing circumstance, unexpected events, and new situations	Demonstrates consistent and strong ability to adapt and "reads-and-flexes" appropriately	Demonstrates consistent ability to adapt and "reads-and-flexes" appropriately	Demonstrates an inconsistent ability to adapt and flex to his or her clients' diverse changing needs	Demonstrates a limited ability to adapt and flex to his or her clients' diverse changing needs	Demonstrates a poor ability to adapt to his or her clients' diverse changing needs, such as being rigid in work with clients
2.K Congruence and genuineness ____ score	Demonstrates ability to be present and to be true to oneself	Demonstrates consistent and strong ability to be genuine and accepting of self and others	Demonstrates consistent ability to be genuine and accepting of self and others	Demonstrates inconsistent ability to be genuine and accepting of self and others	Demonstrates a limited ability to be genuine and accepting of self and others (incongruent)	Demonstrates a poor ability to be genuine and accepting of self and others, such as being disingenuous
____ Total (out of a possible 55 points)						

(*Continued*)

Table 22.2 (*Continued*)

Part 2: Counseling Dispositions and Behaviors

Narrative Feedback From Supervising Instructor/Clinical Supervisor:

Please note the counselor's or trainee's areas of strength, which you have observed:

Please note the counselor's or trainee's areas for development, which you have observed:

Please comment on the counselor's or trainee's general performance during his or her clinical experience to this point:

_____   _____
Counselor's or Trainee's Name (*print*)   Date

_____   _____
Supervisor's Name (*print*)   Date

Date CCS–R was reviewed with Counselor or Trainee _____

_____   _____
Counselor's or Trainee's Signature   Date

_____   _____
Supervisor's Signature   Date

If the supervising instructor/clinical supervisor is concerned about the counselor's or trainee's progress in demonstrating the appropriate counseling competencies, he or she should have another appropriately trained supervisor observe the counselor's or trainee's work with clients to provide additional feedback to the counselor or trainee.

Note. Primary Counseling Disp. = Primary counseling dispositions and behaviors; Specific Skill = Specific counseling skills and therapeutic conditions descriptors; 5 = Exceeds expectations/demonstrates competencies; 4 = Meets expectations/demonstrates competencies; 3 = Near expectations/developing toward competencies; 2 = Below expectations/unacceptable; 1 = Harmful; ACA = American Counseling Association; ASCA = American School Counselor Association; IAMFC = International Association of Marriage and Family Counselors; APA = American Psychological Association; NBCC = National Board for Certified Counselors; CCS–R = Counselor Competencies Scale—Revised.

Table 22.3
Integrative Counseling Theories Paper Rubric

Criterion (CACREP Standard)	Does Not Meet Expectations	Meets Expectations	Exceeds Expectations
Rationale for choosing theory/theories and how the theory/theories does/does not fit with your worldview (2.F.5.a, 2.F.5.n)	Provides minimal evidence and description of the rationale for the theory and may include inaccuracies	Provides adequate evidence and description of the rationale for the theory	Provides comprehensive evidence and detailed description of the rationale for the theory
Key theoretical concepts explored: View of human nature, goals and outcomes of counseling, techniques used with the theory (2.F.5.a)	Provides minimal explanations for one or more key theoretical components and may include inaccuracies	Provides adequate explanations for most key theoretical components	Provides comprehensive explanations for all key theoretical components
Role of the counselor and client identified and explained (2.F.5.a)	Includes a minimal description of the counselor's and client's roles and may include inaccuracies	Includes an adequate description of the counselor's and client's roles	Includes a comprehensive description of the counselor's and client's roles
Theoretical understanding of the change process is explained (2.F.5.a)	Includes a minimal/basic description of theoretical notion of change	Includes an adequate description of theoretical notion of change	Includes a comprehensive description of theoretical notion of change
Multicultural considerations: Examine the inclusion or lack of cultural factors in counseling (2.F.5.a)	Includes a basic description of multicultural factors	Includes an adequate description of multicultural factors	Includes a comprehensive description of multicultural factors
Critique of the theory: Strengths and limitations (2.F.5.a)	Includes minimal strengths and weaknesses of the theory with a lack of literature support	Includes adequate, literature-supported strengths and weaknesses of theory	Includes comprehensive, literature-supported strengths and weaknesses of theory
Quality of paper technicalities	Writing difficulty with several grammar, syntax, and/or APA Style formatting errors	Adequate quality of writing with minimal grammar, syntax, and/or APA Style formatting errors	Excellent quality of writing with few, if any, grammar, syntax, or APA Style formatting errors

Note. CACREP = Council for Accreditation of Counseling and Related Educational Programs; APA = American Psychological Association.

Table 22.4
Consultation Model Rubric

Criterion (CACREP Standard)	Does Not Meet Expectations	Meets Expectations	Exceeds Expectations
Consultation theories, models, and strategies (2.F.5.c)	Insufficient description; does not demonstrate understanding of theories, models, and strategies of consultation; misses several important aspects	Adequate description; demonstrates satisfactory understanding of theories, models, and strategies of consultation	Thorough description; demonstrates an exceptional understanding of theories, models, and strategies of consultation
Consultation practice (2.F.5.c)	Insufficient description; does not demonstrate understanding of consultation implementation; misses several important aspects	Adequate description; demonstrates satisfactory understanding of consultation implementation	Thorough description; demonstrates an exceptional understanding of consultation implementation
Community resources (2.F.5.j)	Insufficient description; does not demonstrate understanding of community-based resources; misses several important aspects	Adequate description; demonstrates satisfactory understanding of community-based resources	Thorough description; demonstrates an exceptional understanding of community-based resources
Quality of paper technicalities	Writing difficulty with several grammar, syntax, and/or APA Style formatting errors	Adequate quality of writing with minimal grammar, syntax, and/or APA Style formatting errors	Excellent quality of writing with few, if any, grammar, syntax, or APA Style formatting errors

Note. CACREP = Council for Accreditation of Counseling and Related Educational Programs; APA = American Psychological Association.

Chapter 23

Group Counseling and Group Work

Jonathan H. Ohrt

Group work is widely accepted as a commonly used, cost-effective counseling modality that results in positive client outcomes in a variety of clinical and educational settings (Burlingame, Fuhriman, & Mosier, 2003; Steen, Bauman, & Smith, 2007). Given the clinical benefits and frequent use of groups with clients, it is important for counselors to receive high-quality education in group work during their entry-level training. Training in group work is emphasized in the Association for Specialists in Group Work's (2000) *Professional Standards for the Training of Group Workers*, and group work is included as an entry-level core standard in the 2016 Standards (CACREP, 2016). Additionally, students in CACREP-accredited programs are required to obtain experience facilitating groups as part of their clinical experience. The authors of both sets of standards have recommended a variety of didactic and experiential approaches to training future group leaders. In addition to the experience of facilitating groups, content in a group class tends to include topics such as group development, group dynamics, therapeutic factors, group stages, leadership styles, and types of groups (Association for Specialists in Group Work, 2000; Corey, Corey, & Corey, 2014). In a study with experienced group leaders who were reflecting on their training, participants reported that planning for a group, developing a leadership style and role, and understanding group processes and dynamics were essential to facilitating groups effectively (Ohrt, Ener, Porter, & Young, 2014).

Counseling in a group requires a unique knowledge base and skill set that are in addition to the competencies required in individual counseling. Thus, counselor educators are tasked with assessing student learning and skills in group work. Counselor educators may develop a variety of learning activities and assessment strategies to ensure that entry-level counseling students complete their training programs with the ability to plan, organize, and execute effective groups in an ethical and diversity-sensitive manner.

In this chapter, I describe three assignments and provide example assessment rubrics for the entry-level core area of group work. The first assignment is designed to provide students with an opportunity to design a group for a specific population with which they would like to work and describe their approach to facilitating the group. The next activity is designed to help students reflect on group processes and dynamics that affect group development through the use of a feature film. The final activity is an opportunity for students to demonstrate group skills and knowledge of theoretically and empirically supported group approaches through a group theory presentation and intervention demonstration.

Group Proposal and Curriculum

SLOs assessed: CACREP 2016 Standards 2.F.6.a, 2.F.6.b, 2.F.6.d, 2.F.6.e, 2.F.6.f, 2.F.6.g

Prepare a group proposal and develop a 6-week curriculum for the proposed group. Select a setting in which you would implement a group for a specific population (e.g., groups designed for children, adolescents, college students, older adults). Select one of the group specializations (i.e., task, psychoeducation, counseling, or psychotherapy) and develop a proposal and curriculum. The group curriculum should consist of six sessions. You may decide to do this in a lesson plan format (example format is included below). The recommended page length is 18–22 pages, and papers should be consistent with APA Style guidelines, including an appropriate title page, headings, margins, and spacing (no abstract is necessary). The proposal should include, at minimum, the following components:

1. *Background and rationale for your group specialization design* (i.e., task, psychoeducation, counseling, or psychotherapy).
2. *Relevant literature to support your rationale* (cite a minimum of five journal articles): Provide a rationale as to why the population you chose needs services.
3. *Objectives of the group:* Identify 3–5 objectives for the group overall and include an objective for each session.
4. *Composition of the group* (i.e., heterogeneous or homogeneous, age or grade level, gender, presenting concerns, how many members will be included in the group).
5. *Logistics to consider when planning the group:* Include an informed consent form. Describe how you will recruit, select, and screen members. Describe the criteria for inclusion in the group and what would cause a member to be inappropriate for the group. Explain when and where the group will take place. Discuss how long the group will last. Use support from the literature to justify your processes.
6. *Ethical and multicultural considerations:* Discuss various ethical concerns related to the group and how you will address them. Discuss how you will attend to diversity within the group.
7. *The theoretical approach you will use in your group:* Describe your theoretical approach to the group with support from the literature. The activities you develop in your curriculum should be congruent with your theoretical approach.
8. *Ways you will attempt to balance process and content in your group:* Discuss how you will attend to group process and balance process with content during group sessions. Also, include the specific content (activities, interventions, topics of discussion) as well as potential process questions for each group session in the curriculum section.
9. *Examples of how you will attend to warm-up, action, and closure phases in your group:* Discuss interventions that you will use in the beginning, working, and closing phases of your group sessions. Also, include "ice-breaker" and warm-up activities, action interventions, and closing activities for each session within the curriculum.
10. *Leadership role and functions:* Discuss your leadership style and your role and responsibilities as a leader during each stage of the group.
11. *Evaluation:* Discuss how termination and follow-up appraisals will be performed to evaluate the effectiveness of the group (e.g., what forms of assessment will you use?). Describe what provisions will be made for individuals who do not progress or who are harmed as a result of the group experience.
12. *Interpersonal learning:* Describe how you will help group members translate interpersonal learning in the group to life beyond the group.

Include a six-session curriculum. The suggested group session format outline is listed below:

- Session topic
- Goal and objectives
- Materials
- Activities/interventions

- Warm-up (check-in, introduction, review topic)
- Working/processing (teach new skill, behavior, etc.; discussion; role-play; processing questions)
- Closing (identify behavioral learning, check-out)

Table 23.1 includes the rubric associated with this assignment.

Group Video Reflection

SLOs assessed: CACREP 2016 Standards 2.F.6.b, 2.F.6.c

Note: This assignment is designed as a final exam. In this example, I use the film *The Breakfast Club* (Tanen & Hughes, 1985). For examples of other feature films that can be used to teach about group work, see Moe, Autry, Olson, and Johnson (2014) and Tyler and Reynolds (1998).

The purpose of this assignment is for you to demonstrate the knowledge about group development that you gained throughout the semester. After viewing the film *The Breakfast Club*, respond to the following in 1–2 paragraphs per question:

1. Discuss the group stages that are evident in the video. Provide examples of how the climate and interactions are indicative of each stage (initial, transition, working, termination).
2. Describe the member roles that are portrayed by the characters in the video. Label the role and provide some examples of how the character exhibits the characteristics of that role. Some characters may exhibit characteristics of multiple roles.
3. Identify the therapeutic factors that appear to be operating for this group. Label the factor and provide examples of how the group was therapeutic for the characters.
4. Discuss content and process. What content was discussed by the characters? What processes were evident (e.g., here-and-now interactions, group development), and what are some examples of how the characters attended to the group process?

Table 23.2 includes the rubric associated with this assignment.

Group Theory Presentation and Demonstration

SLOs assessed: CACREP 2016 Standards 2.F.6.a, 2.F.6.d, 2.F.6.f, 2.F.6.g

Work in groups to present some of the theories and approaches to group counseling. Students are expected to utilize information from the text as well as outside sources such as textbooks or journal articles. The presentation and demonstration should last 40 minutes and include a presentation of the theory, class discussion, and two experiential demonstrations.

1. Briefly present the basic tenets of the identified counseling theory and the role of the group leader within the theory. Present relevant group literature and research on the effectiveness of the theory with various populations. Discuss group-related ethical and multicultural considerations within the theory and the intervention.
2. Engage the class in two role-played group interventions that are congruent with the theory you are presenting. Demonstrate how the group would look by implementing the interventions with you as the group leader and your classmates as the group. Use group skills to effectively facilitate the group activity.
3. Provide the class with a handout that includes the following information about each intervention (this can be presented in a one- to two-page lesson plan style handout; make enough copies for everyone in the class):
   a. a name for the intervention,
   b. the most appropriate client configuration (e.g., children, adolescents, adults, couples, and/or families),
   c. the appropriate age(s),

Table 23.1
Group Proposal and Curriculum Rubric

Criterion (CACREP Standard)	Does Not Meet Expectations	Meets Expectations	Exceeds Expectations
Group program	Lacks clear identification of the group program and population; little or no description of the population	Adequately identifies and clearly explains group program and population; clear description of the populations with attention to several characteristics	Outstanding explanation of group program and population; thorough description of the population with attention to many characteristics
Background and rationale for design (2.F.6.f)	Inadequate discussion of background or rationale for the group design; minimal description of background or weak rationale; few (or no) examples to justify the group; lacks support from the literature	Adequate discussion of background and rationale for the group design; the background and rationale are described; examples to justify the group are included; includes some support from the literature	Outstanding discussion of background and rationale for the group design; thorough description of background and rationale; several examples to justify the group; includes strong support from the literature
Objectives for the group	Inadequate description of objectives; few (or no) objectives are included; or objectives are not clear, specific, or realistic	Adequate description of some objectives; objectives are clear, specific, and realistic	Outstanding description of several objectives; objectives are clear, specific, and realistic
Composition of the group (2.F.6.e)	Insufficient description of group composition; few (or no) elements of group composition are described	Sufficient description of group composition; multiple elements of group composition are described	Excellent description of group composition; several elements of group composition are described
Identification and consideration of group logistics (2.F.6.e, 2.F.6.g)	Inadequate identification and consideration of logistics relevant to planning the proposed group; few (or no) components are included; or the section lacks support from the literature	Adequate identification and consideration of logistics relevant to planning the proposed group; includes multiple components; section includes citations to the literature	Outstanding identification and consideration of logistics relevant to planning the proposed group; includes many components; section includes several citations to the literature
Ethical and multicultural considerations (2.F.6.g)	Insufficient attention to ethical and multicultural aspects of the group; few (or no) examples of strategies to attend to ethics and diversity are included	Sufficient attention to ethical and multicultural aspects of the group; examples of strategies to attend to ethics and diversity are included	Excellent attention to ethical and multicultural aspects of the group; several examples of strategies to attend to ethics and diversity are included
Proposed group counseling theoretical approach (2.F.6.a)	Inadequate discussion of counseling approach in proposed group setting; inconsistent with literature; key concepts from the theory are omitted; empirical support is not provided	Adequate discussion of counseling approach in proposed group setting; consistent with literature; multiple concepts from the theory are included; empirical support is provided	Outstanding discussion of counseling approach in proposed group setting; consistent with literature; most key concepts from the theory are included; empirical support is provided from multiple sources
Process and content in proposed group (2.F.6.b)	Inadequate explanation of group process and content and ways to balance both; lacks specific examples to support the approach	Adequate explanation of group process and content and discusses ways to balance both; provides examples to support the approach	Outstanding explanation of group process and content and discusses ways to balance both; provides multiple examples to support the approach
Attending to warm-up phase of group (2.F.6.b, 2.F.6.d)	Inadequate attention to warm-up phase interventions; lacks specific examples of interventions	Adequate attention to warm-up phase interventions with some examples of interventions	Outstanding attention to warm-up phase interventions with several examples of interventions
Attending to action phase of group (2.F.6.b, 2.F.6.d)	Inadequate attention to action phase interventions; lacks specific examples of interventions	Adequate attention to action phase interventions with some examples of interventions	Outstanding attention to action phase interventions with several examples of interventions
Attending to closure phase of group (2.F.6.b, 2.F.6.d)	Inadequate attention to closure phase interventions; lacks specific examples of interventions	Adequate attention to closure phase interventions with some examples of interventions	Outstanding attention to closure phase interventions with several examples of interventions
Leader's role and functions (2.F.6.b, 2.F.6.d)	Inadequate explanation of leader's role and functions; few (or no) examples of leader functions; lacks citations to the literature	Adequate explanation of leader's role and functions; some examples of leader functions; supports with some citations to the literature	Outstanding explanation of leader's role and function; multiple example of leader functions; supports with multiple citations to the literature

(Continued)

Table 23.1 (*Continued*)
Group Proposal and Curriculum Rubric

Criterion (CACREP Standard)	Does Not Meet Expectations	Meets Expectations	Exceeds Expectations
Evaluation of proposed group (2.F.6.d)	Inadequate explanation of termination and follow-up appraisals to evaluate effectiveness of the group; overly simplistic evaluation methods	Adequate explanation of termination and follow-up appraisals to evaluate effectiveness of the group; sufficient evaluation methods	Outstanding explanation of termination and follow-up appraisals to evaluate effectiveness of the group; multiple comprehensive evaluation methods
Interpersonal learning (2.F.6.d)	Inadequate description of how the leader will help group members translate interpersonal learning to life beyond the group; few (or no) specific examples	Adequate description of how the leader will help group members translate interpersonal learning to life beyond the group; provides specific examples	Outstanding description of how the leader will help group members translate interpersonal learning to life beyond the group; provides multiple specific examples
Quality of sources, writing, and APA Style	Inadequate quality of writing with several grammar, syntax, and/or APA Style formatting errors	Adequate quality of writing with minimal grammar, syntax, and/or APA Style formatting errors	Excellent quality of writing with few, if any, grammar, syntax, or APA Style formatting errors

Note. CACREP = Council for Accreditation of Counseling and Related Educational Programs; APA = American Psychological Association.

d.   the appropriate client issues (for what issues is the activity appropriate?),
e.   the inappropriate client issues (for what issues would this activity be inadvisable to use?),
f.   the source from which you pulled the intervention (cite your sources),
g.   a list of needed materials,
h.   a description of the activity set-up (what needs to be done before meeting with the group?),
i.   a thorough description of the activity, and
j.   the appropriate follow-up/process questions (how to end the activity, process what happens, and transfer learning to life outside the group).

Table 23.3 includes the rubric associated with this assignment.

Table 23.2
Group Video Reflection Rubric

Criterion (CACREP Standard)	Does Not Meet Expectations	Meets Expectations	Exceeds Expectations
Group stages (2.F.6.b)	Inadequate discussion of group stages; lacks specific examples from each stage or misses major key points	Adequate discussion of group stages with specific examples from each stage	Thorough discussion of group stages with multiple specific examples from each stage
Group member roles and characteristics (2.F.6.b)	Inadequate description of group member roles and characteristics; lacks specific examples or misses major key points	Adequate description of group member roles and characteristics with specific examples	Thorough description of group member roles and characteristics with multiple specific examples
Group therapeutic factors (2.F.6.c)	Inadequate description of group therapeutic factors; lacks specific examples or misses major key points	Adequate description of group therapeutic factors with specific examples	Thorough description of group therapeutic factors with multiple specific examples
Group content and process (2.F.6.b)	Inadequate description of group content and process; lacks specific examples or misses major key points	Adequate description of group content and process with specific examples	Thorough description of group content and process with multiple specific examples
Overall writing style and coherence of response	Insufficient quality of writing; response contains several grammatical errors; is difficult to follow	Sufficient quality of writing; response is well-written with minimal grammatical errors and is easy to follow	Outstanding quality of writing; response is well-written with few, if any, grammatical errors and is easy to follow

Note. CACREP = Council for Accreditation of Counseling and Related Educational Program.

Table 23.3
Group Theory Presentation and Demonstration Rubric

Criterion (CACREP Standard)	Does Not Meet Expectations	Meets Expectations	Exceeds Expectations
Presentation—Group theory (2.F.6.a)	Group presents an unclear or inaccurate overview of the tenets of the theory—lacks examples.	Group presents a clear and accurate overview of the tenets of the theory with some examples.	Group presents a clear and accurate overview of the tenets of the theory with multiple examples.
Presentation—Group leader role (2.F.6.a, 2.F.6.d)	Group presents an insufficient overview of the group leader's role and functions within the theory—lacks examples.	Group presents a sufficient overview of the group leader's role and functions within the theory with some examples.	Group presents a thorough overview of the group leader's role and functions within the theory with multiple examples.
Presentation—Ethical and multicultural considerations (2.F.6.g)	Group inadequately addresses ethical and multicultural considerations within the theory and interventions—lacks specific examples.	Group sufficiently addresses ethical and multicultural considerations within the theory and interventions with some examples.	Group thoroughly addresses ethical and multicultural considerations within the theory and interventions with multiple examples.
Presentation—Empirical evidence (2.F.6.a, 2.F.6.d)	Group presents insufficient empirical evidence for the group approach—lacks examples from the literature.	Group sufficiently presents empirical evidence for the group approach with some examples from the literature.	Group thoroughly presents empirical evidence for the group approach with multiple examples from the literature.
Demonstration—Appropriateness of interventions (2.F.6.a, 2.F.6.g)	Inadequate explanation and demonstration of effective, ethical, and diversity-sensitive interventions—inconsistent with the presented theory.	Adequate explanation and demonstration of effective, ethical, and diversity-sensitive interventions—consistent with the presented theory.	Outstanding explanation and demonstration of effective, ethical, and diversity-sensitive interventions—consistent with the presented theory.
Demonstration—Group skills (2.F.6.d)	No or limited demonstration of relevant group skills (e.g., drawing out, linking, rounds, summarizing)—ineffective facilitation of the interventions.	Adequate demonstration of a few group skills (e.g., drawing out, linking, rounds, summarizing). Occasional opportunities to effectively facilitate using group skills may have been missed.	Outstanding demonstration of multiple group skills (e.g., drawing out, linking, rounds, summarizing). Interventions were effectively facilitated.
Handout (2.F.6.a, 2.F.6.f, 2.F.6.g)	Group provides no handout, or handouts are inadequately detailed.	Group provides detailed and practical handouts describing the interventions. Occasional gaps in detail occur, but most content is clearly and practically covered.	Group provides thorough, detailed, and practical handouts detailing the interventions.
Overall quality of presentation	Group lacks interaction or engagement—fails to promote discussion with the class.	Group is sufficiently interactive, engaging, and promotes discussion with the class.	Group is interactive, engaging, and promotes discussion with the class.

Note. CACREP = Council for Accreditation of Counseling and Related Educational Program.

Chapter 24

Assessment and Testing

Rebecca A. Newgent and Molly Watkins

It is important to develop an understanding of what assessment and testing looks like for the counseling profession. Assessment is a broad concept that encompasses several evaluation methods that give counselors an increased understanding of their clients and that aid in treatment planning and progress assessment. Some common assessments include personality assessment, career assessment, intelligence assessment, and ability assessment (Hays, 2013).

Assessment can take many forms. Most commonly, people see assessment as testing. In counseling, tests help measure behaviors, attitudes, thoughts, and feelings but are only one aspect of assessment. Assessment is much more comprehensive. Although assessment can include tests, assessment can also include information from multiple sources. For example, an intake interview is a form of an assessment that provides valuable information regarding the client's mental status, psychosocial history, and current functioning. Teachers, parents, and family members can also provide valuable information regarding a client via interviews and other assessment tools.

If you are a counselor . . . you do assessment. Counselors use assessment in every aspect of their interactions with clients. From the intake assessment through termination, assessment is a necessary element for counselors. The use of assessments by counselors requires knowledge of the historical perspectives, procedures, basic statistical concepts, uses of assessment, and ethical and cultural strategies related to assessment (CACREP 2016 Standard 2.F.7).

CACREP (2016) looks to these Standards as a way in which to help students develop into competent and ethical counselors who have a well-defined professional identity. CACREP has identified the area of Assessment and Testing as one of eight common core curricular experiences that help define professional identity. Consistent with best practices, the assessment of SLOs needs to utilize a variety of tools. That is, it is important to use more than one type of assessment when evaluating student learning.

In this chapter, we provide three assignments and rubrics to assess learning in the counseling core related to Assessment and Testing. The first activity is designed to help master's-level students apply social and cultural factors and ethical strategies related to assessment and analyze results revealed from the assessment procedure. The second activity is a test critique that requires students to critically analyze an assessment and to develop their own evaluation. The final assignment is the comprehensive final examination in which the students must apply all the elements taught in class to develop their own assessment.

Assessment Report

SLOs assessed: CACREP 2016 Standards 2.F.7.e, 2.F.7.f, 2.F.7.m

You will administer the NEO Personality Inventory—3 (McCrae, Costa, & Martin, 2005) and the State-Trait Anxiety Inventory (Spielberger, 1983) to yourself, interpret it, and write up a professional report. At a minimum, you must include the following headings in your report:

- Reason for Referral (1 point)
- Background and History (psychosocial history, medical/counseling background, substance use and abuse, educational and vocational history, and other pertinent information) (4 points)
- Evaluation Procedures (1 point)
- Behavioral Observations (including mental status examination) (1 point)
- Assessment Results (NEO Personality Inventory—3, State-Trait Anxiety Inventory, and Diagnostic Impressions) (9 points)
- Recommendations (1 point)
- Summary (3 points)

The report must be written in the most recent APA Style (if not, −3) and at Bloom's Revised Taxonomy Levels 3–4 (Anderson & Krathwohl, 2001; if not, −3). This assignment will require you to apply (i.e., carry out or use a procedure in a given situation) and analyze (i.e., break material into its constituent parts and determine how the parts relate to one another and to the overall structure and purpose) the elements of this assignment. The total gain for this assignment is 20 points. Table 24.1 includes the rubric associated with this assignment.

Test Critique

SLOs assessed: CACREP 2016 Standards 2.F.7.h, 2.F.7.m

Complete and present one test critique on an assessment you find in *Tests in Print* or the *Mental Measurements Yearbook*. Provide copies of your critique for all class members and instructor(s). Choice of test must be preapproved by instructor.

Table 24.1
Assessment Report Rubric

Criterion (CACREP Standard)	Does Not Meet Expectations	Meets Expectations	Exceeds Expectations
Diagnosis and planning (2.F.7.e)	Demonstrates minimal or inaccurate ability to conceptualize, diagnose, and/or plan; substantial inconsistencies and/or errors; inaccurate summary and/or behavioral observations	Demonstrates some ability to conceptualize, diagnose, and/or plan; some inconsistencies and/or errors; summary and/or behavioral observations need to be more thorough	Demonstrates acceptable ability to conceptualize, diagnose, and plan; no inconsistencies or errors; thorough summary and behavioral observations
Basic concepts (2.F.7.f)	Demonstrates minimal or inaccurate knowledge of basic concepts of testing and assessment; substantial inconsistencies and/or errors; interpretation lacks thoroughness	Demonstrates some knowledge of basic concepts of testing and assessment; some inconsistencies and/or errors; interpretation needs to be more thorough	Demonstrates acceptable knowledge of basic concepts of testing and assessment; no inconsistencies or errors noted; interpretation is thorough
Ethical and cultural strategies (2.F.7.m)	Demonstrates minimal or inaccurate ability to integrate ethical and cultural factors with the interpretation of assessment results; substantial inconsistencies and/or errors; interpretation lacks thoroughness	Demonstrates some ability to integrate ethical and cultural factors with the interpretation of assessment results; some inconsistencies and/or errors; interpretation needs to be more thorough	Demonstrates acceptable ability to integrate ethical and cultural factors with interpretation of assessment results; no inconsistencies or errors noted; interpretation is thorough

Note. CACREP = Council for Accreditation of Counseling and Related Educational Program.

At a minimum, you must include the following in your critique:

- general information (title of the test, include edition and forms if applicable; authors; publisher; dates of publication, include dates of manuals, norms, and supplementary materials; time required to administer; cost of test, booklets, answer sheets, scoring services),
- brief description of the purpose and nature of the test (general type of test: individual, group, performance, aptitude; population for which the test was designed: age range, type of person; nature of the content of the test: subtests and separate scores, item types),
- practical evaluation (qualitative features of test materials: design of test booklet, editorial control, ease of use, attractiveness, durability, appropriateness for intended population; ease of administration: clarity of directions, scoring procedures, computer scoring software, face validity of test, need for test-taker rapport),
- technical evaluation (norms [type of norms/scores, standardization sample; nature, size, representativeness, procedures for obtaining sample, subgroup norms], reliability [type, procedure to establish reliability, long-term stability], validity [type, procedure]),
- reviewer comments from the *Mental Measurements Yearbook* and other sources,
- user qualifications,
- summary evaluation (major strengths/weaknesses; this is your summary), and
- references.

Note: All of the above information may not be available/relevant for all tests. The critique must be written in APA Style and at Bloom's Revised Taxonomy Levels 3–4. This assignment will require you to apply (i.e., carry out or use a procedure in a given situation) and analyze (i.e., break material into its constituent parts and determine how the parts relate to one another and to the overall structure and purpose) the elements of this assignment. Table 24.2 includes the rubric associated with this assignment.

Comprehensive Final Examination

SLOs assessed: CACREP 2016 Standards 2.F.7.a, 2.F.7.f, 2.F.7.g, 2.F.7.i

You are developing an assessment for a special population for a specific purpose. Identify the special population and specified purpose. Then use the information provided to you about this term to develop the assessment. Identify all steps, processes, and procedures that you will use. Also, make sure to include all relevant aspects that relate to the assessment process. This includes all information provided to you in lecture as well as in the text. After you have recorded all the processes you used, provide a complete example of the actual developed assessment.

Table 24.2
Test Critique Rubric

Criterion (CACREP Standard)	Does Not Meet Expectations	Meets Expectations	Exceeds Expectations
Reliability and validity (2.F.7.h)	Demonstrates minimal or inaccurate understanding of reliability and validity; does not report reliability and validity data from empirical studies when available; lacks thoroughness	Demonstrates some understanding of reliability and validity; some errors in reporting reliability and validity data; interpretation needs to be more thorough	Demonstrates acceptable understanding of reliability and validity; reports reliability and validity information accurately; interpretation is thorough
Ethical and cultural strategies (2.F.7.m)	Demonstrates minimal or inaccurate understanding of ethical and cultural strategies; fails to identify ethical and cultural issues related to the selection, administration, and/or interpretation of the assessments and tests	Demonstrates some understanding of ethical and cultural strategies; lacks thoroughness identifying ethical and cultural issues related to the selection, administration, and/or interpretation of the assessments and tests	Demonstrates an acceptable understanding of ethical and cultural strategies related to the selection, administration, and/or interpretation of the assessments and tests
APA Style format	0 points	1 point	2 points
Bloom's Revised Taxonomy Levels 3–4	0 points	1 point	2 points
Substance, thoroughness, and accuracy	0 points	1 point	2 points

Note. CACREP = Council for Accreditation of Counseling and Related Educational Program; APA = American Psychological Association.

You may complete the final examination as an individual or as a group (no more than five students per group). If you choose to complete as a group, you must come to a consensus, as all group members will receive the same grade.

To be eligible to earn the maximum points, you must utilize Bloom's Revised Taxonomy Levels 3–4. Performance below this level will result in a lower grade. APA Style format is required. The assessment must be written in APA Style and at Bloom's Revised Taxonomy Levels 3–4. This assignment will require you to apply (i.e., carry out or use a procedure in a given situation) and analyze (i.e., break material into its constituent parts and determine how the parts relate to one another and to the overall structure and purpose) the elements of this assignment. Table 24.3 includes the rubric associated with this examination.

Table 24.3
Comprehensive Final Examination Rubric

Criterion (CACREP Standard)	Does Not Meet Expectations	Meets Expectations	Exceeds Expectations
Content			
Historical perspectives (2.F.7.a)	Demonstrates minimal or inaccurate understanding of the nature and meaning of assessments; fails to identify required steps, processes, and procedures associated with assessment development	Demonstrates some understanding of the nature and meaning of assessments; does not thoroughly identify required steps, processes, and/or procedures associated with assessment development	Demonstrates acceptable understanding of the nature and meaning of assessments; identifies all required steps, processes, and procedures associated with assessment development
Basic concepts (2.F.7.f)	Demonstrates minimal or inaccurate understanding of basic concepts of standardized and nonstandardized testing; fails to include processes for developing assessment tools for groups and individuals	Demonstrates some understanding of basic concepts of standardized and nonstandardized testing; lacks thoroughness in identifying processes for developing assessment tools for groups and individuals	Demonstrates acceptable understanding of the basic concepts of standardized and nonstandardized testing; includes thorough identification of processes for developing assessment tools for groups and individuals
Statistical concepts (2.F.7.g)	Demonstrates minimal or inaccurate understanding of statistical concepts; fails to include data on scales of measurement, measures of central tendency, indices of variability, shapes and types of distributions, and correlations for the assessment tool	Demonstrates some understanding of statistical concepts; includes limited data on scales of measurement, measures of central tendency, indices of variability, shapes and types of distributions, and correlations for the assessment tool	Demonstrates acceptable understanding of statistical concepts; includes thorough identification of scales of measurement, measures of central tendency, indices of variability, shapes and types of distributions, and correlations for the assessment tool
Relevant use (2.F.7.i)	Demonstrates minimal or inaccurate understanding applying the assessment tool to academic/educational, career, personal, and social development; fails to include purpose of and how to use assessment tool for identified population	Demonstrates limited understanding applying the assessment tool to academic/educational, career, personal, and social development; includes limited application for purpose of and how to use assessment tool for identified population	Demonstrates acceptable understanding applying the assessment tool to academic/educational, career, personal, and social development; includes thorough application for purpose of and how to use assessment tool for identified population
Grading			
Organization and synthesis	Unorganized and fragmented (0 points)	3 points	Well organized and synthesized (6 points)
Clarity	Hazy, rambling, ambiguous (0 points)	3 points	Clear, concise (6 points)
Depth	Superficial understanding (0 points)	3 points	Understanding in-depth (6 points)
Breadth	Limited knowledge (0 points)	3 points	Knowledge in breadth (6 points)
Major concepts	Major concepts not covered (0 points)	3 points	Major concepts covered
Factual support	Opinions, no factual support (0 points)	3 points	Opinion supported by facts (6 points)
APA Style	Lacked compliance with format (0 points)	3 points	APA Style format (6 points)
Bloom's Revised Taxonomy	Blooms Revised Taxonomy Levels 1–2 (0 points)	3 points	Bloom's Revised Taxonomy Levels 3–4 (6 points)

Note. CACREP = Council for Accreditation of Counseling and Related Educational Program; APA = American Psychological Association.

Chapter 25

Research and Program Evaluation

A. Stephen Lenz

Counselor educators are increasingly being asked to emphasize the inclusion of intervention strategies that are supported by rigorous research and outcome data within the student training experience (CACREP, 2016). As a result, the ability of counselors to demonstrate the knowledge and skills to critique or promulgate these outcome driven approaches to counseling are now considered an ethical imperative (ACA, 2014). Although it is not expected that every master's-level graduate cultivate an interest to implement extensive research programs, the CACREP Standards provide a framework for students to be active consumers of research that will inform treatment decisions as well as implement basic strategies for evaluating existing programs and quality of services that clients are receiving. Through implementation of well-developed educational, modeling, and practice activities, counselor educators can foster this understanding and generate enthusiasm that counters the guarded approach to research and program evaluation generally associated with these important activities.

Although research and program evaluation share many of the same components, several authors have insisted that the principal distinction lies in the expressed objectives of each (Benkofske & Heppner, 2008; Daniels, 2010; Fitzpatrick, Sanders, & Worthen, 2011; Posavac, 2011). Benkofske and Heppner (2008) suggested that researchers are primarily concerned with making contributions to a general knowledge base, whereas program evaluators intend to identify what is most efficacious for a particular group of people participating in a particular program. From this perspective, all program evaluations involve implementing research methodology, but not all program evaluation has the intent of contributing to the global knowledge base. In my experience, making this distinction is the principal component to promoting student engagement in research and assessment course material. Following, it is important for students to understand that the question a counselor is attempting to answer indicates the methodology that one should consider implementing. Finally, whether evaluating current research to decide what interventions are appropriate for a client or evaluating the degree that a program is meeting target outcomes, counseling students should be able to identify some important aspects of either approach.

This chapter provides three assignments and associated rubrics to assess SLOs within the domains of master's-level research and program evaluation. The first activity is designed to help students identify evidence-based practices literature and critically appraise characteristics of individual supportive studies (CACREP 2016 Standards 2.F.8.a, 2.F.8.d, 2.F.8.f, 2.F.8.h, 2.F.8.i). The second activity is a pragmatic application of course content to help students consider the relationship between research questions, select appropriate research/evaluation methods, and identify dependent variables of interest (CACREP 2016 Standards 2.F.8.d, 2.F.8.e, 2.F.8.f). The final assignment requires students to apply knowledge and skills about program evaluation to an exemplar case (CACREP 2016 Standards 2.F.8.c, 2.F.8.d, 2.F.8.e, 2.F.8.f, 2.F.8.h, 2.F.8.i).

Identifying and Appraising Evidence-Based Interventions

SLOs assessed: CACREP 2016 Standards 2.F.8.b, 2.F.8.e, 2.F.8.g, 2.F.8.i, 2.F.8.j

This activity is designed to have you identify evidence-based practices within the professional literature and to critically appraise characteristics of individual studies that support claims of efficacy. To complete this task, you should do the following:

1. *Identify an evidence-based practice:*
   a. Use your web browser and navigate to the Substance Abuse and Mental Health Services Administration's National Registry of Evidence-Based Programs and Practices at http://www.nrepp.samhsa.gov/.
   b. Once there, use the Find an Intervention handle to view all interventions endorsed by the Substance Abuse and Mental Health Services Administration as evidence-based.
   c. Select one of the interventions (e.g., Acceptance and Commitment Therapy), review the descriptive information, and select one of the Quality of Research documents for review.
2. *Critically appraise the merits of the study by critiquing the characteristics:*
   a. *Treatment.* Identify and describe the treatment that is the focus of the study. Make sure to describe some fundamental characteristics of the intervention and explains why researchers believe it will be helpful.
   b. *Participant characteristics.* Describe the sample along participant characteristics of age, gender, ethnic identity, affectional orientation, and location.
   c. *Research design.* Identify the research design used in the study. Describe the degree that the implemented design promotes making cause and effect attributions. Identify and describe any longitudinal or follow-up measurement intervals that researchers implemented to support inferences about lasting effects of treatment.
   d. *Intended outcome of treatment.* Identify and describe the dependent variables in your selected study.
   e. *Application of findings to myriad populations.* When considering the findings of your selected study, identify and discuss how applicable the findings would be for providing the intervention to the following individuals:
      i. Men who are military service veterans and who are experiencing symptoms of posttraumatic stress disorder.
      ii. Children who have externalizing disorders and who are experiencing academic difficulties as a result.
      iii. A couple that is experiencing relational problems associated with economic distress.
      iv. A client who is experiencing the symptoms of depression following an acquired disability.
      v. Hispanic/Latino men living in the Pacific Northwest.

Table 25.1 includes the rubric associated with this assignment.

Matching Program Questions to Research Designs

SLOs assessed: CACREP 2016 Standards 2.F.8.e, 2.F.8.f, 2.F.8.g

This activity is designed to provide practice evaluating research questions, selecting appropriate methodologies, and identifying outcome measures. The following will provide a brief scenario related to outcome research or program evaluation in counseling that includes the research question of interest. Given the information about the program or context, complete two tasks:

Table 25.1
Identifying and Appraising Evidence-Based Interventions Rubric

Criterion (CACREP Standard)	Does Not Meet Expectations	Meets Expectations	Exceeds Expectations
Demonstrates ability to identify counseling interventions supported by research (2.F.8.b)	No intervention is identified, or intervention is not one included in the NREPP compendium.	Intervention is identified and is included among those listed in the NREPP compendium.	Intervention is identified, a brief rationale is included for its selection, and a description is provided.
Demonstrates ability to identify and evaluate counseling interventions (2.F.8.e)	No information, or just the name of intervention, is provided.	Intervention is identified and briefly described.	Intervention is identified, and description includes content and process components.
Demonstrates ability to describe culturally relevant context for interpreting research results (2.F.8.j)	Three or fewer of the target characteristics are identified and described.	All five target characteristics are identified and briefly described.	All five target characteristics are identified; description is integrated to form a meaningful depiction.
Demonstrates ability to distinguish between research designs and to evaluate degree of causal inferences (2.F.8.g)	The correct design is not identified or does not include information regarding causality.	The correct design is identified, and limited discussion of causal inference in relation to follow-up or longitudinal data is provided.	The correct strategy is identified, and a cogent discussion about the functional relationship within a design that promotes causal inferences is provided.
Understands outcome analysis and use of data in counseling (2.F.8.i)	Dependent variables are incorrectly identified or are not provided.	Dependent variables are identified and briefly described.	Dependent variables are identified and described and include what measure is used to assess the outcome.
Demonstrates ability to consider the ethical and cultural implications for interpreting results of research (2.F.8.j)	All populations are not addressed, or little understanding about the generalizability of findings to populations is demonstrated.	Applicability of the findings is briefly discussed, and a categorical yes/no understanding of generalizability is demonstrated.	Cogent discussion of generalizability to each population is provided, and cultural considerations are overtly apparent.

Note. CACREP = Council for Accreditation of Counseling and Related Educational Program; NREPP = National Registry of Evidence-Based Programs and Practices.

1. Identify the type of research or program evaluation design that would be most appropriate for answering the questions.
2. Identify at least two measurable outcomes related to the research question.

Scenario 1

Faculty members of an intensive outpatient program for treating eating disorders need to report outcomes to their accrediting body. All clients receive a standardized approach to treatment as part of a 6-week program that includes completing assessments during admission, at termination, and then 1 month after treatment. Administrators at the intensive outpatient program would like to know the following: (a) Do clients report a clinically significant amount of change as a result of treatment? (b) What do clients perceive to be the most effective aspects of the interventions within the program?

Scenario 2

A school counselor has been asked to implement a wellness intervention with teachers at an urban elementary school. The counselor's school has historically struggled to meet achievement testing benchmarks. Although they have support of administrators and pay is slightly above average for the area, teacher turnover is an alarming 28% annually, with burnout being the most frequently cited reason for leaving. The school counselor's principal has indicated that if an effective program can be identified, they would provide funding for extended implementation. With a program already in mind, the school counselor wants to determine the following: (a) How effective is a holistic wellness program for decreasing burnout among elementary school teachers? (b) How effective is a holistic wellness program for increasing work–life balance among elementary school teachers?

Scenario 3

A program evaluator has been asked to provide services to an afterschool program for girls located within an urban metropolitan area. The program is primarily grant-funded and is being reviewed to determine whether outcomes warrant extended funding for expansion to other areas of the city. In particular, the program director is being asked to provide data reflecting efficacy of a group-based conflict resolution intervention for decreasing attitudes toward violence, number of conduct-related referrals at school, use of prosocial problem-solving strategies, and grades. The group meets three times per week for 6 weeks, and on the other days, girls meet with tutors for homework assistance.

Table 25.2 includes the rubric associated with this assignment.

An Exercise in Program Evaluation Planning

SLOs assessed: CACREP 2016 Standards 2.F.8.d, 2.F.8.e, 2.F.8.f, 2.F.8.g, 2.F.8.h, 2.F.8.i, 2.F.8.j

This activity is designed to promote mastery for planning program evaluation activities. After reviewing the brief scenario, answer the questions listed below. Make sure to be thorough in your response by not just identifying important concepts but by providing illustrative examples.

Scenario

You have been asked to evaluate a week-long, overnight leadership retreat for executive employees who work for a large shipping and express delivery company located in the mid-Southern region of the United States. With this scenario in mind,

1. What outcomes do you think would be important to consider?
2. If you were developing a survey to address the outcomes you identified in Question 1, what would some of your items be?
3. What type of research method may be best to collect your data, and why?
4. On the basis of the design selected in Question 3, what type of data analysis would you conduct and why?
5. Given the design you selected and the analysis plan you have developed, what are the limitations related to the generalizability of your findings?
6. Who are the stakeholders to whom you would provide a report?
7. What are some cultural considerations related to population, setting, and regional location that would be important to be mindful of while completing the evaluation?

Table 25.3 includes the rubric associated with this assignment.

Table 25.2
Matching Program Questions to Research Designs Rubric

Criterion (CACREP Standard)	Does Not Meet Expectations	Meets Expectations	Exceeds Expectations
Demonstrates knowledge of qualitative, quantitative, or mixed research methods (2.F.8.f)	Selected design is not conducive for answering research questions.	Selected design is conducive for answering research questions; brief rationale is provided.	Selected design is conducive for answering research questions; thorough rationale is provided.
Demonstrates knowledge of designs used in research and program evaluation (2.F.8.g)	Selected design is not conducive for answering research questions.	Selected design is conducive for answering research questions; brief rationale is provided.	Selected design is conducive for answering research questions; thorough rationale is provided.
Demonstrates ability to identify measurable outcomes related to the research questions (2.F.8.e)	No measurable outcomes are identified, or outcomes are not measurable given the design.	Measurable outcomes identified are consistent with provided design.	Measurable outcomes identified are consistent with provided design; example assessments are provided.

Note. This rubric is intended to be used across scenarios. CACREP = Council for Accreditation of Counseling and Related Educational Programs.

Table 25.3
An Exercise in Program Evaluation Planning Rubric

Criterion (CACREP Standard)	Does Not Meet Expectations	Meets Expectations	Exceeds Expectations
Demonstrates ability to identify measurable outcomes related to the research questions (2.F.8.e)	No measurable outcome is identified, or outcomes are not measurable given the design.	Measurable outcomes identified are consistent with provided design.	Measurable outcomes identified are consistent with provided design; example assessments are provided.
Demonstrates knowledge of how to develop surveys to assess outcomes (2.F.8.d)	Items do not complement the outcomes identified in Question 1 or do not complement all outcomes identified.	Items complement the outcomes identified in Question 1, but connection between outcome and item is not explicitly detailed.	Items complement the outcomes identified in Question 1 and connection between outcome and item is explicitly detailed.
Demonstrates knowledge of how to implement research methods to evaluate programs (2.F.8.f, 2.F.8.g)	Selected design is not conducive for answering research questions.	Selected design is conducive for answering research questions; brief rationale is provided.	Selected design is conducive for answering research questions; thorough rationale is provided.
Demonstrates knowledge of data analysis strategies used to evaluate program outcomes (2.F.8.h)	Selected analysis strategy is not congruent with the design choice.	Selected analysis is conducive for answering research questions; brief rationale is provided.	Selected analysis is conducive for answering research questions; thorough rationale is provided.
Demonstrates knowledge of use of outcome data and limitations to generalizability (2.F.8.i)	Limitations of design and statements about generalizability are underdeveloped or inaccurate.	Basic statements about generalizability are included and accurate.	Cogent description of design limitations is provided.
Demonstrates knowledge of culturally relevant considerations for completing program evaluation and reporting findings (2.F.8.j)	Minimal or no discussion is provided regarding population, setting, and regional factors.	Identification of population, setting, and regional factors is provided, with brief discussion of each area.	Identification of population, setting, and regional factors is provided, with discussion that integrates all features meaningfully.

Note. CACREP = Council for Accreditation of Counseling and Related Educational Programs.

Chapter 26

Addiction Counseling

Cortney Stark, Kristopher M. Goodrich, and Heather C. Sands

The CACREP 2016 Standards for counseling programs requires specific competencies for students planning to enter the profession as substance abuse counselors, as well as those entering into other counseling specialties. They allow for CITs to understand addiction within a broader context of mental health and equally within the contexts of school; marriage, family, and couple counseling; and rehabilitation counseling. To meet the changing demands of the addictions field in counseling, the CACREP Standards articulate a multisystem approach to counselor comprehension and treatment of substance abuse. These Standards promote biopsychosocial awareness as well as an understanding of the many systemic forces influencing the development of addiction and the recovery process.

The multisystemic approach embraces the continuum of etiologies that informs counselors' understanding of addiction and treatment. From the disease model to the harm reduction paradigm, these Standards legitimize addiction treatment from an array of perspectives. The recent changes in CACREP Standards for addiction counseling incorporate harm reduction principles, acknowledging reduction of adverse consequences of drug use on the individual and society as a legitimate goal for treatment. As a counseling strategy, harm reduction utilizes cognitive-behavioral and solution-focused principles. Overall, this perspective provides a low-threshold entrance into treatment services, meeting the client where he or she is in the recovery and change process rather than demanding abstinence. This perspective has been incorporated with existing perspectives of addiction into better understanding clients' points of view and needs for clinical care. Although the CACREP 2016 Standards do not articulate or prioritize one perspective of addiction over another, the most current Standards have increased focus on the multisystemic praxis of addiction.

Artifacts are structured so as to engage CITs first in relatively simple, less structured discourse, followed by increasingly complex tasks that require the integration of content and application of skills (Bonwell, 1993, p. 2). Each artifact builds on the knowledge and awareness cultivated during prior activities, other counseling related coursework, and personal and professional life experiences. They require students to engage in the recursive recall of information acquired through assigned readings, class discussion, and activities. Therefore, students benefit from these assignments by not only engaging the information through comprehension and application but also by analyzing and synthesizing new knowledge and understanding (Bloom, 1956) while revising taken-for-granted cognitive schema.

Web-Enhanced Environment: Discussion Board

SLOs assessed: CACREP 2016 Standards 5.A.1.b, 5.A.1.c, 5.A.3.d

The purpose of these web-enhanced discussion board posts is to assess students' comprehension, skill mastery, and receptivity to new perspectives at the beginning of the semester, with reassessment of student development at the midterm and at the close of the semester. Within each post, students' level of awareness and understanding regarding the addictive process and harm reduction approach to the conceptualization and treatment of addiction is evaluated.

Post 1 Prompt

What is your understanding of what constitutes addiction as well as how and why a person becomes addicted? What is your current understanding, or what are your current beliefs, about harm reduction and the role of abstinence in recovery? What are some strengths and limitations you have noticed in the Harm Reduction Model and the role of abstinence in recovery?

Post 2 Prompt

What are your beliefs regarding applicability of harm reduction programs or strategies? If harm reduction and abstinence only fall on opposite ends of a continuum (see Figure 26.1), where do you stand in relation to support of the aforementioned models (Moral Model—Abstinence Only, Disease Model, Harm Reduction Model)? Support your selection of a substance abuse model by articulating two or more of the following principles according to your chosen conceptualization of addiction: wellness, prevention, consultation, education, or advocacy.

Considering your experiences over the course of the semester, what is your understanding of what constitutes addiction as well as how and why a person becomes addicted? How have specific aspects of the course influenced your thoughts, feelings, and beliefs about addictions, the harm reduction perspective, and the role of abstinence in recovery?

Discussion Board Posts 1 and 3: Learning Objective

Student evinces understanding of theories and models of addiction related to substance abuse and other addictions (CACREP 2016 Standard 5.A.1.b):

Exceeds Expectations (4)
- Exhibits advanced awareness and understanding of harm reduction and abstinence only as models for conceptualizing substance abuse.
- Engages in critical evaluation of the strengths and limitations of each perspective.

Disease Model	Moral Model	Harm Reduction Model
Abstinence as Goal	**Abstinence Only**	**Reduction of Individual and Social Harms as Goal**
Need to reduce use by educating individuals regarding ill effects of drugs. Prefer treatment over incarceration.	Need to reduce use by reducing availability of substances and by criminalizing and penalizing use.	Educate individuals about infectious diseases and safe use practices. The longer the individual survives, the greater the likelihood he or she will progress through the stages of change and achieve recovery.

Figure 26.1
Etiology of Addiction Continuum

- Articulates personal beliefs and reflection.
- Discussion board post consists of at least 3–4 complete paragraphs, with no grammatical or syntax errors, and proper APA Style citations where appropriate.

Meets Expectations (3)
- Shows sufficient understanding of harm reduction and abstinence only as models for conceptualizing substance abuse.
- Provides some articulation of strengths or limitations of each perspective.
- Articulates personal beliefs and reflection.
- Discussion board post consists of at least 2–3 paragraphs, with minor grammatical or syntax errors, and attempted APA Style citations where appropriate.

Needs Some Improvement (2)
- Evinces basic understanding of harm reduction or abstinence only as models for conceptualizing substance abuse.
- Mentions but does not fully articulate strengths or limitations of harm reduction or abstinence only as models.
- Provides some indication of personal reflection.
- Discussion board post consists of 2–3 paragraphs, with minor grammatical or syntax errors, and attempted APA Style citations where appropriate.

Needs Substantial Improvement (1)
- Does not demonstrate a basic understanding of harm reduction or abstinence only as models for conceptualizing substance abuse.
- Exhibits misunderstanding of the strengths and limitations of harm reduction or abstinence only as models.
- Fails to provide personal reflection or provides only personal reflection without other criteria.
- Discussion board post consists of 1–2 paragraphs, with major grammatical or syntax errors, and no attempted APA Style citations.

Not Evident (0)
- Student does not submit discussion board post, or
- Student provides incomplete (no paragraphs), incomprehensible, or inaccurate understanding of the topic.

Discussion Board Post 2: Learning Objective

Student exhibits understanding of principles of wellness, prevention, consultation, education, and advocacy in addiction as well as techniques and interventions related to substance abuse and other addictions (CACREP 2016 Standards 5.A.1.c, 5.A.3.d):

Exceeds Expectations (4)
- Exhibits advanced awareness and understanding of the applicability of harm reduction programs and strategies in the treatment and conceptualization of substance abuse.
- Evinces engagement in self-assessment and evaluation of cognitive schema regarding addiction.
- Indicates awareness of other perspectives.
- Articulates advanced understanding of the Moral Model, the Disease Model, and the Harm Reduction Model in conceptualization of substance abuse.
- Indicates the specific model with which he or she identifies, and addresses two or more of the following elements in justification of selection: wellness, prevention, consultation, or advocacy.
- Discussion board post consists of at least 3–4 complete paragraphs, with no grammatical or syntax errors, and proper APA Style citations where appropriate.

Meets Expectations (3)
- Shows sufficient awareness and understanding of the applicability of harm reduction programs and strategies in the treatment and conceptualization of substance abuse.
- Evinces basic engagement in self-assessment and evaluation of cognitive schema regarding addiction.

- Indicates awareness of other perspectives.
- Articulates sufficient understanding of the Moral Model, the Disease Model, and the Harm Reduction Model in conceptualization of substance abuse.
- Indicates the model with which he or she identifies, and addresses one of the following elements in justification of selection: wellness, prevention, consultation, advocacy, or education.
- Discussion board post consists of at least 2–3 paragraphs, with minor grammatical or syntax errors, and attempted APA Style citations where appropriate.

Needs Some Improvement (2)
- Evinces basic understanding of the applicability of harm reduction programs and strategies in the conceptualization of substance abuse.
- Mentions but does not fully articulate self-assessment or evaluation of one's own cognitive schema regarding addiction.
- Fails to indicate awareness of other perspectives.
- Articulates understanding of two of the following models in conceptualization of substance abuse: the Moral Model, the Disease Model, or the Harm Reduction Model.
- Indicates the model with which he or she identifies, but fails to address any of the following elements in justification of selection: wellness, prevention, consultation, advocacy, or education.
- Discussion board post consists of 2–3 paragraphs, with minor grammatical or syntax errors, and attempted APA Style citations where appropriate.

Needs Substantial Improvement (1)
- No basic understanding of the applicability of harm reduction programs and strategies is evinced.
- Does not adequately articulate self-assessment of one's own cognitive schema regarding addiction.
- Exhibits misunderstanding of at least one or more of the following models: the Moral Model, the Disease Model, or the Harm Reduction Model.
- Indicates the model with which he or she identifies, but fails to justify selection.
- Discussion board post consists of 1–2 paragraphs, with major grammatical or syntax errors, and no attempted APA Style citations.

Not Evident (0)
- Student does not submit discussion board post, or
- Student provides incomplete (no paragraphs), incomprehensible, or inaccurate understanding of the topic.

Client Case Conceptualization

SLOs assessed: CACREP 2016 Standards 5.A.2.b, 5.A.2.i, 5.A.2.l, 5.A.2.d, 5.A.3.b, 5.A.3.c, 5.A.3.e, 5.A.3.f, 5.A.3.g, 5.A.3.h

The purpose of this assignment is to ask students to critically engage with the client's case, assessing the presenting problem and treatment concerns on both macro- and microlevels. For this artifact, educators are encouraged to select a case example in which the client's presenting problem consists of substance abuse with a co-occurring disorder. Although our preference is to utilize the case of "Yola and the Man" provided in Keim and Wells's (2009) casebook, other case examples are available and suitable for an assignment of this type. One example is to ask students to review the YouTube video *Darkina* (EmpowHER, 2011), as discussed in the third artifact, and to write up their responses on the basis of that video. Students will analyze the selected case study using the following areas of focus:

- diagnosis;
- counseling;
- prevention;
- intervention;
- knowledge of comorbidity;
- differential diagnosis and associated medical issues;
- screening and assessment;

- legal and ethical conditions; and
- institutional, historical, and political conditions.

Review the provided client case example. The client discussed in the case study has been diagnosed with drug and/or alcohol dependence with co-occurring serious mental illness. After reviewing this case, construct a six- to eight-page paper conceptualizing the client's case as if you were his or her clinician. Use the Areas of Evaluation section to assist you in this process.

Areas of Evaluation

Areas of evaluation include the following:

1. *Diagnosis, counseling, prevention, and intervention:* On the basis of the client's presumed diagnosis of alcohol and/or drug dependence with a serious mental illness, describe three counseling strategies you would use and why you would use them.
2. *Knowledge of comorbidity, differential diagnosis, and/or associated medical issues:* Consider how the client's substance use disorder may mimic or coexist with medical or psychological disorders or disabilities. What might be the disease concept and etiology of his or her co-occurring disorder?
3. *Screening and assessment:* Discuss which standard screening and assessment instrument you might utilize, as well as why, to identify any substance use disorder and process addiction that the client might have.
4. *Legal and ethical conditions:* How might your work address legal or ethical issues using the *ACA Code of Ethics* (ACA, 2014); current state law; and public policies at the local, state, and national levels?
5. *Institutional, historical, and political conditions:* What institutional, historical, and current political conditions might affect the client's case (e.g., institutional racism, political climate related to immigration, poverty, welfare, and disability)? What strategies could you utilize to support the client through advocacy (e.g., public policy and government relations on local, state, and national levels to enhance equity, increase funding, and promote programs that affect clients and the practice of clinical mental health, addiction, rehabilitation, or couples and family counseling)?

Grading Rubric

Follow the instructions in the assignment description, and proceed by addressing each area of evaluation, which will be assessed on the basis of content addressed by the student. The case study as a whole will be assessed on the basis of organization and clarity. The assignment has a total potential score of 25 points. Points will be deducted for inadequate presentation in these areas. Expectations of content and organization are elaborated below:

Organization
- Proficient use of grammar, syntactical formatting, sentence cohesion, punctuation, and spelling.
- Using the guiding questions, address each area of evaluation: symptoms and diagnoses, counseling strategies, screening and assessment, legal and ethical issues, and advocacy concerns.
- Follow APA Style format.

Content
- Well-informed articulation of each area of evaluation: symptoms and diagnoses, counseling strategies, screening and assessment, legal and ethical issues, and advocacy concerns.
- All information presented is supported by scholarly/academic literature.
- Clear evolution of clinical judgment through the examination of the case study; student supports interpretation and perceptions with related literature, examples of trends in the field, and addiction-related resources (i.e., publications by the Substance Abuse and Mental Health Services Administration or the National Institute on Drug Addiction).

Table 26.1 includes the rubric associated with this assignment.

Table 26.1
Client Case Conceptualization Rubric

Area for Evaluation (CACREP Standard)	Instructor Evaluation of Student Assignment: Organization and Content	Student Score[a]
Symptoms and diagnoses (5.A.2.i, 5.A.3.c, 5.A.2.b)	☐ Discusses symptomology experienced by the client, on the basis of the stated diagnosis ☐ Describes three counseling strategies and their application to the client and client's presenting problem(s); explains rationale for the selection of each strategy	_____/4 points
Counseling strategies (5.A.3.e, 5.A.3.f, 5.A.3.g)	☐ Articulates how the client's substance use disorder may mimic or coexist with medical or psychological disorders or disabilities ☐ Discusses the disease concept of addiction ☐ Explains perceived etiology of client's co-occurring disorder	_____/3 points
Screening and assessment (5.A.3.b, 5.A.3.c)	☐ Identifies a standard screening and assessment instrument ☐ Explains rationale for selected instrument and how to utilize it to identify substance abuse or process addiction	_____/2 points
Legal and ethical issues (5.A.2.l, 5.A.3.h)	☐ Identifies and articulates specific ethical and legal issues ☐ Cites *ACA Code of Ethics* (ACA, 2014) ☐ Cites state law ☐ Cites public policy at the local, state, or national level ☐ Addresses legal and ethical considerations regarding the treatment of court-referred clients	_____/5 points
Advocacy concerns (5.A.3.h, 5.A.2.d)	☐ Addresses all guiding questions as listed in assignment description ☐ Discusses advocacy strategies that could be utilized to support the client ☐ Discusses how regulatory policy and substance abuse policy influence addiction treatment delivery Student addresses how each of the following influence the client's experience: ☐ Institutional conditions ☐ Historical context ☐ Political conditions	_____/6 points
Structure and content	☐ Follows APA Style format ☐ Evinces proficient use of grammar, proper syntax, and transitions ☐ Meets six- to eight-page length requirement ☐ Sufficiently addresses all areas of evaluation ☐ Paper is well organized, with transitions between topics	_____/5 points

Note. Each box is worth 1 point, except for in the first category (Symptoms and diagnoses), in which each box is worth 2 points for a possible total of 4. CACREP = Council for Accreditation of Counseling and Related Educational Programs; ACA = American Counseling Association; APA = American Psychological Association.
[a]Total points possible per category indicated after slash.

In-Class Exercise: Darkina Shares Her Story

SLOs assessed: CACREP 2016 Standards 5.A.2.b, 5.A.2.c, 5.A.2.e, 5.A.2.j, 5.A.3.g

The purpose of the following in-class exercise is to provide a provocative case study via video interview that enables students to consider the applicability of harm reduction strategies. This structured exercise enables students to interact and discuss with other learners how the real-world application of harm reduction interventions might appear. The use of Darkina's interviews (EmpowHER, 2011) also encourages students to look beyond the stigma associated with substance abuse and sex-work and honor the unique lived experience and humanity of each individual struggling with an addictive disorder. This exercise may best fit more advanced counseling coursework, as it requires the basic understanding of the etiologies of addiction, evolution of addiction policy and practice in the United States, the Stages of Change Model (Prochaska, DiClemente & Norcross, 1992), the ethics of utilizing harm reduction strategies, and harm reduction resources and services.

1. Show the vignette *Darkina: Drug Addiction: How Did You Get Help?* (EmpowHER, 2011; http://www.empowher.com/users/darkina). Check link prior to class presentation; if no longer viable, other video interview case studies are available via https://www.youtube.com/.

2. Provide the class with the following discussion prompts:
   - Outline Darkina's journey in recovery, to include traumatic experiences, major life events mentioned, and milestones in addiction and recovery.
   - What does Darkina's experience cycling through the stages of change look like?
   - How did different institutions and agencies work to reduce harm, build resources, and help Darkina come to the current place in her recovery?
   - What biopsychosocial factors does Darkina identify as contributing to her substance abuse?
   - How might harm reduction help, or harm, the recovery process for someone like Darkina? At what stages in Darkina's change process might harm reduction have been helpful (e.g., when she was actively using, working in the sex industry, in the precontemplation stage of change [this is not yet a problem], needle exchange/condoms and safe-sex and use practices)? At what stages are harm reduction strategies not helpful? How do you know when harm reduction strategies are appropriate?
3. Facilitate class discussion; incorporate information, awareness, and understanding gained through previous class sessions.

Darkina Shares Her Story Rubric

Exceeds Expectations (3)
- Student actively engages in discussion through direct participation in dialogue, providing relevant contributions while indicating engagement with both verbal and nonverbal cues.
- Discussion contribution indicates the integration of previously learned concepts from the course, with new information and ideas.
- Student is respectful of alternative perspectives.
- Student addresses two or more of the aforementioned discussion questions.
- Student addresses at least two of the aforementioned student learning objectives.

Meets Expectations (2)
- Student engages in discussion through contribution to class dialogue; contribution is relevant.
- Discussion contribution indicates the integration of previously learned concepts from the course, with new information and ideas.
- Student is respectful of alternative perspectives.
- Student addresses one or more of the aforementioned discussion questions.
- Student addresses at least one of the aforementioned student learning objectives.

Needs Improvement (1)
- Student passively engages in class activity by attending class session; student indicates engagement with nonverbal cues.
- Student provides no direct contribution to class dialogue.
- Student is respectful of others' perspectives.
- Student fails to address aforementioned discussion questions or learning objectives.

Not Evident (0)
- Student fails to attend class session, or
- Student attends class session and is disrespectful of others' perspectives.

Treatment Facility Report

SLOs assessed: CACREP 2016 Standards 5.A.1.c, 5.A.2.a, 5.A.2.d, 5.A.2.l, 5.A.3.d, 5.A.3.h

The purpose of this assignment is to increase student familiarity with available resources for the treatment of individuals with addictive disorders, meeting addiction counseling CACREP 2016 Standard 2.g by raising student awareness of "culturally relevant education programs that raise awareness and support addiction and substance abuse prevention and the recovery process." The assignment also challenges students to move outside of their zone of comfort by making a cold contact with an agency with which they are unfamiliar.

Contact a substance abuse treatment facility, either by phone or in person, with whom the student is not currently familiar. Identify yourself as a [College or University] student and request a brief interview regarding this agency's services. You may speak with the facilities director, a clinical supervisor, or a counselor.

Following contact with the site, write a two- to three-page paper describing the facility, population, treatment strategies, and legal or ethical issues that need attention. Include the following areas:

- *Informational interview contact:* Provide your contact's name, title or level of licensure, position within the agency, and phone number.
- *Facility description*: Describe the facility. What did it look like (e.g., well-kept, dirty, welcoming)? Where is it located? Is the location easily accessible for the population that it is serving? How is the facility being funded to operate?
- *Population description:* Describe the population. What is the population distribution (e.g., gender identity/expression, affectual orientation, ability, socioeconomic status, race/ethnicity)? Which substances does this facility see most commonly? Are there eligibility requirements for clients to be helped? If so, what are they?
- *Treatment strategies:* Describe treatment strategies. What are the primary treatment methods being used? How do they assess the efficacy of their methods? What challenges do they commonly face in treatment? How do they utilize multicultural competencies among diverse populations? How do they manage emergencies and crises?
- *Ethical/legal issues:* Describe common legal or ethical issues that the facility faces. What is its relationship with the court system? You can include mandated referrals here, if any.
- *Personal experiences:* Describe your personal experiences and interpretations of this experience.

Grading Rubric

Follow the instructions in the assignment description, and proceed by addressing each area of evaluation, which will be assessed on the basis of content addressed by student. The assignment as a whole will be assessed on the basis of organization and clarity. Each area is worth 5 points, for a total of 35 points possible. Points will be deducted for inadequate presentation in these areas. Expectations of content and organization are elaborated as follows:

Organization
- Proficient use of grammar, syntactical formatting, sentence cohesion, punctuation, and spelling.
- Using the guiding questions, address each area of evaluation: facility description, population description, treatment strategies, ethical/legal considerations, professional issues, advocacy issues, and personal analysis.
- Follow APA Style format.

Content
- Well-informed articulation of each area for evaluation: facility description, population description, treatment strategies, ethical/legal considerations, professional issues, advocacy issues, and personal analysis.
- All information presented is supported by personal communication, facility documents, and additional scholarly/academic literature.

Table 26.2 includes the rubric associated with this assignment.

Psychopharmacology Hunt

SLO assessed: CACREP 2016 Standard 5.A.2.h

The purpose of this assignment is to familiarize students with those psychopharmacological medications used in the treatment of mental health conditions and addictive disorders. The assignment's format is such that students may refer back to their paper as practicing counselors. Students are required to post their pharmacological report in an online discussion board so that other students may be privy to the discoveries of their classmates; students are welcome to print others' pharmacology entries for their own future reference.

Table 26.2
Treatment Facility Report Rubric

Area for Evaluation (CACREP Standard)	Instructor Evaluation of Student Assignment: Organization and Content	Student Score[a]
Facility description (5.A.2.a)	☐ Describes nature of services ☐ Provides facility location information ☐ Addresses client's ability to access facility ☐ Outlines facility's funding sources ☐ Paints picture of the roles and settings of addictions counselors	_____/5 points
Population description (5.A.2.j)	☐ Discusses clientele distribution, to include age, socioeconomic status, affectual orientation, race or ethnicity (2 points possible) ☐ Describes substances commonly abused in client population ☐ Provides facility's treatment eligibility requirements ☐ Outlines cultural factors relevant to addiction and addictive behavior—namely, multicultural elements of selected client population	_____/5 points
Treatment strategies (5.A.3.d; 5.A.3.e; 5.A.3.f; 5.A.3.g)	☐ Describes facility's primary techniques and interventions for the treatment of substance abuse and/or other addictions ☐ Articulates facility's strategies for reducing the negative effects of substance abuse and dependence as well as addictive disorders ☐ Discusses how the agency assesses the efficacy of its methods ☐ Addresses how facility's treatment strategies emphasize the benefits of recovery and/or harm of continued addictive behaviors ☐ Discusses challenges commonly faced by clients ☐ Outlines facility's crisis management plan	_____/6 points
Legal and ethical issues (5.A.2.l, 5.A.3.h)	☐ Discusses legal issues ☐ Discusses ethical considerations specific to addictions counseling ☐ Lists any mandated referrals ☐ Addresses legal and ethical considerations regarding the treatment of court-referred clients (2 points possible)	_____/5 points
Personal experiences	☐ Describes personal perceptions ☐ Articulates emotional experience ☐ Discusses interpretation of experience at facility (2 points possible)	_____/4 points
Structure and content	☐ Follows APA Style format ☐ Evinces proficient use of grammar, proper syntax, and transitions ☐ Meets page length requirement ☐ Sufficiently addresses all areas of evaluation ☐ Paper is well organized, with transitions between topic	_____/5 points

Note. Each box is worth 1 point, unless otherwise stated. CACREP = Council for Accreditation of Counseling and Related Educational Programs; APA = American Psychological Association.
[a]Total points possible per category indicated after slash.

Students will conduct a scavenger hunt to find information about commonly prescribed psychopharmacological medications, and/or medications used in the treatment of addictions, or commonly abused prescription medication. Students decide which medications they wish to explore, utilize the assignment guide/grading rubric provided below as a guide for formatting, and then post their final results on the Blackboard Discussion board page for the course so that all students can be made privy to the information that other students found in this assignment (and can take for their own future records).

Table 26.3 includes the rubric associated with this assignment.

Final Paper and Presentation: Implementation of a Harm Reduction Strategy

SLOs assessed: CACREP 2016 Standards 5.A.1.b, 5.A.2.a

The purpose of this artifact is to engage students in the process of integrating the knowledge, awareness, and skills gained throughout the course of the semester. The final paper allows students to summarize and apply new knowledge to a real-world scenario. Students are asked to research a local human services agency and to describe a harm reduction strategy that they believe would best fit

Table 26.3
Psychopharmacology Hunt Rubric

Key Concepts	Instructor Evaluation of Student Assignment: Organization and Content	Student Score[a]
Drug name, classification, or drug family	☐ Provides brand name of psychopharmacological drug ☐ Indicates generic name of selected drug ☐ States drug's classification or family	_____/6 points
Indications for use	☐ Explains what legitimate uses or conditions the drug may be prescribed for (4 points possible)	_____/4 points
Diversion status	☐ Indicates whether prescription drug is considered commonly abused If commonly abused, describe the following using http://www.drugabuse.gov/drugs-abuse/commonly-abused-drugs-charts/commonly-abused-prescription-drugs-chart ☐ Schedule ☐ Intoxication effects ☐ Potential health consequences	_____/8 points
Contraindications or drug interactions	☐ Describes those prescription and nonprescription drugs with which the psychopharmacological medication interacts ☐ Describes the result of drug interactions ☐ Indicates those foods or medications with which the selected psychopharmacological drug is contraindicated	_____/6 points
Side effects	☐ Outlines important side effects attributed to use of this medication (4 points possible)	_____/4 points
Treatment populations and problems	☐ Discusses what medical conditions, presenting problems, and diagnoses this medication is considered appropriate for (4 points possible)	_____/4 points
Counseling implications	☐ Describes potential referrals for a client who is prescribed this medication ☐ Indicates whether a counselor working with an individual prescribed this medication should provide coordination of care ☐ Addresses possible ethical or legal concerns when working with an individual prescribed this medication, such as the need for having a Release of Information with the client's prescribing physician ☐ Lists any potential triggers for relapse caused by this medication	_____/8 points

Note. Unless otherwise noted, 2 points are possible per criteria.

[a]Total points possible per category indicated after slash.

this agency and its treatment population. Students are asked to consider how an alteration of policy or perspective could provide a local agency's clientele with harm reduction services.

Understanding the harm reduction perspective, select a harm reduction strategy and explain how you would institute this strategy at a local human services agency. For this project, select a local human services agency (this may include substance abuse treatment centers, not-for-profit charities, counseling agencies, hospitals, etc.). Be sure to describe the strategy, the agency, how the strategy would be implemented, and why you feel this strategy would be a good fit for the agency and the population that it serves.

You will be required to turn in a 5- to 10-page paper in APA Style summarizing the project described in the previous paragraph. You should utilize at least three to five scholarly sources to inform and support your argument. You will also provide a 10- to 15-minute presentation to the class explaining your chosen strategy and covering the aforementioned information. PowerPoint slides and brochures/handouts from your agency of choice will be helpful additions to bring for your presentation.

Harm Reduction Final Paper Criteria

Exemplary (10 points per criterion met)
☐ Is submitted on or before due date
☐ Utilizes at least 3–5 scholarly sources (peer reviewed journals or publications; *may use class readings*)
☐ Is a minimum of five pages in length, not including title page or references

☐ Follows APA Style format, with minimal errors (no more than three missing APA Style formatting elements)

☐ Spelling, punctuation, and grammar are generally correct (no more than three mistakes)

☐ There is a clear thesis

☐ Transitions are thoughtful

☐ Appropriate headers are used, such as the following examples: Introduction, Description of Agency, Population Served, Harm Reduction Strategy, Implementation/Rationale, and Discussion/Personal Reaction

☐ Provides clear rationale for selection of agency, selection of harm reduction strategy, and its applicability to the population served

☐ Indicates understanding of harm reduction principles and their applicability to at-risk populations

Competent (8 points per criterion met)

☐ Is submitted on or before due date

☐ Utilizes at least three sources, not all scholarly

☐ Is a minimum of five pages in length, not including title page or references

☐ Follows APA Style format, with moderate errors (missing more than three APA Style formatting elements)

☐ Spelling, punctuation, and grammar are generally correct (more than three mistakes)

☐ Thesis is identifiable, not directly stated

☐ Includes necessary transitions

☐ Includes headers and subheadings, mostly appropriate to content

☐ Paper shows understanding of harm reduction strategies and of agency of choice, but lacks depth

☐ Paragraphs occasionally lack focus or coherence

Developing (7 points per criterion met)

☐ Submitted after due date

☐ Utilizes less than three scholarly sources, or utilizes all unscholarly resources

☐ Is less than five pages in length, not including title page or references

☐ Fails to follow APA Style format; no APA Style formatting elements are present

☐ Disregard for appropriate spelling, punctuation, and grammar

☐ No clear thesis is stated

☐ Missing transitions between paragraphs and sections

☐ Lack of appropriate headings

☐ Fails to provide rationale for selected agency or harm reduction strategy

☐ Indicates a lack of understanding of harm reduction principles

Harm Reduction Presentation Criteria

High Mastery (10 points per criterion met)

☐ Presentation fully describes student's rationale for chosen agency and harm reduction strategy

☐ Presentation provides comprehensive description of agency and strategy

☐ Student provides plan for implementation (covers practical implications: budget barriers/support, location, staff; political climate: supportive or unsupportive)

☐ Presentation provides complete description of at-risk population served by agency and benefit of proposed strategy

☐ Presenter is well-prepared, enhancing presentation with use of handouts, brochures, and/or PowerPoint presentation

☐ Presentation is 10–15 minutes in length

Average Mastery (8 points per criterion met)

☐ Presentation fails to fully describe student's rationale for chosen agency and harm reduction strategy

☐ Presentation provides some information regarding student's agency and strategy of choice

☐ Student's plan for implementation is evolving, not comprehensive, and fails to provide necessary practical implications

- ☐ Presentation provides brief description of population served by agency
- ☐ Presenter is prepared and has basic PowerPoint presentation
- ☐ Student's presentation is at least 10 minutes in length

Low Mastery (6 points per criterion met)
- ☐ Presentation fails to describe student's rationale for chosen agency and harm reduction strategy
- ☐ Presentation provides little background information for the student's chosen agency, and fails to provide evidence of comprehension of harm reduction strategy or principles
- ☐ Student does not provide clear plan for implementation of harm reduction strategy
- ☐ Presentation does not provide description of the special needs of the at-risk population served by agency; does not provide explanation of benefits of proposed strategy
- ☐ Presenter is ill-prepared and provides no PowerPoint presentation or handouts
- ☐ Student's presentation is less than 10 minutes in length

Chapter 27

Career Counseling

Melissa J. Fickling

Students who choose to specialize in career counseling likely possess an appreciation for the significant roles of work and career in human experience. Thus, instructors of specialty career counseling courses have the pleasure of expecting that their students will have at least some investment in the topic of career development—something not all instructors of career development experience in the core course (Lara et al., 2011; Osborn & Dames, 2013). It is appropriate, then, that the CACREP 2016 Standards require students seeking to specialize in career counseling to be exposed to knowledge, skills, and practices beyond those required in the core curricular experiences. Instructors of these specialty career counseling courses should provide students with multiple opportunities to understand the foundational, contextual, and practice domains of career counseling, including an understanding of how these domains can interact and inform ethical and effective career counseling work.

One piece of knowledge that should be familiar to students of career counseling is the profession's history of advocacy and social justice, beginning with Frank Parsons's work with the Boston youth and immigrant populations in the early 20th century (O'Brien, 2001; Parsons, 1909). Despite this well-known foundation of social justice, more can be done today to ensure that career counselors are competently serving diverse populations (Evans & Larrabee, 2002; Hansen, 2003; Tang, 2003). The ACA and NCDA ethic codes (ACA, 2014; NCDA, 2009) call for counselors and career professionals to advocate at multiple levels (e.g., individual, group, institutional, and societal) when appropriate. Both associations define *advocacy* as the removal of barriers and obstacles that inhibit client access, growth, and development (ACA, 2014; NCDA, 2009).

Multicultural counseling skills are crucial to competent career counseling (Heppner & Fu, 2011; NCDA, 2009; Vespia, Fitzpatrick, Fouad, Kantamneni, & Chen, 2010). Multicultural counseling involves understanding clients as members of "historical, cultural, economic, political, and psychosocial contexts" (ACA, 2014, p. 20). Vespia et al. (2010) found that multicultural training predicted both self-reported and externally rated multicultural competence among a sample of career counselors. They also found a discrepancy between self-reported and external evaluations of multicultural behaviors, indicating that there may be a gap between self-perceptions of competence and actual practice (Vespia et al., 2010). Additional opportunities for students to actively conceptualize and understand cultural considerations in career development could influence actual practice after students begin their practicum, internship, and postgraduate clinical experiences. The activities in this section are designed to give students such experience.

There is relatively wide agreement that career counseling has traditionally emphasized intrapsychic and individual influences to career development rather than systemic level influences (Blustein, Medvide, & Wan, 2011; Heppner & O'Brien, 2006; McIlveen & Patton, 2006; Prilleltensky & Stead, 2012; Sampson, Dozier, & Colvin, 2011). Further, recent research indicates that career counselors may be intervening primarily at the individual rather than systemic level, despite being aware of social injustices affecting clients and desiring greater skill in advocacy (Arthur, Collins, Marshall, & McMahon, 2013; Arthur, Collins, McMahon, & Marshall, 2009; McMahon, Arthur, & Collins, 2008). Concepts such as career choice and voluntary transition may be neither applicable nor available to all people; therefore, career counselors must be prepared to take on multiple roles and to intervene at multiple levels (Blustein, 2006; Blustein et al., 2011; Duffy & Dik, 2009; Gainor, 2005; Prilleltensky & Stead, 2012; Sampson et al., 2011; Savickas, 2011; Tang, 2003).

Career counseling is multifaceted because clients are diverse and because employment and labor are complex, socially located experiences (Blustein et al., 2011; Browne & Misra, 2003). Assignments in career counseling courses should reflect this level of diversity and complexity and provide students with needed skills and experiences to prepare them for clinical practice. In addition, students specializing in career counseling will likely be the strongest advocates for career counseling and clients and should therefore have ample opportunity to develop advocacy skills (CACREP, 2016; Hansen, 2003). The activities in this section are designed to give students experience promoting the work of career counseling and advocating with and for clients. The activities outlined below emphasize (a) advocacy for career counseling; (b) cultural and social influences on career development; and (c) teaching employability, job search, and research skills to clients using up-to-date technology and resources.

Public Service Announcement/Ad Campaign for Career Counseling

SLOs assessed: CACREP 2016 Standards 5.B.1.a, 5.B.1.c, 5.B.2.a, 5.B.2.b, 5.B.3.e

This assignment encompasses Standards across all three domains: foundational, contextual, and practice. This assignment could be completed individually, in small groups, or as a class. The instructor could also elect to create a friendly contest in which classmates or other students, staff, and faculty in the counseling department vote for the most effective video. This assignment could also be connected with an ACA or division contest that would serve an additional objective of increasing student familiarity with ACA, NCDA, and other professional counseling associations.

For this assignment, you will create a video public service announcement in which you promote the profession of career counseling. Your audience may be potential clients, employers, policy makers, or the general public. The video should be 5–10 minutes in length; should be of high video and audio quality; and should have a clear, central message. Your goal should be to educate individuals about career counseling and to convince them to consider career counseling for their own or their constituents' career development needs. Be sure to include the following components:

- An engaging and creative delivery.
- Brief history and development of career counseling.
- Description of the various roles of a career counselor, including the core principles and values of the profession.
- Ways in which career counselors are advocates.
- Description of career counseling activities and services. Some questions you may want to address, but do not necessarily have to, include the following: Where can I find a career counselor? What can I expect in career counseling? Will I be expected to take tests? Will my counselor be able to help me? Will my counselor get me a job?
- By the end of your video, your intended audience should have a good idea of who career counselors are, what they do, and who they serve.

Table 27.1 includes the rubric associated with this assignment.

Table 27.1
Ad Campaign for Career Counseling Rubric

Objective	Does Not Meet Expectations	Fully Meets or Exceeds Expectations	Score[a]
Provide a brief history of career counseling	Fails to include relevant information regarding the development of the career counseling profession	Provides concise but relevant information about the history of the profession and connects themes to current roles, values, and tenets of career counseling	_____/20 points
Explains advocacy in career counseling	Fails to adequately explain what is unique about career counseling or how career counselors serve in multiple roles, including the advocate role	Provides a thorough and convincing rationale for why career counseling is important and effective	_____/20 points
Creativity and clarity of communication	Lacks a cohesive message or theme; lacks originality or an effective way of capturing the audience's attention; video is less than 5 minutes or more than 10 minutes long	Captures the attention of the intended audience and conveys a clear message about the value, importance, and/or effectiveness of career counseling, citing relevant research as appropriate; video is between 5 and 10 minutes in length	_____/20 points
Accurately describes career counseling activities and services	Description of career counseling activities and services lacks depth and breadth; provides only basic information; fails to consider the diversity of persons who may be seeking career counseling services	Sophisticated knowledge of the variety of settings where career counseling takes place as well as the variety of services available; considers accessibility for individuals from diverse populations, developmental levels, and socioeconomic statuses	_____/20 points
Effective use of technology	Video is of poor quality and is not well edited; video would be inappropriate for broad dissemination in its current format; video is not accessible to persons with a visual or hearing impairment; video uses professional jargon that is not relevant to the general public; video fails to incorporate music, visual effects, text, voice, and/or images	Audio and video quality is of a professional level and would be appropriate for broad dissemination; video makes excellent use of music, visual effects, text, voice, and/or images; video is accessible to persons with a visual or hearing impairment; video uses appropriate and accessible language (avoids the use of professional jargon)	_____/20 points
Total score			_____/100 points

[a]Total points possible per category indicated after slash.

Cultural Case Study

SLOs assessed: CACREP 2016 Standards 5.B.2.c, 5.B.2.d, 5.B.2.e, 5.B.2.f

This assignment focuses on the contextual dimension domain. This assignment was designed as a group project that culminates in a 30- to 45-minute presentation made to the larger class. In this assignment, students will develop their ability to conceptualize the career counseling needs of diverse populations as well as consider those clients within a broader, global context of work and career.

Choose a cultural group that you would like to research in regard to historic and current economic and employment trends. For example, you could research economic and employment related issues and trends for Black women in the United States; lesbian, gay, bisexual, and transgender (LGBT) youths; people living in poverty in the rural U.S. South; refugees; or Latino immigrants in the United States. If exploring U.S. populations, be sure to utilize publications, reports, and databases from the U.S. Department of Labor and Bureau of Labor Statistics. The U.S. Census may also be a helpful resource as you begin this project.

- Provide an historic overview of your population's relationship with labor (which can be paid or unpaid). Discuss relevant cultural, political, or economic forces that have shaped access to work, including globalization.
- Address how work and mental health intersect for your population of focus.
- Discuss how race, class, gender, and other social identity categories may interact with work and career development for your population of focus.
- Engage class members by facilitating an experiential component (e.g., discussion questions, case study, video, role plays).

Table 27.2 includes the rubric associated with this assignment.

Table 27.2
Cultural Case Study Rubric

Objective	Does Not Meet Expectations	Fully Meets or Exceeds Expectations	Score[a]
Historic overview/ context	Fails to contextualize contemporary labor and employment issues for the population of focus	Provides a comprehensive historical context for present day employment and labor trends for the population of focus	_____/20 points
Impact of globalization	Fails to consider the impact of globalization on access to work and living wages; does not consider cultural, political, or economic forces	Provides an in-depth analysis of relevant cultural, political, or economic forces that have shaped access to work, including globalization	_____/20 points
Work and mental health	Fails to address how work and mental health intersect for the population of focus; does not consider whether or how career development issues relate to overall mental health and wellness	Considers how career and mental health are related for this population, including engagement with counseling or career counseling as well as cultural norms regarding mental health and counseling	_____/20 points
Intersectionality and career development	Presenters do not address the diversity within the population of focus or consider the intersection of identity categories and how these could influence or be influenced by career development, work, employment, and/or mental health	Presenters speak to the complexity of identity within the population of focus and how the social constructions of race, class, gender, and other identity categories may interact with career development, work, employment, and/or mental health	_____/20 points
Experiential component	Does not effectively integrate an experiential component to address diverse learning styles in the audience; experiential activity does not connect the theoretical components of the topic with practical application or knowledge integration	Includes an experiential component that effectively engages the audience and encourages practice and/or application of material covered	_____/20 points
Total score			_____/100 points

[a]Total points possible per category indicated after slash.

Job Search Workshop

SLOs assessed: CACREP 2016 Standards 5.B.3.c, 5.B.3.d, 5.B.3.f, 5.B.3.g

This project focuses on the practice domain of career counseling. Career counselors fulfill a variety of roles. One significant role may be that of educator, particularly when it comes to educating clients about career development and employment resources that are increasingly located online. Workshops and group work can be a cost-effective way to reach clients. In this individual assignment, you will gain experience with program planning and outreach by developing a workshop designed to teach clients how to use technology skills to access reliable career resources.

Technology skills are increasingly important in today's job market. For many clients, using and learning new technology can be a source of anxiety and a barrier to gaining and maintaining paid employment. For this project, you will identify career-related resources relevant to a population of interest. Your finished project will contain two parts: (a) a complete workshop curriculum and (b) a proposal in the form of a letter to an agency in the community where you would like to implement your program.

You will design a workshop that utilizes technology to teach employability or job search skills to members of your community. Your workshop must be experiential, meaning your participants should get to practice using the technology you are teaching. In addition to creating the curriculum and outline for this program, you will write up a proposal to a local community agency or a non-profit agency that might be interested in hosting your workshop at their site. In this proposal, you should outline the resources you will need to complete this workshop (e.g., number of computers, Internet access, staff support). Your proposal should also describe how you plan to advertise your workshop and to coordinate registration and payment, if applicable. Your proposal and workshop curriculum together should be thorough enough that a counselor who is unfamiliar with the content and proposed structure should be able to read your materials and execute your workshop exactly as you have planned.

Table 27.3 includes the rubric associated with this assignment.

Table 27.3
Job Search Workshop Rubric

Objective	Does Not Meet Expectations	Fully Meets or Exceeds Expectations	Score[a]
Workshop curriculum —Clarity of Instruction	Outline for workshop is incomplete or confusing; does not include a variety of methods (e.g., lecture, demonstration, practice, video) appropriate for diverse abilities and learning styles	Provides a clear and easy to follow outline (e.g., PowerPoint) for the content to be covered during the workshop; utilizes effective teaching approaches for diverse abilities and learning styles	_____/20 points
Workshop curriculum —Appropriate resources	Teaches resources that are inappropriate for the targeted user or are out of date	Utilizes reliable and up-to-date resources that are relevant and essential for the population of focus	_____/20 points
Workshop curriculum— Clear goals and objectives	Lacks clear and cohesive goals and objectives to guide the workshop content; unclear rationale for inclusion of specific resources or technologies	Includes learning objectives for workshop participants; provides a clear rationale for including specific resources or technologies	_____/20 points
Proposal to community agency —Rationale	Fails to provide the agency or site a strong rationale for why the program is needed and why it would benefit their clients	Provides a strong and clear rationale for the need for the program and why the proposed agency or site would be an appropriate location for the program; explains the potential benefit to the agency or site and its clients for hosting the workshop	_____/20 points
Proposal to community agency —Resources	Does not include a well-thought-out or comprehensive list of acquired and needed resources (e.g., staff, space, technology, supplies)	Provides a comprehensive plan for running the program; lists needed resources (e.g., staff, space, technology, supplies) and resources already obtained	_____/20 points
Total score			_____/100 points

[a]Total points possible per category indicated after slash.

Chapter 28

Clinical Mental Health Counseling

Elizabeth A. Prosek

CMHCs must be prepared to work in a variety of settings along the continuum of care, from inpatient crisis stabilization to individual counseling of clients experiencing normal developmental milestones. Students may enter a counseling program with a limited scope of practice in clinical mental health counseling. Therefore, counselor educators are challenged to illuminate the multifaceted roles and functions of a counselor in the community setting. Moreover, in alignment with current issues in the counseling profession (see Kaplan & Gladding, 2011), educators seek to cultivate a strong professional identity among counseling students. CMHCs are able to conceptualize their clients and communities with cultural sensitivity.

In the CMHC core, master's students must achieve competence in 23 standards across three domains (foundations, contextual dimensions, and practice). Courses most appropriate to assess the CMHC standards might include professional orientation, diagnosis and treatment planning, and CMHC specialty area. To meet a multitude of student learning styles, I recommend activities that highlight different learning strengths. There is a balance of structured evaluation methods (e.g., quiz) and assignments that empower students to further investigate topics of importance to them (e.g., public advocacy). My intention is to foster relativistic learning and student-driven motivation to complete activities.

In this chapter, I provide five assignments and rubrics to assess learning in CMHC. The first activity is designed for students to demonstrate their ability to apply legal and ethical codes to realistic counseling dilemmas. The second activity is intended to empower students to become advocates in the profession, writing their local legislators letters of support for counseling-related initiatives. I encourage the second activity to be linked to a group advocacy project in which students gain the skills to present public policy information in a poster session conference format. The third activity is an opportunity for students to use creativity and media sources to demonstrate their clinical decision-making skills. Moreover, the complex assignment requires several elements of standard clinical, administrative procedures including a biopsychosocial report, diagnostic summary, and treatment plan. The fourth assignment is an evaluation of psychopharmacological knowledge. Finally, the fifth assignment is an intentional effort to have students interact with local mental health agencies. This assignment has two parts as well. First, students are exposed to the functions of a clinical mental health agency, applying key concepts to the real-world setting. In the second phase of the assignment, students incorporate information that they learned and collected from classmates to analyze the services provided in the local community.

Contact me by e-mail (Elizabeth.Prosek@unt.edu) if you would like access to examples and templates that may assist counselor educators to implement the activities in class.

Ethical Decision Making

SLOs assessed: CACREP 2016 Standards 5.C.2.j, 5.C.2.l, 5.C.2.m

Prepare a paper in response to three ethical dilemmas relevant to CMHC. For each case, clearly and concisely apply the steps of an ethical decision-making model to resolve the dilemma. Be mindful to identify relevant ethical codes and legal standards at the national and state levels. Furthermore, responses incorporate attention to cultural factors that require consideration in the ethical resolution.

Papers must be prepared in accordance with APA Style and should not exceed 15 pages, including title and reference page(s). Students are expected to integrate at least five original, scholarly resources into the paper to demonstrate knowledge of relevant professional issues in clinical mental health counseling. Table 28.1 includes the rubric associated with this assignment.

Public Policy and Advocacy Project

SLOs assessed: CACREP 2016 Standards 5.C.2.i, 5.C.2.k, 5.C.3.e

Part I: Individual Assignment

In this assignment, students are expected to read and become familiar with ACA legislative agenda, American Mental Health Counselor Association public policy, and state public policy. From this knowledge, students identify one issue that they are personally invested in that advocates for client well-being and/or for the counseling profession. Students write a letter to their identified representative advocating for the identified issue on behalf of the profession. The letter should

- demonstrate knowledge of the public policy;
- indicate how policy will affect the quality and accessibility of mental health services; and
- follow the guidelines recommended by ACA, the American Mental Health Counselor Association, and/or the state division for communicating with Congress.

Table 28.1
Ethical Decision-Making Rubric

Criterion (CACREP Standard)	Does Not Meet Expectations	Meets Expectations	Exceeds Expectations
Legal and ethical considerations specific to clinical mental health counseling (5.C.2.l)	Inaccurate application of an ethical decision-making model; may show inadequate incorporation of ethical and legal codes; overlooked codes that affect an ethical resolution of dilemma	Thorough application of an ethical decision-making model; demonstrates an adequate incorporation of ethical and legal codes; if a few minor codes are overlooked, it does detract from overall response to dilemma	Thoughtful and accurate application of an ethical decision-making model; demonstrates exceptional incorporation of pertinent ethical and legal codes; cites ethical and legal codes from multiple organizations (e.g., national, state) to develop holistic analysis
Record keeping, third-party reimbursement, and other practice and management issues in clinical mental health counseling (5.C.2.m)	Overlooks the documentation process of the ethical decision; missed opportunity to include appropriate community partners in the resolution of dilemma	Alludes to documentation process of the ethical decision; demonstrates adequate incorporation of other community partners as applicable to each case	Thoughtful and clear report of how the ethical decision is documented in the clinical record; demonstrates exceptional incorporation of other community partners as applicable to each case
Cultural factors relevant to clinical mental health counseling (5.C.2.j)	Overlooks cultural factors in the ethical decision-making process	Alludes to cultural factors in the ethical decision-making process as relevant to each case	Thoughtful and well-stated inclusion of cultural factors in the ethical decision-making process as relevant to each case

Note. CACREP = Council for Accreditation of Counseling and Related Educational Programs.

Students write a one-page reflection regarding the public policies and how they continue to advocate for the profession. Students are evaluated on their ability to support client/professional advocacy; understanding of public policy; ability to advocate as CMHCs; knowledge of how public policy affects quality and accessibility of mental health services; and format of letter, including writing style.

Students with international student status are encouraged, if they chose, to write an advocacy letter applicable to the public policy of their identified home country.

Part II: Group Assignment

To practice how to communicate public policy to others and to advocate for clients and the profession, a group of three students create a poster presentation representing one public policy issue of choice. The poster must include the pertinent information regarding the public policy issue, connections to ethical codes, and suggestions on what the public (i.e., other counselors) can do to advocate. Be sure to include citations and reference information per APA Style. Each student in the group must be able to speak to the issue during the mini poster presentation "conference." Table 28.2 includes the rubric associated with this assignment.

Fictional Case Study

SLOs assessed: CACREP 2016 Standards 5.C.1.c, 5.C.1.d, 5.C.1.e, 5.C.2.b, 5.C.2.d, 5.C.2.e, 5.C.2.f, 5.C.2.g, 5.C.2.j, 5.C.2.m, 5.C.3.a, 5.C.3.b

Select a fictional character from a book, television program, or film to serve as the basis for a comprehensive case study. Then do the following:

- Write a biopsychosocial history as part of an expanded, narrative-style mental status report.
  –Use Seligman (2004) and Polanski and Hinkle (2000) for formatting guidelines.
  –Be sure to use professional language.
  –The report should explicitly attend to historical–social–political–cultural contexts.
- Identify, if applicable, a mental health disorder diagnosis using the *Diagnostic and Statistical Manual of Mental Disorders* (5th ed.; *DSM–5*; American Psychiatric Association, 2013).
  –Include justification with particular attention to differential diagnosis and issues of culture.
  –If deferring diagnosis or recommending no diagnosis, be sure to include detailed explanation of decision in the justification.
- Create a comprehensive, evidence-based treatment plan with justification.
  –Treatment plans include a total of 3–5 objectives.

Table 28.2
Public Policy and Advocacy Project Rubric

Criterion (CACREP Standard)	Does Not Meet Expectations	Meets Expectations	Exceeds Expectations
Legislation and government policy relevant to mental health counseling (5.C.2.i)	Simplified letter and/or reflection paper that overlooks connections between policy and impact to mental health counseling services	Thorough letter and/or reflection paper that demonstrates adequate understanding of how public policy affects mental health counseling services	Thoughtful and well-written letter and/or reflection paper that demonstrates exceptional understanding of how public policy affects mental health counseling services
Professional organizations, preparation standards, and credentials relevant to the practice of clinical mental health counseling (5.C.2.k)	Overlooks the preparation standards and credentials required of clinical mental health counselors as relevant to the chosen public policy	Alludes to the preparation standards and credentials required of clinical mental health counselors as relevant to the chosen public policy	Thoughtful incorporation of the preparation standards and credentials required of clinical mental health counselors as relevant to the chosen public policy
Strategies to advocate for persons with mental health issues (5.C.3.e)	Simple and/or inaccurate suggestions of how counselors can advocate as presented in the poster session	Alludes to ways in which counselors can advocate as presented in the poster session; overlooks strategies beyond letter writing	Thoughtfully suggests ways in which counselors can advocate as presented in the poster session

Note. CACREP = Council for Accreditation of Counseling and Related Educational Programs.

–Attention to assessments must include the World Health Organization Disability Assessment Schedule 2.0 (World Health Organization, 2010) and the *DSM–5*.

–Provide therapeutic details congruent with your identified theoretical orientation.

–Justification includes support from the counseling literature (minimum of five scholarly sources).

Although students make take creative liberties when developing profile information not originally included in the book, television program, or film source, all clinical data included in the report must be written using professional language. Students should include all clinical data in the biopsychosocial report that support the identified mental health disorder diagnosis. Table 28.3 includes the rubric associated with this assignment.

Psychopharmacological Medication Quiz

SLOs assessed: CACREP 2016 Standard 5.C.2.h

Each week in class, treatment options associated with mental health disorders are discussed, which include the potential for appropriate referral and consultation for prescribed psychopharmacological medication. This quiz assesses your ability to classify commonly prescribed psychopharmacological medications as well as to articulate the potential side effects for prescribed medications. The quiz is available _[insert availability]_ . Students are responsible to take the quiz before _[insert date near end of the semester]_ . Students may use class notes and books, but they cannot consult with other peers. There is a 45-minute time limit associated with the quiz; therefore, create a space in which you can concentrate before beginning.

Understanding of classifications, indications, and contraindications of commonly prescribed psychopharmacological medications for appropriate medical referral and consultation (5.C.2.h) is assessed as follows:

- *Does Not Meet Expectations*—Simplified understanding and applicable knowledge of psychopharmacological medications, as evidenced by missing six or more items on the exam (not including bonus questions).
- *Meets Expectations*—Thorough understanding and applicable knowledge of psychopharmacological medications, as evidenced by 3–5 items missed on the exam (not including bonus questions).
- *Exceeds Expectations*—Thoughtful understanding and applicable knowledge of psychopharmacological medications, as evidenced by 0–2 items missed on the exam (not including bonus questions).

For a copy of the psychopharmacology quiz, e-mail the chapter author.

Agency Profile and Community Analysis

SLOs assessed: CACREP 2016 Standards 5.C.1.a, 5.C.1.b, 5.C.1.c, 5.C.2.a, 5.C.2.c, 5.C.2.j, 5.C.3.c, 5.C.3.e

Part I: Agency Profile

Students conduct an in-depth interview of a public or nonprofit community agency that serves a population or provides a service that is of interest to them. Students briefly present information about their chosen agency to the class, including a handout for all classmates. The handouts serve as resources for the community analysis paper. Handouts are approximately 2 pages in length and follow the template provided. Potential interview questions are also provided to help students guide the interview process. The presentation is limited to 4 minutes; therefore, verbally share the unique features of the agency knowing that all pertinent information is included on the handout. For a copy of the profile template, e-mail the chapter author.

Table 28.3
Fictional Case Study Rubric

Criterion (CACREP Standard)	Does Not Meet Expectations	Meets Expectations	Exceeds Expectations
Principles, models, and documentation formats of biopsychosocial case conceptualization and treatment planning (5.C.1.c)	Simplified development of a biopsychosocial case conceptualization of client; overlooks importance of professional language and clear, concise sentence structure, which may lead to confusion when reading client's story	Adequately develops a biopsychosocial case conceptualization of client; a few minor errors in sentence structure or word choices do not distract from overall professionalism in the document	Thoughtfully develops a biopsychosocial case conceptualization of client; exemplar attention to professional language and accuracy of word choices in describing the client's presenting concerns and history
Neurobiological and medical foundation and etiology of addiction and co-occurring disorders (5.C.1.d)	In differential diagnosis, overlooks possibility for co-occurring disorders; limited, or omitted, attention to how a counselor may establish the etiology of symptoms	In differential diagnosis, adequately discusses potential for co-occurring disorders; less attention is paid to how a counselor may establish the etiology of symptoms	In differential diagnosis, thoughtfully discusses potential for co-occurring disorders; can identify questions to ask of client to effectively establish the etiology of symptoms
Psychological tests and assessments specific to clinical mental health counseling (5.C.1.e)	In treatment plan, overlooks potential for test or assessment use beyond the standard use of WHODAS 2.0	In treatment plan, identifies at least one test or assessment appropriate for the salient symptoms presented (beyond the WHODAS 2.0); may not clearly support choice of assessments based on the psychometric properties and support from literature	In treatment plan, thoughtfully identifies tests and assessments appropriate for the salient symptoms presented; justifies choice of assessments based on the psychometric properties and support from literature
Etiology, nomenclature, treatment, referral, and prevention of mental and emotional disorders (5.C.2.b)	In treatment plan, demonstrates simplified understanding of etiology and prevention by overlooking appropriate referrals to adjunct services congruent to client's presenting concerns	In treatment plan, adequately demonstrates understanding of etiology and prevention by providing some referrals to adjunct services; however, may miss opportunity for a referral that is most congruent to client's presenting concerns	In treatment plan, thoughtfully demonstrates understanding of etiology and prevention by providing appropriate referrals to adjunct services congruent to client's presenting concerns
Diagnostic process, including differential diagnosis and the use of diagnostic classification systems such as the *DSM* and *ICD* (5.C.2.d)	In diagnostic process, simplified clinical decision-making process results in mismatch of data provided in case and criteria of a diagnostic classification system; overlooks use of examples from case to support each criterion; the missed opportunities create potential for misdiagnosis	In diagnostic process, adequately connects data presented in case to the criteria of a diagnostic classification system; may miss a few opportunities to provide examples from case to support each criterion; the missed opportunities do not create potential for a misdiagnosis	In diagnostic process, thoughtfully connects data presented in case to the criteria of a diagnostic classification system; accurately provides detailed examples from case to support each criterion
Potential for substance use disorders to mimic and/or co-occur with a variety of neurological, medical, and psychological disorders (5.C.2.e)	In differential diagnosis, overlooks potential for substance use to resemble symptoms of a mental health disorder	In differential diagnosis, adequately addresses potential for substance use to resemble symptoms of a mental health disorder; provides limited evidence to support choices in diagnosis	In differential diagnosis, thoughtfully addresses potential for substance use to resemble symptoms of a mental health disorder; provides evidence to support choices in diagnosis
Impact of crisis and trauma on individuals with mental health diagnoses (5.C.2.f)	In biopsychosocial report, overlooks how crisis or trauma may affect the client; simplified conceptualization overlooks potential for symptoms to be a normal response to crisis	In biopsychosocial report, alludes to how crisis or trauma may affect the client; limited attention to potential for symptoms to be a normal response to crisis	In biopsychosocial report, thoughtfully conceptualizes how crisis or trauma may affect the client; clearly identifies whether the symptoms are a normal response to the crisis and avoids pathologizing the client; or identifies how symptoms accurately reflect a mental health disorder given the experience of the client

(Continued)

Table 28.3 (*Continued*)
Fictional Case Study Rubric

Criterion (CACREP Standard)	Does Not Meet Expectations	Meets Expectations	Exceeds Expectations
Impact of biological/neuro-logical mechanisms on mental health (5.C.2.g)	In differential diagnosis, over-looks potential for medical explanation of mental health symptoms	In differential diagnosis, ad-equately discusses potential for medical explanation of mental health symptoms; simplified use of support in description of choice made in diagnosis	In differential diagnosis, thoughtfully discusses poten-tial for medical explanation of mental health symptoms; clearly supports choices made in diagnosis
Cultural factors relevant to clini-cal mental health counseling (5.C.2.j)	In biopsychosocial history report, simplifies the importance of historical–social–political–cul-tural contexts in a client's life; overlooks potential for cultural factors to affect symptoms	In biopsychosocial history report, adequately attends to historical–social–political–cul-tural context of client's life; alludes to how cultural factors may affect symptoms but does not clearly develop case	In biopsychosocial history re-port, thoughtfully and explic-itly attends to historical–so-cial–political–cultural context of client's life; connects cultural factors to presentation of symptoms, if applicable
Record keeping, third-party reimbursement, and other practice and management issues in clinical mental health counseling (5.C.2.m)	Treatment plan is simplified in development; overlooks details that greatly affect potential for third-party reimbursement	Treatment plan is adequately developed; with few minor adjustments, the treatment plan format would ensure compliance with third-party reimbursement expectations	Treatment plan is thoughtfully developed; detailed format ensures compliance with third-party reimbursement expectations
Intake interview, mental status evaluation, biopsychosocial history, mental health history, and psychological assess-ment for treatment planning and caseload management (5.C.3.a)	In biopsychosocial report, simpli-fied attention to important elements of client history; mental status evaluation overlooks attention to suicidal and homicidal ideation, reality testing, and hallucinations or delusions; does not reflect un-derstanding of how document-ing nonpresent symptoms is as important as identifying those symptoms present	In biopsychosocial report, ad-equately includes information pertinent from the clinical interview, including attention to client's treatment history; mental status evaluation is accurate and reflects atten-tion to suicidal and homicidal ideation, reality testing, and hallucinations or delusions; may miss opportunity to report key elements that are not present	In biopsychosocial report, thoughtfully includes infor-mation pertinent from the clinical interview, including attention to client's treat-ment history; mental status evaluation is accurate and reflects attention to suicidal and homicidal ideation, reality testing, and hallucinations or delusions; accurately describes key elements that are not pres-ent as well as present
Techniques and interventions for prevention and treatment of a broad range of mental health issues (5.C.3.b)	In treatment plan, identifies sim-plified therapeutic techniques to be used in treatment of client; overlooks attention to counselor's theoretical orienta-tion; treatment interventions are not necessarily congruent with needs of client	In treatment plan, adequately identifies therapeutic tech-niques to be used in treatment of client; clear attention to counselor's theoretical ori-entation; however, may miss opportunities to demonstrate flexibility in orientation to best serve needs of client	In treatment plan, thoughtfully identifies therapeutic tech-niques to be used in treatment of client; exemplar attention to counselor's theoretical ori-entation, balanced with needs of client

Note. CACREP = Council for Accreditation of Counseling and Related Educational Programs; WHODAS 2.0 = World Health Organization Disability Assessment Schedule 2.0; *DSM = Diagnostic and Statistical Manual of Mental Disorders; ICD = International Classification of Diseases.*

Part II: Community Analysis

Use your experience within your own agency profile and your observations of peers' reports and handouts to construct an analysis by completing the following:

- Identify principles of CMHC in the local area.
- Identify how the five required regulations of the Community Mental Health Act of 1963 can be observed at the local community's agencies.
- Provide observations of how the local community's mental health counseling services illustrate the continuum of care and delivery modalities.
- Provide general trends and gaps of service delivery in the local area.
- Choose one community counseling model discussed in class; from this model, identify areas of strength and recommendations for improvement for the local area.

Papers must be prepared in accordance with APA Style and should not exceed 15 pages, including title and reference page(s). Students are expected to integrate agency profile handouts, class readings, and scholarly resources into the paper to exemplify knowledge of CMHC systems in the local community. Table 28.4 includes the rubric associated with this assignment.

Table 28.4
Agency Profile and Community Analysis Rubric

Criterion (CACREP Standard)	Does Not Meet Expectations	Meets Expectations	Exceeds Expectations
Roles and settings of mental health counselors (5.C.2.a)	Overlooks key elements of the agency profile handout	Adequate completion of the agency profile handout; potential for minor errors in the application of key terms to agency setting	Thoughtfully and clearly completes the agency profile handout
Strategies for interfacing with the legal system regarding court-referred clients (5.C.3.c)	Does not identify or explain how the agency does or does not coordinate with the legal system	Alludes to how the agency coordinates with the legal system; potential for limited clarity	Thoughtfully incorporates how the agency coordinates with the legal system regarding court-referred clients in the completion of the agency profile handout
Principles of clinical mental health counseling, including prevention, intervention, consultation, education, and advocacy, and networks that promote mental health and wellness	Overlooks several opportunities to identify how local agencies provide prevention, intervention, consultation, education, and advocacy services; may incorrectly identify, or omit, examples from the local community	Identifies how local agencies provide prevention, intervention, consultation, education, and advocacy services; simplified examples may not fully capture the scope of practice in the local community	Thoughtfully identifies how local agencies provide prevention, intervention, consultation, education, and advocacy services; provides clear examples from agency profile handouts
History and development of clinical mental health counseling (5.C.1.a)	Overlooks several opportunities to identify how historical federal legislation (i.e., CMHC Act of 1963) influences the practice of clinical mental health counselors in the local community setting; may incorrectly identify, or omit, examples from the local community	Adequately addresses how historical federal legislation (i.e., CMHC Act of 1963) influences the practice of clinical mental health counselors in the local community setting; simplified examples may not fully capture the scope of practice in the local community	Thoughtfully conceptualizes how historical federal legislation (i.e., CMHC Act of 1963) influences the practice of clinical mental health counselors in the local community setting; provides clear examples from local agencies
Cultural factors relevant to clinical mental health counseling (5.C.2.j)	Overlooks several opportunities to identify how clinical mental health agencies adapt services to be more culturally sensitive to the local community; may omit examples from local agencies	Alludes to how clinical mental health agencies adapt services to be more culturally sensitive to the local community; simplified examples may not fully capture the scope of practice at local agencies	Thoughtfully conceptualizes how clinical mental health agencies adapt services to be more culturally sensitive to the local community; provides clear examples from local agencies
Mental health service delivery modalities within the continuum of care, such as inpatient, outpatient, partial treatment, and aftercare and the mental health counseling services networks (5.C.2.c)	Overlooks several opportunities to identify how clinical mental health agencies deliver services within the scope of the continuum of care; may incorrectly identify, or omit, examples from the local community setting	Adequately identifies how clinical mental health agencies deliver services within the scope of the continuum of care; simplified example may not fully capture the scope of practice in the local community setting	Thoughtfully identifies how clinical mental health agencies deliver services within the scope of the continuum of care; provides clear examples from the local community setting
Theories and models related to clinical mental health counseling (5.C.1.b)	Simplified conceptualization of the local community setting from a chosen model of clinical mental health counseling; overlooks opportunity to create explanation; limited connections made between key elements of the model and the local community	Adequately conceptualizes the local community setting from a chosen model of clinical mental health counseling; simplified explanation may leave gaps in the application of the model to the local community	Thoughtfully conceptualizes the local community setting from a chosen model of clinical mental health counseling; provides exemplar explanation, connecting key elements of the model to the local community
Strategies to advocate for persons with mental health issues (5.C.3.e)	Simplified exploration of the trends and gaps of the services provided in the local community setting; overlooks opportunity to develop suggestions for how counselors may advocate or address gaps in services	Adequately explores trends and gaps of the services provided in the local community setting; develops some suggestions for how counselors may advocate or address gaps in services	Thoughtfully explores trends and gaps of the services provided in the local community setting; develops persuasive suggestions for how counselors may advocate or address gaps in services

Note. CACREP = Council for Accreditation of Counseling and Related Educational Programs; CMH = Clinical Mental Health.

Chapter 29

Clinical
Rehabilitation Counseling

Michael J. Walsh

Central to the clinical rehabilitation counseling standards is the notion that rehabilitation counselors should be able to appropriately engage clients in an evaluation process; conceptualize clients as individuals with unique strengths, values, and abilities; and work with the clients to enhance and improve their overall functioning. These skills involve professional knowledge, to be sure, but they also call for an ability to understand and apply this knowledge in specific ways.

In pedagogical terms, Bloom's Revised Taxonomy (Anderson & Krathwohl, 2001) lends a helpful framework for conceptualizing levels of thinking. The higher the level of thinking, the more complex the conceptual process and the more developed the ideas that result from that process.

According to Bloom's Revised Taxonomy, the highest level of thinking is Creating. This level may be especially helpful in thinking about the education of clinical rehabilitation counselors. Because clinical rehabilitation counseling often involves helping people with many different types of disabilities—often involving intricately complicated biological, psychological, social, and medical issues—creativity in thinking and knowledge application are critical skills. The assignments below are designed to mirror the complexity involved with clinical rehabilitation counseling casework. They are also designed to help students build the higher order critical thinking skills needed to be successful with these complex clinical cases.

The exercises in this chapter seek to engage students in the process of methodically and scientifically gathering data; analyzing that data; and then developing detailed, creative, and practical recommendations that the client may use to improve his or her overall functioning. The background and process of each assignment are provided, along with the assignment itself. Finally, a rubric is provided for the evaluation of the assignment.

The following assignment is an example of a case-driven diagnostic exercise. This exercise is used as the capstone project for a classification and assessment course in which rehabilitation counseling students interview and gather clinical and assessment data on a particular client. This assignment and this course are based in a Learning Community model in which the group acts as a learning community to facilitate the gathering of information and clinical data, whereas each student works to formulate his or her own comprehensive diagnosis and rehabilitation plan.

Diagnostic Report and Comprehensive Rehabilitation Plan

SLOs assessed: CACREP 2016 Standards 5.D.1.d, 5.D.1.f, 5.D.1.g, 5.D.2.f, 5.D.3.a, 5.D.2.m, 5.D.2.o

Over the course of the semester, the learning community will participate in the development of a case study. Each student will act as the counselor, and the instructor will role play the client. This case study will mirror, as closely as possible, an actual case development process in which a client is referred, clinical interviews are conducted, testing is done, and the results of the clinical interviews and testing are used to formulate a diagnosis and detailed rehabilitation recommendations.

In Week 5 of the semester, students will receive the "referral" on the case. This brief introduction is designed to give the most basic case information prior to the first client meeting. A reason for referral will be given in that brief introduction. This is designed to mirror a real-world scenario in which a counselor has been referred a case.

The learning community will then "meet" the client for the first time as a group that week. Each student should think about what information he or she would like to gather and should ask those questions in the initial interview.

After that interview, the learning community, as a group, will process and discuss what they learned while planning for the next week's interview. Thereafter, each week, a different student will lead the clinical interview with the client. This student will be the lead interviewer for that week. This student will be responsible for reaching out to the learning community prior to the meeting to determine any specific information gathering that is needed. The learning community as a whole is also responsible for getting any specific questions or informational requests to the lead interviewer prior to class each week. The second part of each class meeting time from Week 6 onward will be devoted to clinical interviewing time. In this way, the learning community will work together to develop their clinical investigatory and decision-making skills. Each student will be responsible for developing his or her own diagnostic impressions and formulating his or her own principle project, but the group will work through the clinical interview process together. The idea behind this aspect of the assignment is to build skills in gathering and developing information from client interactions as well as to build skills in recognizing client strengths in clinical interactions. Students will also begin to develop and refine their own personal clinical decision-making skills. Instructor and learning community feedback will be provided throughout this process.

In the same way, the learning community, as a group, will determine which standardized instruments may be helpful for use with this particular person. The learning community will be provided the results of this testing, and each student will be responsible for interpreting the test scores in the context of the case. Students will be responsible for mining the test data for strengths on which they may base the steps of the rehabilitation plan. The rehabilitation plan is a detailed list of practical steps that the clients can take to use their strengths to help to enhance their overall functioning. For example, if the testing data indicate that a client has strengths in using words and in oral expression, but the client is really struggling in social settings, one potential rehabilitation recommendation might be that the client use his or her speaking skills to engage with peers by organizing study groups. The instructor will help each student to develop his or her conceptualization of the case and his or her rehabilitation plan recommendations. The idea here is to develop skills in recognizing client strengths and figuring out how clients might use those strengths to improve their functioning. Students will develop the items listed below.

A. Diagnostic Letter and Rehabilitation Plan (Sample Provided in Course Materials)

The diagnostic letter is a comprehensive report on the results of your diagnostic findings related to the case study. This letter should include the following sections:

- *Reason for referral* (provided in case introduction)
- *Present status* (what you were able to learn from the client and/or his or her family)
- *Testing instruments used* (What instruments were used and why. In what ways were they helpful?)
- *Testing observations* (what you were able to observe about the person's behavior during testing—that information will be provided with the test scores)
- *Test scores* (the actual test scores reported to the index level)
- *Interpretation of those scores* (what these scores suggest about the client)
- *Summary of your diagnostic impressions* (your diagnostic impressions of the case, the client's unique strengths and desires, and your *DSM–5* [American Psychiatric Association, 2003] diagnosis)
- *Rehabilitation recommendations* (practical, detailed suggestions for the clients based on their unique strengths that will help them to improve their overall functioning; this includes the role of family, social support systems, and community connections in the rehabilitation and recovery process)

B. Process Paper

The process paper details each student's individual process for thinking through the case and each decision-making process involved in the differential diagnosis process.

- Students will record what they learned of the biopsychosocial history of the client.
- Students will detail the mental status evaluation of the client at each interview session as well as their own biopsychosocial evaluation process. Students will also record each of the client's unique strengths and desires, explaining how they have worked these strengths and desires into their diagnostic process and rehabilitation recommendations.
- It is recommended that students keep detailed case logs in which they can record their thinking and clinical decision making along the way. This will make the writing of the process paper much easier when that time comes. It will also help the student to track his or her own decision making and thought process.

C. Research Paper

Students will prepare a research paper, not to exceed 15 pages in length, in which they explore the diagnoses assigned to the fictional case study.

- This paper should present relevant information concerning the causes of the disorder, the differentiating criteria, the progression of the disorder, contributing physical considerations, implications for assessment, and treatment considerations that justify assignment of the particular diagnosis. The prevalence and etiology of the disorder is explored and explained in the context of the current case. The research related to the presenting issues is provided and critically evaluated. The research found is applied to this case in appropriate ways, and the student demonstrates good understanding of how the research applies and the ways in which this case may agree, confound, or conflict with the professional literature.
- This paper must follow APA Style and should be representative of the student's best clinical and professional writing. A minimum of 10 citations in support of the research done and points made must be provided.

Table 29.1 includes the rubric associated with this assignment.

Comprehensive Clinical Rehabilitation Counseling

SLOs assessed: CACREP 2016 Standard 5.D, 5.D.1.b, 5.D.1.g, 5.D.2.a, 5.D.2.b, 5.D.2.c, 5.D.2.i, 5.D.2.k, 5.D.2.n, 5.D.2.o, 5.D.2.q, 5.D.2.r, 5.D.2.w, 5.D.3.a, 5.D.3.b, and 5.D.3.e

The following assignment is an example of a case-study-driven comprehensive clinical rehabilitation counseling assessment. This is used to help students to showcase their learned knowledge and skills in two broad areas of clinical rehabilitation counseling: disability and vocation. This is typically used with a third question that specifically addresses areas of counseling, but as those areas are ably represented in other chapters in this text, the assignment and rubric presented here are limited to just two areas of rehabilitation.

This assignment asks students to read a case study and then to respond to questions based on these two broad areas. Each question has subareas designed to assess specific areas of rehabilitation counseling knowledge and/or skills. Each subquestion is noted with the standard measured.

This case-driven approach seeks to mimic the realities of working with actual clients in a rehabilitation counseling setting. This design also seeks to engage students in the cognitive processes needed to develop effective rehabilitation plans and to work effectively with clients.

Instructions to Students

This exercise involves working with a case study and conceptualizing the case within two broad areas of clinical rehabilitation counseling. The courses associated with each area of rehabilitation are listed next to each question number. This indicates that you may have learned knowledge or gained skills

Table 29.1
Diagnostic Report and Comprehensive Rehabilitation Plan Rubric

Criterion (CACREP Standard)	Does Not Meet Expectations	Meets Expectations	Exceeds Expectations
Diagnostic process (5.D.2.m, 5.D.3.b)	Demonstrates minimal or inaccurate understanding of diagnosis and differential diagnosis; inconsistencies in presentation; poor support for diagnostic conclusions	Demonstrates acceptable understanding of diagnosis and differential diagnosis; if present, inconsistencies are minor and do not interfere with overall understanding; adequate support for diagnostic conclusions	Demonstrates exceptional understanding of diagnosis and differential diagnosis; no inconsistencies noted; outstanding support of diagnostic conclusions
Biopsychosocial case conceptualization (5.D.1.d)	Poor use or understanding of biopsychosocial case conceptualization; did not consider one or more phases	Good conceptualization of the case on the biological, psychological, and social levels; all phases considered and addressed in the context of the client	Thoughtful and well considered conceptualization; all phases considered and utilized to advance the in-depth understanding of the client and the client's everyday functioning
Treatment planning/rehabilitation recommendations (5.D.1.d)	Poor understanding or communication of the ways in which the client may use his or her strengths to improve his or her overall functioning	Good use of client strengths to address significant client functional issues; detailed recommendations made that may be of practical use to the client	Excellent use of client strengths to address overall functioning; student identified specific strengths within the clinical and testing data and showed creativity in developing and presenting detailed and practical steps that a client may use to improve his or her overall functioning
Screening and assessment instruments (5.D.1.g)	Shows poor understanding of the choice of instruments used in the case	Shows good understanding of the choice of instruments used in the case and the ways in which the instrument was helpful in the diagnostic process	Shows an excellent understanding of the choice of instruments used in the case; goes on to describe in detail the ways in which the instrument was helpful; offers good recommendations for further testing, if appropriate
Impact on holistic functioning (i.e., physical, spiritual, sexual, vocational, social, relational, and recreational) (5.D.2.m)	Demonstrates little understanding of the ways in which the person's functioning is affected by the presenting issues or is missing some domains of functioning	Demonstrates good understanding of the ways in which the client's functioning is being affected by the presenting issues; all domains of functioning are considered	Demonstrates exceptional understanding of the ways in which the client's functioning is being affected by the presenting issues; provides in-depth analysis of those areas affected
Family, social networks and community (5.D.2.o)	Demonstrates or communicates little understanding of the ways in which family, social relationships, and community connections can be used to enhance the functioning of the client	Demonstrates or communicates good understanding of the ways in which family, social relationships, and community connections can be used to enhance the functioning of the client	Demonstrates or communicates excellent understanding of the ways in which family, social relationships, and community connections can be used to enhance the functioning of the client; provides detailed analysis
Research applications (5.D.1.f)	Demonstrates or communicates poor research and/or poor understanding of the prevalence, etiology, and effects of the presenting issues; research is poorly documented and/or poorly critically evaluated	Demonstrates or communicates good research and good understanding of the prevalence, etiology, and effects of the presenting issues; research is well documented and critically evaluated	Demonstrates or communicates excellent research and understanding of the prevalence, etiology, and effects of the presenting issues; research is well documented and tied back to the case in meaningful ways

Note. CACREP = Council for Accreditation of Counseling and Related Educational Programs.

in those courses that will help you to answer the questions posed. Question 1 deals with disability issues, and Question 2 deals with the vocational aspects of rehabilitation. Each question has subparts designed to measure a specific area of rehabilitation knowledge or skills. This is your opportunity to showcase what you have learned while applying this knowledge and these skills to a specific case.

Please answer the following questions in paragraph format. Each question has several parts. Please number each part of your answer to correspond to the section you are addressing. Your answers will be evaluated on the basis of your responsiveness to all parts of the question, your ability to demonstrate a grasp on both the details and general concepts appropriate to the scenario presented, and your ability to integrate and apply information from all parts of your rehabilitation counseling preparation.

Both of the content-area questions will be awarded 0–5 points on the basis of the criteria mentioned earlier. Each part of the question is scored from 0 to 1 on the basis of the thoroughness and accuracy of the response. Examinees must score 4 points or higher on each question to pass the question. Examinees will be required to rewrite their answer to an alternative question when a score of less than 4 points has been earned on a particular question. You will have 2 hours to respond to these questions. Please manage your time wisely.

Case Study

Thuy is a 33-year-old mother of two who came to the United States from Vietnam when she was 18 years of age. She became an American citizen 3 years ago and decided at that time to make English the primary language in her home. Thuy's children are bilingual, but Thuy has had difficulty learning her new language and, as a result, has worked jobs that did not require her to converse. She enrolled in an English course at the local community college. The guidance/career counselors and teachers were impressed with Thuy's motivation and her interest in school. They encouraged her to think about taking the GED (General Educational Development) and perhaps obtaining a college degree.

Thuy was anxious to pursue her dream of further education and looked forward to a time when she could quit her three jobs cleaning motel rooms. She talked to her children and friends about being a teacher of English in the elementary school.

Her first English class was challenging, but she was able to pick up the pronunciation and conversational phrases easily. Writing the language was much more difficult. Thuy had not been able to write well in Vietnamese and avoided activities that required her to express herself in written form. She rarely read books, magazines, or newspapers, explaining that they were really of little interest to her.

By the second semester, Thuy found that the classes and her heavy work schedule were becoming unmanageable. She ran from one job to another in her husband's rusty Ford pickup truck, held together by baling wire and duct tape. She rarely slept more than 3 hours because she was working, caring for her children, and attending English classes.

Then the unthinkable happened. Thuy had been exhausted after her shift and felt weak and short of breath. It was raining, and she tried to keep on driving even though she was dizzy and felt herself becoming nauseated. Thuy's truck hit a pool of water on the road and spun off the road, throwing Thuy out of the window and across the pavement. When the emergency workers arrived, Thuy had stopped breathing and was in cardiac arrest. They rushed her to the hospital.

Thuy had suffered a heart attack and had broken her lumbar (L) vertebrae at L2 and L3. Fortunately she suffered only a mild concussion, but she was covered from head to toe with abrasions and asphalt burn. Two years later, she comes to your office for help in getting a job.

Question 1
Disability Issues (Introduction to Rehabilitation Counseling, Psychosocial Aspects of Disability, Medical Aspects of Disability, Case Management)
Thuy has only a manual wheelchair, and she is wheeled into your office by her oldest son. Her medical records explain that she experienced a fracture of the vertebrae at L2 and L3 and a partial spinal cord injury in the same area. Her heart attack was caused by a congenital condition affecting the aortic valve. Thuy's lack of insurance coverage is preventing her from getting the medical treatment that would best treat this condition.

1. What government program(s) would be available to help Thuy acquire the medical treatment she desperately needs? How would Thuy apply, and what might she expect to receive if she is determined to be eligible? (CACREP 2016 Standards 5.D.2.c, 5.D.2.r)
2. Thuy's children are 11 and 14 years of age. Her husband is a person who has an alcohol problem and works occasionally as a landscaper. Thuy's jobs have covered most of the expenses for the family. They live in a Vietnamese community but have no relatives in this country. Discuss

three strategies that you might pursue to help this family address the many lifestyle changes that are the result of Thuy's disability. (CACREP 2016 Standards 5.D.3.e, 5.D.2.o)

3. What physical limitations might you expect Thuy to have as a result of her spinal cord injury? Discuss the implications of the partial injury as opposed to a complete injury to the spinal cord. (CACREP 2016 Standard 5.D.2.i)

4. What types of adaptive equipment or other aids might assist Thuy in a return to work, her household duties, and her mobility? (CACREP 2016 Standard 5.D.2.q)

5. Identify three agencies other than the one(s) you have mentioned in your response to Section 1 that would be able to assist Thuy and her family with their many needs. Discuss the services they would be able to provide and the way in which these services would fall into the full rehabilitation plan that you have designed for this client. (CACREP 2016 Standards 5.D.2.a, 5.D.2.b)

6. Discuss the ways in which Thuy may be affected by issues of handicapism, ableism, power, privilege, and oppression. What strategies might you use to help Thuy to manage those issues? (CACREP 2016 Standard 5.D.2.k)

Question 2
Vocational Aspects (Introduction to Rehabilitation Research and Assessment, Occupational Analysis, Career Development, Rehabilitation Assessment)

1. Thuy needs to be trained for a new job. Given her lack of transferable skills, her limited education, and the problems she was experiencing with school, you feel that a full vocational evaluation would be useful. What specific questions do you need answered to help identify job possibilities, and what specific instruments or evaluation procedures would you suggest to the evaluator to help you gain the information you need? Name at least four instruments or evaluation methods, and discuss the rationale for your selection. (CACREP 2016 Standards 5.D.1.g, 5.D.2.n, 5.D.3.b)

2. Following the evaluation, you find out that Thuy has a learning disorder. Her full scale IQ is 102, and her performance IQ is 78. If the mean of the IQ test is 100, and the standard deviation is 15, discuss where Thuy's scores fall in comparison with most other people her age. (CACREP 2016 Standard 5.D.3.a)

3. Discuss the influence of language and culture on the scores of standardized tests. How would you address these issues in designing the vocational evaluation? (CACREP 2016 Standard 5.D.1.g)

4. Apply one career theory to Thuy's situation and discuss the way in which culture and social factors affect Thuy's overall career development? (CACREP 2016 Standards 5.D.1.b, 5.D.2.o)

5. Thuy has seemed somewhat reluctant to talk with you about her needs and her family situation. You find that your ability to work with her is frequently hampered by misunderstandings that could be related to differences in culture or language barriers. You are interested in learning more about effective strategies for helping individuals from Thuy's culture find employment. What three rehabilitation journals would you explore for more information? What other sources might you pursue to further research your questions? (CACREP 2016 Standard 5.D.2.o)

6. What ethical issues do you see involved in this case? Discuss any and all applicable ethical principles and the ways in which you may go about making good ethical decisions in this case. (CACREP 2016 Standard 5.D.2.w)

Table 29.2 includes the rubric associated with this assignment regarding Question 1, and Table 29.3 includes the rubric associated with this assignment regarding Question 2.

Table 29.2
Comprehensive Case Study Question 1 Rubric

Criterion (CACREP Standard)	Does Not Meet Expectations	Meets Expectations	Exceeds Expectations
Rehabilitation service delivery systems, including housing, independent living, case management, public benefits programs, educational programs, and public/proprietary vocational rehabilitation programs (5.D.2.c)	Poor use or understanding of rehabilitation services systems; does not consider one or more aspect that would be appropriate	Good understanding and application of knowledge of rehabilitation systems; all aspects considered and addressed in the context of the client	Excellent understanding and application of the knowledge shown; applied to the case in thoughtful and meaningful ways; all services recommended are likely to help the client significantly
Legislation and government policy relevant to rehabilitation counseling (5.D.2.r)	Poor understanding or communication of the ways in which the client may take advantage of legislation and government policy related to disability and function	Good use of the knowledge of government legislation to address significant client functional issues; made recommendations that may be of practical use to the client	Excellent use of legislation knowledge to address overall functioning; identifies specific legislation and programs to address significant client functional issues; shows creativity in developing and presenting detailed and practical steps that clients may take to avail themselves of the services or benefits available
Strategies to consult with and educate employers, educators, and families regarding accessibility, Americans with Disabilities Act compliance, and accommodations (5.D.3.e)	Student shows poor understanding or communication of the ways in which the family may be involved in advocating for Thuy and themselves given Thuy's disability	Students shows good understanding of the impact of the disability and the ways in which the family may be involved	Student shows an excellent understanding of the impact of the disability and the ways in which the family may be involved to make a positive impact for the client; student extends that model to include other professionals and rehabilitation systems
Role of family, social networks, and community in the provision of services for and treatment of people with disabilities (5.D.2.o)	Demonstrates or communicates little understanding of the ways in which family, social relationships, and community connections can be used to enhance the functioning of the client	Demonstrates or communicates good understanding of the ways in which family, social relationships, and community connections can be used to enhance the functioning of the client	Demonstrates or communicates excellent understanding of the ways in which family, social relationships, and community connections can be used to enhance the functioning of the client; provides detailed analysis
Impact of biological/neurological mechanisms on disability (5.D.2.i)	Demonstrates or communicates poor understanding of biological and functional aspects of disability and spinal cord injury	Demonstrates or communicates good understanding of biological and functional aspects of disability and spinal cord injury and applies that information well in the context of the case	Demonstrates or communicates excellent understanding of biological and functional aspects of disability and spinal cord injury; applies that information to the case in meaningful ways; uses that connection to make recommendations to maximize client functioning and autonomy
Assistive technology to reduce or eliminate barriers and functional limitations (5.D.2.q)	Demonstrates or communicates an inadequate understanding of assistive technology and ways in which it can be used to maximize client function	Demonstrates or communicates a good understanding of assistive technology and ways in which it can be used to maximize client function	Demonstrates or communicates an excellent understanding of assistive technology and ways in which it can be used to maximize client function; applies that information to the case in creative and thoughtful ways
Roles and settings of clinical rehabilitation counselors (5.D.2.a)	Demonstrates or communicates an inadequate understanding of the role of the rehabilitation counselor within the rehabilitation system and the ways in which counselors can help clients to maximize function	Demonstrates good understanding of the role of the rehabilitation counselor within the rehabilitation system and the ways in which counselors can help clients to maximize function	Demonstrates excellent understanding of the role of the rehabilitation counselor within the rehabilitation system and the ways in which counselors can help clients to maximize function

(Continued)

Table 29.2 (*Continued*)
Comprehensive Case Study Question 1 Rubric

Criterion (CACREP Standard)	Does Not Meet Expectations	Meets Expectations	Exceeds Expectations
Relationships between clinical rehabilitation counselors and medical and allied health professionals, including interdisciplinary treatment team (5.D.2.b)	Demonstrates or communicates poor understanding of the relationships between allied health professionals and the ways in which those relationships may fit together in the case context to help maximize client outcomes	Demonstrates or communicates good understanding of the relationships between allied health professionals and the ways in which those relationships may fit together in the case context to help maximize client outcomes	Demonstrates or communicates excellent understanding of the relationships between allied health professionals and the ways in which those relationships may fit together in the case context to help maximize client outcomes; applies knowledge creatively and productively to the case, showing excellent critical thinking skills and clinical judgment
Effects of discrimination, handicapism, ableism, power, privilege, and oppression on clients' lives and careers (5.D.2.k)	Demonstrates or communicates poor understanding of the effects of handicapism, ableism, power, privilege, and oppression	Demonstrates good understanding of the effects of handicapism, ableism, power, privilege, and oppression and applies that understanding to this case	Demonstrates good understanding of the effects of handicapism, ableism, power, privilege, and oppression and applies that understanding to this case; takes that understanding and uses it to make meaningful recommendations that will maximize client quality of life
Theories and models related to rehabilitation counseling (5.D.1.b)	Demonstrates or communicates an inadequate understanding of career theories and ways in which they can be used with clients in rehabilitation settings	Demonstrates or communicates a good understanding of career theories and ways in which they can be used with clients in rehabilitation settings; applies that knowledge to the case	Demonstrates or communicates a good understanding of career theories and ways in which they can be used with clients in rehabilitation settings; applies that knowledge to the case; displays excellent critical thinking and creative skills in applying knowledge to this case
Role of family, social networks, and community in the provision of services for and treatment of people with disabilities (5.D.2.o)	Demonstrates or communicates an inadequate understanding of social networks and the ways in which they can affect career development	Demonstrates or communicates a good understanding of social networks and the ways in which they can affect career development; applies that information to the case	Demonstrates or communicates a good understanding of social networks and the ways in which they can affect career development; applies that information to the case; makes meaningful recommendations that foster good client outcomes.

Note. CACREP = Council for Accreditation of Counseling and Related Educational Programs.

Table 29.3
Comprehensive Case Study Question 2 Rubric

Criterion (CACREP Standard)	Does Not Meet Expectations	Meets Expectations	Exceeds Expectations
Screening and assessment instruments (5.D.1.g)	Demonstrates or communicates poor understanding of the use of screening instruments in rehabilitation services systems; does not consider one or more aspect(s) that would be appropriate	Demonstrates good understanding of the use of screening instruments in rehabilitation services systems; does not consider one or more aspect(s) that would be appropriate	Demonstrates excellent understanding of the use of screening instruments in rehabilitation services systems; applies learned material to the case in thoughtful and meaningful ways; all services recommended are likely to help the client significantly
Transferable skills, functional assessments, and work-related supports (5.D.2.n)	Demonstrates poor understanding or communication of the use of TSA and other functional skills assessments in the vocational process	Demonstrates good understanding or communication of the use of TSA and other functional skills assessments in the vocational process; applies this knowledge well to the case	Demonstrates excellent understanding or communication of the use of TSA and other functional skills assessments in the vocational process; shows excellent creative and critical thinking skills in applying the information to the case in meaningful ways
Career and work-related assessments (5.D.3.b)	Demonstrates or communicates poor understanding of the use of career and work-related instruments and evaluation procedures and/or their potential use in this case	Demonstrates or communicates good understanding of the use of career and work-related instruments and evaluation procedures and/or their potential use in this case	Demonstrates or communicates excellent understanding of the use of career and work-related instruments and evaluation procedures and/or their potential use in this case; applies knowledge creatively and productively to the case, showing excellent critical thinking skills and clinical judgment
Psychoeducational assessments (5.D.3.b)	Demonstrates or communicates poor understanding of the role of psychoeducational assessments in the rehabilitation process	Demonstrates or communicates good understanding of the role of psychoeducational assessments in the rehabilitation process; applies the knowledge well to the case	Demonstrates or communicates good understanding of the role of psychoeducational assessments in the rehabilitation process; applies the knowledge well to the case; demonstrates excellent critical thinking skills and clinical judgment in using this knowledge to make meaningful recommendations for client success
Screening and assessment (5.D.1.g)	Demonstrates or communicates poor understanding of the impact of language and culture on standardized tests and the ways in which those issues affect test validity and reliability with specific populations	Demonstrates or communicates good understanding of the impact of language and culture on standardized tests and the ways in which those issues affect test validity and reliability with specific populations; applies that information well to the case	Demonstrates or communicates good understanding of the impact of language and culture on standardized tests and the ways in which those issues affect test validity and reliability with specific populations; applies that information well to the case; demonstrates excellent critical thinking in vocational design choices
Role of family, social networks, and community in the provision of services for and treatment of people with disabilities (5.D.2.o)	Demonstrates or communicates poor understanding of the ways in which community and family networks can be combined with rehabilitation research to facilitate client outcomes	Demonstrates or communicates good understanding of the ways in which community and family networks can be combined with rehabilitation research to facilitate client outcomes; applies that knowledge to the case well	Demonstrates or communicates good understanding of the ways in which community and family networks can be combined with rehabilitation research to facilitate client outcomes; applies that knowledge to the case well; exhibits creative and critical thinking skills in developing meaningful recommendations for client success

(Continued)

Table 29.3 (*Continued*)
Comprehensive Case Study Question 2 Rubric

Criterion (CACREP Standard)	Does Not Meet Expectations	Meets Expectations	Exceeds Expectations
Legal and ethical considerations specific to clinical rehabilitation counseling (5.D.2.w)	Demonstrates or communicates poor understanding of the legal and ethical aspects of clinical rehabilitation counseling	Demonstrates or communicates good understanding of the legal and ethical aspects of clinical rehabilitation counseling; applies that knowledge well to case	Demonstrates or communicates good understanding of the legal and ethical aspects of clinical rehabilitation counseling; applies that knowledge well to case; displays excellent ethical decision-making and critical-thinking skills

Note. CACREP = Council for Accreditation of Counseling and Related Educational Programs; TSA = transferable skills analysis.

Chapter 30

College Counseling and Student Affairs

Joshua C. Watson

There is a growing body of evidence suggesting that today's college and university students are struggling with emotional and behavioral problems at an increasingly higher rate than students in past generations have experienced (Brunner, Wallace, Reymann, Sellers, & McCabe, 2014). As a result, the need for college counselors has never been greater. In terms of practice, the role of the college counselor has become quite multifaceted as the scope and complexity of college counseling programs have expanded considerably in recent years. Today, college counselors are expected to wear many hats. In addition to having to manage growing caseloads with increased levels of client severity, college counselors also must involve themselves in marketing and public relations efforts, networking and collaboration initiatives with campus and community resource providers, campus-wide programming, and crisis management and disaster mental health services (Smith et al., 2007). Furthermore, college counselors are being asked to perform these increased duties in light of decreases in staffing and funding. According to Much, Wagener, and Hellenbrand (2010), "the dynamic nature of working in a university or college counseling center creates special challenges for mental health providers" (p. 32). As a result, those individuals choosing to work in a college counseling center must be well-versed and trained to perform a variety of roles and functions.

The CACREP (2016) College Counseling and Student Affairs Standards reflect the multifaceted nature of the college counseling profession. Standards for training and practice address the many ways that college counselors work to support the educational mission of their institution, including consultation (Standard 5.E.2.c), preventive and developmental interventions (Standard 5.E.2.n), student needs advocacy (Standard 5.E.2.j), program development (Standard 5.E.3.a), outreach programming (Standard 5.E.3.b), consultation with faculty and staff (Standard 5.E.3.a), crisis management (Standard 5.E.2.b), and clinical treatment (Standard 5.E.2.d). The Standards, which have emerged following several iterations, combine elements of counseling and student affairs training, and they represent the importance of college counselors collaborating with other units across the institution and addressing the whole student in their counseling activities. As a result, counselor educators who are training students to work on university campuses should provide these students with diverse learning opportunities that allow them to build the skill set needed to function in the university setting. Applied examples and problem-based activities provide the greatest amount of opportunity for students to understand the connection between theory and practice.

In this chapter, three assignments with College Counseling and Student Affairs themes are presented. In addition, evaluation rubrics are provided to facilitate the assessment of student learning across the college counseling curriculum. The first assignment provides students with an opportunity to put theory to practice. Students will choose a unique subpopulation represented on college and university campuses today and use contemporary theories or student development to help understand the student's developmental status and discuss how they would work with that individual in a counseling setting. The second assignment gives students the opportunity to plan their own counseling program. Given a set budget, students will need to develop a proposal that describes a mental health program they would like to implement that would benefit their campus-based community. In addition to describing the program, students will need to explain how they determined the need for the program, what resources would be required to effectively run the program, how the program will be marketed, and how the success of the program will be marketed. The final assignment is related to program evaluation. Students will be asked to evaluate a counseling program being offered on a college campus using the principles of sound program evaluation that they have learned in their coursework.

Applied Student Development Theory

SLOs assessed: CACREP 2016 Standards 5.E.1.b, 5.E.1.d, 5.E.2.m, 5.E.2.n, 5.E.3.b

This assignment is designed to provide practice applying existing theory to the lived experiences of college students. Identify a student subpopulation on campus, and describe how you would counsel that individual using one of the student developmental theories discussed in class as a framework. Examples of student subpopulations might include the following: first-year students, nontraditional students, international students, undocumented students, first-generation students, graduate students, or minority status students. In your paper, you will be asked to support your rationale for the theory chosen and its appropriateness for the student subpopulation that you identify.

In your paper, be sure to include the following section headings:

1. *Student Conceptualization*—provide a brief overview of the demographics and background of the student subpopulation you chose to examine. Describe what makes this group special and unique.
2. *Theoretical Framework*—identify the theory you chose to guide your understanding of the student subpopulation you selected. This should include an overview of the major theoretical tenets associated with your theory.
3. *Treatment Plan*—describe the counseling program you will create for this subpopulation. Be sure to include what is involved in the program, how it will be implemented, how it will be marketed to your target population, and who will participate in the facilitation of this program.
4. *Strengths and Limitations*—discuss the strengths and limitations of your program, especially as it relates to meeting the unique needs of the student subpopulation you chose to study.
5. *Prognosis and Expected Outcome*—describe what you expect to occur as a result of your work counseling this student. Be sure to address how you plan to assess whether goals have been met and whether counseling has been successful.

Papers should be written in accordance with current APA Style guidelines (12-point, Times New Roman font; double-spaced; 1-inch margins; etc.). In total, your final submission should be 15–20 pages in length, including a title page, abstract, and references. Note that any references used should be drawn from professional counseling/student affairs journals that are no more than 10 years old.

Papers will be evaluated using the following rubric. Students are encouraged to review the evaluation criteria and to format their papers accordingly. Table 30.1 includes the rubric associated with this assignment.

College Counseling Program Implementation

SLOs assessed: CACREP 2016 Standards 5.E.1.b, 5.E.1.d, 5.E.2.n, 5.E.3.c, 5.E.3.d

As a staff counselor at a local university counseling center, you have been asked to identify a particular mental health service that you would like to deliver to students. Assume that administration has

Table 30.1
Applied Student Development Theory Rubric

Criterion (CACREP Standard)	Does Not Meet Expectations	Meets Expectations	Exceeds Expectations
Conceptualization of student development (5.E.1.d)	Significant problems with conceptualization, such as irreconcilable discrepancies or missing key issues	Provides a useful description of key issues for developing treatment plan; few (or no) inconsistencies	All elements of case conceptualization clearly fit to create a unified understanding to guide counseling process; sophisticated conceptualization that identifies subtle issues
Application of student development theory (5.E.1.b)	Content is incomplete; several major components of the theory were left out of the discussion or were incorrectly applied to the client in the case study	Content is not comprehensive; major theoretical points are stated, but they are not discussed or supported in the context of this case study	Content is accurate and applied correctly; major theoretical points are stated and discussed in the context of the case study
Treatment plan (5.E.2.m)	Treatment plan is devoid of any logical strategies or techniques related to the theory being used	Treatment plan designed for this client contains a variety of strategies; however, some may not be related to the theory being used	Treatment plan designed for this client utilizes a variety of strategies that are supported in the professional literature
Evaluation of theory strengths and limitations (5.E.3.b)	Strengths and limitations of the chosen theory are not addressed at all; no consideration for how these will be addressed in the treatment plan	Cursory attention is paid to strengths and limitations of the theory; these issues are not addressed in the treatment plan developed	The strengths and limitations of the chosen development theory are critically reviewed and addressed in the treatment plan
Prognosis and expected outcome (5.E.2.n)	A prognosis for the client is not provided; there is disconnect between how the treatment plan is described and how the client is expected to benefit from counseling	A prognosis is given, but it appears to be vague and without much detail; expected outcomes appear to be loosely tied to the treatment plan	A clear and concise prognosis is given; expected outcomes are detailed in relation to the components of the treatment plan designed to address the components

Note. CACREP = Council for Accreditation of Counseling and Related Educational Programs.

provided you with a budget ample enough to create such a mental health program that effectively fills a void in the campus community. Some examples might include the following: peer helper training, stress management, suicide prevention, mental health screenings, or the development of a mobile crisis stabilization team. Create a proposal that you would submit to the university administration detailing what you would like to implement. Although there is not a standard format that the university uses for such proposals, you likely would want to be sure to include the following components:

1. Needs assessment (how will you identify what is lacking, and needed, on campus)
2. Mission statement (what will be the charge or focus of your project)
3. Goals and/or objectives
4. Program (what are the actual working components or activities that make up your program)
5. Working knowledge, skills, and resource supports needed to be successful
6. Funding sources that could be partnered with to ensure the sustainability of this program in the future (provide a listing of local, state, or national agencies that might be interested in funding such a project)
7. Environmental supports (what community resources can be used to enhance or supplement your proposed campus-based program)
8. Marketing strategies employed to attract students to your program
9. Program evaluation (how will you know whether your project has been successful)

As you formulate your program proposal, make sure you are reviewing the relevant professional literature and including it in your narrative. In addition to your proposal, submit no more than two marketing items (flyers, mailings, posters, etc.) that you might use in promoting your new program to students on campus.

Your written proposal should adhere to current APA Style guidelines (12-point, Times New Roman font; double-spaced; 1-inch margins; etc.) and should not exceed 10 pages in length excluding title page and references. Table 30.2 includes the rubric associated with this assignment.

Table 30.2
College Counseling Program Implementation Rubric

Criterion (CACREP Standard)	Does Not Meet Expectations	Meets Expectations	Exceeds Expectations
Needs assessment (5.E.1.d)	No input was sought from any stakeholders in terms of program objectives	Input was sought from stakeholders and was partially used to develop the program	Input was sought from all relevant stakeholders and was used to develop the program
Mission statement (5.E.1.d)	Statement does not identify the functions of the program or its greater purpose; does not align with the mission of the counseling center or the university	Statement addresses the program purpose and whom it is intended to serve; aligns with the mission of the counseling center and the university	Statement is clear, concise, and specific to the program, and it addresses the larger impact of the program
Goals and objectives	Describes a process rather than an outcome and is not aligned with the program mission statement; unclear how evaluator will determine when the outcome is met	Goals are observable and measureable; they encompass the mission of the program and, although appropriate, may be vague and in need of revisions	Several measureable outcomes are identified; action verbs are used to describe the level of mastery expected; aligns completely with program mission
Description of program (5.E.1.b)	Many key items are not addressed, or the descriptions provided are incomplete or faulty; the program does not appear to align at all with stated goals and objectives	Not all key items are addressed, or the descriptions of these items are somewhat incomplete; loosely aligned with program goals and objectives	All key items are included, and descriptions are reasonably complete; program activities are aligned with program goals and objectives
Resource inventory (5.E.2.n)	Program does not appear to take advantage of all available resources; key assets are neither identified nor utilized	Program appears to recognize the availability of key resources on campus, but no plan to actively use them exists	Program recognizes the availability of key resources on campus and actively incorporates them into program activities
Funding sources	The proposal does not include any consideration as to how the program can be funded in the future	General suggestions for future funding sources are included, but no specific sources are identified	A clear understanding of where future funding for this program can come from is shared
Environmental supports (5.E.2.n)	No consideration is given to including outside resources; program does not include off campus stakeholders	Consideration is given to including outside resources, but a definite plan for doing so is not clearly articulated	Collaboration with outside resources is included in the program, and a clear vision for how this will occur is detailed
Marketing strategies (5.E.3.d)	No clear marketing strategy exists; directions for reaching target population appear disjointed and ineffective	A clear marketing strategy is in place; directions for reaching target population are somewhat vague	A clear marketing strategy is in place; specific direction for reaching target population is provided
Program evaluation	Evaluation design is not clearly specified; design does not allow for the evaluation questions to be answered; limitations are not addressed or are addressed in an incomplete fashion	Evaluation design is not clearly specified; design allows for evaluation questions to be partially addressed, and limitations are described but incompletely	Evaluation design is clearly specified and allows for complete answering of all evaluation questions; limitations are addressed and clearly described

Note. CACREP = Council for Accreditation of Counseling and Related Educational Programs.

Campus-Based Program Evaluation

SLOs assessed: CACREP 2016 Standards 5.E.1.e, 5.E.2.h, 5.E.2.l, 5.E.3.e

In this assignment, you are tasked with developing a practical, evidence-based program evaluation model for an existing program, a program that is under development, or an area of unmet need relevant to the current needs of students enrolled at a 4-year college or university. To successfully complete this assignment, you will need to integrate and apply the principles of sound program evaluation discussed in class and course readings to present a model that addresses the following: (a) the formulation of a specific mental health or student issue affecting students on college campuses, (b) the design of a program model based on evidence-based practices selected to address these specific issues, and (c) the research concepts and methods used to evaluate the impact of the program for those students whom the target program was intended to serve.

Separate headings should be used for each of the major components of your paper. Components included in your paper must include, but at are not limited to, the following:

- *Overview of the Institution*—Describe the college or university at which the program will take place. What are the salient characteristics of the institution? What does the student body look like at this institution?
- *Problem Statement*—What is the issue identified? Why is it important that college counselors address this issue?
- *Goals and Objectives*—What are the expected outcomes of the program? How will the campus community benefit from the implementation of such a program?
- *Model*—What is the logic model being used for this program? How was it (or will it be) initially conceptualized?
- *Methods*—What activities or interventions will be implemented in the program? What does the research say about these activities or interventions?
- *Evaluation*—How will you be able to document that the program is effective? What data would you collect to assess goal attainment? What research design would be most appropriate?
- *Sustainability*—Discuss the strengths and limitations of the program and how it can be continued in the future (consider funding and staffing issues).

Papers should be written in accordance with current APA Style guidelines (12-point, Times New Roman font; double-spaced; 1-inch margins; etc.). In total, your final submission should be 20–25 pages in length, including a title page, abstract, and references. Note that any references used should be drawn from professional counseling/student affairs journals that are no more than 10 years old.

Papers will be evaluated using the enclosed rubric. Students are encouraged to review the evaluation criteria and to format their papers accordingly. Table 30.3 includes the rubric associated with this assignment.

Table 30.3
Campus-Based Program Evaluation Rubric

Criterion (CACREP Standard)	Does Not Meet Expectations	Meets Expectations	Exceeds Expectations
Overview of the institution (5.E.2.h)	The institution is poorly defined, and the unique characteristics of the institution are not addressed in the program	The institution is well defined, and most unique characteristics of the institution are addressed in the program	The institution is well defined, and all unique characteristics of the institution are addressed in the program
Problem statement	Problem statement is disjointed and hard to follow; it does not appear to be specific to the program or represent the big picture need for the program	Problem statement is understandable but somewhat wordy; it is specific to the program being evaluated, but the big picture need for the program is vague	Problem statement is concise, understandable, specific to the program being evaluated, and conveys the big picture need for the program
Goals and objectives (5.E.1.e)	No or unclear goals and objectives are stated; none are student learning focused and/or objectives-oriented	Most goals and objectives are clearly stated in measurable terms, are student learning focused, and are objectives-oriented; the number of goals and objectives is appropriate, with most reflecting student well-being	All goals and objectives are clearly stated in measurable terms, are student learning focused, and are objectives-oriented; the number of goals and objectives is appropriate, with all goals and objectives reflecting student well-being
Logic model (5.E.2.l)	No logical relationships between any of the resources, activities, and outcomes are addressed and accounted for	Logical relationships between most of the resources, activities, and outcomes are addressed and accounted for	Logical relationships between all resources, activities, and outcomes are addressed and accounted for
Method (5.E.3.e)	Program lacks information on methods, procedures, timelines, and responsible parties; the program has not been implemented, or no clear plan for how it will be implemented exists	Most methods, procedures, timelines, and responsible parties are in place and are clearly stated; the majority of the program has been implemented, or a clear plan for implementation is firmly in place.	All methods, procedures, timelines, and responsible parties are in place and are clearly stated; the program has been fully implemented or an established and agreed on implementation plan is in place
Evaluation	Evaluation methods do not appear to be appropriate to the program described; only one source of data is used	Evaluation methods are appropriate and address questions generally related to the program; data will be collected from some, but not all, possible resources	Evaluation methods are appropriate and address the right questions; data will be collected from all possible resources
Sustainability	There is no description of how the program will be continued beyond the initial phase, how it will be funded, or what parties will be involved	Consideration is given to the continuation of the program beyond the initial phase, yet details are lacking in terms of how it will be funded and who will be involved	A well-thought-out plan for continuing the program after the initial phase is presented, including where funding will come from and what parties will be involved

Note. CACREP = Council for Accreditation of Counseling and Related Educational Programs.

Chapter 31

Marriage, Couples, and Family Counseling

Ryan G. Carlson

Family of origin, family context, and interpersonal relationships are foundational concepts for marriage, couples, and family counselors. Family theories and techniques aim to understand clients through their interactions with others, thus separating the family systems epistemology from individual-oriented approaches. Successfully implementing such family theories often requires students to examine their own family systems, thus becoming more aware of how their family dynamics contribute to current interpersonal functioning (e.g., Trusty, Skowron, Watts, & Parrillo, 2004). Supervision models for family counseling students often incorporate reflective practices, such as understanding systemic concepts like differentiation, and the parallel process (Carlson & Lambie, 2012). Therefore, counselor educators may utilize both experiential and reflective approaches when teaching students to use self-awareness as marriage, couple, and family counselors.

Traditional teaching models for theory, and subsequent practice, generally include the "theory-of-the-week" approach. Such an approach identifies one theory each week, providing students with a didactic overview of the theory's foundational concepts. Traditional approaches may not be as conducive to training systemic-oriented counselors because they do not provide opportunities for students to reflect on how their perceptions of concepts have been influenced by family dynamics. A reflection of how family dynamic influences current perspectives, especially concerning family therapy curriculum taught in the classroom setting, may be helpful in training students to be aware of their own family influences, thus increasing their chances of adopting a systemic framework with clients. Conversely, an experiential framework that includes discussion and opportunities to experience theoretical concepts may provide more opportunities for class reflection. Consoli and Jester (2005) presented an integrative approach to teaching traditional counseling theories to students, whereas Fraenkel and Pinsof (2001) discussed family-therapy integration for family counseling students. Each approach offers a framework for helping students learn the broader concepts of theory, as well as compare and contrast theory, contributing to a more pragmatic framework. As such, students may be more apt to discuss experiences related to the broader concepts and to use those experiences in application.

The three assignments presented in the MCFC chapter are designed to help students through a process of (a) understanding content, (b) experiencing the content through reflection, and (c) identifying how the content and experience contribute to the student's developing identity as a counselor. The first activity is specific toward students learning approaches to counseling couples. The activity aims to help students experience meeting with couples and assessing the couple relationship from a strength-based perspective. The second assignment will help students to critically examine family therapy conducted by experts. Students might often assume therapy is good and effective simply because it is conducted by an expert. This experience will provide students an opportunity to demonstrate their understanding of theory and to evaluate the overall effectiveness of the approach. Finally, the third assignment provides an opportunity for students to experience the family genogram, understand resulting patterns, and integrate those patterns into current interpersonal functioning.

Couple Interview and Assessment

SLOs assessed: CACREP 2016 Standards 5.F.1.e, 5.F.2.c, 5.F.2.m, 5.F.3.a, 5.F.3.c, 5.F.3.d

Identify three distinctly different couples (e.g., race/cultural difference, sexual orientation, developmental life cycle stage) who are willing to let you assess and interview them regarding their relationship. Be sure to inform couples that you will change their names in your write-up to help protect their identity. Prior to the interview, couples should be reminded that this is a class assignment and not a counseling session. Therefore, questions will be designed to understand important aspects of the couple relationship rather than explore deficits within the relationship.

Administer a couple assessment, such as the Relationship Assessment Scale (Hendrick, 1998); conduct a genogram with each member of the couple that includes basic information about each person's family (e.g., substance abuse, mental health, culture, religion, and relational history); and ask general relationship questions from a strength-based perspective (e.g., "What do you consider to be an important story about your relationship?" "Tell the story of how you met." "What do you see as your greatest couple strengths?").

Provide a written summary of your results in no less than 10 pages. Papers must adhere to APA Style. The summary should present the following information: (a) insight into couple dynamics, such as the overall patterns and strengths you identify within each couple; (b) results of the assessment, providing a brief interpretation of the couple's score; (c) transgenerational influences gathered from the couple genogram; (d) cultural factors within the relationship that could affect the couple's functioning; and (e) a section outlining a treatment approach for each couple, as if you were planning to counsel each couple. The treatment approach should include a specific theory and relevant techniques. Theory and techniques chosen should be supported by relevant peer-reviewed literature. Table 31.1 includes the rubric associated with this assignment.

Expert Family Theory Video Review and Critique

SLOs assessed: CACREP 2016 Standards 5.F.1.b, 5.F.1.e, 5.F.3.a, 5.F.3.c

Choose from one of the core family therapies (e.g., Structural, Strategic, Milan, Bowen Family Systems, Solution-Focused Family Therapy, Symbolic-Experiential, Human-Validation Process, Narrative, Object Relations) and use library or online resources to identify a video of a well-known therapist conducting counseling utilizing the chosen theory. Your college or university library may offer some videos for check-out or might subscribe to an online video library resource (e.g., http://alexanderstreet.com/products/counseling-and-therapy-video-series). Some instructors or counseling programs may own a collection of videos that could be checked out by students for purposes of completing the assignment.

After viewing the video, provide a review and critique of the session observed. The review should adhere to APA Style and should provide an overview of the following: (a) statement of theory reviewed and its core underpinnings, (b) client's presenting concerns, (c) review of techniques utilized by the counselor leading the session, (d) discussion of perceived effectiveness (do you think the therapy was effective, why or why not?), (e) limitations of the theory as well as cultural considerations, and (f) personal reaction to the therapy. Table 31.2 includes the rubric associated with this assignment.

Genogram and Reflection

SLOs assessed: CACREP 2016 Standards 5.F.2.c, 5.F.2.h, 5.F.2.j, 5.F.2.k, 5.F. 2.l

Complete a three-generation genogram on the student's family of origin (e.g., Butler, 2008). The

Table 31.1
Couple Interview and Assessment Rubric

Criterion (CACREP Standard)	Does Not Meet Expectations	Meets Expectations	Exceeds Expectations
Overall interpretation of couple dynamics (e.g., strengths and insights) (5.F.1.e)	Does not provide an interpretation of couple dynamics based on the information gathered, or the interpretation does not appear to match the questions asked, or an interpretation was not included	Identifies couple's strengths and appears to have an understanding of the couple's overall functioning; the interpretation provided matches the questions asked of the couples during the interview	Provides a thorough and in-depth conceptualization of the couple's overall functioning, including strengths, and how these strengths contribute to couple functioning
Use of relationship assessment (5.F.3.a)	Does not use a relationship assessment, or the assessment includes information about the couple not relevant to the assignment, or the assessment results are not clearly included in the summary	Implements a relevant assessment and demonstrates an understanding of the assessment results, providing a description of how the results contribute to couple functioning	Implementes a relevant assessment; demonstrates an understanding of the assessment results; provides in-depth description of results; tied results to other areas of information gathered during the interview
Use of genogram and transgenerational patterns identified (5.F.2.c)	Genogram is not comprehensive or does not include information relevant to the interview	Genogram includes relevant information and identifies transgenerational patterns	Genogram contains relevant information, identifies transgenerational patterns, and integrates the patterns into other assessed areas to contribute to more in-depth conceptualization of the couple
Cultural factors influencing the couples (5.F.2.m)	Does not identify cultural factors or expand on contribution of the influence of cultural factors	Identifies cultural factors and their potential influence on couple dynamics	Demonstrates an in-depth awareness of cultural influences on couple dynamics, and demonstrates an understanding of how culture contributed to couples' responses in other areas of the interview
Treatment plan and approach (5.F.3.d)	Does not develop a complete or relevant treatment plan	Treatment plan is complete and includes a theoretical approach, along with potential goals and techniques	Treatment plan is comprehensive, is supported through the relevant literature, and includes methods to evaluate its effectiveness throughout the course of counseling

Note. CACREP = Council for Accreditation of Counseling and Related Educational Programs.

genogram should include relevant names, birth dates, illnesses, and so forth for respective family members. Additionally, the genogram should chart family characteristics including, but not limited to, substance abuse, mental illness, physical illness, religious/spiritual beliefs, culture, and types of employment (e.g., business, teaching). Include a legend to accompany the symbols chosen to represent characteristics on the genogram.

Write a minimum of a three-page paper describing the family patterns and dynamics observed in the genogram. The paper should adhere to APA Style. In addition to identifying specific family generational patterns, the paper should include the following: (a) a reflection describing how those patterns contribute to personal and professional characteristics, (b) family life-cycle development factors exhibiting influence on the family (e.g., substance abuse, career changes, cultural factors, health factors), and (c) potential areas of growth (e.g., biases, triggers) that the student may experience as a counselor. Table 31.3 includes the rubric associated with this assignment.

Table 31.2
Expert Family Theory Video Review and Critique Rubric

Criterion (CACREP Standard)	Does Not Meet Expectations	Meets Expectations	Exceeds Expectations
Family theory and foundational principles (5.F.1.b)	Does not review a family theory or does not demonstrate understanding of the family theory	Reviews a family theory and demonstrates an understanding of the family theory	Reviews a family theory, demonstrates an understanding of the family theory, and shows evidence of understanding how the expert incorporated the theory into the counseling session
Client's presenting concerns (5.F.1.e)	Does not accurately identify the client's presenting concerns	Demonstrates an understanding of the client's presenting concerns	Demonstrates an understanding of the client's presenting concerns and an in-depth understanding of the strategies that the expert used to assess the clients' overall functioning (e.g., questions asked)
Identification and review of techniques observed (5.F.3.c)	Does not identify techniques or does not accurately identify techniques observed	Accurately identifies techniques implemented by the expert counselor	Accurately identifies techniques implemented by the expert counselor, and demonstrates an understanding of how those techniques relate to the theory as well as the goal of implementing with the client
Assessment of therapy effectiveness (5.F.3.a)	Does not demonstrate an ability to assess the effectiveness of the therapy session	Assesses the effectiveness of the therapy session and provides a justification for the assessment	Assesses the effectiveness of the therapy session, and provides a justification for the assessment as well as potential resources that may benefit the client
Limitations and cultural components (5.F.2.m)	Does not identify limitations, or limitations or cultural considerations are not accurate	Accurately identifies potential limitations of the theory as well as potential cultural influences	Accurately identifies potential limitations of the theory and potential cultural influences, and demonstrates an understanding of the theory's stance on cultural differences
Personal reaction	Does not provide a personal reflection, or the reflection is not in-depth	Provides an in-depth personal reflection	Provides an in-depth personal reflection, demonstrating an awareness of personal biases and areas of growth

Note. CACREP = Council for Accreditation of Counseling and Related Educational Programs.

Table 31.3
Genogram and Reflection Rubric

Criterion (CACREP Standard)	Does Not Meet Expectations	Meets Expectations	Exceeds Expectations
Genogram (5.F.2.c)	Genogram does not include three generations or does not include relevant family characteristics	Genogram represents multigenerational family of origin patterns over three generations	Genogram represents multigenerational family of origin patterns over three generations, including in-depth family characteristics, and a clear legend making the genogram easy to follow
Personal and professional patterns	Does not identify overall family patterns	Identifies family patterns and can relate to personal and professional experiences	Identifies family patterns and demonstrates an in-depth awareness of how they contribute to student's current interpersonal interactions
Family life-cycle development factors (5.F.2.h, 5.F.2.j, 5.F.2.k, 5.F.2.l)	Does not include information in the genogram, or does not comment in the paper on life-cycle factors influencing the family	Genogram and paper include relevant life-cycle factors and briefly discuss their influence on the family	Genogram and paper include relevant life-cycle factors and provide an in-depth discussion of their influence on the family
Potential growth areas	Does not include potential biases or areas for growth	Discusses some areas of growth and biases resulting from family of origin patterns	Demonstrates and in-depth understanding of areas of growth and biases resulting from family of origin patterns

Note. CACREP = Council for Accreditation of Counseling and Related Educational Programs.

Chapter 32

School Counseling

Brandie M. Oliver and Nick R. Abel

The primary role of professional school counselors (PSCs) is to promote the academic, career, and personal/social development of students in PK–12 educational settings (ASCA, n.d.). PSCs are called to reach all students by providing services via a well-designed CSCP that parallels ASCA's (2012) National Model. In such a way, PSCs ensure that students are systematically provided with services in all three developmental domains via direct services, such as individual counseling, small group counseling, and classroom guidance, as well as through indirect methods, such as consultation, coordination, leadership, advocacy, and the use of data (ASCA, 2012).

To design, implement, and manage an effective CSCP, PSCs must collaborate with key stakeholders in their school communities (e.g., administrators, teachers, parents, and support staff) to identify the needs of students and to foster a unified commitment to a common set of goals. PSCs then act as key members of the educational team and help lead school transformation by following ethical standards, using data to remain accountable, and managing a CSCP designed to target the student development goals identified by the stakeholder group.

With an increasingly diverse student population, another critical element to effective and ethical school counseling is the need for multicultural counseling. PSCs are charged with the responsibility of understanding and continuing to focus on multicultural issues within their school systems and within the world so that they can be social advocates for all youths, families, and the school community. Multicultural counseling competence is an area that needs constant professional development, as our country's fabric is continually transforming and changing. It is critical that PSCs develop strategies and interventions based on data. In the event that data reveal gaps in service or access to specific student populations, then the PSCs must utilize their advocacy skills to ensure that these student groups' needs are being met.

Given the complexity of the job, it should come as no surprise to counselor educators that preparing future PSCs is a challenging task—one that requires more than 35 CACREP Specialty Standards. In addition, school counseling is a fast-changing profession that must quickly respond to the needs of students and families while also sharing the burdens of school accountability that affect other K–12 educators. As such, in addition to preparing future PSCs according to the CACREP 2016 Standards, counselor educators must be keenly aware of current trends in education and student development as well as complementary standards and best practices for PSC training put forth by influential organizations such as ASCA (2012), Education Trust (n.d.), and the College Board's National Office for School Counselor Advocacy (2010). To put it simply, there is no shortage of material to cover in a master's-level training program in school counseling; the real challenge is developing ways to address the most critical standards.

Candidate Portfolio

SLOs assessed: CACREP 2016 Standards 5.G.2.a, 5.G.2.b, 5.G.2.e, 5.G.2.l, 5.G.3.c, 5.G.3.d, 5.G.3.e, 5.G.3.f, 5.G.3.h, 5.G.3.k, 5.G.3.n

Throughout your clinical experiences, you will create a portfolio demonstrating your competency in the following areas related to school counseling CACREP Standards:

1. Demonstrate the ability to articulate and model an appropriate school counselor identity
2. Develop, implement, and evaluate a developmental guidance lesson for students
3. Develop, implement, and evaluate a student academic intervention to promote educational improvement for students
4. Develop, implement, and evaluate a career development activity to promote career information and/or awareness for students
5. Demonstrate the ability to provide group counseling for those students experiencing academic and/or personal/social problems that interfere with learning
6. Demonstrate the ability to provide crisis intervention in a school setting
7. Demonstrate the ability to address multicultural counseling issues, including possible effects of ability levels, language, culture, race, stereotyping, family, socioeconomic status, gender, and sexual identity
8. Demonstrate the ability to work with parents, guardians, and families to act on behalf of their children to address challenges that affect student success in school

Portfolios must address the following components for each of the eight competency areas:

1. *Description*: Describe in detail the activity/program/event.
2. *Artifacts*: Provide artifacts (limit of two) that support or verify the activity/program/event. Examples include lesson plans, name badges, e-mails from a teacher, and so forth. Artifacts are not required for Area 6 (Crisis Intervention).
3. *Use of data*: Describe how you used data to plan and evaluate your intervention. How did you determine that there was a need for this activity/program/event? How did you measure its effectiveness? Provide copies of tests/assessments, raw data, and results of data analysis as available. Posttest-only data are acceptable, but perception (pre-/posttest) or outcome data are preferred. Data are not required for Areas 1 (Counselor Identity) and 6 (Crisis Intervention).
4. *Reflection*: Thoroughly reflect on each area, including the impact that your work had on students and your school counselor identity.

The scoring for the Candidate Portfolio Rubric follows:

1 = *Emerging* (needs improvement; performance and supporting evidence indicate that the student does not yet appear to understand the underlying concepts of the Standard and/or has not demonstrated application of the Standard in an educational setting)
2 = *Proficient* (meets expectations; performance and supporting evidence indicate that the student clearly understands the underlying concepts of the Standard and has demonstrated sound, appropriate application in an educational setting)
3 = *Distinguished* (exceptional; this rating is reserved for those who have clearly demonstrated exceptional mastery of the Standard on the basis of the depth and clarity of their portfolio reflections and the strength of their supporting evidence)

Table 32.1 includes the rubric associated with this portfolio.

Table 32.1
Candidate Portfolio Rubric

Criterion	Description	Artifacts	Use of Data	Reflection
Demonstrate the ability to articulate and model an appropriate school counselor identity			N/A	
Develop, implement, and evaluate a developmental guidance lesson for students				
Develop, implement, and evaluate a student academic intervention to promote educational improvement for students				
Develop, implement, and evaluate a career development activity to promote career information and/or awareness for students				
Demonstrate the ability to provide group counseling for those students experiencing academic and/or personal/social problems that interfere with learning				
Demonstrate the ability to provide crisis intervention when appropriate		N/A	N/A	
Demonstrate the ability to address multicultural counseling issues, including possible effects of ability levels, culture, race, stereotyping, family, socioeconomic status, gender, and sexual identity				
Demonstrate the ability to work with parents, guardians, and families to act on behalf of their children to address challenges that affect student success in school				

Note. N/A = not applicable.

Digital Storytelling Project

SLOs assessed: CACREP 2016 Standards 5.G.2.a, 5.G.2.l, 5.G.2.n

Develop/design a digital project describing and explaining your unique counseling identity—including your philosophy, outlook, and expectations as a future PSC—on the basis of what you learned in this course. At a minimum, you must include the following: discussion of your school counselor identity (components described earlier); reflection on your growth this semester, stance on at least one important ethical issue (informed consent, confidentiality, abuse/neglect, etc.), roles and responsibilities of a school counselor, dispositions/attitudes you will display as a school counselor, and reflection on the ED 553 course. Examples will be provided, but try to make this unique to you—and be creative! Table 32.2 includes the rubric associated with this assignment.

Comprehensive School Counseling Program (CSCP) Project

SLOs assessed: CACREP 2016 Standards 5.G.1.b, 5.G.2.a, 5.G.2.d, 5.G.2.f, 5.G.2.j, 5.G.3.a, 5.G.3.b, 5.G.3.c, 5.G.3.d, 5.G.3.k, 5.G.3.l, 5.G.3.n, 5.G.3.o

This group project is intended to provide you with the experience of designing a comprehensive school counseling program. This project includes, but is not limited to, the following: defining a vision and mission statement, program goals and objectives, the use of data to plan and assess programs, designing curriculum, lesson planning, classroom guidance delivery, and collaboration. The collaborative project also incorporates critical thinking, problem solving, leadership, and advocacy skills. The purpose of the assignment is for student counselors to work together in a problem-based learning environment to develop a sample comprehensive developmental guidance program.

During this project, you will need to find data about a school as well as statements from various stakeholders about certain concerns and needs and issues of finances and community activity. The program should nest within the following parameters: student developmental level, ASCA Standards and state-level standards, and the assigned school's and community's needs.

Table 32.2
Digital Storytelling Project Rubric

Criterion (CACREP Standard)	Exemplary	Satisfactory	Unacceptable
Dramatic question/counselor identity (5.G.2.a)	A meaningful dramatic question (counselor identity) is asked and answered within the context of the story; clearly articulates appropriate school counselor identity, including appropriate roles and responsibilities; demonstrates understanding of role of advocacy for a PSC	A dramatic question (counselor identity) is hinted at but not clearly established within the context of the story; school counselor identity is somewhat unclear and/or includes some inappropriate roles/responsibilities; missing vital roles/components of an effective PSC	Little or no attempt is made to pose a dramatic question (counselor identity) or to answer it; school counselor identity is completely unclear and/or includes many inappropriate roles/responsibilities; does not communicate the need for advocacy in role of PSC
Legal/ethical issue (5.G.2.n)	Mentions at least one important ethical issue that may be encountered as a PSC; provides stance on that ethical issue; sound reasoning and evidence for the stance are provided	Mentions at least one important ethical issue that may be encountered as a PSC; but provides a minimal stance on that issue; or provides only minimal reasoning and evidence for the stance	Does not mention an important ethical issue that may be encountered as a PSC; or does not provide a stance on that ethical issue; or does not provide sound reasoning and evidence for the stance
Professional content (5.G.2.1)	Story references importance of appropriate professional organizations; creator articulates the credentials required to become a PSC	Story references one professional organization; creator does not mention credentials required to become a PSC	Story does not include knowledge of professional organizations; creator does not mention credentials required to become a PSC
Reflection on growth	Includes meaningful discussion of growth experienced this semester	Includes some discussion of growth this semester	Little to no discussion of growth this semester
Presentation elements (e.g., voice-over is meaningful and matches images well, audio soundtrack is appropriate)	Voice-over is meaningful and helps the audience "get into" the story; voice over matches slides/images well; images create a distinct atmosphere or tone that matches different parts of the story; images may communicate symbolism and/or metaphors; music stirs a rich emotional response that matches the story line well; images are coordinated with the music; story is told with exactly the right amount of detail throughout; story does not seem too short or too long	Voice-over is sometimes meaningful, but audience is not consistently engaged; sometimes noticeable that the pacing does not fit the story line; an attempt is made to use images to create an atmosphere/tone, but it needs more work; image choice is logical; music is okay: not distracting, but it does not add much to the story; music is not coordinated with images; story needs more editing; story is noticeably long or short in more than one section	Voice-over is not meaningful or does not connect with the story-line or the audience; voice-over frequently does not match slides or fit the storyline; little or no attempt is made to use images to create an appropriate atmosphere/tone; music is distracting, inappropriate, or not used; story needs extensive editing; story is too long or too short to be interesting

Note. CACREP = Council for Accreditation of Counseling and Related Educational Programs; PSC = professional school counselor.

Comprehensive school guidance counseling plan/program will include the following:

- School name
- School demographics/information
  – Provide the reader with an overview of your school and school community
  – Snapshot of school data (number of students, student–teacher ratio, socioeconomic status, free/reduced lunch, gender, graduation rate, etc.); this snapshot will help frame your proposed plan
- Vision statement
- Mission statement
- Benefits statement/philosophy/beliefs
- Advisory council roster
  – Who should be on the advisory council? What are the titles/roles of an ideal advisory council?

- Data reports: Your assigned school has collected the following information in each of the categories below; you need to provide baseline data for a specified group of students (i.e., ninth grade)
  –Achievement
  –Student choice
  –Guidance
  –Counseling
- Program priorities (at least two within each area): After your team spends time analyzing the data reports, the team should discuss and decide on
  –minimum of two priorities per area; priorities are areas of concern that
  –your team has decided need to be further addressed in your school; these priorities would be based on the gaps that were discovered in the data
  –Achievement: Example: Graduation rates
  –Student choice: Example: Number of ESL (English as a second language) students enrolled in AP (advanced placement) courses
  –Guidance: Example: Number of students have successfully completed 4-year plan (typically academic and/or career domain)
  –Counseling: Example: Social/emotional: Number of students who self-reported need for anger management
- Goals: Using the program priorities, the team will decide on two goals within each area; these goals should be SMART (Specific, Measurable, Attainable, Realistic, Time-oriented)
  –Achievement
  –Student choice
- Guidance
  –Counseling
- Guidance activities
  –Lesson plans (career, academic, social/emotional)—what goal does this address? Your group needs to select one of the goals developed and create a guidance unit to address this goal. You will need at least four lessons for this unit. Each lesson should build on the previous lesson. Remember these lessons do not always need to be administered by the PSC . . . think of other parties who could be involved (teacher, parent, community member)
  –Narrative on each lesson plan: Please discuss learning styles/developmental assets/multiple intelligences/classroom management plans for this unit and your teaching of the guidance curriculum
- Counseling activities
  –What group/individual counseling and/or peer facilitation do you foresee as needed, and what goal(s) would be addressed? Please discuss what counseling activities your council deems appropriate and an overall plan of how these activities will be accomplished (Narrative only)
- Social justice activity: Select a problem or issue that you found apparent within the school that highlights an inequity in access (base this decision on data). You will provide that topic to the instructor for approval before you begin. Example: Disproportionality within discipline or student choices, school failure, and so forth
  –Briefly discuss how you would conduct additional student needs assessment for that topic. Next, create a needs assessment to be used (students, parents, teachers/staff, community); this needs assessment should connect with the information that you desire to gain
  –Develop one prevention activity and one intervention activity you would recommend and outline how you would conduct an outcomes assessment for each of the activities you just identified
  –Discuss the school wide implications, including presenting a school wide advocacy plan and a plan for a teacher in-service
  –Evaluate the legal and ethical issues of that topic
  –Discuss the insights you have gained in terms of systemic issues relative to that topic (in terms of families, schools, and communities)
- Narrative descriptions: How will your program address the following?

You need to provide a brief narrative explaining the PSC role of each of the following components:

> –Counseling services
> –Consultation services
> –Referral services
> –Crisis response role
> –Student assistance team role
> –School improvement role
> –Role in closing achievement gaps
> –Role as advocate for individual students
> –How school counselor networks with school personnel
> –How school counselor networks with community
> –How school counselor networks with profession (professional development)

- Other items
  - –Counseling calendar: Include at least four activities per month
  - –One MEASURE (Mission, Element, Analyze, Stakeholders-Unite, Results, Educate) document completed; show one of the activities that you would recommend to address one of the identified goals of your plan
  - –Need to include a template you will use for your self-study/program audit
  - –Time use document; ask the school counselor at your assigned school to track his or her time for at least 1 day

Table 32.3 includes the rubric associated with this assignment.

Table 32.3
Comprehensive School Counseling Program (CSCP) Project Rubric

Final Project Rubric (CACREP Standard)	Exemplary	Satisfactory	Unacceptable
Foundational principles (5.G.1.b, 5.G.2.a, 5.G.2.d, 5.G.3.a, 5.G.3.d)	Project thoroughly and clearly articulates a comprehensive model of school counseling based on the ASCA National Model	Project somewhat articulates a comprehensive model of school counseling based on the ASCA National Model	Project missing multiple elements to articulate a comprehensive model of school counseling based on the ASCA National Model
	Clear mission, vision, and beliefs statement (philosophy)	Mission, vision, and beliefs statement (philosophy) included—missing some key language	Unclear mission, vision, and beliefs statement (philosophy) or missing these elements
	Project clearly demonstrates the importance of PSC role through development of a CSCP and the overall academic mission of the school	Project somewhat demonstrates the importance of PSC role through development of a CSCP and the overall academic mission of the school	Project does not demonstrate the importance of PSC role through development of a CSCP and the overall academic mission of the school
Delivery principles: Program priorities/goals (5.G.3.c, 5.G.3.d, 5.G.3.k, 5.G.3.l)	Project includes guidance unit addressing one of the three domains—at least four lessons included; lesson plans are comprehensive; crosswalking standards are included; differentiated instruction is discussed; assessments are included	Project includes guidance unit addressing one of the three domains—at least three lessons included; lesson plans vaguely cover items listed; missing some components such as crosswalking standards, differentiated instruction suggestions, and/or assessments	Project missing key elements of guidance unit addressing one of the three domains—lesson plans are missing or lack multiple components required
	Professional development topic is planned and linked to overall goal of CSCP	Professional development topic briefly discussed/planned and does not directly link to overall goal of CSCP	Missing key elements of the professional development topic/plan; no clear link to overall program goal
	Counseling: group/individual counseling and/or peer facilitation discussed; needs and goal link to program goals/priorities; overall plan of how these activities will be accomplished clearly is explained	Counseling: group/individual counseling and/or peer facilitation discussed; not a clear linkage to the needs and goals of CSCP	Missing key elements of the ways in which to address counseling goals/activities
	Activities within the delivery system are designed clearly and link to program priorities/goals that will affect student achievement, close the achievement gap, and promote for academic success for all students	Activities within the delivery system are designed and somewhat link to program priorities/goals that will affect student achievement, close the achievement gap, and promote for academic success for all students	Activities within the delivery system do not link to CSCP program
Management principles data (5.G.2.f, 5.G.3.k, 5.G.3.l, 5.G.3.n, 5.G.3.o)	Uses data in a meaningful way; includes appropriate data charts and clearly links data to overall program	Uses data; includes appropriate data charts, and somewhat links data to overall program	Data are not used in a meaningful way; missing appropriate data charts; data do not link to overall program
	Comprehensive advisory council	Suggested advisory council lacking some key players	Advisory council not well done—missing multiple key players
	Management agreements ensure effective implementation of the delivery system	Management agreements somewhat describe effective implementation of the delivery system	Missing management agreements
	Clearly defined program priorities and goals; goals are linked directly to student achievement, closing the achievement gap, and promoting academic success for all students	Program priorities and goals are somewhat defined; goals are somewhat linked to student achievement and closing the achievement gap	Unclear program priorities and goals; goals do not directly link to student achievement and closing the achievement gap
	Comprehensive action plans included	Action plans included—missing some elements	Missing action plans, or action plans are missing multiple elements for effectiveness

(Continued)

Table 32.3 (*Continued*)
Comprehensive School Counseling Program (CSCP) Project Rubric

Final Project Rubric (CACREP Standard)	Exemplary	Satisfactory	Unacceptable
Management principles data (5.G.2.f, 5.G.3.k, 5.G.3.l, 5.G.3.n, 5.G.3.o) *(Continued)*	Time use study explained; template included; thorough explanation of suggested use of time to effectively implement CSCP provided	Time use study explained; template included; brief explanation of suggested use of time to effectively implement CSCP provided	Missing time use study information
	Calendar included with activities listed	Calendar included—missing activities	No calendar included
Accountability, collaboration, and leadership (5.G.2.a, 5.G.2.d, 5.G.2.j, 5.G.3.l, 5.G.3.n, 5.G.3.o)	Thorough discussion of program audit, and template to be used is included	Brief discussion of program audit, and template to be used is included	Lack of discussion of program audit, and template to be used is missing
	MEASURE document is fully explained and is linked to program effectiveness; includes clear vision of collaboration with multiple parties	MEASURE document is explained and is somewhat linked to program effectiveness; brief discussion of collaboration with some parties is provided	MEASURE document is missing key elements and is unable to link to program effectiveness; collaboration with other parties is unclear
	Program components clearly identify PSC leadership in school community including curriculum development, implementation, and ways in which CSCP will be reviewed to demonstrate effectiveness	Program components somewhat identify PSC leadership in school community including curriculum development, implementation, and ways in which CSCP will be reviewed to demonstrate effectiveness	Program components lack a vision of PSC leadership in school community; not able to identify how PSC would be involved in curriculum development, implementation, and ways in which CSCP will be reviewed to demonstrate effectiveness
Advocacy, systemic change, narrative responses (5.G.2.f, 5.G.3.b, 5.G.3.k)	Advocacy initiatives clearly connect with program proposed; clear rationale	Advocacy initiatives somewhat connect with program proposed; rationale briefly explained	Advocacy initiatives do not connect with program proposed; lacks rationale
	In-depth narrative responses that fully explain each item	Narrative responses somewhat explain each item	Narrative responses lack clarity and depth
	PSC fully engaged in design, implementation, management, and evaluation of a comprehensive developmental school counseling program	PSC partially engaged in design, implementation, management, and evaluation of a comprehensive developmental school counseling program	PSC lack of engagement in design, implementation, management, and evaluation of a comprehensive developmental school counseling program

Note. CACREP = Council for Accreditation of Counseling and Related Educational Programs; ASCA = American School Counselor Association; PSC = professional school counselor; MEASURE = Mission, Element, Analyze, Stakeholders-Unite, Results, Educate.

Chapter 33

Counselor Education and Supervision—Counseling

Carrie A. Wachter Morris, Paula J. Swindle, and Laura M. Gonzalez

Doctoral students in counselor education will typically begin their programs with a basic understanding of counseling theory and be capable of identifying their own theoretical orientation. Therefore, a theories class at this level should go beyond a "theory-of-the-week" approach to extend theoretical foundations learned at the master's level through in-depth exploration of theories (CACREP 2016 Standard 6.B.1.a). This includes integration of counseling theories (Standard 6.B.1.b), conceptualization of clients from multiple theoretical perspectives (Standard 6.B.1.c), identification of evidence-based counseling practices (Standard 6.B.1.d), and development of methods for evaluation of counseling effectiveness (Standard 6.B.1.e). Further, doctoral students will need to be able to use that knowledge to train master's students how in thinking critically about theory, and they need to be aware of ethical and culturally relevant counseling across multiple settings (Standard 6.B.1.f). In other words, doctoral students need to be not only consumers of theory but critical analysts contributing to our theoretical knowledge base.

For these reasons, doctoral-level theories courses should look different than their master's-level counterparts in terms of the breadth and depth of what is covered. Doctoral students build their theoretical knowledge and expertise through interpretation of primary texts and cutting-edge research on topics, dissecting assumptions and critically analyzing applicability of theories to particular settings and populations. Doctoral students can also engage with theories with an eye toward applicability to diverse clients, conceptualizing client presenting concerns through multiple theoretical lenses to see how theories may explain change in different ways.

Aside from the content of counseling theories coursework, program faculty can design assignments and discussion points to support doctoral students' identity development as scholars and researchers. We encourage faculty to think of doctoral-level counseling theories courses as opportunities to augment other professional orientation activities because they will be engaging with previously taught content in a vastly different way. Building on a strong practitioner foundation and discussing differences in doctoral- and master's-level use of theories is a way to help students see themselves in new roles at the beginning of their doctoral programs.

It is with these points in mind that we present the following assignments. The suggested assignments in this chapter build on each other and allow students to explore a chosen counseling theory in depth, provide a critique of existing research into the efficacy of the approach, provide a framing of the approach within the research, share this knowledge in a research presentation, and present and guide discussion in applying theory to a role-play. The final assignment is geared toward an in-depth deconstruction of a theory and application of that to building an intervention that supports change through the constructs of the theory.

Counseling Theories Academic Research Paper and Presentation

SLOs assessed: CACREP 2016 Standards 6.B.1.a, 6.B.1.d, 6.B.1.f

Students will delve into one of the major counseling theories, reporting what they have learned via a 15-page research paper and a 45-minute presentation to their class.

The paper should include at least 20 academic references and be written in APA Style. The following concepts should be covered in the academic research paper:

1. A thorough critique of the theory or one significant component of the theory based on the existing research (e.g., What does the latest research say? What is the evidence base regarding effectiveness? Are there any off-shoots or recent extensions to the theory? What is missing in the theory? What is missing in the research? What are the common factors of change present?).
2. Discussion of the applicability of the theory to different populations and presenting concerns, grounded in empirical research (e.g., With what populations/presenting issues does this theory work best? Where does it not apply? For example, would Gestalt theory be an effective approach with clients who have experienced trauma, and how does the research address this?).
3. Discussion regarding multicultural issues regarding this theory.
4. Discussion of ethical considerations regarding this theory.

The presentation is an opportunity to share the information you have learned in your research paper with your classmates. Presentations should last approximately 45 minutes and should cover all the components required for your paper. Be sure to provide examples of applicability, multicultural issues, and ethical considerations to help in translating your learning to your classmates. In addition, prepare a one- to two-page handout with a summary of your presentation. Presentation slides should contain overview information only and should not be a copy-and-paste wall of text from your paper. Tables 33.1 and 33.2 include the rubrics associated with this assignment.

Table 33.1
Counseling Theories Academic Research Paper Rubric

Criterion	Does Not Meet Expectations	Meets Expectations	Exceeds Expectations
Provides appropriate overall critique of theory	Does not demonstrate critical approach but merely gives overview of theory; does not address missing components	Exhibits critical thinking in approach to theory; utilizes recent research; mentions some missing components or provides new research questions	Exhibits in-depth critical approach to theory; utilizes and reviews recent literature; addresses and explains missing components of theory; exhibits high level of thought in providing new research questions
Presents appropriate applicability of theory	Does not address application or describes without empirical basis	Provides application of theory; describes target population or limitations; some reference to empirical research	Provides well-articulated application of theory grounded in the literature; describes target and challenging populations/ presenting issues; backs up application with empirical research
Addresses multicultural issues	Does not consider or address multicultural issues	Provides insight into multicultural issues of theory	Provides in-depth critical awareness of cultural issues and how theory might have limitations or need to be adapted
Addresses ethical concerns	Does not address ethical issues	Provides overview of some areas of ethical concern	In-depth discussion of ethical issues associated with the theory
APA Style	Consistent mistakes in APA Style	APA Style used consistently throughout with few minor errors	Paper follows APA Style with no errors
Includes 20 academic references	Reference page lists fewer than 20 entries, or many entries are not academic writings	Lists at least 20 references, majority of which are academic publications	Uses more than 20 peer-reviewed academic references

Note. APA = American Psychological Association.

Table 33.2
Counseling Theories Academic Research Presentation Rubric

Criterion	Does Not Meet Expectations	Meets Expectations	Exceeds Expectations
Presents an appropriate overall critique of theory	Does not demonstrate critical approach but merely gives overview of theory; does not address missing components	Exhibits critical thinking in approach to theory; utilizes recent research; mentions some missing components of theory or provides new research questions	Exhibits in-depth critical approach to theory; utilizes and reviews recent literature; addresses and explains missing components of theory; exhibits high level of thought in providing new research questions
Presents appropriate applicability of theory	Does not address application or describes without empirical basis; no examples are provided	Provides application of theory; describes target population or limitations; some reference to empirical research is provided; some examples are provided	Provides well-articulated application of theory grounded in the literature; describes target and challenging populations/presenting issues; backs-up application with empirical research; multiple examples are provided
Addresses multicultural issues	Does not consider or address multicultural issues	Provides insight into multicultural issues of theory; general examples are provided	Provides in-depth critical awareness of cultural issues and how theory might have limitations or need to be adapted; specific examples are given
Addresses ethical concerns	Does not address any ethical issues	Provides overview of areas of ethical concerns; provides examples	Provides in-depth discussion of ethical issues associated with the theory; provides several examples
Professional presentation style	Significant deficits in professionalism; is unprepared; uses inappropriate language; volume is difficult to hear	Maintains professionalism throughout majority of presentation, but may lack engagement or have moments of less professionalism	High level of professionalism, well-prepared; smooth delivery; audience is engaged throughout
Appropriate use of slides	Slides are unreadable; too much information is contained per slide	Slides are adequate to present information; slides may occasionally be too wordy	Slides are used in effective manner to present overview and to guide discussion; uses creativity such as appropriate animations or charts/other graphics
Appropriate handout	Does not have handout, or handout does not summarize topic	Provides class with acceptable one- to two-page handout with summary of topic	Exhibits high level of writing in summarizing topic in one- to two-page handout provided

Counseling Theory Role-Play

SLOs assessed: CACREP 2016 Standards 6.B.1.a, 6.B.1.c, 6.B.1.e, 6.B.1.f

Note to instructors: If doing an assignment such as the academic research paper and presentation, this assignment would ideally be due after all presentations have been made. For the purposes of this example, we assume that the previous assignment was also given.

Students will prepare a scripted role-play of a 10- to 15-minute segment of a counseling session that demonstrates their selected theory in practice. Students have freedom to design a role-play that uses their theory appropriately or may construct a role-play that demonstrates the challenges, limitations, or inappropriateness of using the theory with a population or presenting issue that does not work well with the theory. Be creative.

After the role-play is presented, the student will facilitate a 10- to 15-minute discussion on the appropriateness, challenges, limitations, ethical concerns, or multicultural concerns present in using this theory in this situation. This should be an in-depth, critical discussion of the application of the theory, and it should build on previous work on the academic research paper and presentation. It should be clear from the role-play session which theory the student is using. Students should bring two copies of the role-play to class on the assigned day.

Note to instructors: Collect all copies of the role-play and assign each a number. Pairs of students will then draw a number to see which role-play they will read. This will allow the author to remain anonymous and for the class to decipher which theory is being presented by watching the role-play. You may want to get creative and ask each person to make signs with identifying information for the "client" to wear that display demographics so that those are clear whether they differ significantly from those of the individual presenting the role-play. After the class correctly identifies the theory being presented, the author of that role-play will facilitate a discussion of the role-play. Table 33.3 includes the rubric associated with this assignment.

Logic Models and Career, Group, and Multicultural Counseling Theories

SLOs assessed: CACREP 2016 Standards 6.B.1.a, 6.B.1.b, 6.B.1.d, 6.B.1.e, 6.B.1.f

For this assignment, students will be divided into three groups. Each group will be responsible for updating the class on scholarly discourse related to career, group, or multicultural counseling theories, then developing and applying a Logic Model (Theory of Change; see resource list for examples) to one of those areas. Each group will identify and distribute one reading to classmates at least 1 week in advance of the due date; this will be read in conjunction with the other selected readings for the week.

Part I

Your group will complete the following steps:

1. Present an overview of your chosen career development, group, or multicultural counseling theory;
2. Deconstruct the theory to identify its basic assumptions or building blocks, especially as it relates to how change may occur;
3. Describe how the theory can be used to conceptualize target behaviors/conditions and/or a target population; and
4. Describe how this theory fits with the research base on career, group, or multicultural counseling theories, as illustrated by your previous learning or the other readings on the topic (listed on the syllabus).

You will have 60–75 minutes in class.

Part II

Your group will will complete the following steps:

1. Describe and justify a Logic Model/Theory of Change related to a chosen career, group, or multicultural counseling issue.

Table 33.3
Counseling Theory Role-Play Rubric

Criterion	Does Not Meet Expectations	Meets Expectations	Exceeds Expectations
Appropriate scripting of role-play	Extremely unclear which theory is being applied; segment is too short (< 5 minutes)	Meets time expectations (10–15 minutes); appropriate and clear application of theory; presents ethical or multicultural issue for discussion	Meets time expectations (10–15 minutes); clear presentation of theory use by counselor role; provides engaging or creative content for class discussion; presents ethical or multicultural issue for discussion
Facilitation of discussion	Surface level presentation of theory; lack of preparation for discussion or takes over discussion and turns it into a presentation rather than a discussion	Demonstrates preparation to facilitate discussion; guides class in exploring issues presented in role-play	Strong facilitation of discussion; asks questions that prompt class to apply critical thinking and critical approach to theory; guides deep exploration of ethical or multicultural issues; exhibits comfort in facilitation role; allows discussion from class and does not take over

2. Complete a chart similar to the sample Logic Model table format (available at http://www.uwex.edu/ces/pdande/evaluation/evallogicmodelworksheets.html) and provide it to your classmates at least 48 hours before class.
3. Describe at least two ways of evaluating the effectiveness of the Logic Model/Theory of Change that you are presenting.
4. Explain the process used by the group to develop its Logic Model/Theory of Change; discuss potential limitations and implications to the Logic Model/Theory of Change (including use for evaluating outcomes or generating research ideas).

You will have 75–90 minutes in class. This part of the assignment differs from the first in that you have already described the theory—now you are showing that you could use this theory to generate research questions and strategies for improving outcomes for clients or participants.

PowerPoint or Prezi presentations are required in that they will facilitate your ability to convey the eight goals (listed above) in a clear manner and will allow the instructors to assign a grade for your group's efforts. Tables 33.4 and 33.5 include the rubrics associated with this assignment.

Table 33.4
Logic Models and Theories: Part I Rubric

Criterion	Does Not Meet Expectations	Meets Expectations	Exceeds Expectations
Overview of chosen theory	Description of theory is unclear or inaccurate.	Overview of theory is accurate and clear	Overview of theory is thorough and clear, providing strong introduction to major theoretical concepts
Deconstruction of theory	Weak deconstruction; inaccurate or incomplete presentation of underpinnings of theory	Basic knowledge of underpinnings of theory presented accurately	Well-articulated; clearly knowledgeable of underpinnings of theory
Conceptualization of target behaviors and/or population	Inaccurate conceptualization or description of target behaviors or misunderstanding of target population	Fundamental and accurate presentation of target behaviors and basic description of population	Strong conceptualization of target behaviors and thorough description of target population including consideration of cultural issues
Description of fit with research base on group	Little to no description of research base or no connection of topic to research base	Provides general overview of research base and connects to topic	Comprehensive understanding of research base with appropriate examples of current research and how they relate to topic
Presentation effectiveness	Disorganized, unclear, or displays lack of preparation in presentation	Presenter is prepared and organized with clear understanding of topic	Engaging presentation style with clear articulation of material; uses creativity in presentation

Table 33.5
Logic Models and Theories: Part II Rubric

Criterion	Does Not Meet Expectations	Meets Expectations	Exceeds Expectations
Description of LM/ToC	Description of LM/ToC is not understandable or clear to reader	LM/ToC is clearly articulated and easy for reader to follow and understand	Exceptional description of LM/ToC; accessible to readers at all levels of familiarity with topic
Completed LM provided 48 hours in advance	LM is not provided to classmates prior to class or is provided less than 48 hours in advance; LM is unclear or incompletely constructed	LM is clear and is provided to classmates 48 hours or more in advance of class	LM visual is thorough and well-developed; it is provided to classmates at least 48 hours in advance
Description of process of development of LM/ToC	Does not describe process of developing LM/ToC, or description is unclear	Provides clear and basic description of development of LM/ToC	Provides robust and methodical description of development process for LM/ToC
Describe at least two ways of evaluating the effectiveness of the LM/ToC	Does not provide at least two ways of evaluation effectiveness of LM/ToC	Presents two reasonable ways of evaluating effectiveness of LM/ToC	Describes more than two ways of evaluating the effectiveness of LM/ToC; description is well-articulated and clear
Potential limitations of LM/ToC	Does not address any potential limitations of LM/ToC	Addresses at least one limitation of LM/ToC	Addresses and describes potential limitations of LM/ToC
Presentation effectiveness	Disorganized, unclear, or displays lack of preparation in presentation	Presenter is prepared and organized with clear understanding of topic	Engaging presentation style with clear articulation of material; uses creativity in presentation

Note. LM = Logic Model; ToC = Theory of Change.

Chapter 34

Counselor Education and Supervision—Supervision

Jodi L. Tangen and L. DiAnne Borders

Clinical supervision has been defined both in terms of structure and process (Borders & Brown, 2005). Structurally, *supervision* is defined as "an intervention provided by a more senior member of a profession to a more junior colleague or colleagues who typically (but not always) are members of that same profession" (Bernard & Goodyear, 2014, p. 9). Building on this definition, Borders and Brown (2005) defined *supervision* from a process perspective as an educational endeavor occurring within a specific and intentional learning environment. We situate the following assignments within the process-oriented definition of clinical supervision and supervision-of-supervision. Thus, we emphasize the *educational* process of counselor educators teaching new doctoral-level supervisors to supervise from an educational lens.

Supervision is considered an important component of doctoral professional identity (CACREP, 2016). However, before exploring the standards and associated assignments for doctoral-level supervisors, it is important to consider who these doctoral-level supervisors are on the basis of their developmental trajectory. According to Watkins (1990, 1993), new supervisors, much like new counselors, progress through a fairly predictable series of four stages: (a) *role shock*, (b) *role recovery/transition*, (c) *role consolidation*, and (d) *role mastery*. During the role shock stage, new supervisors are unclear of their supervisor identity and lack confidence. Their confidence and awareness increase as they move into the second stage of role recovery/transition. In the role consolidation stage, supervisors experience consistent levels of confidence and establish a supervision identity. Finally, supervisors in role mastery work from an integrated supervision style. There is some empirical evidence for the first stage. For example, Gazzola, De Stefano, Thériault, and Audet (2013) found that new supervisors struggled to manage gatekeeping responsibilities, manage multiple processes, establish a supervisory stance, navigate self-doubt, and handle dynamics with other supervisors. On the basis of these findings, it is important that counselor educators carefully attend to doctoral-level supervisors' educational and developmental needs.

In recent writings on best practices of supervision, Borders (2014) and Borders et al. (2014) cited supervisor preparation/training as an important procedural element of supervision. It is interesting to note that researchers (Bernard, 2014; Borders, 2010; Goodyear, 2014; Watkins & Scaturo, 2013, 2014) have cited the lack of attention toward the pedagogy—or perhaps more appropriately termed *andragogy*—of supervision. Borders et al. (1991) explored the educational process of supervision by creating a comprehensive curriculum guide for training supervisors, with specific topics situated within the three areas of self-awareness, theoretical and conceptual knowledge, and skills and techniques. More recently, Borders (2010) applied three key principles of the science of learning (from Bransford, Brown, & Cocking, 2000) to supervision, stating that supervision training must

(a) consider learners' prior knowledge, (b) aid in helping supervisors organize new knowledge, and (c) stimulate metacognitive thinking.

It is based on this recent application of the science of learning that we present the following three supervision assignments. The first assignment is ongoing and requires doctoral students to intervene on the basis of their prior levels of knowledge (either before becoming supervisors or as they learn more concepts throughout the course). This assignment is appropriate for a didactic supervision course before supervision practicum or internship, and it is believed that throughout the duration of the assignment, doctoral-level supervisors will gain increasing foundational understanding of what it means to be a clinical supervisor. The second assignment is intended to help doctoral-level supervisors create clear conceptual frameworks around specific supervision interventions, which inevitably enhances the organization of their mental schemata. This assignment is appropriate for the conclusion of a didactic supervision course or the middle of supervision practicum or internship. Finally, the third assignment is intended to capitalize on doctoral-level students' metacognitive abilities as they engage in deeper levels of self-reflection at the conclusion of supervision practicum or internship. It is with assignments such as these that we believe the spirit of supervision as a distinctly developmental and educational process can be actualized.

Supervision Simulation

SLOs assessed: CACREP 2016 Standards 6.B.2.c, 6.B.2.d, 6.B.2.f, 6.B.2.h, 6.B.2.i, 6.B.2.j, 6.B.2.k

At the beginning of the semester, you will draw the name and description of a fictitious supervisee out of a hat, and you will have the opportunity to consider how you might intervene with this supervisee for the next 10 weeks. This assignment provides you with the opportunity to think more intentionally about supervision interventions before working with actual supervisees.

Each week, you will be given a new update on your supervisee and will be asked to consider how you might intervene with the supervisee given this new information. Each week you will (a) write a one-page (single-spaced, 500 words) journal entry describing how you might intervene with your supervisee each week (you may include a sample dialogue of what you might say to the supervisee), (b) briefly (5 minutes) describe the situation and the interventions you chose to implement to your doctoral-level peers in class the following week, and (c) ask for your peers' feedback and suggestions on interventions you could have implemented. (By including your peers in this process, you can learn more about how they might approach your situation and learn about the different situations they are facing with their fictitious supervisees.)

Specific themes of supervision will emerge in your supervisee updates each week. Thus, in your journal entries, make sure to address the following themes. Example updates of the fictitious supervisee "Corrine" are included below.

Week 1 themes include the following:

- Introductions and rapport building (supervisory relationship, multicultural dynamics).
- Professional paperwork (supervisor disclosure statement).
- Orientation to supervision (roles and responsibilities of supervisor, purpose of supervision).
- Expectations for the supervisee (course requirements/responsibilities of supervisee, your expectations, meeting dates and times).
- *Example:*

  For the next 10 weeks, you will be supervising Corrine Chung. Corrine is a 23-year-old Korean American woman who majored in psychology as an undergraduate. Her professors have said that she is quiet, intelligent, and studious. However, one of her professors expressed concern about Corrine's anxiety and said that this might interfere with her counseling ability. In addition, another professor stated that Corrine sometimes struggles with perfectionism, which may interfere with her willingness to take risks. On the basis of this information, how might you approach Corrine in your first supervision session?

Week 2 themes include the following:

- Initial assessment of supervisee's developmental level.
- Supervision interventions based on supervisee's developmental level.

- *Example:*

  You just received your first recording of Corrine's counseling work. You noticed that she seemed really anxious. She was soft-spoken and seemed shaky throughout the session with the client. When she comes into supervision, she is quiet and trembling, seemingly really concerned about your initial impression of her. On the basis of your assessment of her development, how might you intervene with Corrine?

Week 3 themes include the following:

- Supervisee's struggle with a specific skill.
- Appropriate use of the teacher role to address deficit in the skill.
- *Example:*

  Corrine turned in her second recording to you, and you noted that she used lots of closed-ended questions. After a while, the client appeared annoyed with Corrine's questions and started responding by saying, "I don't know" to everything. Corrine seemed flustered when the client responded in this manner. When Corrine comes to supervision, she still appears to be flustered and confused by what happened. How might you help Corrine become more aware of this skill deficit and teach her a new way of being with her client?

Week 4 themes include the following:

- Supervisee's lapse in professional behavior.
- Ethical response to supervisee's mistake.
- *Example:*

  Corrine contacted you a week ago and said that she was a little behind on her paperwork. You told her that she could have an extra day to submit the paperwork, and she still has not completed it. Corrine is typically conscientious, so you are a little confused by her lack of response. How will you address this with her in the next supervision session?

Week 5 themes include the following:

- Supervisee's personal issues.
- Appropriate use of the counselor role to respond to supervisee's personal issues.
- *Example:*

  After your intervention with Corrine last week, she completed her paperwork in a timely manner. However, when she comes into supervision this week, she looks drawn and tired. You ask her how she is doing, and she immediately starts crying. She starts telling you all about the recent break-up with her girlfriend, which has left her devastated. How do you respond to Corrine? (Also, this is the first time you learn Corrine's apparent sexual/affectional orientation, so take this into consideration.)

Week 6 themes include the following:

- Supervisee's resistance/defensiveness.
- Supervision interventions to address resistance/defensiveness.
- *Example:*

  Corrine submitted another recording to you, and in this one, you noticed that she seemed triggered when a client said that he was very religious. Corrine responded by telling him that he was old-fashioned and narrow-minded. When Corrine comes to supervision and you try to talk about this issue with her, she starts to become defensive and resistant with you. How do you respond to this?

Week 7 themes include the following:

- Relationship rupture between you and the supervisee based on cultural differences.
- Supervision interventions to address rupture.
- *Example:*

  Corrine was clearly angry with you last week when you tried to talk to her about her response to her client's religion. When she comes in this week for supervision, she is quiet and withdrawn, and you are aware that she is still angry with you. How do you address this relationship rupture? (Consider Corrine's multicultural background as well [ethnicity/race, age, religion, sexual orientation, gender].)

Week 8 themes include the following:

- Supervisee's struggles with case conceptualization.
- Appropriate use of the teacher and/or consultant role to help the supervisee develop greater cognitive complexity.
- *Example:*
  Your response to Corrine last week successfully repaired your relationship. In the recording that she submitted this week, she is much more sensitive to the client's religious beliefs. However, when she comes into supervision, it becomes evident that she struggles to conceptualize the client from a more holistic perspective. She often forgets to consider systemic-level issues in her conceptualizations. How can you help her do this?

Week 9 themes include the following:

- Evaluation with the supervisee.
- Approaches for delivering various types of feedback.
- *Example:*
  It is time for your evaluation with Corrine. You have noticed great improvement in her skills and conceptualizations. However, you are still a little concerned about how she reacted to the client who identified as religious. How can you address this concern in your evaluation of Corrine? Should she pass the course?

Week 10 themes include the following:

- Termination with the supervisee.
- Interventions to address supervisee's response to termination.
- *Example:*
  After repairing your relationship with Corrine a few weeks ago, she seems to trust you more, and recently, she said that she is going to miss having you as a supervisor. How do you effectively terminate with her?

Five Fictitious Supervisees for Counselor Educators to Use With Doctoral Supervisors

(Fictitious supervisees were not created to resemble any actual supervisees that the authors may have encountered. Any likeness to actual supervisees is purely coincidental.)

Week 1 Themes: Introduction, Paperwork, Orientation, Expectations

Week 1—Jenny Jamison
For the next 10 weeks, you will be supervising Jenny Jamison. Jenny is a 22-year-old Caucasian American woman. On the basis of reports from other professors, you have learned that Jenny is the daughter of a wealthy congressman and has lived a rather comfortable lifestyle. In her multicultural counseling course, Jenny also openly stated that she is Baptist and is strongly against same-sex marriage. When you inquire more into this, her professor said that Jenny stated that she was still open to counseling LGBT populations. Her professors also said that Jenny is hard-working, polite, and responsible. On the basis of this information, how might you approach your first supervision session with Jenny?

Week 1—Jamal Carter
Jamal is a 33-year-old African American man. On the basis of reports from other professors, Jamal is humorous—but respectful at the same time. One professor said that he was really impressed with how creative Jamal was, and another professor commented on his friendliness, stating, "Everyone adores Jamal." Professors did not have any concerning feedback about him. On the basis of this information, how do you approach your first supervision session with Jamal?

Week 1—Sheryl Garcia
Sheryl is a 41-year-old Latina woman. On the basis of reports from other professors, Sheryl had a rough time last semester because of her recent divorce. She is also the single parent of a 4-year-old

daughter. One professor stated that Sheryl is dedicated to counseling, as she has decided to leave her business career to become a counselor. Another professor affirmed her commitment to the profession; however, this professor also expressed some concerns about Sheryl's somewhat negative perceptions of men. The professor acknowledged and affirmed Sheryl's feminist identity; however, the professor said that Sheryl is sometimes a little too vocal about her feminist beliefs. On the basis of this information, how do you approach your first supervision session with Sheryl?

Week 1—Andy Marcelli

Andy is a 23-year-old Italian American man. On the basis of reports from other professors, Andy is polite, somewhat quiet, and kind-hearted. Academically, they said that he seemed to be a fairly average student. His advisor, however, said that Andy admitted that he struggles with dyslexia and that Andy seemed ashamed of his struggles. His advisor suggested that you not broach this issue with him, as it seems that Andy is able to complete his assignments successfully. On the basis of this information, how do you approach your first supervision session with Andy?

Week 1—Amelia Walker

Amelia is a 26-year-old international student from London, England. Other professors express concern about Amelia's progress thus far. They said that she comes to class late almost every week, frequently turns in assignments late, and has even told professors to "bugger off" when they remind her of assignments. Her advisor says that she wonders whether something is going on with Amelia personally, as her previous academic records (before attending school in the United States) were exemplary. On the basis of this information, how do you approach your first supervision session with Amelia?

Week 2 Themes: Development

Week 2—Jenny Jamison

Jenny submits her first recording to you, and in it, she is working with an older adult woman. Throughout the session, Jenny jumps from topic to topic, clearly anxious about working with this client. When she comes to supervision, she says that she had no idea how to work with the client because the client is much older. She asks you for specific direction. On the basis of her developmental level, how do you intervene with Jenny?

Week 2—Jamal Carter

Jamal submits his first recording to you, and in it, he is working with a 15-year-old male client. Jamal appears at ease in the session and quickly develops rapport with the client. The client easily opens up to Jamal and begins telling him how angry he is about his parents' divorce. Jamal listens patiently and expertly reflects his anger. When Jamal comes to supervision, he says that he experienced some countertransference with the client. How would you initially gauge Jamal's developmental level and intervene accordingly?

Week 2—Sheryl Garcia

Sheryl submits her first recording to you, and in it, she is working with a 30-year-old Chinese American woman. Sheryl does not make eye contact with the client, speaks rapidly and in a high-pitched voice, and uncomfortably shifts in her seat many times. In addition, she nods her head excessively and repeatedly uses the minimal encourager, "Right . . . right . . . right." How would you initially gauge Sheryl's developmental level and intervene accordingly?

Week 2—Andy Marcelli

Andy submits his first recording to you, and in it, he is working with a 22-year-old male client. Andy rushes through the intake paperwork, often not asking the client to expand on his answers. The intake is completed in 30 minutes, and afterward, Andy awkwardly stalls with the client for the remaining 30 minutes. He starts a conversation about weather patterns in Alaska, and the client looks at him with confusion. On the basis of this information, how would you initially gauge Andy's developmental level and intervene accordingly?

Week 2—Amelia Walker

Amelia submits her first recording to you, and in it, she is working with a 19-year-old female client who expresses significant suicidal ideation. Amelia does not seem concerned about the issue and asks no follow-up questions. She simply tells the client, "You aren't really going to do that, though." Later, she tells jokes to the client, to which the client smiles, and Amelia says, "See, you're fine." On the basis of this information, how would you initially gauge Amelia's developmental level and intervene accordingly?

Week 3 Themes: Skill Deficits, Teacher Role

Week 3—Jenny Jamison

Jenny submits her second recording to you, and in this one, she starts giving the older female client advice about what to do in her marriage. The client is clearly distraught and sad, and Jenny tells her that she just needs to talk to her husband. How can you teach Jenny how to reflect the client's emotions instead of giving advice?

Week 3—Jamal Carter

Jamal submits his second recording to you where he is working with a 25-year-old female client. In the recording, the client begins sobbing, and Jamal shifts uncomfortably in his seat and keeps repeating, "There, there, don't cry now." His statement confuses you, as he seemed to reflect anger really well with his client last week. How do you teach Jamal how to reflect sadness and respond appropriately to his client's tears?

Week 3—Sheryl Garcia

Sheryl submits her second recording to you, and in it, she is working with a 20-year-old woman who recently lost her mother to cancer. As the client cries, Sheryl begins speaking rapidly, repeatedly saying, "Oh you poor thing!" She then encourages the client to "look on the bright side" of the situation. How do you teach Sheryl the skills to respond more empathically to her client?

Week 3—Andy Marcelli

Andy submits his second recording to you, and in it, he is again working with the same 22-year-old male client. This time, he acknowledges the awkwardness of the last session and asks the client what he wants to discuss. The client starts discussing his troubling relationships with his friends. Andy responds by asking somewhat irrelevant questions—some of which are closed-ended. For example, "What is your friend's full name? Does your friend have siblings? Does your friend live close to you?" The client answers his questions; however, he seems to become impatient with Andy. How do you teach Andy the skills to respond in a more appropriate manner?

Week 3—Amelia Walker

Amelia submits her second recording to you, and in it, she is working with a 55-year-old female client who was just diagnosed with cancer. The client is clearly distraught. Amelia tells her, "It can't be that bad. At least you didn't have to move across the country by yourself!" The client looks at her quite shocked, and Amelia tries to recover by saying, "Well, yeah, I suppose you might be kind of sad about this." How do you address this interaction with Amelia and teach her the skills to respond to a client in this situation?

Week 4 Themes: Professional Behavior, Ethical Response

Week 4—Jenny Jamison

In your next session with Jenny, she tells you that she has had some concerns about child abuse with a client. You ask her more about the situation, and you agree that she may need to report this information. Jenny is concerned about betraying the client, and you remind her that these types of situations constitute limits to confidentiality. Jenny then tells you that she forgot to outline the limits of confidentiality with the client. She apologizes profusely and seems genuinely upset. How do you respond to her?

Week 4—Jamal Carter

Jamal submits another recording of him working with his 25-year-old female client. In this session, the client is clearly feeling much better. At one point in the session, she leans forward and tells Jamal that he is "kind of cute." He laughs and responds in a similarly flirtatious manner: "You are too."

When he comes to supervision, he does not mention this interaction at all. How do you broach the subject with him?

Week 4—Sheryl Garcia

Midweek, you receive a call from a clinic staff member, stating that Sheryl's client is waiting for her. You try to find Sheryl, but she is nowhere to be found. You finally call her on her telephone, and she says that she decided to stay home with her daughter for a mental health day. You remind her of her appointment with her client, and she nonchalantly says that she forgot. How do you respond to Sheryl in the moment and in your next supervision session with her?

Week 4—Andy Marcelli

Throughout the past few weeks, Andy has been submitting client notes with multiple grammatical and spelling errors. You remember what Andy's advisor told you about the dyslexia, and you let the first few notes slide without requiring him to fix them. However, the issue is becoming worse, and in some cases, his notes are difficult even to understand. You realize that you need to intervene. How do you approach Andy in the next session?

Week 4—Amelia Walker

Midweek, you go to the coffee shop and you see Amelia there with an older female who looks somewhat familiar. After closer inspection, you realize that is the same 55-year-old female client that she saw last week. In your next supervision session with Amelia, you broach the subject, and she tells you not to make such a big deal out of it. She defends herself, stating that you told her that she was not kind to her client the previous week, so she decided to make it up to her by taking her out for tea. How do you respond to Amelia?

Week 5 Themes: Supervisee Personal Issues, Counselor Role

Week 5—Jenny Jamison

Jenny was clearly upset by her forgetfulness around limits of confidentiality last week. When she comes in for supervision this week, she still appears upset and begins apologizing again. She starts crying and says that she is really worried about your evaluation of her. She says that when she was growing up, her parents were strict with her, and she is worried that you are going to be the same way with her. How do you appropriately respond to Jenny's personal issues using the counselor role?

Week 5—Jamal Carter

When Jamal comes into supervision this week, he says that he had another session with his 15-year-old male client. He again references his own countertransference. However, as opposed to last time, he becomes heated and describes his anger toward his own father. He continues to escalate until his voice is loud. You are surprised by his reaction, as he is typically even-tempered. How do you respond to him using the counselor role?

Week 5—Sheryl Garcia

When Sheryl comes to supervision this week, she appears tired and withdrawn. You ask her how everything is going, and she immediately starts crying. She says that she is really overwhelmed with school, work, and parenting responsibilities, and is not sure that she can continue in the program. How do you respond to Sheryl using the counselor role?

Week 5—Andy Marcelli

In your last supervision session with Andy, he apologized for the spelling and grammatical mistakes, stating that writing has never been his strong suit, but he promises to make improvements. He does not mention the dyslexia. Throughout the week, his notes continue to be replete with errors. You gently confront him again, and he becomes quiet. You ask him how you can help him with this, and he says that you cannot. He becomes emotional (unlike his usual presentation) and says that all throughout his academic life, his father has reviewed all of his assignments and helped him fix them (even in undergraduate and graduate school). He discloses his struggles with dyslexia and tells you that he is "completely hopeless." How do you respond to Andy using the counselor role?

Week 5—Amelia Walker

This week, Amelia does not show up for individual supervision. You call her, and she does not answer her phone. The next day, you call her again, and she sounds groggy and tired. She reluctantly agrees to come in and see you. When she comes, she seems to be under the influence of drugs. How do you respond to Amelia in the moment, and do you use the counselor role?

Week 6 Themes: Supervisee Resistance/Defensiveness

Week 6—Jenny Jamison

Jenny submits a recording this week where she was working with a gay man. At first, she is her usual empathic and accepting counselor self with the client. However, when the client tells her that he has a male partner, she immediately freezes, and her tone becomes clipped. When she comes to supervision, you broach this subject with her, and she says that his sexual orientation does not bother her at all. You sense some resistance and defensiveness in her. How do you respond to her?

Week 6—Jamal Carter

Jamal submits a recording of him working with a 30-year-old African American male client. Throughout the session, Jamal is friendly with the client, often calling him "buddy," making jokes, and laughing with him. When Jamal comes into supervision, you tell him that he seemed to act more like a friend than a counselor. Jamal tells you that this is not true; he was simply trying to build rapport with the client. How do you respond to Jamal's apparent resistance/defensiveness?

Week 6—Sheryl Garcia

Your supervision session with Sheryl last week really helped her feel less overwhelmed. This week, she submits a tape of her working with a 25-year-old female client. In the session, the client states that the male-dominated society is the root of all evil and violence in America. Sheryl tells the client that she agrees with her and believes that changes need to be made. For the remainder of the session, Sheryl and the client discuss the perils of patriarchy. In supervision, you try to talk about the situation and help her become more aware of her values and the ways they might be affecting the session. Sheryl openly tells you that you are wrong and that everyone should be feminist. She leaves the session telling you that you are either for her or against her. What should you do?

Week 6—Andy Marcelli

In your next session with Andy, he says that he really appreciates your kindness from last week. He then proceeds to tell you what a wonderful supervisor you are—kind, gentle, forgiving, and accepting. Andy further states that he wants to become just like you as a counselor. At first, you really appreciate his kind words. Then you remember that effusive supervisor praise can be a subtle form of supervisee resistance. Do you think this is the case with Andy? If so, how do you approach him?

Week 6—Amelia Walker

Last week, you appropriately consulted with many faculty members about your continued concerns about Amelia. You decide that this week, you really need to confront Amelia about the many concerns that you have witnessed over the last 5 weeks. When you mention that she seemed under the influence of drugs last week, she blatantly denies this. She responds by recounting all of her clients' progress over the past few weeks, stating that they could not have made this type of progress without her as a counselor. How do you respond to Amelia?

Week 7 Themes: Relationship Rupture and Repair, Cultural Differences

Week 7—Jenny Jamison

Jenny comes into supervision this week and immediately tells you that she is really upset with you. She says that you were right last week and that she is actually uncomfortable counseling LGBT individuals. She states that she should not be required to counsel LGBT individuals if it contradicts with her religious beliefs. How do you respond to Jenny?

Week 7—Jamal Carter

You spot check Jamal's subsequent work with his 30-year-old African American client, and again in the newest session, he acts more like a friend than a counselor. When Jamal comes to supervision, you try to give him this feedback again. He turns to you angrily and tells you that you just do not understand how African American men build rapport with each other. How do you respond to Jamal?

Week 7—Sheryl Garcia

Midweek, you are notified by another faculty member that Sheryl has approached the Department Chair and said that you have perpetuated misogyny. She comes into supervision and does not mention this to you. You finally ask her about it, and she says that equality is important to her and that she will not work with a supervisor who does not believe in equality as strongly as she does. How do you respond to Sheryl?

Week 7—Andy Marcelli

Last week, you decided to confront some of Andy's effusive praise, and he became really hurt that you might perceive his words as disingenuous. He also mentioned that, as a man, it was difficult for him to tell you those kind words. When he comes into supervision this week, he is fairly cool toward you and does not engage much in the session. How do you respond to Andy?

Week 7—Amelia Walker

This week, Amelia comes into supervision with a list of responses to everything that you discussed with her last week. She does not take responsibility for any of her actions, instead stating that your evaluation is simply a representation of your hatred of the United Kingdom and international students. How do you respond to Amelia?

Week 8 Themes: Case Conceptualization, Cognitive Complexity, Teacher/Consultant Role

Week 8—Jenny Jamison

After last week, it seems as though Jenny is still a little upset with you. However, when she comes into supervision, she says that she is having trouble conceptualizing one of her 10-year-old clients who is being bullied at school. How do you help Jenny conceptualize the client using the teacher and/or consultant role?

Week 8—Jamal Carter

You and Jamal seem to have repaired your relationship last week. This week, he comes to supervision and tells you that the parent of one of his clients recently passed away. Jamal tells you that he does not know how to conceptualize and respond to the client's grief. How do you help Jamal conceptualize the client's grief using the teacher and/or consultant role?

Week 8—Sheryl Garcia

It seems that you and Sheryl have repaired your relationship last week. She even sent you some feminist literature to read throughout the week. In the next session, she demonstrates greater openness, stating that she wants to learn how to conceptualize her 25-year-old female client from a theory other than feminism. How do you help Sheryl conceptualize her client from different theories using the teacher and/or consultant role?

Week 8—Andy Marcelli

Your approach with Andy last week really seems to have repaired your relationship. When he comes to supervision this week, he seems excited to work with you. He says that he recently met with a woman who was struggling with disordered eating and asks for your help conceptualizing her from a specific theory. How do you help Andy conceptualize from the teacher and/or consultant role?

Week 8—Amelia Walker

Amelia comes into supervision guarded this week. She does not mention anything that happened last week, and instead, she asks for help conceptualizing a 20-year-old client who is struggling with procrastination. Do you help her conceptualize from a teacher and/or consultant role? Do you address what happened with her last week?

Week 9 Themes: Evaluation, Feedback

Week 9—Jenny Jamison

Although Jenny scored well on the midterm evaluation, you are concerned about your final evaluation with her (given her reluctance to counsel LGBT populations). How do you evaluate her and provide her with this feedback. Should she pass the course?

Week 9—Jamal Carter

It is your final evaluation session with Jamal. On the basis of what you have experienced with him throughout the semester, how would you evaluate him and what feedback would you provide? Should he pass the course?

Week 9—Sheryl Garcia

It is your final evaluation session with Sheryl. She has demonstrated greater openness to other theories (beyond feminism), but you are still a little concerned about this issue. How do you evaluate her and provide her with this feedback? Should she pass the course?

Week 9—Andy Marcelli

It is your final evaluation session with Andy. He has demonstrated great improvement as a counselor. He is empathic and accepting of clients and can use a variety of skills. Furthermore, he has been trying a few new academic approaches, and his case notes have improved. However, there are still some mistakes in each one. How do you evaluate him and provide him with feedback? Should he pass the course?

Week 9—Amelia Walker

It is your final evaluation session with Amelia. In her midterm evaluation, you documented the many concerns that you had about Amelia's professional and personal behaviors. You have also consulted many times with faculty members about everything. Since then, Amelia has yet to take any responsibility for her actions. How do you evaluate her and provide her with feedback? Should she pass the course?

Week 10 Themes: Termination

Week 10—Jenny Jamison

For the past few weeks, it seems that your relationship with Jenny has deteriorated. Now it is time for you to terminate your time together. How do you approach your termination with her?

Week 10—Jamal Carter

Last week during the final evaluation, Jamal told you that you really meant a lot to him. He said that it is not often that he is really authentic with people; however, he was authentic with you. You were touched by his statement. On the basis of this information, how would you approach your termination with Jamal this week?

Week 10—Sheryl Garcia

In your final supervision session with Sheryl, she tells you that she has learned a lot from you and appreciates your guidance and support. She does not appear to be upset about this being your last session together. On the basis of this information, how would you approach your termination with Sheryl?

Week 10—Andy Marcelli

During the final evaluation last week, Andy tells you that you have really made a difference in his life, and he asks whether he can keep in touch with you. He appears to be genuinely sad about your termination. On the basis of this information, how would you approach your termination with Andy this week?

Week 10—Amelia Walker
In your final evaluation session with Amelia, you broach the subject of termination, and her response is, "It is probably good for both of us to end our time together." On the basis of this information, how would you approach your termination with Amelia?

Tables 34.1 and 34.2 include the rubrics associated with this assignment.

Supervision Interventions Manual

SLOs assessed: CACREP 2016 Standards 6.B.2.c, 6.B.2.d, 6.B.2.f

After a while, supervisors sometimes find themselves using the same types of interventions with supervisees. It is important that supervisors continue to stretch themselves and intervene according to each supervisee's idiosyncratic needs. Together as a class, we will create a manual of supervision interventions that you can reference when you find yourself stuck.

To create this, each student will be responsible for creating a one- to two-page description of a supervision intervention (only one student per intervention). These interventions could be around teaching skills, addressing conceptualization, broadening self-awareness, and/or addressing professional behaviors. Examples of interventions you could use are described below. However, you may create your own supervision interventions.

- Role-playing
- Teaching a skill in a step-by-step manner
- Using interpersonal process recall
- Modeling
- Thinking aloud
- Using graphic organizers
- Socratic questioning
- Visualizing/using mindfulness
- Conducting live supervision
- Using creative interventions (e.g., sand tray, art, music)
- Using humor
- Self-disclosing
- Using metaphors
- Conceptualizing clients from multiple theories

When creating the page(s), use short descriptions and bulleted lists. You must include each of the following in your page(s):

1. A brief definition of the intervention.
2. A description of the supervisee with whom this intervention would be most appropriate on the basis of developmental level and other characteristics (e.g., with a beginning-level supervisee, with a supervisee who is defensive, with a supervisee who struggles to understand conceptualization, with a supervisee who lacks self-awareness).
3. A description of the intervention focus (on the basis of the four areas of Bernard's Discrimination Model; see Bernard & Goodyear, 2014; Borders & Brown, 2005): (a) counseling performance skills, (b) conceptualization skills, (c) personalization skills, and (d) professional role skills. A description is also needed of the most appropriate supervision role for the intervention (on the basis of the three roles of Bernard's Discrimination Model): (a) teacher, (b) counselor, and (c) consultant.
4. A step-by-step outline of how the intervention is conducted.
5. A description of intended outcome of the intervention.

Table 34.3 includes the rubric associated with this assignment.

Table 34.1
Supervision Simulation Weekly Journals Rubric

Criterion (CACREP Standard)	Does Not Meet Expectations	Meets Expectations	Exceeds Expectations
Week 1: Introduction, paperwork, orientation, and expectations of supervision (6.B.2.h)	Journal entry does not include or inadequately includes introduction, paperwork, orientation, and expectations of supervision; evidences minimal thought and consideration	Journal entry includes introduction, paperwork, orientation, and expectations of supervision; evidences average levels of thought and consideration	Journal entry includes introduction, paperwork, orientation, and expectations of supervision; evidences high levels of thought and consideration; is insightful, informed, intentional, and/or creative
Week 2: Developmental level (6.B.2.f)	Journal entry does not include or inadequately includes assessment of supervisee's developmental level; evidences minimal thought and consideration	Journal entry includes assessment of supervisee's developmental level; evidences average levels of thought and consideration	Journal entry includes assessment of supervisee's developmental level; evidences high levels of thought and consideration; is insightful, informed, intentional, and/or creative
Week 3: Skill deficit using teacher role (6.B.2.c, 6.B.2.d)	Journal entry does not include or inadequately includes teacher-oriented intervention to address skill deficit; evidences minimal thought and consideration	Journal entry includes teacher-oriented intervention to address skill deficit; evidences average levels of thought and consideration	Journal entry includes teacher-oriented intervention to address skill deficit; evidences high levels of thought and consideration; is insightful, informed, intentional, and/or creative
Week 4: Professional behavior and ethics (6.B.2.j, 6.B.2.k)	Journal entry does not include or inadequately includes attention toward supervisee's professional behavior and ethics; evidences minimal thought and consideration	Journal entry includes attention toward supervisee's professional behavior and ethics; evidences average levels of thought and consideration	Journal entry includes attention toward supervisee's professional behavior and ethics; evidences high levels of thought and consideration; is insightful, informed, intentional, and/or creative
Week 5: Personal issues using the counselor role (6.B.2.c)	Journal entry does not include or inadequately includes counselor-oriented intervention to address supervisee's personal issues; evidences minimal thought and consideration	Journal entry includes counselor-oriented intervention to address supervisee's personal issues; evidences average levels of thought and consideration	Journal entry includes counselor-oriented intervention to address supervisee's personal issues; evidences high levels of thought and consideration; is insightful, informed, intentional, and/or creative
Week 6: Resistance/defensiveness (6.B.2.c)	Journal entry does not include or inadequately includes attention toward supervisee's resistance/defensiveness; evidences minimal thought and consideration	Journal entry includes attention toward supervisee's resistance/defensiveness; evidences average levels of thought and consideration	Journal entry includes attention toward supervisee's resistance/defensiveness; evidences high levels of thought and consideration; is insightful, informed, intentional, and/or creative
Week 7: Supervisory relationship rupture and cultural differences (6.B.2.c, 6.B.2.k)	Journal entry does not include or inadequately includes attention toward the supervisory relationship rupture and cultural differences; evidences minimal thought and consideration	Journal entry includes attention toward the supervisory relationship rupture and cultural differences; evidences average levels of thought and consideration	Journal entry includes attention toward the supervisory relationship rupture and cultural differences; evidences high levels of thought and consideration; is insightful, informed, intentional, and/or creative
Week 8: Case conceptualization and cognitive complexity using teacher/consultant role (6.B.2.c)	Journal entry does not include or inadequately includes teacher/consultant-oriented interventions to address case conceptualization and cognitive complexity; evidences minimal thought and consideration	Journal entry includes teacher/consultant-oriented interventions to address case conceptualization and cognitive complexity; evidences average levels of thought and consideration	Journal entry includes teacher/consultant-oriented interventions to address case conceptualization and cognitive complexity; evidences high levels of thought and consideration; is insightful, informed, intentional, and/or creative

(Continued)

Table 34.1 (*Continued*)
Supervision Simulation Weekly Journals Rubric

Criterion (CACREP Standard)	Does Not Meet Expectations	Meets Expectations	Exceeds Expectations
Week 9: Evaluation and feedback (6.B.2.i)	Journal entry does not include or inadequately includes attention toward evaluation and feedback; evidences minimal thought and consideration	Journal entry includes attention toward evaluation and feedback; evidences average levels of thought and consideration	Journal entry includes attention toward evaluation and feedback; evidences high levels of thought and consideration; is insightful, informed, intentional, and/or creative
Week 10: Termination (6.B.2.c)	Journal entry does not include or inadequately includes attention toward termination; evidences minimal thought and consideration	Journal entry includes attention toward termination; evidences average levels of thought and consideration	Journal entry includes attention toward termination; evidences high levels of thought and consideration; is insightful, informed, intentional, and/or creative
Journal quality	Journal is disorganized and/or unfocused; demonstrates limited ability in writing mechanics; does not follow page limit	Journal is organized and focused; demonstrates acceptable use of writing mechanics; follows page limit	Journal is well organized and focused; demonstrates mastery of writing mechanics; follows page limit

Note. CACREP = Council for Accreditation of Counseling and Related Educational Programs.

Letter to a New Supervisor

SLOs assessed: CACREP 2016 Standards 6.B.2.a, 6.B.2.b, 6.B.2.c, 6.B.2.e

You have undoubtedly learned quite a bit about supervision (and yourself as a supervisor) throughout the semester. Now is your opportunity to share your knowledge with new supervisors. To that end, you are invited to write a personal letter to a new supervisor who will be taking this course next semester. Remember that this individual does not yet know about supervision, so your descriptions need to be geared toward a novice.

Please address the following six areas in the letter:

1. Describe the purpose of clinical supervision. What is it? Why is it important? How is it similar to and/or different from counseling? How did your understanding of clinical supervision change throughout the semester?

Table 34.2
Supervision Simulation Class Participation Rubric

Criterion	Does Not Meet Expectations	Meets Expectations	Exceeds Expectations
Updates peers each week on the situation and the interventions chosen	Does not update or inadequately updates peers on supervisee's progress or chosen interventions; evidences minimal thought and consideration	Adequately updates peers on supervisee's progress and chosen interventions; evidences average levels of thought and consideration	Clearly updates peers on supervisee's progress and chosen interventions; evidences high levels of thought and consideration; is insightful, informed, intentional, and/or creative
Considers peers' feedback and suggestions	Does not consider and/or is defensive with peers' feedback and suggestions	Thoughtfully considers peers' feedback and suggestions	Thoughtfully considers peers' feedback and suggestions, engages with peers, and incorporates their feedback in future sessions
Provides peers with feedback and suggestions	Does not provide peers with feedback and suggestions or inappropriately provides peers with feedback or suggestions	Thoughtfully provides peers with feedback and suggestions	Thoughtfully provides peers with feedback and suggestions; feedback is insightful, informed, intentional, and/or creative

Table 34.3
Supervision Interventions Manual Rubric

Criterion (CACREP Standard)	Does Not Meet Expectations	Meets Expectations	Exceeds Expectations
Definition of the intervention (6.B.2.d)	Document does not include, inadequately includes, or inaccurately includes definition of the intervention; evidences minimal thought and consideration	Document includes accurate definition of the intervention; evidences average levels of thought and consideration	Document includes accurate definition of the intervention; evidences high levels of thought and consideration; is insightful, informed, intentional, and/or creative
Description of supervisee with whom intervention is appropriate (considering development and other characteristics) (6.B.2.f)	Document does not include, inadequately includes, or inaccurately includes description of supervisee with whom the intervention is appropriate; evidences minimal thought and consideration	Document includes accurate description of the supervisee with whom the intervention is appropriate; evidences average levels of thought and consideration	Document includes accurate description of the supervisee with whom the intervention is appropriate; evidences high levels of thought and consideration; is insightful, informed, intentional, and/or creative
Description of the intervention focus and appropriate supervision role (6.B.2.c)	Document does not include, inadequately includes, or inaccurately includes description of the intervention focus and appropriate supervision role; evidences minimal thought and consideration	Document includes accurate description of the intervention focus and appropriate supervision role; evidences average levels of thought and consideration	Document includes accurate description of the intervention focus and appropriate supervision role; evidences high levels of thought and consideration; is insightful, informed, intentional, and/or creative
Step-by-step outline of intervention (6.B.2.d)	Document does not include, inadequately includes, or inaccurately includes step-by-step outline of the intervention; evidences minimal thought and consideration	Document includes accurate step-by-step outline of the intervention; evidences average levels of thought and consideration	Document includes accurate step-by-step outline of the intervention; evidences high levels of thought and consideration; is insightful, informed, intentional, and/or creative
Description of intended outcome (6.B.2.d)	Document does not include, inadequately includes, or inaccurately includes description of the intended outcome; evidences minimal thought and consideration	Document includes accurate description of the intended outcome; evidences average levels of thought and consideration	Document includes accurate description of the intended outcome; evidences high levels of thought and consideration; is insightful, informed, intentional, and/or creative
Writing quality	Document is disorganized and/or unfocused; demonstrates limited ability in writing mechanics; does not follow page limit	Document is organized and focused; demonstrates acceptable use of writing mechanics; follows page limit	Document is well organized and focused; demonstrates mastery of writing mechanics; follows page limit

Note. CACREP = Council for Accreditation of Counseling and Related Educational Programs.

2. Describe the various models of clinical supervision that you used in your work this semester. What was your experience using these models? Were there any that you did not use? Why or why not?

3. Describe the importance of the supervisory relationship. How did you foster effective supervisory relationships with your supervisees this semester? Did you encounter any difficulties with boundaries or ruptures in the relationship? If so, how did you intervene?

4. Describe your personal style of supervision as you currently understand it. When did you begin to discern your own personal style? Is there an example situation with one of your supervisees that illustrates your emerging supervision style? Is there a specific metaphor that might illuminate your personal style of supervision?

5. Describe your greatest learning challenge throughout the semester. Did you overcome this challenge, and, if so, how? If not, what do you think is needed to help you move forward?

6. Finally, provide some words of wisdom and encouragement. What do you wish someone would have told you before you became a supervisor?

Table 34.4 includes the rubric associated with this assignment.

Table 34.4
Letter to a New Supervisor Rubric

Criterion (CACREP Standard)	Does Not Meet Expectations	Meets Expectations	Exceeds Expectations
Description of purpose of clinical supervision (6.B.2.a)	Letter does not include, inadequately includes, or inaccurately includes description of the purpose of clinical supervision; evidences minimal thought and consideration	Letter includes accurate description of the purpose of clinical supervision; evidences average levels of thought and consideration	Letter includes accurate description of the purpose of clinical supervision; evidences high levels of thought and consideration; is insightful, informed, and/or creative
Descriptions of supervision models (6.B.2.b)	Letter does not include, inadequately includes, or inaccurately includes descriptions of supervision models; evidences minimal thought and consideration	Letter includes accurate descriptions of supervision models; evidences average levels of thought and consideration	Letter includes accurate descriptions of supervision models; evidences high levels of thought and consideration; is insightful, informed, and/or creative
Description of the importance of the supervisory relationship (6.B.2.c)	Letter does not include or inadequately includes description of the importance of the supervisory relationship; evidences minimal thought and consideration	Letter includes description of the importance of the supervisory relationship; evidences average levels of thought and consideration	Letter includes description of the importance of the supervisory relationship; evidences high levels of thought and consideration; is insightful, informed, and/or creative
Description of personal style of supervision (6.B.2.e)	Letter does not include or inadequately includes description of personal style of supervision; evidences minimal thought and consideration	Letter includes description of personal style of supervision; evidences average levels of thought and consideration	Letter includes description of personal style of supervision; evidences high levels of thought and consideration; is insightful, informed, and/or creative
Description of learning challenges	Letter does not include or inadequately includes description of learning challenges; evidences minimal thought and consideration	Letter includes description of learning challenges; evidences average levels of thought and consideration	Letter includes description of learning challenges; evidences high levels of thought and consideration; is insightful, informed, and/or creative
Words of wisdom and encouragement	Letter does not include or inadequately includes words of wisdom and encouragement; evidences minimal thought and consideration	Letter includes words of wisdom and encouragement; evidences average levels of thought and consideration	Letter includes words of wisdom and encouragement; evidences high levels of thought and consideration; is insightful, informed, and/or creative
Willingness to share personal experiences	Letter evidences minimal willingness to share personal experiences; follow-up questions are not adequately answered	Letter evidences moderate willingness to share personal experiences; follow-up questions are addressed in a thoughtful manner	Letter evidences sufficient willingness to share personal experiences; follow-up questions are addressed in a highly thoughtful, insightful, and reflective manner
Letter quality	Letter is disorganized and/or unfocused; demonstrates limited ability in writing mechanics	Letter is organized and focused; demonstrates acceptable use of writing mechanics	Letter is well organized and focused; demonstrates mastery of writing mechanics

Note. CACREP = Council for Accreditation of Counseling and Related Educational Programs.

Chapter 35

Counselor Education and Supervision—Teaching

Casey A. Barrio Minton and Carrie A. Wachter Morris

Unlike nearly all other core areas of the master's and doctoral counseling curriculum, counselor educators may need to draw a substantial portion of content in the teaching area of the doctoral core from other fields. Although counselor education has a clearly identifiable body of literature around teaching and learning (see Barrio Minton et al., 2014, for an overview), counselor education as a field lacks depth in incorporation of pedagogical models and methods (CACREP 2016 Standard 6.B.3.b), models of adult learning (Standard 6.B.3.c), instructional design (Standard 6.B.3.d), and approaches to online instruction (Standard 6.B.3.e). In their 10-year review of counselor education pedagogy articles, Barrio Minton et al. (2014) found only one article specific to preparing counselor educators to teach, and only 14.78% of the 230 peer-reviewed articles were clearly grounded in learning theory and instructional research. To ensure intentional development of learning experiences and quality assessment practices, we need to use other literature bases to inform our work around the pedagogy of counselor education. Educational psychology, teacher education, higher education, and education technology all have relevant and useful content that can be adapted to fit the needs of counselor education and to prepare doctoral students to digest primary sources about learning theories and to use them to make sound, intentional decisions for the courses they teach.

Although much of the foundational, theoretical content of teaching and learning may be drawn from other professional literature bases, counselor education has a rich body of literature specific to teaching issues in counselor education. Counselor educators can draw from the profession's unique, established bodies of literature regarding the roles and responsibilities of counselor educators (CACREP 2016 Standard 6.B.3.a), remediation and gatekeeping (Standard 6.B.3.f), and ethical and sociocultural considerations in teaching (Standard 6.B.3.h). Despite the wealth of literature in some of these areas—particularly remediation and gatekeeping—doctoral students may not have the opportunity to hone their skills in vivo during their own training programs. Unless they have a student with a concern who is brought to the faculty, conversations about gatekeeping and remediation may remain hypothetical. Even if they do participate in the remediation and gatekeeping process, legal and privacy considerations may mean that doctoral students are not privy to the more specific happenings behind closed doors. This means that counselor educators must take particular care in assessment of learning in critical areas that doctoral students will face in their careers. Counselor educators may craft specialized assignments and case studies to help guide conversation and application of relevant codes of ethics and university policies to approximate and assess learning around this content.

In this chapter, we provide three assignments and rubrics to assess learning in the doctoral core related to teaching. The first activity is designed to help doctoral students examine a learning or instructional theory from both primary and secondary sources and apply that theory to counselor education. The second activity is a practical portfolio that requires students to articulate their beliefs about teaching and learning, design a counselor education course, and describe how the course reflects the students' philosophy of teaching as well as best practices of counselor education and instructional design. The final assignment is a sample instrument that one may use to observe teaching practice in a teaching internship.

Learning Theory Primer

SLOs assessed: CACREP 2016 Standards 6.B.3.a, 6.B.3.b, 6.B.3.c, 6.B.3.d, 6.B.3.h, 6.B.4.h

Prepare an instructional primer to help counselor educators understand and apply a specific learning theory or model to counselor education. You may select from learning theories and models listed on http://www.learning-theories.com/ or propose a learning theory or model not listed. The theory should fit into one of the following paradigms:

- behaviorist theories;
- cognitivist theories;
- constructivist, social, and situational theories;
- motivational and humanist theories;
- critical and transformative theories; or
- design (instructional) theories and models.

At a minimum, you must include the following headings in your paper:

- Theory Overview (include attention to theoretical view of student learning and theory-based teaching techniques),
- Evidence Base,
- Critical Review (include attention to consistency with philosophical foundations of counseling, relevance to adult learning, quality of evidence base, and cultural considerations),
- Implications for Counselor Educators (include attention to curriculum design, potential in online instruction, and assessment of learning), and
- Resources for Continuing Education.

Papers must be prepared in accordance with APA Style and should not exceed 25 pages, including title, abstract, and references. Give careful attention to primary theoretical sources as well as empirical sources. This assignment will require you to reach beyond the professional counseling literature to build the resource. Table 35.1 includes the rubric associated with this assignment.

Course Design Portfolio

SLOs assessed: CACREP 2016 Standards 6.B.3.a, 6.B.3.b, 6.B.3.d, 6.B.3.g, 6.B.3.h, 6.B.4.h

This major assignment has several components that will guide you through articulating your beliefs about teaching and learning, identifying your roles and responsibilities as a counselor educator, and designing a course in an intentional manner. Submit the following:

- Your philosophy of teaching and learning in counselor education (see O'Neal, Meizlish, & Kaplan, 2007)
- CACREP-compliant syllabus for a required or elective course other than practicum or internship
- Curriculum map illustrating connections between course outcomes, readings, methods, and learning assessments

Table 35.1
Learning Theory Primer Rubric

Criterion (CACREP Standard)	Does Not Meet Expectations	Meets Expectations	Exceeds Expectations
Knowledge of learning theory (6.B.3.b)	Demonstrates minimal or inaccurate understanding of theory; substantial inconsistencies in presentation; poor support of claims via primary sources	Demonstrates acceptable understanding of theory; if present, inconsistencies are minor and do not interfere with overall understanding; good support of claims via primary sources	Demonstrates exceptional understanding of theory; no inconsistencies noted; outstanding support of claims via primary sources
Critical review: Professional counseling identity (6.B.3.a)	Overly simplified review with poor support for claims; may show inadequate understanding of professional counseling identity, roles, and responsibilities	Thorough and relevant review with adequate support for claims; shows adequate understanding of professional counseling identity, roles, and responsibilities	Thoughtful and well stated in all sections; clear, persuasive, and engaging with outstanding support for claims; shows strong integration with professional counseling identity, roles, and responsibilities
Critical review: Adult development and learning (6.B.3.c)	Overly simplified review with poor support for claims; may show inadequate connection to models of adult development and learning	Thorough and relevant review with adequate support for claims; shows adequate connection to models of adult development and learning	Thoughtful and well stated in all sections; clear, persuasive, and engaging with outstanding support for claims; shows strong integration with models of adult development and learning
Critical review: Quality of evidence base	Overly simplified review with poor support for claims; may show inadequate understanding of research base	Thorough and relevant review with adequate support for claims; shows adequate connection to evidence base	Thoughtful and well stated in all sections; clear, persuasive, and engaging with outstanding support for claims; shows strong understanding of evidence base
Critical review: Cultural considerations (6.B.3.h)	Overly simplified review with poor support for claims; may show inadequate understanding of cultural considerations	Thorough and relevant review with adequate support for claims; shows adequate connection to cultural considerations	Thoughtful and well stated in all sections; clear, persuasive, and engaging with outstanding support for claims; shows strong integration with cultural considerations
Implications: Curriculum design (6.B.3.d)	Overly simplified, abstract, or inaccurate applications to recommendations for curriculum design	Several concrete and meaningful recommendations for curriculum design; if present, theoretical inconsistencies are minor and do not detract from overall message	Demonstrates exceptional ability to provide concrete and meaningful recommendations for curriculum design; no inconsistencies noted
Implications: Online instruction (6.B.3.e)	Overly simplified, abstract, or inaccurate applications to online instruction	Several concrete and meaningful recommendations for online instruction; if present, theoretical inconsistencies are minor and do not detract from overall message	Demonstrates exceptional ability to provide concrete and meaningful recommendations for online instruction; no theoretical inconsistencies noted
Implications: Assessment of learning (6.B.3.g)	Overly simplified, abstract, or inaccurate applications to recommendations for assessment of learning	Several concrete and meaningful recommendations for assessment of learning; if present, theoretical inconsistencies are minor and do not detract from overall message	Demonstrates exceptional ability to provide concrete and meaningful recommendations for assessment of learning; no theoretical inconsistencies noted
Quality of writing (6.B.4.h)	Persistent difficulty with writing results in difficulty conveying meaning; difficulty may include two or more of the following: focus, logic, organization, style, grammar, or APA Style; writing is not consistent with published material	Occasional difficulty with writing, but meaning is clear overall; difficulty may include one or more of the following: focus, logic, organization, style, grammar, or APA Style; writing is mostly consistent with published material	Exceptional, precise quality of writing; excels in the following areas: focus, logic, organization, style, grammar, and APA Style; writing is consistent with published material

Note. CACREP = Council for Accreditation of Counseling and Related Educational Programs; APA = American Psychological Association.

- Teaching artifacts: Lesson plan and materials for at least two class periods
- Justification paper in which you
  - Discuss how methods of instruction and student evaluation are congruent with your philosophy of teaching and learning, the professional literature, and the CACREP 2016 Standards
  - Discuss how you will address ethical, legal, and multicultural issues specific to your course

Table 35.2 includes the rubric associated with this assignment.

Teaching Observation

SLOs assessed: CACREP 2016 Standards 6.B.3.a, 6.B.3.d, C.7

Just as the counselor preparation process should culminate with increasingly complex field experience opportunities, the teaching preparation process should culminate with increasingly complex teaching opportunities in which the candidate takes responsibility for a class period, portion of course under supervision of a faculty member, or entire undergraduate course experience. Counselor educators may utilize the following assessment tools to assess teaching skill and to provide feedback after a single teaching observation or a series of teaching observations. This Classroom Observation Guide is adapted from the Committee on the Evaluation of Teaching Excellence (2010); the full version of the form includes guidance regarding pre- and postobservation conferences. Similar observation forms are readily available via many university teaching and learning centers. Table 35.3 includes the teaching observation form.

Table 35.2
Course Design Portfolio Rubric

Criterion (CACREP Standard)	Does Not Meet Expectations	Meets Expectations	Exceeds Expectations
Philosophy of teaching	Philosophy includes minimal attention to or meaningful integration of at least two of the following: professional identity as counselor educator, philosophical/theoretical foundations, goals for student learning, enactment of goals, assessment of goals, or creating an inclusive learning environment (see O'Neal et al., 2007).	Philosophy includes adequate attention to and integration of all or all but one of the following: professional identity as counselor educator, philosophical/theoretical foundations, goals for student learning, enactment of goals, assessment of goals, and creating an inclusive learning environment (see O'Neal et al., 2007).	Philosophy includes clear, concise, and compelling integration to all of the following: professional identity as counselor educator, philosophical/theoretical foundations, goals for student learning, enactment of goals, assessment of goals, and creating an inclusive learning environment (see O'Neal et al., 2007).
Syllabus	Syllabus includes minimal attention to or meaningful integration of at least two of the following: "(1) content areas, (2) knowledge and skills outcomes, (3) methods of instruction, (4) required text(s) and/or reading(s), (5) student performance evaluation criteria and procedures, and (6) a disability accommodation and procedure statement" (CACREP, 2016, p. 6). Syllabus may not reflect best practice related to teaching in the content area.	Syllabus includes adequate attention to and integration of all or all but one of the following: "(1) content areas, (2) knowledge and skills outcomes, (3) methods of instruction, (4) required text(s) and/or reading(s), (5) student performance evaluation criteria and procedures, and (6) a disability accommodation and procedure statement" (CACREP, 2016, p. 6). Syllabus reflects some elements of best practice related to teaching in the content area.	Syllabus includes clear, concise, and consistent attention to and integration of all of the following: "(1) content areas, (2) knowledge and skills outcomes, (3) methods of instruction, (4) required text(s) and/or reading(s), (5) student performance evaluation criteria and procedures, and (6) a disability accommodation and procedure statement" (CACREP, 2016, p. 6). Syllabus reflects consistent attention to best practice related to teaching in the content area.
Curriculum map	Curriculum map demonstrates minimal linkages among several aspects of the course design (i.e., outcomes, readings, methods, and learning assessments).	Curriculum map demonstrates clear linkages among nearly all aspects of the course design (i.e., outcomes, readings, methods, and learning assessments).	Curriculum map demonstrates clear and intentional linkages among all aspects of the course design (i.e., outcomes, readings, methods, and learning assessments).
Teaching artifacts	Artifacts are lacking in intentionality, creativity, or professional counseling identity. Artifacts may not be realistic or well-aligned to students' developmental needs, cultural perspectives, and learning style preferences.	Overall, artifacts convey an appropriate level of intentionality, creativity, and professional counseling identity. With few exceptions, artifacts are realistic and mostly aligned to students' developmental needs, cultural perspectives, and learning style preferences.	High-quality artifacts convey intentionality, creativity, and strong professional counseling identity. Artifacts are realistic and well-aligned to students' developmental needs, cultural perspectives, and learning style preferences.
Justification paper	Justification paper lacks adequate grounding in general teaching and learning literature and/or counselor education literature. The author may struggle to demonstrate ability in one or more of the following: navigate abstract and concrete teaching tasks with intentionality, demonstrate multicultural competence, or attend to ethical issues in teaching.	Justification paper provides evidence of grounding in general teaching and learning literature as well as counselor education literature. The author demonstrates ability to navigate abstract and concrete teaching tasks with intentionality, demonstrate multicultural competence, and attend to ethical issues in teaching.	Justification paper provides evidence of exceptional grounding in general teaching and learning literature as well as counselor education literature. The author's demonstrates outstanding ability to navigate both abstract and concrete teaching tasks with intentionality, demonstrate multicultural competence, and attend to ethical issues in teaching.

(Continued)

Table 35.2 (*Continued*)
Course Design Portfolio Rubric

Criterion (CACREP Standard)	Does Not Meet Expectations	Meets Expectations	Exceeds Expectations
Cohesiveness of portfolio contents	Portfolio lacks adequate portrayal of student's identity as a counselor educator. There are significant disconnects or contradictions among teaching philosophy, syllabus, curriculum map, teaching artifacts, and/or justification paper.	Portfolio provides adequate portrayal of the student's identity as a counselor educator. Although materials are generally clear and consistent, there are occasional disconnects or contradictions among teaching philosophy, syllabus, curriculum map, teaching artifacts, and/or justification paper.	Portfolio provides a well-articulated, insightful, clear, and detailed picture of student's identity as a counselor educator. Themes from the philosophy of teaching are clearly applicable to the syllabus, curriculum map, and teaching artifacts, and they are illuminated in the justification paper.
Quality of writing (6.B.4.h)	Persistent difficulty with writing results in difficulty conveying meaning. Difficulty may include two or more of the following: focus, logic, organization, style, grammar, or APA Style. Writing is not consistent with published material.	Occasional difficulty with writing, but meaning is clear overall. Difficulty may include one or more of the following: focus, logic, organization, style, grammar, or APA Style. Writing is mostly consistent with published material.	Quality of writing is exceptional and precise and excels in the following areas: focus, logic, organization, style, grammar, and APA Style. Writing is consistent with published material.

Note. Depending on the nature of the experience, one could construct or locate a rubric for each element of the portfolio (e.g., philosophy of teaching, syllabus, teaching artifacts). In this case, we chose to include one overarching rubric for the course-based portfolio. CACREP = Council for Accreditation of Counseling and Related Educational Programs; APA = American Psychological Association.

Table 35.3
Teaching Observation Form

Use the following key to assess each item in the rubric below:

Yes = The indicator was observed.

No = The indicator was not observed.

N/A = *Not applicable.* The indicator was not applicable for this class or in this setting.

Organization

Provides students with a complete course syllabus	☐ Yes	☐ No	☐ N/A
Is prepared for class	☐ Yes	☐ No	☐ N/A
Reviews material from previous class with students	☐ Yes	☐ No	☐ N/A
States class goals or objectives	☐ Yes	☐ No	☐ N/A
Uses class time efficiently	☐ Yes	☐ No	☐ N/A
Organizes learning materials or activities effectively	☐ Yes	☐ No	☐ N/A
Summarizes material and/or provides closure	☐ Yes	☐ No	☐ N/A

Instructional Methods

Uses teaching technique(s) appropriate to the instructional goals for this class	☐ Yes	☐ No	☐ N/A
Invites class discussion	☐ Yes	☐ No	☐ N/A
Uses multimedia effectively	☐ Yes	☐ No	☐ N/A
Provides clear directions for group work/labs/exercises	☐ Yes	☐ No	☐ N/A
Assesses student learning	☐ Yes	☐ No	☐ N/A

Content or Subject Knowledge

Appears knowledgeable about subject matter	☐ Yes	☐ No	☐ N/A
Points out any potential bias	☐ Yes	☐ No	☐ N/A
Uses examples and/or illustrations to explain content	☐ Yes	☐ No	☐ N/A
Addresses diversity or ethics when relevant to content	☐ Yes	☐ No	☐ N/A

Communication Skills

Is enthusiastic about the subject matter	☐ Yes	☐ No	☐ N/A
Makes material interesting to students	☐ Yes	☐ No	☐ N/A
Responds to questions clearly and promptly	☐ Yes	☐ No	☐ N/A
Uses speech that is audible, distinct, and appropriately paced	☐ Yes	☐ No	☐ N/A
Demonstrates adequate command of English or the language of the course	☐ Yes	☐ No	☐ N/A
Uses classroom space well	☐ Yes	☐ No	☐ N/A

Student Interaction

Encourages student participation	☐ Yes	☐ No	☐ N/A
Manages student interactions effectively	☐ Yes	☐ No	☐ N/A
Welcomes and respects diverse viewpoints	☐ Yes	☐ No	☐ N/A
Treats students equitably	☐ Yes	☐ No	☐ N/A
Motivates students	☐ Yes	☐ No	☐ N/A

Chapter 36

Counselor Education and Supervision—Research

Carrie A. Wachter Morris, Laura M. Gonzalez, Kelly L. Wester, and Casey A. Barrio Minton

The nature and quality of research in counseling and counselor education have been the subject of critique for at least the past 20 years (e.g., Fong & Malone, 1994; Thompson & Snyder, 1998; Vacha-Haase & Thompson, 2011; Wester, Borders, Boul, & Horton, 2013). As the counseling profession has grown out of infancy, navigated adolescence, and prepares for adulthood, it must face the challenge of addressing opportunities for growth related to research. Because of the consistency in identified gaps in research competence, counseling still has strides to make to increase the rigor and variety of research produced (see Wester et al., 2013).

Research is a core focus of the CACREP 2016 Doctoral Standards, but the importance of competence and proficiency in research transcends accreditation requirements. Recently, research competencies have been developed for the counseling field. Wester and Borders (2014) highlighted 160 research competencies that emerged from a Delphi methodology study with a panel of counseling research experts. They suggested that acquirement of research competencies is developmental throughout one's career but highlight the importance of having knowledge of the breadth of research methodologies and analysis. Wester and Borders stressed that having breadth of knowledge allows counseling researchers to know all possibilities available to answer research questions; however, the competencies lead to the need to have in-depth knowledge and skill of the methodologies and analyses selected by the researcher. As Sink and Mvududu (2010) noted, "If the ultimate goal of most counseling-related research is to positively affect the profession and the work of practitioners and their clients, knowing the basics and the nuances of quality research is indispensable" (pp. 1–2).

Even with this indispensability, Okech, Astramovich, Johnson, Hoskins, and Rubel (2006) found that nearly one third of counselor educators did not feel well prepared in quantitative research methods. Approximately two thirds did not feel well prepared in qualitative research methods (Okech et al., 2006). Of the participants surveyed in the study, 51.3% reported that doctoral students should have more quantitative research training, and 57.6% reported that doctoral students should have more qualitative research training. Nearly all of the participants (93.7%) reported that mentoring was an important part of research training.

Research mentoring can take place both within and outside the academic curriculum. ACES adopted the *Guidelines for Research Mentorship* (Borders et al., 2012), which can be infused into the doctoral curriculum. These research mentorship guidelines have specific roles and responsibilities for research mentors and mentees, and they are a basis for counselor educators and counselor education programs to think critically about how formal and hidden curricula prepare doctoral students to complete and disseminate rigorous research.

The assignments in this chapter are designed to build research competence through focus on methodologies and creation of conceptual frameworks, leading to a larger research proposal. The first assignment prompts students to do in-depth research on a specific methodology of interest while also exposing them to a variety of other methodologies. The second assignment is tailored to help students get into the literature regarding constructs of interest and develop a conceptual framework to describe the relationships among those constructs. The final assignment is a three-chapter proposal that could build off the first assignments and that supports progress toward developing a research idea for student dissertations.

Methodology Intensive

SLOs assessed: CACREP 2016 Standards 6.B.4.a, 6.B.4.b, 6.B.4.c, 6.B.4.d, 6.B.4.e, 6.B.4.f

Create a 40-minute professional presentation regarding an approved research methodology. This will require that you become familiar enough with a research method to teach it to colleagues. Although duplication of topics will not be allowed, we may negotiate collaboration on more in-depth intensives.

This professional presentation will equip participants with a working knowledge of key research methodologies in counseling research. Presenters should assume that participants are doctoral candidates and counselor educators who have a research background and wish to refresh on practical aspects of design. The presentation will be offered as part of a research summit. The sponsors have asked you to fit your topic to the following specifications:

- Title: _____ Design in Counseling: A Practical Guide
- Presentations should be practical and well-referenced and should answer the following questions:
  –What are key philosophical assumptions or underpinnings to the method?
  –What are key characteristics of the method?
  –What are key questions or situations that might lead one to select this method?
  –How might a researcher go about using the method?
  –What are key data collection and analysis procedures or considerations?
  –What are validity considerations associated with the method?
  –Overall, what are the method's greatest advantages and disadvantages?
- Presenters must provide handouts that include the following:
  –a summary of critical information,
  –original sources/references for learning more about the method, and
  –references for sample articles utilizing the method.

Ideally, students will present on a method that they most expect to use for dissertation. In the likely event that several students are interested in the same topic, we may

- decide to present a multistaged presentation in which each student takes responsibility for a 40-minute segment, and the class learns about the method in additional depth; or
- select topics based on a lottery system.

Potential topics include, but are not limited to, the following: randomized controlled trials, quasi-experimental, meta-analysis, instrument construction, survey/descriptive, narrative, phenomenological, case study, grounded theory, ethnography, mixed methods, single case, action research, between-groups, within-subjects, time series designs, process research, analogue research, outcome research, and content analysis.

Methodology intensives will be evaluated on the basis of comprehensiveness, knowledge of research design, knowledge of data analysis, utilization of resources, handout quality, and quality of communication. Table 36.1 includes the rubric associated with this assignment.

Table 36.1
Methodology Intensive Rubric

Criterion	Does Not Meet Expectations	Meets Expectations	Exceeds Expectations
Knowledge of research design	Description of research design contains inaccurate information. Student is unable to accurately and adequately address key assumptions and characteristics of selected research design.	Components and underlying assumptions of research design are described adequately and accurately but may lack sophistication.	All required components of the research design are articulated accurately and eloquently. Members of the audience come away with a clear understanding of the research design and when to use it.
Knowledge of data analysis	Description of data analysis is flawed or incomplete. Student is unable to accurately and adequately address key considerations in data analysis.	Description of data analysis is adequate and accurate. Student accurately addresses key considerations in data analysis, but description lacks sophistication.	Description of data analysis is eloquent so that members of the audience come away with a clear understanding of the analyses most often used within the research design.
Handout quality	Handouts are not provided or lack required components.	Handouts cover all required information.	Handouts are thorough but concise, with all required elements clearly presented.
Quality of presentation	Student has persistent difficulty with presentation skills and conveying meaning. Presentation is not consistent with the quality expected from a national conference presentation.	Student has occasional difficulty conveying meaning or professional poise, but presentation is successful. Presentation is mostly consistent with the quality expected from a national conference presentation.	Presentation is exceptional. Points made are clear, presentation is engaging, and material is presented clearly and specifically. Presentation quality is consistent with what would be expected at a national conference.

Conceptual Framework for Your Research Agenda

SLOs assessed: CACREP 2016 Standard 6.B.4.h

The purpose of this assignment is to create a conceptual framework through which you could address your own research questions. This can be particularly useful in helping you test out a possible dissertation idea.

In a brief paper (five to six pages), describe your conception or model of what is out there that you plan to study as well as what is going on with these things and why—a tentative theory of the phenomena that you are investigating. Although this may look different for each of you, it should explain (a) the key factors, constructs, or variables that you would like to study; (b) the presumed relationships among them; (c) past theories or explanations; and (d) why this brings you to a new question of importance to counseling. You may include a hand-drawn or computer generated image if this helps to clarify Point b.

This is different from a literature review describing a topic because you are hypothesizing relationships—how one set of variables may affect another. These relationships do not have to be proven by other scholars—this is your chance to make an original contribution and show how you are generating a new perspective on a research question in counseling. The paper will be graded on the basis of the rubric provided. It is a good idea to keep notes about thoughts and questions that occur to you as you are reading to make this assignment directed and concise. Table 36.2 includes the rubric associated with this assignment.

Research Project Proposal

SLOs assessed: CACREP 2016 Standards 6.B.4.a, 6.B.4.g, 6.B.4.h, 6.B.4.j, 6.B.4.k, 6.B.4.l

Prepare a fully developed proposal for a viable study. The proposal is to include the following sections: Introduction, Review of the Literature, and Methodology. The proposal should be as complete as possible. The following outline with objectives is for your use as a guide in developing your research proposal. This is a proposal that could technically mimic that of which you will eventually submit for a dissertation proposal and/or a grant proposal. The paper should be 16–20 pages in length

Table 36.2
Conceptual Framework for Your Research Agenda Rubric

Criterion (CACREP Standard)	Does Not Meet Expectations	Meets Expectations	Exceeds Expectations
Key factors and constructs	Key factors and constructs are omitted or undefined. Minimal or no relationship is described between variables. Attention to foundational theories or explanations of relationship between constructs is cursory or unclear.	Key factors and constructs include definitions and adequate attention to the relationships between them. Those relationships or proposed relationships are based on past theories or explanations, but some gaps in explanation may be present.	Key factors and constructs are clearly and concisely defined. Relationships are detailed with clear language. Diagram provided includes all key factors and the relationships described between them. Relationships are clearly and concisely tied to the literature in a relevant and meaningful way.
Importance to counseling	No or minimal justification is provided for the importance of the new question(s) generated by the conceptual model to the counseling field at large.	Adequate justification is provided for the importance of the new question(s) generated by the conceptual model. Justification may lack some clarity in writing or links but is understandable and relevant to the field.	Justification is provided for the importance of the new question(s) generated by conceptual model. Questions are clear, concise, and relevant to current issues in the counseling field.
Quality of construction of conceptual model	Conceptual model is drawn from only one source, with no novel additional thoughts or concepts from the student. No evidence is provided for the relationships proposed. Major assumptions of the model are unclear or unnamed.	Conceptual model is drawn from several sources, and there is evidence of the student's thoughts and additions in the construction of the model. Adequate evidence is provided, but there might be an occasional gap in the description of underlying assumptions of the model.	Conceptual model is clearly a well-based and well-constructed synthesis of a variety of sources and the student's own hypotheses. Evidence and assumptions underpinning the conceptual model are thorough and clearly stated.
Quality of writing (6.B.4.H)	Persistent difficulty with writing results in difficulty conveying meaning. Difficulty may include two or more of the following: focus, logic, organization, style, grammar, or APA Style. Writing is not consistent with published material.	Student has occasional difficulty with writing, but meaning is clear overall. Difficulty may include one or more of the following: focus, logic, organization, style, grammar, or APA Style. Writing is mostly consistent with published material.	Quality of writing is exceptional and precise and excels in the following areas: focus, logic, organization, style, grammar, and APA Style. Writing is consistent with published material.

Note. CACREP = Council for Accreditation of Counseling and Related Educational Programs; APA = American Psychological Association.

(not including cover page, abstract, and references), be in 12-point font, have 1-inch margins, and follow APA Style.

This paper is designed to allow you to conceptualize a proposed research agenda from the material studied in class. This assignment is not to be a critique of your research idea but instead to be a proposal for your research idea. In this assignment, you should do the following:

- review, synthesize, and critique related literature that supports your investigation;
- provide a theoretical framework and/or a conceptual model that frames your research problem;
- state your proposed research problem;
- discuss the need for and significance of the study;
- specify the research questions that you will be addressing;
- describe the research methodology that will be used to address your research question; and
- discuss data analysis methods that will be used to answer the research questions, given the methodology.

Start the paper with the introduction section, in which you should provide background information on the topic, issue(s), and focus of the research. In the literature review section, you should also discuss your research issue/problem from the perspective of a theory and status of the research in the literature—this latter section may also include the significance of and need for the study. You will need to ensure that you have provided specific illustrations to support and/or explain your points. This may require hypothesizing about the topic, particularly concerning issues not yet addressed in the literature. Conclude the paper with the methodology section (i.e., How will the research be conducted?). An outline is provided below:

- Chapter 1: Introduction (approximately 4–5 pages)
  –Statement of the problem
  –Purpose of the study
  –Significance of the study
  –Questions to be addressed (i.e., focus of research)
  –Definition of terms
- Chapter 2: Review of the literature (approximately 6–7 pages)
- Chapter 3: Methodology (approximately 8 pages)
  –Introductory paragraph
  –Research questions and hypotheses
  –Population and samples
  –Instruments
  –Procedures and/or treatment
  –Analysis of data (this will be fairly short in this project)
  –Limitations of the study

Table 36.3 includes the rubric associated with this assignment.

Table 36.3
Research Project Proposal Rubric

Criterion (CACREP Standard)	Does Not Meet Expectations	Meets Expectations	Exceeds Expectations
Introduction	Introduction is overly simplified or absent. Required sections are minimally addressed or absent.	All required sections are present and adequately addressed. Significance of the study is supported and logical.	Literature supports the purpose and significance of the study, and the focus of the research is well-developed.
Literature review	Overly simplified review is provided with poor support for claims. The review may show inadequate understanding of the literature grounding the proposed study. Conceptual/theoretical framework is absent or unclear.	Thorough and relevant review is provided with adequate support for claims. Conceptual/theoretical framework is present and developed, but it may have occasional gaps in presentation to the reader.	Review is thoughtful and well stated in all sections. Review is clear, persuasive, and engaging with outstanding support for claims. Conceptual/theoretical framework is exceptionally written and clearly integrated.
Methodology	Required sections of methodology are unclear or absent. Methodology does not match research questions.	All required sections are present and adequately addressed. Methodology matches research questions.	All required sections are well-articulated and clear. Methodology, sampling procedures, instruments, and data analysis sections are clearly the most appropriate way to answer the research questions. Rationale is backed up by the methodology literature.
Quality of writing (6.B.4.h)	Persistent difficulty with writing results in difficulty conveying meaning. Difficulty may include two or more of the following: focus, logic, organization, style, grammar, or APA Style. Writing is not consistent with published material.	Student has occasional difficulty with writing, but meaning is clear overall. Difficulty may include one or more of the following: focus, logic, organization, style, grammar, or APA Style. Writing is mostly consistent with published material.	Quality of writing is exceptional and precise and excels in the following areas: focus, logic, organization, style, grammar, and APA Style. Writing is consistent with published material.

Note. CACREP = Council for Accreditation of Counseling and Related Educational Programs; APA = American Psychological Association.

Chapter 37

Counselor Education and Supervision— Leadership and Advocacy

Donna M. Gibson

Although leadership and advocacy are integrated into some of the master's curriculum, they are integral to every aspect of the doctoral curriculum. The purpose of these standards at the doctoral level is to build on the student's knowledge, skills, and sense of responsibility in promoting the profession through counseling, teaching, and service. Different leadership models, theories, and strategies are presented in counselor education and supervision courses to expose doctoral students to possible ways of making meaning and eventual application to their work (CACREP 2016 Standards 6.B.5.a, 6.B.5.k, 6.B.5.l). Transformational leadership, participatory leadership, and servant leadership are some of the theories that can be introduced, but attention also needs to be given to how leadership is developed and acted on in counselor education and the counseling profession (Standards 6.B.5.b, 6.B.5.c, 6.B.5.e). Assignments and internship requirements need to incorporate aspects of leadership that are connected to curriculum standards, program assessment and evaluation activities, and crisis responses and intervention (Standards 6.B.5.d, 6.B.5.f, 6.B.5.g). Counselor educators may need to draw leadership theory information from other fields that focus on leadership, as there are few resources in the counselor education profession. Chi Sigma Iota International (http://www.csi-net.org/) offers some resources on leadership development, professional identity development, and advocacy.

In the area of advocacy, there is an assumption in the doctoral standards and curriculum that students have been exposed to specific information and experiences to help them develop their multicultural awareness and advocacy skills. Doctoral students, at a minimum, should be knowledgeable of the domains of the ACA Advocacy Competencies (J. A. Lewis, Arnold, House, & Toporek, 2002) and how each of these may look in action both as a counselor (see Lee & Rodgers, 2009) and as a counselor educator (CACREP 2016 Standards 6.B.5.j, 6.B.5.i). Counselor educators need to assess this knowledge carefully to ensure that doctoral students understand how advocacy is enacted by counselors, as this will influence their ability to encourage and support supervisees' advocacy efforts. Similar to the leadership standards, the purpose of the advocacy standards is to increase doctoral students' sense of responsibility for the profession in their roles of educator, supervisor, and scholar. Training doctoral students in the political aspects of higher education will help them learn what advocacy efforts can be most effective in this arena. Counselor educators can mentor doctoral students in these aspects as well as offer assignments and internships in research, leadership, and advocacy that require students to conduct research or literature reviews that represent a form of advocacy within the profession.

In this chapter, three assignments and rubrics to assess learning in the doctoral core related to leadership and advocacy are offered. The first assignment is designed to help doctoral students self-label as a leader and identify leadership practices and skills that they possess or are in the process of developing. The second assignment is application based, which makes it optimal for advanced practicum or counseling internship. It requires students to use consultation skills to evaluate crisis responses, including the role of the leader in the crisis response. Advocacy strategies are also identified in the recommendations for crisis response. The third assignment is designed to use with a Counselor Education and Supervision Internship focused on leadership and advocacy. The doctoral student, in consultation with his or her faculty internship supervisor, researches a current issue relevant to the counseling profession, designs an advocacy plan, implements the plan, and evaluates the plan.

Leadership Philosophy

SLOs assessed: CACREP 2016 Standards 6.B.5.a, 6.B.5.b., 6.B.5.c, 6.B.5.e, 6.B.5.f, 6.B.5.k, 6.B.5.l

Develop and write a philosophy that incorporates aspects of one to two different leadership theories that represent your leadership style as a counselor educator and supervisor. The philosophy should include specific leadership skills that will be used in your role as a counselor educator in higher education as well as leadership skills that will be necessary within professional counseling organizations. Ethical and culturally relevant leadership and advocacy practices need to be highlighted. Table 37.1 includes the rubric associated with this assignment.

Crisis and Consultation Presentation and Paper

SLOs assessed: CACREP 2016 Standards 6.B.4.h, 6.B.5.f, 6.B.5.g, 6.B.5.i, 6.B.5.l

In conjunction with their practicum sites, students will identify a crisis that has occurred in their site's past. This could include several different levels of crisis, such as individual, systemic, and/or catastrophic. Using the text of Collins and Collins (2005) and other appropriate research, students will identify whether any crisis model/theory was utilized in responding to this crisis. Key stakehold-

Table 37.1
Leadership Philosophy Rubric

Criterion (CACREP Standard)	Does Not Meet Expectations	Meets Expectations	Exceeds Expectations
Knowledge of leadership theory/model (6.B.5.a, 6.B.5.e) and examples related to leadership theory and personal style of leadership	Leadership theory and personal leadership style are not articulated or, if articulated, are basic or lack reflectivity (reflection). Student does not describe theory/model relevant to counselor education or leadership in professional organizations.	Leadership theory and personal leadership style are articulated but lack connection to each other. Examples are provided but do not illustrate leadership theory.	Leadership theory and personal style of leadership are specific and clearly relevant to counselor education and professional organizations. Examples provided illustrate integration of leadership theory and personal style.
Knowledge and application of specific leadership development, skills, and practices in counselor education (higher education) and professional organizations (6.B.5.a, 6.B.5.b, 6.B.5.c, 6.B.5.f)	Specific leadership development, skills, and practices are not articulated or are articulated in a general manner.	Leadership development, skills, and practices in counselor education and professional organizations are delineated, but specific information is not included in a consistent manner.	Leadership development, skills, and practices in both counselor education and professional organizations are discussed specifically and consistently.
Knowledge of ethical and culturally relevant leadership practices (6.B.5.k, 6.B.5.l) are illustrated in examples	Specific leadership practices and strategies are not connected to ethical and multicultural considerations.	Specific leadership practices and strategies are connected loosely to ethical and multicultural considerations. Examples may not illustrate this specifically.	Specific leadership practices and strategies are connected directly to ethical and multicultural considerations. Examples illustrate this specifically.

Note. CACREP = Council for Accreditation of Counseling and Related Educational Programs.

ers in the crisis response will be interviewed to determine the perception of the effectiveness of the response (for the leader and team responses).

Students will present the crisis scenario, response, and reflections of key stakeholders in a PowerPoint presentation. Additionally, students will provide their analysis of the response as well as research-based recommendations for increased effectiveness for similar future crises and implementation of advocacy strategies.

Students will provide an accompanying paper that will serve as a case example manuscript to be submitted to a journal that is appropriate for the content. A minimum of 15 references (at least 10 peer-refereed) will be required for the manuscript. There will be a 25-page maximum, and APA Style should be utilized. Table 37.2 includes the rubric associated with this assignment.

Leadership and Advocacy Plan and Project

SLOs assessed: CACREP 2016 Standards 6.B.5.d, 6.B.5.h, 6.B.5.i, 6.C.1

This project is intended for doctoral students completing an internship focused on leadership and/or advocacy. The intern needs to choose a topical or political issue in counseling and to investigate how this issue is affecting the work of counselors and the counseling profession. On the basis of this research, the intern will determine the role of counselors and counselor educators in advocating on behalf of the profession and professional identity. Specific advocacy and leadership practices need to be delineated and acted on. Consultation with faculty internship supervisor is required. The plan (APA Style format) will include the components listed in the rubric in Table 37.3.

Table 37.2
Crisis and Consultation Presentation and Paper Rubric

Criterion (CACREP Standard)	Does Not Meet Expectations	Meets Expectations	Exceeds Expectations
Presentation of Crisis Content			
Information about the crisis event is presented, including the following elements: • What was the crisis? • Who was affected by the crisis? • What was the response? • Who led the response? • Who was involved in the response? • How did the crisis affect those involved (during and after event)? • How did the responders evaluate their response? • What consultation strategies did the student use in acquiring information? (6.B.5.f, 6.B.5.g)	All questions in the crisis content are not answered.	All questions in the crisis content are answered but not adequately or specifically enough to understand the scope and impact of the crisis event.	All questions in the crisis content are answered comprehensively. The crisis event, response, leadership, and impact of event and response are understood.
Presentation of the Crisis Model Application			
The student will choose 1–2 crisis models to apply to the reported crisis event: • What is (are) the crisis model(s)? • Why should the model apply to the event (how appropriate is it for the type of crisis event?)? • How would it apply? • What are the similarities/differences between the event and model? • What are the similarities/differences between the event response and model recommended response?	All questions in the crisis model application are not answered.	All questions in the crisis model application are answered but not adequately enough to understand the crisis model applied and/or the rationale for the application of the chosen model. Similarities and differences between event and model as well as between the response and the model are not delineated specifically.	All questions in the crisis model application are answered comprehensively. References are provided and are in the correct APA Style format.
Presentation of Crisis Response Recommendations			
Utilizing the chosen crisis model(s) and the application of the model for fit and evaluation of crisis response to the event, evidence-based recommendations are made.	All recommendations are not based on cited research.	Five recommendations are presented, but not all are appropriate on the basis of the crisis model.	Five recommendations are provided and discussed comprehensively with rationale for use during and after crisis.
Five research-based and specific recommendations to type of crisis are presented. The recommendations should include appropriate responses when crisis is occurring as well as recommendations for helping survivors after the crisis. Counseling interventions are appropriate for postcrisis recommendations.		Ethical and cultural advocacy practices are not represented in the recommendation.	Recommendations represent ethical and cultural advocacy practices at the individual, system, or policy level.
Recommendations should include ethical and culturally relevant advocacy practices that illustrate advocating at the individual, system, or policy level. (6.B.5.i, 6.B.5.l)		Research is cited, but there are fewer than five references and/or APA Style format is not applied appropriately.	At least five research-based, peer-refereed journal articles are used for recommendations. APA Style format is applied correctly.

(Continued)

Table 37.2 (*Continued*)
Crisis and Consultation Presentation and Paper Rubric

Criterion (CACREP Standard)	Does Not Meet Expectations	Meets Expectations	Exceeds Expectations
Journal Manuscript			
All elements of the presentation will be included in the manuscript. The formatting elements of the manuscript should include the following: • Title page • Running head with page numbers • Abstract • Body of the manuscript • Appropriate headings • References • 1-inch margins • 12-point font • Double-spaced throughout	Does not include all of the elements listed in the journal manuscript requirements.	Meets the majority of the elements listed in the journal manuscript requirements.	All elements listed in the journal manuscript requirements are included.
The presentation outline can be utilized to outline the content of manuscript with an appropriate introduction to the type of crisis event (citing relevant literature regarding type of crisis). The content should flow logically, and transitions between sections should be present.	Several writing errors are present (e.g., grammar, spelling, wording, sentence structure).	Few writing errors are present (e.g., fewer than three).	No significant writing errors are present (e.g., sentence structure issues).
A minimum of 15 references (at least 10 peer-refereed) is required, and the references should be in the correct APA Style format—avoid website addresses as well as Wiki and unsubstantiated resources. (6.B.4.h)	Formatting errors are present.	With few exceptions, formatting is correct for manuscript and APA Style references.	Formatting is correct for manuscript and APA Style references.

Note. CACREP = Council for Accreditation of Counseling and Related Educational Programs; APA = American Psychological Association.

Table 37.3
Leadership and Advocacy Plan and Project Rubric

Criterion (CACREP Standard)	Does Not Meet Expectations	Meets Expectations	Exceeds Expectations
Current issue and research (6.B.5.d, 6.B.5.h)	The current issue is not explained or connected in relevance to the work of counselors or to the counseling profession.	The current issue is explained, but the relevance to the counseling profession and the work of counselors is not connected specifically.	The current issue is explained as to its relevance to the counseling profession, the work of counselors, and accreditation standards.
	Five resources are not included.	Five resources are included, but not all are peer-refereed.	Five peer-refereed journal articles are included as a minimum to explain the issue's relevance.
Leadership/advocacy strategies (6.B.5.i)	The roles of the counselor educator and/or counselor are not described.	The roles of the counselor educator and/or counselor are described but are not specific to leadership and advocacy.	The roles of the counselor educator and/or counselor are described in terms of leadership and advocacy.
	Leadership or advocacy strategies are not described.	Leadership or advocacy strategies are described but not in terms of what is needed to implement the advocacy plan.	Specific leadership and advocacy strategies/practices required for implementation of the advocacy plan are described.
	Five resources are not included.	Five resources are included, but not all are peer-refereed.	Five peer-refereed journal articles to support roles/strategies/practices are included.
Implementation of advocacy plan	Plan is not included, implemented, or evaluated.	Some of the elements of the advocacy plan are included, but sufficient detail is not delineated.	Detailed advocacy plan is described to include the following elements: • Purpose of plan • Persons involved in advocacy plan (i.e., roles and relevance) • Possible consequences of action • Timeline of implementation • Evaluation of plan (i.e., how will plan and implementation be evaluated?) • Results of implementation (What happened?) • Recommendations based on results and evaluation (What to do differently/similarly? What are the next steps for advocacy?)

Note. CACREP = Council for Accreditation of Counseling and Related Educational Programs.

References

Allen, M. J. (2004). *Assessing academic programs in higher education.* Bolton, MA: Anker.

Ambrose, S. A., Bridges, M. W., DiPietro, M., Lovett, M. C., & Norman, M. K. (2010). *How learning works: Seven research-based principles for smart teaching.* San Francisco, CA: Jossey-Bass.

American Association of Suicidology. (2003). *Know the warning signs of suicide.* Retrieved from http://www.suicidology.org/resources/warning-signs

American Counseling Association. (2014). *ACA code of ethics.* Alexandria, VA: Author.

American Educational Research Association, American Psychological Association, & National Council on Measurement in Education. (1999). *Standards for educational and psychological testing.* Washington, DC: American Educational Research Association.

American Psychiatric Association. (2013). *Diagnostic and statistical manual of mental disorders* (5th ed.). Arlington, VA: Author.

American Psychological Association. (2010). *Publication manual of the American Psychological Association* (6th ed.). Washington, DC: Author.

American School Counselor Association. (n.d.). *The role of the professional school counselor.* Retrieved from https://www.schoolcounselor.org/asca/media/asca/home/RoleStatement.pdf

American School Counselor Association. (2012). *The ASCA National Model: A framework for school counseling programs* (3rd ed.). Alexandria, VA: Author.

Anderson, L. W., & Krathwohl, D. R. (Eds.). (2001). A *taxonomy for learning, teaching, and assessing: A revision of Bloom's taxonomy of educational objectives.* New York, NY: Longman Publishing.

Andrade, H. G. (2005). Teaching with rubrics: The good, the bad, and the ugly. *College Teaching, 53,* 27–31.

Arredondo, P., Toporek, M. S., Brown, S., Jones, J., Locke, D. C., Sanchez, J., & Stadler, H. (1996). *Operationalization of the multicultural counseling competencies.* Alexandria, VA: Association for Multicultural Counseling and Development.

Arthur, N., Collins, S., Marshall, C., & McMahon, M. (2013). Social justice competencies and career development practices. *Canadian Journal of Counselling and Psychotherapy, 47,* 136–154.

Arthur, N., Collins, S., McMahon, M., & Marshall, C. (2009). Career practitioners' views of social justice and barriers for practice. *Canadian Journal of Career Development, 8,* 22–31.

Association for Counselor Education and Supervision. (2011). *Best practices in clinical supervision*. Retrieved from http://www.acesonline.net/sites/default/files/ACES-Best-Practices-in-clinical-supervision-document-FINAL.pdf

Association for Counselor Education and Supervision & National Career Development Association. (2000). *Preparing counselors for career development in the new millennium*. Retrieved from http://ncda.org/aws/NCDA/pt/sp/guidelines

Association for Specialists in Group Work. (2000). Association for Specialists in Group Work: Professional standards for the training of group workers. *The Journal for Specialists in Group Work, 25*, 327–342.

Association for Spiritual, Ethical, and Religious Values in Counseling. (2009). *Spiritual competencies*. Retrieved from http://www.aservic.org/resources/spiritual-competencies/

Association of American Colleges and Universities. (2008). *Our students' best work: A framework for accountability worthy of our mission* (2nd ed.). Washington, DC: Author.

Baggerly, J., & Osborn, D. (2013). A survey of counselor education comprehensive exam types and procedures: Recommendations for clinical supervisors and counseling faculty. *The Clinical Supervisor, 32*, 90–104. doi:10.1080/07325223.2013.780933

Baker, G. R., Jankowski, N. A., Provezis, S., & Kinzie, J. (2012). *Using assessment results: Promising practices of institutions that do it well*. Retrieved from http://www.learningoutcomesassessment.org/documents/CrossCase_FINAL1.pdf

Baltimore, M. L., Hickson, J., George, J. D., & Crutchfield, L. B. (1996). Portfolio assessment: A model for counselor education. *Counselor Education and Supervision, 36*, 113–121. doi:10.1002/j.1556-6978.1996.tb00377.x

Banta, T. W., Griffin, M., Flateby, T. L., & Kahn, S. (2009). *Three promising alternatives for assessing college students' knowledge and skills*. Retrieved from http://learningoutcomesassessment.org/documents/AlternativesforAssessment.pdf

Barrio Minton, C. A., & Gibson, D. M. (2012). Evaluating student learning outcomes in counselor education: Recommendations and process considerations. *Counseling Outcome Research and Evaluation, 3*, 73–91. doi:10.1177/2150137812452561

Barrio Minton, C. A., Wachter Morris, C. A., & Yaites, L. D. (2014). Teaching and learning in counselor education: A ten-year content analysis. *Counselor Education and Supervision, 53*, 162–177. doi:10.1002/j.1556-6978.2014.00055.x

Bartle, L., & Bradwin, M. G. (2006). The comprehensive examination: Study groups and their effectiveness—A message to counselor education faculty and graduate students. *Education, 127*, 69–73.

Benkofske, M., & Heppner, C. C. (2008). Program evaluation. In P. P. Heppner, B. E. Wampold, & D. M. Kivlighan (Eds.), *Research design in counseling* (3rd ed., pp. 511–537). Belmont, CA: Thompson Higher Education.

Bernard, J. M. (2014). The use of supervision notes as a targeted training strategy. *American Journal of Psychotherapy, 68*, 195–212.

Bernard, J. M., & Goodyear, R. K. (2014). *Fundamentals of clinical supervision* (5th ed.). Boston, MA: Pearson.

Bhat, C. S. (2005). Enhancing counseling gatekeeping with performance appraisal protocols. *International Journal for the Advancement of Counselling, 27*, 399–411. doi:10.1007/s10447-005-8202-z

Blaich, C., & Wise, K. (2011). *From gathering to using assessment results: Lessons from the Wabash National Study*. Retrieved from http://www.learningoutcomeassessment.org/documents/Wabash_001.pdf

Bloom, B. S. (1956). *Taxonomy of educational objectives: Handbook I. The cognitive domain*. New York, NY: David McKay.

Blum, L. D. (2010). The "all-but-the-dissertation" student and the psychology of the doctoral dissertation. *Journal of College Student Psychotherapy, 24*, 74–85. doi:10.1080/87568220903558554

Blustein, D. L. (2006). *The psychology of working*. Mahwah, NJ: Erlbaum.

Blustein, D. L., Medvide, M. B., & Wan, C. M. (2011). A critical perspective of contemporary unemployment policy and practices. *Journal of Career Development, 39,* 341–356.

Bonwell, C. (1993). *Active learning: Creating excitement in the classroom.* Retrieved from http:// files.eric.ed.gov/fulltext/ED336049.pdf

Boote, D. N., & Beile, P. (2005). Scholars before researchers: On the centrality of the dissertation literature review in research preparation. *Educational Researcher, 34,* 3–15. doi:10.3102/0013189X034006003

Borders, L. D. (2010). Principles of best practices for clinical supervisor training programs. In J. R. Culbreth & L. L. Brown (Eds.), *State of the art in clinical supervision* (pp. 127–150). New York, NY: Routledge.

Borders, L. D. (2014). "Best practices in clinical supervision": Another step in delineating effective supervision practice. *American Journal of Psychotherapy, 68,* 151–162.

Borders, L. D., Bernard, J. M., Dye, H. A., Fong, M. L., Henderson, P., & Nance, D. W. (1991). Curriculum guide for training counseling supervisors: Rationale, development, and implementation. *Counselor Education and Supervision, 31,* 58–80.

Borders, L. D., & Brown, L. L. (2005). *The new handbook of counseling supervision.* Mahwah, NJ: Erlbaum.

Borders, L. D., Glosoff, H. L., Welfare, L. E., Hays, D. G., DeKruyf, L., Fernando, D. M., & Page, B. (2014). Best practices in clinical supervision: Evolution of a counseling specialty. *The Clinical Supervisor, 33,* 26–44.

Borders, L. D., Wester, K. L., Granello, D. H., Chang, C. Y., Hays, D. G., Pepperell, J., & Spurgeon, S. L. (2012). Association for Counselor Education and Supervision guidelines for research mentorship: Development and implementation. *Counselor Education and Supervision, 51,* 162–175. doi:10.1002/j.1556-6978.2012.00012.x

Boyer, E. L. (1990). *Scholarship reconsidered: Priorities of the professoriate.* New York, NY: Jossey-Bass.

Bransford, J. D., Brown, A. L., & Cocking, R. R. (Eds.). (2000). *How people learn: Brain, mind, experience, and school.* Washington, DC: National Academy Press.

Brown, M. (2013). A content analysis of problematic behavior in counselor education programs. *Counselor Education and Supervision, 52,* 179–192. doi:10.1002/j.1556-6978.2013.00036.x

Browne, I., & Misra, J. (2003). The intersection of gender and race in the labor market. *Annual Review of Sociology, 29,* 487–513.

Brunner, J. L., Wallace, D. L., Reymann, L. S., Sellers, J. J., & McCabe, A. G. (2014). College counseling today: Contemporary students and how counseling centers meet their needs. *Journal of College Student Psychotherapy, 28,* 257–324. doi:10.1080/87568225.2014.948770

Burkard, A. W., Knox, S., DeWalt, T., Fuller, S., Hill, C., & Schlosser, L. Z. (2014). Dissertation experiences of doctoral graduates from professional psychology programs. *Counselling Psychology Quarterly, 27,* 19–54. doi:10.1080/09515070.2013.821596

Burke, S. K., & Snead, J. T. (2014). Faculty opinions on the use of master's degree end of program assessments. *Journal of Education for Library and Information Science, 55,* 26–39.

Burlingame, G. M., Fuhriman, A., & Mosier, J. (2003). The differential effectiveness of group psychotherapy: A meta-analytic perspective. *Group Dynamics: Theory, Research, and Practice, 7,* 3–12.

Butler, J. F. (2008). The family diagram and genogram: Comparisons and contrasts. *The American Journal of Family Therapy, 36,* 169–180.

Cabrera, A., Weerts, D., & Zulick, B. (2005). Making an impact with alumni surveys. *New Directions for Institutional Research, 126,* 5–17. doi:10.1002/ir.144

Cain, T. R. (2014). *Assessment and academic freedom: In concert, not conflict.* Retrieved from http:// www.learningoutcomesassessment.org/documents/OP2211-17-14.pdf

Calderon, O. (2013). Direct and indirect measures of learning outcomes in an MSW program: What do we actually measure? *Journal of Social Work Education, 49,* 408–419. doi:10.1080/104377 97.2013.796767

Cambridge, B. L. (2001). Fostering the scholarship of teaching and learning: Communities of practice. In D. A. Lieberman & C. Wehlburg (Eds.), *To improve the academy* (Vol. 19, pp. 3–16). Bolton, MA: Anker.

Carlson, R. G., & Lambie, G. W. (2012). Systemic-developmental supervisions: A clinical supervisory approach for family counseling student interns. *The Family Journal, 20,* 29–36.

Carney, J. S., Cobia, D. C., & Shannon, D. M. (1996). The use of portfolios in the clinical and comprehensive evaluation of counselors-in-training. *Counselor Education and Supervision, 36,* 122–132.

Carriveau, R. S. (2010). *Connecting the dots: Developing student learning outcomes and outcome based assessments.* Denton: University of North Texas.

Chang, C. Y., Gnilka, P., & O'Hara, C. (2014). Social justice counseling. In D. G. Hays & B. T. Erford (Eds.), *Developing multicultural counseling competency: A systems approach* (pp. 58–81). Columbus, OH: Pearson Merrill Prentice Hall.

Coleman, H. L. K., Morris, D., & Norton, R. A. (2006). Developing multicultural counseling competence through the use of portfolios. *Journal of Multicultural Counseling and Development, 34,* 27–37. doi:10.1002/j.2161-1912.2006.tb00024.x

Collins, B. G., & Collins, T. M. (2005). *Crisis and trauma: Developmental–ecological intervention.* Belmont, CA: Brooks/Cole.

Commission on the Future of Higher Education. (2006). *A test of leadership: Charting the future of U.S. higher education.* Washington, DC: U.S. Department of Education.

Committee on the Evaluation of Teaching Excellence. (2010). *Final report.* Retrieved from https://spot.unt.edu/sites/default/files/Committee_Evaluation_Teaching_Excellence_2010_0.pdf

Community Mental Health Act, Pub. L. No. 88-164, 77 Stat. 282 (1963).

Consoli, A. J., & Jester, C. M. (2005). A model for teaching psychotherapy theory through an integrative structure. *Journal of Psychotherapy Integration, 15,* 358–373.

Corey, M. S., Corey, G., & Corey, C. (2014). *Groups: Process and practice* (9th ed.). Belmont, CA: Brooks/Cole.

Council for Accreditation of Counseling and Related Educational Programs. (1994). *1994 CACREP accreditation manual.* Alexandria, VA: Author.

Council for Accreditation of Counseling and Related Educational Programs. (2001). *2001 standards.* Alexandria, VA: Author.

Council for Accreditation of Counseling and Related Educational Programs. (2009). *2009 standards.* Retrieved from http://www.cacrep.org/wp-content/uploads/2013/12/2009-Standards.pdf

Council for Accreditation of Counseling and Related Educational Programs. (2016). *2016 standards.* Retrieved from http://www.cacrep.org/wp-content/uploads/2012/10/2016-CACREP-Standards.pdf

Council for Higher Education Accreditation. (2010). *Recognition of accrediting organizations: Policies and procedures.* Retrieved from http://www.chea.org/pdf/Recognition_Policy-June_28_2010-FINAL.pdf

Council for Higher Education Accreditation. (2011). *Accreditation and accountability: Looking back and looking ahead.* Retrieved from http://www.chea.org/pdf/accred_account.pdf

Council of Counseling Psychology Training Programs. (2006). *Counseling psychology model training values statement addressing diversity.* Retrieved from http://www.ccptp.org/ccptp-model-training-vales-statement-addressing-diversity

Council of Regional Accrediting Commissions. (2003). *Regional accreditation and student learning: Principles for good practices.* Retrieved from https://www.msche.org/documents/regnlsl.pdf

Daniels, M. H. (2010). Systematic program evaluation: The foundation of program quality. In C. J. Sheperis, J. S. Young, & M. H. Daniels (Eds.), *Counseling research: Quantitative, qualitative, and mixed methods* (pp. 173–186). Upper Saddle River, NJ: Pearson.

Deets, J. (2000). Maps and curriculum decision making. *Journal of Curriculum and Supervision, 15,* 359–371.

Dipietro, B. J. C., Drexler, W., Kennedy, K., Buraphadeja, V., Liu, F., & Dawson, K. (2010). Using wikis to collaboratively prepare for qualifying examinations: An example of implementation in an advanced graduate program. *TechTrends, 54,* 25–32.

Disposition. (n.d.). In *Merriam-Webster's online dictionary* (11th ed.). Retrieved from http://www. merriam-webster.com/dictionary/disposition

Dollarhide, C. T. (2013). Using a values-based taxonomy in counselor education. *Counseling and Values, 58,* 221–236. doi:10.1002/j.2161-007X.2013.00035.x

Dougherty, A. M. (2005). *Psychological consultation and collaboration in school and community settings* (4th ed.). Belmont, CA: Thomson Brooks/Cole.

Driscoll, A., & Wood, S. (2007). *Developing outcomes-based assessment for learner-centered education: A faculty introduction.* Sterling, VA: Stylus.

Duffy, R. D., & Dik, B. J. (2009). Beyond the self: External influences in the career development process. *The Career Development Quarterly, 58,* 29–43.

Education Trust. (n.d.). *Ten essential elements for change in school counselor preparation programs.* Retrieved from http://edtrust.org/wp-content/uploads/2014/09/Elements-of-Change_0.pdf

Eisenberg, T. (1965). Are doctoral comprehensive examinations necessary? *American Psychologist, 20,* 168–169. doi:10.1037/h0020945

EmpowHER. (2011). *Darkina* [Video files]. Retrieved from http://www.empowher.com/users/darkina

Evans, K. M., & Larrabee, M. J. (2002). Teaching the multicultural counseling competencies and revised career counseling competencies simultaneously. *Journal of Multicultural Counseling and Development, 30,* 21–39.

Ewell, P. T. (2009). *Assessment, accountability, and improvement: Revisiting the tension.* Retrieved from http://www.learningoutcomeassessment.org/documents/PeterEwell_005.pdf

Ewell, P., Paulson, K., & Kinzie, J. (2011). *Down and in: Assessment practices at the program level.* Retrieved from http://www.learningoutcomesassessment.org/documents/NILOAsurveyreport2011.pdf

Fernando, D. M., & Hulse-Killacky, D. (2006). Getting to the point: Using research meetings and the inverted triangle visual to develop a dissertation research question. *Counselor Education and Supervision, 46,* 103–115.

Fitzpatrick, J. L., Sanders, J. R., & Worthen, B. R. (2011). *Program evaluation: Alternative approaches and practical guidelines* (4th ed.). Upper Saddle River, NJ: Pearson.

Flynn, S. V., Chasek, C. L., Harper, I. F., Murphy, K. M., & Jorgensen, M. F. (2012). A qualitative inquiry of the counseling dissertation process. *Counselor Education and Supervision, 51,* 242–255. doi:10.1002/j.1556-6978.2012.00018.x

Fong, M., & Malone, C. (1994). Defeating ourselves: Common errors in counseling research. *Counselor Education and Supervision, 33,* 356–362. *doi:*10.1002/j.1556-6978.1994.tb00303.x

Foster, J. M., Leppma, M., & Hutchinson, T. S. (2014). Students' perspectives on gatekeeping in counselor education: A case study. *Counselor Education and Supervision, 53,* 190–203. doi:10.1002/j.1556-6978.2014.00057.x

Foster, V. A., & McAdams, C. R., III. (2009). A framework for creating a climate of transparency for professional performance assessment: Fostering student investment in gatekeeping. *Counselor Education and Supervision, 48,* 271–285. doi:10.1002/j.1556-6978.2009.tb00080.x

Fraenkel, P., & Pinsof, W. M. (2001). Teaching family therapy-centered integration: Assimilation and beyond. *Journal of Psychotherapy Integration, 11,* 59–85.

Gainor, K. A. (2005). Social justice: The moral imperative of vocational psychology. *The Counseling Psychologist, 33,* 180–188.

Gazzola, N., De Stefano, J., Thériault, A., & Audet, C. T. (2013). Learning to be supervisors: A qualitative investigation of difficulties experienced by supervisors-in-training. *The Clinical Supervisor, 32,* 15–39. doi:10.1080/07325223.2013.778678

Gibbons, M. M., Cochran, L., Spurgeon, S., & Diambra, J. E. (2013). The human factor: Student reactions to the integration of personal dispositions into a counseling program. *Journal of Humanistic Counseling, 52*, 5–22. doi:10.1002/J.2161-1939.2013.00029.x

Gibson, D. M., Dollarhide, C. T., & Moss, J. M. (2010). Professional identity development: A grounded theory of transformational tasks of new counselors. *Counselor Education and Supervision, 50*, 21–38.

Goodrich, K. M., & Shin, R. Q. (2013). A culturally responsive intervention for addressing problematic behaviors in counseling students. *Counselor Education and Supervision, 52*, 43–55. doi:10.1002/j.1556-6978.2013.00027.x

Goodyear, R. K. (2014). Supervision as pedagogy: Attending to its essential instructional and learning processes. *The Clinical Supervisor, 33*, 82–99. doi:10.1080/07325223.2014.918914

Graham, G., & Megarry, B. (2005). The social care work portfolio: An aid to integrated learning and reflection in social care training. *Social Work Education, 24*, 769–780. doi:10.1080/02615470500238686

Granello, D. H., & Hazler, R. J. (1998). A developmental rationale for curriculum order and teaching styles in counselor education programs. *Counselor Education and Supervision, 38*, 89–105.

Guli, L. A. (2005). Evidence-based parent consultation with school-related outcomes. *School Psychology Quarterly, 20*, 455–472. doi:10.1521/scpq.2005.20.4.455

Hamilton, P., Johnson, R., & Poudrier, C. (2010). Measuring educational quality by appraising theses and dissertations: Pitfalls and remedies. *Teaching in Higher Education, 15*, 567–577. doi:10.1080/13562517.2010.491905

Hanna, F. J., & Cardona, B. (2012). Multicultural counseling beyond the relationship: Expanding the repertoire with techniques. *Journal of Counseling & Development, 91*, 349–357. doi:10.1002/j.1556-6676.2013.00104.x

Hansen, L. S. (2003). Career counselors as advocates and change agents for equality. *The Career Development Quarterly, 52*, 43–53.

Harden, R. M. (2001). AMEE Guide No. 21: Curriculum mapping: A tool for transparent and authentic teaching and learning. *Medical Teacher, 23*, 123–137. doi:10.1080/01421590120036547

Hatfield, S. (2009). *Assessing your program-level assessment plan*. Manhattan, KS: IDEA Center.

Hays, D. G. (2013). *Assessment in counseling: A guide to the use of psychological assessment procedures* (5th ed.). Alexandria, VA: American Counseling Association.

Heath, L., DeHoek, A., & Locatelli, S. (2012). Indirect measures in evaluation: On not knowing what we don't know. *Practical Assessment, Research & Evaluation, 17*, 1–6.

Henderson, K. L., & Dufrene, R. L. (2011). Student remediation: Practical considerations for counselor educators and supervisors. From *VISTAS Online*. Retrieved from http://www.counseling.org/resources/library/vistas/2011-v-online/Article_45.pdf

Henderson, K. L., & Dufrene, R. L. (2012). Student behaviors associated with remediation: A content analysis. *Counseling Outcome Research and Evaluation, 3*, 48–60. doi:10.1177/2150137812437364

Hendrick, S. S. (1998). The Relationship Assessment Scale. *Journal of Social and Personal Relationships, 15*, 137–142.

Heppner, M. J., & Fu, C. (2011). The gendered context of vocational self-construction. In P. J. Hartung & L. M. Subich (Eds.), *Developing self in work and career: Concepts, cases, and contexts* (pp. 177–192). Washington, DC: American Psychological Association.

Heppner, M. J., & O'Brien, K. M. (2006). Women and poverty: A holistic approach to vocational intervention. In W. B. Walsh & M. J. Heppner (Eds.), *Handbook of career counseling for women* (2nd ed., pp. 75–102). Mahwah, NJ: Erlbaum.

Hoey, J. J., & Gardner, D. C. (1999). Using surveys of alumni and their employers to improve an institution. *New Directions for Institutional Research, 101*, 43–59.

Homrich, A. M., Delorenzi, L. D., Bloom, Z. D., & Godbee, B. (2014). Making the case for standards of conduct in clinical training. *Counselor Education and Supervision, 53*, 126–144. doi:10.1002/j.1556-6978.2014.00053.x

Huba, M. E., & Freed, J. E. (1999). *Learner-centered assessment on college campuses: Shifting the focus from teaching to learning.* Old Tappan, NJ: Pearson Education.

Hutchings, P. (2010). *Opening the doors to faculty involvement in assessment.* Retrieved from http://www.learningoutcomesassessment.org/documents/PatHutchings_0004.pdf

International Assembly for Collegiate Business Education. (2014). *Checklist for writing intended student learning outcomes statements.* Retrieved from http://iacbe.org/pdf/checklist-writing-islos.pdf

Ivey, A. E. (1986). *Developmental therapy: Theory into practice.* San Francisco, CA: Jossey-Bass.

Ivey, A. E., & Ivey, M. B. (2005). Wellness and the *DSM–IV–TR*: A developmental approach for clients in severe distress. In J. E. Myers & T. J. Sweeney (Eds.), *Counseling for wellness: Theory, research, and practice* (pp. 217–224). Alexandria, VA: American Counseling Association.

Ivey, A. E., Ivey, M. B., Myers, J. E., & Sweeney, T. J. (2005). *Developmental counseling and therapy: Promoting wellness over the lifespan.* New York, NY: Houghton-Mifflin.

Jacobs, H. H. (1997). *Mapping the big picture: Integrating curriculum and assessment K–12.* Alexandria, VA: Association for Supervision and Curriculum Development.

Jacobs, H. H. (2005). *Getting results with curriculum mapping.* Alexandria, VA: Association for Supervision and Curriculum Development.

James, S. H., & Greenwalt, B. C. (2001). Documenting success and achievement: Presentation and working portfolios for counselors. *Journal of Counseling & Development, 79,* 161–165. doi:10.1002/j.1556-6676.2001.tb01955.x

Jensen, J. L., McDaniel, M. A., Woodard, S. M., & Kummer, T. A. (2014). Teaching to the test . . . or testing to teach: Exams requiring higher order thinking skills encourage greater conceptual understanding. *Educational Psychology Review, 26,* 307–329. doi:10.1007/s10648-013-9248-9

Jonson, J. (2006). *Guidebook for programmatic assessment of student learning outcomes.* Lincoln: University of Nebraska–Lincoln.

Jonsson, A., & Svingby, G. (2007). The use of scoring rubrics: Reliability, validity and educational consequences. *Educational Research Review, 2,* 130–144.

Kaplan, D. M., & Gladding, S. T. (2011). A vision for the future of counseling: The 20/20 Principles for Unifying and Strengthening the Profession. *Journal of Counseling & Development, 89,* 367–372. doi:10.1002/j.1556-6678.2011.tb00101.x

Keim, J., & Wells, K. (2009). *Case studies in ethics, diagnosis, and treatment: Images of client's lives.* Eau Claire, WI: PESI.

Kelley, C., Tong, P, & Choi, B.-J. (2010). A review of assessment of student learning programs at AACSB schools: A dean's perspective. *Journal of Education for Business, 85,* 299–306. doi:10.1080/08832320903449519

Kirkpatrick, D. L. (1959). Techniques for evaluating training programs. *Journal of the American Society of Training Directors, 13,* 3–9.

Knox, S., Burkard, A. W., Janecek, J., Pruitt, N. T., Fuller, S. L., & Hill, C. E. (2011). Positive and problematic dissertation experiences: The faculty perspective. *Counselling Psychology Quarterly, 24,* 55–69. doi:10.1080/09515070.2011.559796

Koltz, R. L., Odegard, M. A., Provost, K. B., Smith, T., & Kleist, D. (2010). Picture perfect: Using photo-voice to explore four doctoral students' comprehensive examination experiences. *Journal of Creativity in Mental Health, 5,* 389–411. doi:10.1080/15401383.2010.527797

Koppang, A. (2004). Curriculum mapping: Building collaboration and communication. *Intervention in School and Clinic, 39,* 154–161. doi:10.1177/10534512040390030401

Kress, V. E., & Protivnak, J. J. (2009). Professional development plans to remedy problematic counseling student behaviors. *Counselor Education and Supervision, 48,* 154–167.

Kruger, J., & Dunning, D. (1999). Unskilled and unaware of it: How difficulties in recognizing one's own incompetence lead to inflated self-assessments. *Journal of Personality and Social Psychology, 77,* 1121–1134. doi:10.1037/0022-3514.77.6.1121

Kübler-Ross, E. (1969). *On death and dying.* New York, NY: McMillan.

Kuh, G. D., & Ewell, P. T. (2010). The state of learning outcomes assessment in the United States. *Higher Education Management and Policy, 22,* 9–28.

Kuh, G., & Ikenberry, S. (2009). *More than you think, less than we need: Learning outcomes assessment in American higher education.* Retrieved from http://www.learningoutcomeassessment. org/documents/niloafullreportfinal2.pdf

Kuh, G. D., Jankowski, N. A., Ikenberry, S. O., & Kinzie, J. (2014). *Knowing what students know and can do: The current state of learning outcomes assessment at U.S. colleges and universities.* Retrieved from http://www.learningoutcomeassessment.org/documents/2013%20Survey%20Report%20Final.pdf

Ladany, N., & O'Shaughnessy, T. (2014). Training and supervision in career counseling. In P. J. Hartung, M. L. Savickas, & W. B. Walsh (Eds.), *APA handbook of career intervention: Vol. 1. Foundations* (pp. 375–387). Washington, DC: American Psychological Association.

Lambert, A. D., & Miller, A. L. (2014). Lower response rates on alumni surveys might not mean lower response representativeness. *Educational Research Quarterly, 37,* 38–51.

Lambert, M. J., & Barley, D. E. (2001). Research summary on the therapeutic relationship and psychotherapy outcome. *Psychotherapy, 38,* 357–361.

Lambie, G. W., Mullen, P. R., Swank, J. M., & Blount, A. (2015). *The Counseling Competencies Scale: Validation and refinement.* Manuscript submitted for publication.

Lara, T. M., Kline, W. B., & Paulson, D. (2011). Attitudes regarding career counseling: Perceptions and experiences of counselors-in-training. *The Career Development Quarterly, 59,* 428–440.

Lee, C. C., & Rodgers, R. A. (2009). Counselor advocacy: Affecting systemic change in the public arena. *Journal of Counseling & Development, 87,* 284–287.

Lewis, J. A., Arnold, M. S., House, R., & Toporek, R. L. (2002). *ACA advocacy competencies.* Retrieved from http://www.counseling.org/Resources/Competencies/Advocacy_Competencies.pdf

Lewis, R. G., & Smith, H. D. (1994). *Total quality in higher education.* Delray Beach, FL: St. Lucie Press.

Li, C.-S., Trusty, J., Lampe, R., & Lin, Y. F. (2008). Remediation and termination of impaired students in CACREP-accredited counseling programs. *International Journal of Leadership Preparation, 3*(2). Retrieved from http://cnx.org/content/m17376/latest/

Loughead, T. (1997). The doctoral comprehensive examination: Fine-tuning the process. *Counselor Education and Supervision, 37,* 140–148. doi:10.1002/j.1556-6978.1997.tb00539.x

Lovitts, B. E. (2005). How to grade a dissertation. *Academe, 91,* 18–23.

Lumley, T. (2002). Assessment criteria in a large-scale writing test: What do they really mean to the raters? *Language Testing, 19,* 246–277.

Marzano, R. J. (2002). A comparison of selected methods of scoring classroom assessments. *Applied Measurement in Evaluation, 15,* 249–267.

Maxwell, T. W., & Kupczyk-Romanczuk, G. (2009). Producing the professional doctorate: The portfolio as a legitimate alternative to the dissertation. *Innovations in Education and Teaching International, 46,* 135–145. doi:10.1080/14703290902843760

McAdams, C. R., & Foster, V. A. (2007). A guide to just and fair remediation of performance deficiencies. *Counselor Education and Supervision, 47,* 2–13.

McAdams, C. R., & Robertson, D. L. (2012). An informed look at doctoral vivas (oral examinations) in the preparation of counselor educators. *Counselor Education and Supervision, 51,* 176–189.

McAdams, C. R., Robertson, D. L., & Foster, V. A. (2013). Doctoral oral examinations and contemporary counselor education: Are they compatible? *Counselor Education and Supervision, 52,* 270–283. doi:10.1002/j.1556-6978.2013.00042.x

McCrae, R. R., Costa P. T., Jr., & Martin, T. A. (2005). The NEO–PI–3: A more readable Revised NEO Personality Inventory. *Journal of Personality Assessment, 84,* 261–270.

McIlveen, P., & Patton, W. (2006). A critical reflection on career development. *International Journal for Educational and Vocational Guidance, 6,* 15–27.

McIntosh, P. (1989, July/August). White privilege: Unpacking the invisible knapsack. *Peace and Freedom Magazine.* Retrieved from http://nationalseedproject.org/images/documents/ Knapsack_plus_Notes-Peggy_McIntosh.pdf

McKinney, K. (2004). *What is the scholarship of teaching and learning (SoTL) and what can SoTL do for you and your department/school?* Retrieved from http://www.issotl.com/issotl15/sites/default/files/chairDeanHandout.pdf

McKinney, K. (2007). *Enhancing learning through the scholarship of teaching and learning: The challenges and joys of juggling.* Bolton, MA: Anker.

McLaughlin, J. A., & Jordan, G. B. (2010). Using Logic Models. In J. S. Wholey, H. P. Hatry, & N. E. Newcomer (Eds.), *Handbook of practical program evaluation* (3rd ed., pp. 55–80). San Francisco, CA: Jossey-Bass.

McMahon, M., Arthur, N., & Collins, S. (2008). Social justice and career development: Views and experiences of Australian career development practitioners. *Australian Journal of Career Development, 17,* 15–25.

Meyer, B., & Latham, N. (2008). Implementing electronic portfolios: Benefits, challenges, and suggestions. *Educause Quarterly, 1,* 34–41.

Meyers, N. M., & Nulty, D. D. (2009). How to use (five) curriculum design principles to align authentic learning environments, assessment, students' approaches to thinking and learning outcomes. *Assessment & Evaluation in Higher Education, 34,* 565–577. doi:10.1080/02602930802226502

Miller, M. A. (2012). *From denial to acceptance: The stages of assessment.* Retrieved from http://www.learningoutcomesassessment.org/documents/MillerOcPaper13.pdf

Mizikaci, F. (2006). A systems approach to program evaluation model for quality in higher education. *Quality Assurance in Education, 14,* 37–53. doi:10.1108/09684880610643601

Moe, J., Autry, L., Olson, J. S., & Johnson, K. F. (2014). Teaching group work with *The Great Debaters. Counselor Education and Supervision, 53,* 204–218. doi:10.1002/j.1556-6978.2014.00058.x

Moskal, B. M., & Leydens, J. A. (2000). Scoring rubric development: Validity and reliability. *Practical Assessment, Research & Evaluation, 7,* Article 10.

Much, K., Wagener, A. M., & Hellenbrand, M. (2010). Practicing in the 21st century college counseling center. *Journal of College Student Psychotherapy, 24,* 32–38. doi:10.1080/87568220903400138

Mueller, J. (2014). *Authentic assessment toolbox.* Retrieved from http://jfmueller.faculty.noctrl.edu/toolbox/tasks.htm

Myers, J. E., & Sweeney, T. J. (2008). Wellness counseling: The evidence base for practice. *Journal of Counseling & Development, 86,* 482–493. doi:10.1002/j.1556-6678.x008xtb00536.x

National Career Development Association. (2009). *Minimum competencies for multicultural career counseling and development.* Retrieved from http://ncda.org/aws/NCDA/pt/sp/guidelines

National Council for Accreditation of Teacher Education. (2014). *NCATE glossary.* Retrieved from http://www.ncate.org/Standards/UnitStandards/Glossary/tabid/477/Default.aspx

National Office for School Counselor Advocacy. (2010). *Eight components of college and career readiness counseling.* Retrieved from http://nosca.collegeboard.org/eight-components

Newcomer, K. E., Hatry, H. P., & Wholey, J. S. (2010). Planning and designing useful evaluations. In J. S. Wholey, H. P. Hatry, & N. E. Newcomer (Eds.), *Handbook of practical program evaluation* (3rd ed., pp. 5–29). San Francisco, CA: Jossey-Bass.

New Leadership Alliance for Student Learning and Accountability. (2012). *Committing to quality: Guidelines for assessment and accountability in higher education.* Washington, DC: Author.

Oakleaf, M., Belanger, J., & Graham, C. (2013, April). Choosing and using assessment management systems: What librarians need to know. In *Proceedings of the ACRL 15th National Conference* (pp. 97–106). Retrieved from http://www.ala.org/acrl/sites/ala.org.acrl/files/content/conferences/confsandpreconfs/2013/papers/OakleafBelangerGraham_Choosing.pdf

O'Brien, K. M. (2001). The legacy of Parsons: Career counselors and vocational psychologists as agents of social change. *The Career Development Quarterly, 50,* 66–76.

Office of Academic Planning and Assessment. (2001). *Program-based review and assessment: Tools and techniques for program improvement.* Retrieved from http://www.umass.edu/oapa/oapa/publications/online_handbooks/program_based.pdf

Office of Planning and Institutional Effectiveness. (2014, Spring). *Learning outcomes assessment handbook: A guide to learning outcomes assessment at Marymount University*. Retrieved from http://www.marymount.edu/marymount.edu/media/Home/Faculty-and-Staff/AssessmentHandbookSpring2014.pdf

Ohrt, J. H., Ener, E., Porter, J., & Young, T. L. (2014). Group leader reflections on their training and experience: Implications for group counselor educators and supervisors. *The Journal for Specialists in Group Work, 39*, 95–124.

Okech, E. A., Astramovich, R. L., Johnson, M. M., Hoskins, W. J., & Rubel, D. J. (2006). Doctoral research training of counselor education faculty. *Counselor Education and Supervision, 46*, 131–145. doi:10.1002/j.1556-6978.2006.tb00018.x

O'Neal, C., Meizlish, D., & Kaplan, M. (2007). *Writing a statement of teaching philosophy for the academic job search* (CLRT Occasional Papers No. 23). Available from http://www.crlt.umich.edu/sites/default/files/resource_files/CRLT_no23.pdf

Orr, J. J., & Smith, J. (2013). *Social and cultural issues in counseling syllabus*. Unpublished manuscript.

Osborn, D. S. (2009). Teaching career theories, career assessments, and career information. *Career Planning and Adult Development Journal, 25*, 71–81.

Osborn, D. S., & Dames, L. S. (2013). Teaching graduate career classes: A national survey of career instructors. *Counselor Education and Supervision, 52*, 297–310.

Owens, E. W., & Neale-McFall, C. W. (2014). Counselor identity development: Toward a model for the formation of professional identity. *Journal of Counselor Leadership and Advocacy, 1*, 16–27.

Parke, C. S. (2001). An approach that examines sources of misfit to improve performance assessment items and rubrics. *Educational Assessment, 7*, 201–225.

Parsons, F. (1909). *Choosing a vocation*. Boston, MA: Houghton Mifflin.

Patton, M. Q. (2003). *Qualitative evaluation checklist*. Retrieved from https://cyfernetsearch.org/sites/default/files/Patton,%202003.pdf

Patton, S. (2013, October 14). Graduate students urge changes in comprehensive exams. *Chronicle of Higher Education, 60*, A16–A17.

Peach, B. E., Mukherjee, A., & Hornyak, M. (2007). Assessing critical thinking: A college's journey and lessons learned. *Journal of Education of Business, 82*, 313–320.

Pease-Carter, C., & Barrio Minton, C. A. (2012). Counseling program informed consent practices: A survey of student preferences. *Counselor Education and Supervision, 51*, 308–319. doi:10.1002/j.1556-6978.2012.00023.x

Pedersen, P. B. (1991). Multiculturalism as a fourth force in counseling. *Journal of Counseling and Development, 70*, 483–487.

Peterson, S. E., Bowman, R. L., Myer, R. A., & Maidl, C. M. (1992). A survey of comprehensive examination practices among doctoral programs in counseling. *Counselor Education and Supervision, 32*, 116–129. doi:10.1002/j.1556-6978.1992.tb00181.x

Plaza, C. M., Draugalis, J. R., Slack, M. K., Skrepnek, G. H., & Sauer, K. A. (2007). Curriculum mapping in program assessment and evaluation. *American Journal of Pharmaceutical Education, 71*, 1–8.

Polanski, P. J., & Hinkle, J. S. (2000). The Mental Status Examination: Its use by professional counselors. *Journal of Counseling & Development, 78*, 357–364. doi:10.1002/j.1556

Pope, M., & Minor, C. W. (Eds.). (2000). *Experiential activities for teaching career counseling classes and for facilitating career groups*. Columbus, OH: National Career Development Association.

Posavac, E. J. (2011). *Program evaluation: Methods and case studies* (8th ed.). Upper Saddle River, NJ: Pearson.

Praslova, L. (2010). Adaptation of Kirkpatrick's four level model of training criteria to assessment of learning outcomes and program evaluation in higher education. *Educational Assessment, Evaluation and Accountability, 22*, 215–225. doi:10.1007/s11092-010-9098-7

Prilleltensky, I., & Stead, G. B. (2012). Critical psychology and career development: Unpacking the adjust-challenge dilemma. *Journal of Career Development, 39*, 321–340.

Prochaska, J., DiClemente, C., & Norcross, J. (1992). In search of how people change: Applications to addictive behaviors. *American Psychologist, 47,* 1102–1114.

Provezis, S. (2010). *Regional accreditation and student learning outcomes: Mapping the territory.* Retrieved from http://www.learningoutcomesassessment.org/documents/Provezis.pdf

Reddy, Y. M. (2007). Effect of rubrics on enhancement of student learning. *Educate, 7,* 3–17.

Reddy, Y. M., & Andrade, H. (2010). A review of rubric use in higher education. *Assessment and Evaluation in Higher Education, 35,* 435–448. doi:10.1080/02602930902862859

RiCharde, R. S. (2009). *Data management and data management tools.* Retrieved from http://www.usf.edu/provost/documents/assessment/resources-considerationsforselectingdatamanagementandtools.pdf

Rockquemore, K. A., Brunsma, D. L., & Delgado, D. J. (2009). Racing to theory or retheorizing race? Understanding the struggle to build a multiracial identity theory. *Journal of Social Issues, 65,* 13–34. doi:10.1111/j.1540-4560.2008.01585.x

Sampson, J. P., Dozier, V. C., & Colvin, G. P. (2011). Translating career theory to practice: The risk of unintentional social injustice. *Journal of Counseling & Development, 89,* 326–337.

Savickas, M. L. (2011). New questions for vocational psychology: Premises, paradigms, and practices. *Journal of Career Assessment, 19,* 251–258.

Schmidt, E., Homeyer, L., & Walker, J. (2009). Predictors of success on the Counselor Preparation Comprehensive Examination. *Counselor Education and Supervision, 48,* 226–238. doi:10.1002/j.1556-6978.2009.tb00077.x

Seligman, L. (2004). Intake interviews and their role in diagnosis and treatment planning. In *Diagnosis and treatment planning in counseling* (3rd ed., pp. 138–159). New York, NY: Kluwer.

Sink, C. A., & Mvududu, N. H. (2010). Statistical power, sampling, and effect sizes: Three keys to research relevancy. *Counseling Outcome Research and Evaluation, 1,* 1–18. doi:10.1177/2150137810373613

Smith, T. B., Dean, B., Floyd, S., Silva, C., Yamashita, M., Durtschi, J., & Heaps, R. A. (2007). Pressing issues in college counseling: A survey of American College Counseling Association members. *Journal of College Counseling, 10,* 64–78. doi:10.1002/j.2161-1882.2007.tb00007.x

Spielberger, C. D. (1983). *State-Trait Anxiety Inventory.* Palo Alto, CA: Consulting Psychologists Press.

Spruill, D. A., & Benshoff, J. M. (2000). Helping beginning counselors develop a personal theory of counseling. *Counselor Education and Supervision, 40,* 70–80. doi:10.1002/j.1556-6978.2000.tb01800.x

Spurgeon, S. L., Gibbons, M. M., & Cochran, J. L. (2012). Creating personal dispositions for a professional counseling program. *Counseling and Values, 57,* 96–109.

Steen, S., Bauman, S., & Smith, J. (2007). Professional school counselors and the practice of group work. *Professional School Counseling, 11,* 72–80.

Stevens, D. D., & Levi, A. J. (2005). *Introduction to rubrics: An assessment tool to save grading time, convey effective feedback, and promote student learning.* Sterling, VA: Stylus.

Stiehl, R., & Lewchuk, L. (2008a). *The assessment primer: Creating a flow of learning evidence.* Corvallis, OR: The Learning Organization.

Stiehl, R., & Lewchuk, L. (2008b). *The outcomes primer: Reconstructing the college curriculum* (3rd ed.). Corvallis, OR: The Learning Organization.

Strudler, N., & Wetzel, K. (2005). The diffusion of electronic portfolios in teacher education: Issues of initiation and implementation. *Journal of Research on Technology in Education, 37,* 411–433.

Suskie, L. (2009). *Assessing student learning: A common sense guide* (2nd ed.). San Francisco, CA: Jossey-Bass.

Swank, J. M., & Lambie, G. W. (2012). The assessment of CACREP core curricular areas and student learning outcomes using the Counseling Competencies Scale. *Counseling Outcome Research and Evaluation, 3,* 116–127. doi:10.1177/2150137812452560

Swank, J. M., Lambie, G. W., & Witta, E. L. (2012). An exploratory investigation of the Counseling Competencies Scale: A measure of counseling skills, dispositions, and behaviors. *Counselor Education and Supervision, 51,* 189–206. doi:10.1002/j.1556-6978.2012.00014.x

Swank, J. M., & Smith-Adcock, S. (2014). Gatekeeping during admissions: A survey of counselor education programs. *Counselor Education and Supervision, 53,* 47–61. doi:10.1002/j.1556-6978.2014.00048.x

Swigonski, M., Ward, K., Mama, R. S., Rodgers, J., & Belicose, R. (2006). An agenda for the future: Student portfolios in social work education. *Social Work Education, 25,* 812–823. doi:10.1080/02615470600915860

Tamase, K. (1989). Introspective developmental counseling. *Bulletin of Nara University of Education, 38,* 166–177.

Tanen, N. (Producer), & Hughes, J. (Producer & Director). (1985). *The breakfast club* [Motion picture]. Universal City, CA: MCA Home Video.

Tang, M. (2003). Career counseling in the future: Constructing, collaborating, advocating. *The Career Development Quarterly, 52,* 61–69.

Taylor-Powell, E., Jones, A. L., & Henert, E. (2002). *Enhancing program performance with Logic Models.* Retrieved from http://www.uwex.edu/ces/lmcourse/

Taylor-Powell, E., Steele, S., & Douglah, M. (1996). *Planning a program evaluation* (G3658-1). Retrieved from http://learningstore.uwex.edu/assets/pdfs/G3658-1.PDF

Texas Education Agency. (2012). *Texas Examinations of Educator Standards (TExES) Program: Preparation manual: School counselor (152).* Retrieved from http://cms.texes-ets.org/files/9713/5722/8070/school_counselor_152.pdf

Thompson, B., & Snyder, P. A. (1998). Statistical significance and reliability analyses in recent *Journal of Counseling & Development* research articles. *Journal of Counseling & Development, 76,* 436–441. *doi*:10.1002/j.1556-6676.1998.tb02702.x

Thyer, B. A. (2003). A student portfolio approach to conducting doctoral social work comprehensive examinations. *Journal of Teaching in Social Work, 23,* 117–126. doi:10.1300/J067v23n03_10

Toman, S. (2012). Career counseling: A process-based teaching approach for training career counselors. In D. M. Perera-Diltz & K. C. MacCluskie (Eds.), *The counselor educator's survival guide: Designing and teaching outstanding courses in community mental health counseling and school counseling* (pp. 187–205). New York, NY: Routledge.

Trusty, J., Skowron, E. A., Watts, R. E., & Parrillo, A. L. (2004). Modeling the effects of counselor-trainees' perceptions of early childhood on trainees' social influence attributes. *The Family Journal, 12,* 6–13.

Tyler, J. M., & Reynolds, T. (1998). Using feature films to teach group counseling. *The Journal for Specialists in Group Work, 23,* 7–21. doi:10.1080/01933929808411378

Uchiyama, K. P., & Radin, J. L. (2008). Curriculum mapping in higher education: A vehicle for collaboration. *Innovative Higher Education, 33,* 271–280. doi:10.1007/s10755-008-9078-8

Urofsky, R. I. (2009, Fall). CACREP board issues guiding statements on student learning outcomes. *The CACREP Connection.* Retrieved from http://www.cacrep.org/wp-content/uploads/2012/07/Connection-Fall-20091.pdf

Urofsky, R. I., & Bobby, C. L. (2012). The evolution of a student learning outcomes focus in the CACREP standards in relation to accountability in higher education. *Counseling Outcome Research and Evaluation, 3,* 63–72. doi:10.1177/2150137812452562

Vacc, N. A., & Loesch, L. C. (2000). *Professional orientation to counseling.* Philadelphia, PA: Brunner-Routledge.

Vacha-Haase, T., Davenport, D. S., & Kerewsky, S. D. (2004). Problematic students: Gatekeeping practices of academic professional psychology programs. *Professional Psychology: Research and Practice, 35,* 115–122. doi:10.1037/0735-7028.35.2.115

Vacha-Haase, T., & Thompson, B. (2011). Score reliability: A retrospective look back at 12 years of reliability generalization studies. *Measurement and Evaluation in Counseling and Development, 44,* 159–168. *doi*:10.1177/0748175611409845

Vespia, K. M., Fitzpatrick, M. E., Fouad, N. A., Kantamneni, N., & Chen, Y.-L. (2010). Multicultural career counseling: A national survey of competencies and practices. *The Career Development Quarterly, 59,* 54–71.

Wachter, C. A. (2007). *Counseling multicultural and diverse populations syllabus.* Unpublished manuscript.

Wakimoto, D. K., & Lewis, R. E. (2014). Graduate student perceptions of eportfolios: Uses for reflection, development, and assessment. *The Internet and Higher Education, 21,* 53–58. doi:10.1016/j.iheduc.2014.01.002

Watkins, C. (1990). Development of the psychotherapy supervisor. *Psychotherapy: Theory, Research, Practice, Training, 27,* 553–560. doi:10.1037/0033-3204.27.4.553

Watkins, C. (1993). Development of the psychotherapy supervisor: Concepts, assumptions, and hypotheses of the supervisor complexity model. *American Journal of Psychotherapy, 47,* 58–74.

Watkins, C. J., & Scaturo, D. J. (2013). Toward an integrative, learning-based model of psychotherapy supervision: Supervisory alliance, educational interventions, and supervisee learning/relearning. *Journal of Psychotherapy Integration, 23,* 75–95. doi:10.1037/a0031330

Watkins, C. J., & Scaturo, D. J. (2014). Proposal for a common language, educationally-informed model of psychoanalytic supervision. *Psychoanalytic Inquiry, 34,* 619–633. doi:10.1080/07351690.2014.924374

Weldy, T. G., & Turnipseed, D. L. (2010). Assessing and improving learning in business schools: Direct and indirect measures of learning. *Journal of Education for Business, 85,* 268–273. doi:10.1080/08832320903449535

Wester, K. L., & Borders, L. D. (2014). Research competencies in counseling: A Delphi study. *Journal of Counseling & Development, 92,* 447–458.

Wester, K. L., Borders, L. D., Boul, S., & Horton, E. (2013). Research quality: Critique of quantitative articles in the *Journal of Counseling & Development. Journal of Counseling & Development, 91,* 280–290. doi:10.1002/j.1556-6676.2013.00096.x

Wetzel, K., & Strudler, N. (2005). The diffusion of electronic portfolios in teacher education: Next steps and recommendations from accomplished users. *Journal of Research on Technology in Education, 38,* 231–243.

Whiston, S. C. (2013). *Principles and applications of assessment in counseling* (4th ed.). Belmont, CA: Brooks/Cole.

Wilkerson, K. (2006). Impaired students: Applying the therapeutic process model to graduate training programs. *Counselor Education and Supervision, 45,* 207–218. doi:10.1002/j.1556-6978.2006.tb00143.x

Williams, L., & Rink, J. (2003). Teacher competency using observational scoring rubrics. *Journal of Teaching in Physical Education, 22,* 552–572.

Winterowd, C. L., Adams, E. M., Miville, M. L., & Mintz, L. B. (2009). Operationalizing, instilling, and assessing counseling psychology training values related to diversity in academic programs. *The Counseling Psychologist, 37,* 676–704. doi:10.1177/0011000009331936

World Health Organization. (2010). *Measuring health and disability: Manual for WHO Disability Assessment Schedule: WHODAS 2.0.* Retrieved from http://whqlibdoc.who.int/publications/2010/9789241547598_eng.pdf

Young, M. E. (2012). *Learning the art of helping: Building blocks and techniques* (5th ed.). Upper Saddle River, NJ: Pearson Education.

Zalaquett, C. P., Fuerth, K. M., Stein, C., Ivey, A. E., & Ivey, M. B. (2008). Reframing the *DSM–IV–TR* from a multicultural/social justice perspective. *Journal of Counseling & Development, 86,* 364–371.

Ziomek-Daigle, J., & Christensen, T. M. (2010). An emergent theory of gatekeeping practices in counselor education. *Journal of Counseling & Development, 88,* 407–415. doi:10.1002/j.1556-6678.2010.tb00040.x

Index

Figures and tables are indicated by f and t following the page number.

A

(Continued)

I

J

K

L

M

(*Continued*)